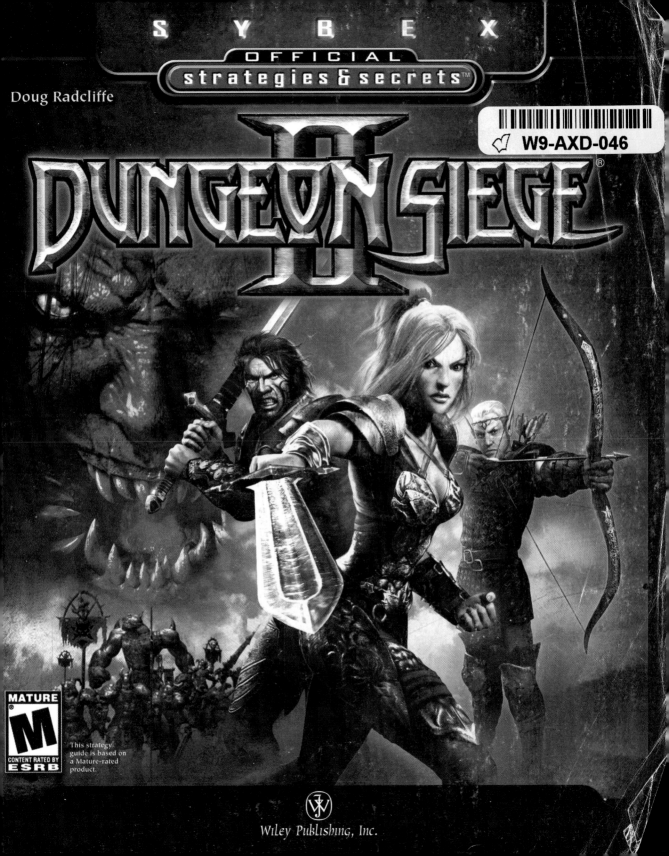

SYBEX

OFFICIAL
strategies & secrets™

Doug Radcliffe

W9-AXD-046

DUNGEON SIEGE
II

Wiley Publishing, Inc.

Acquisitions and Developmental Editor:
Willem Knibbe

Production Editor: Patrick Cunningham

Copy Editor: Candace English

Production Manager: Tim Tate

Vice President and Executive Group Publisher:
Richard Swadley

Vice President and Publisher: Joseph B. Wikert

Vice President and Publisher: Dan Brodnitz

Book Design: Susan Honeywell, Patrick Cunningham,
and Judy Fung

Compositor: Susan Honeywell

Proofreader: Candace English

Cover Design: Richard Miller, Calyx Design

Copyright © 2005 by Wiley Publishing, Inc.,
Indianapolis, IN

ISBN-13: 978-0-7821-4356-0
ISBN-10: 0-7821-4356-3

Please be advised that the ESRB rating icons "EC", "K-A",
"T", "M", "AO" and "RP" are copyrighted works and cer-
tification marks owned by the Entertainment Software
Association and the Entertainment Software Rating
Board and may only be used with their permission
and authority. Under no circumstances may the rating
icons be self-applied or used in connection within any
product that has not been rated by the ESRB. For information regarding whether a product has been rated by
the ESRB, please call the ESRB at 1-800-0771-3772 or
visit www. Esrb.org. For information regarding licensing
issues, please call the ESA at 916-522-3250. The ESRB
did not rate this strategy guide; the logo on the cover is
the rating assigned to the game only.

For general information on our other products and
services or to obtain technical support, please contact our Customer Care Department within the U.S. at
(800) 762-2974, outside the U.S. at (317) 572-3993 or
fax (317) 572-4002.

Wiley also publishes its books in a variety of electronic formats. Some content that appears in print
may not be available in electronic books.

Manufactured in the United States of America

10 9 8 7 6 5 4 3 2 1

Dedication

For Alyssa, brighter than morning sun.

Acknowledgements

At Wiley, I have to thank Willem Knibbe, a great friend. Thanks as always for your dedication. Thanks to Patrick Cunningham, Susan Honeywell, and Judy Fung for using the dozens and dozens of maps, tips, and tables and crafting an amazing guide. Thanks to Candace English for asking all the right questions.

Many thanks to the Gas Powered Games team and congratulations for creating one of the most detailed and engrossing games ever. Specific thanks to Bert Bingham for being patient with my countless emails and questions and his help unraveling *Dungeon Siege II*'s impressive depth. Thanks to Sarah Boulian, Jerry Pritchard, John Cutter, Kelly Kristek, Matt Mahon, Matt Gillikin, Jessica St. Croix, Ryan Gibson, Chris Burns, and Grant Roberts for their designer tips and help on numerous elements of this guide. I'd also like to thank Daniel Achtermann, Paul Dahlke, and Matt Kittleson for invaluable assistance with the guide's statistics section. Thanks also to Wes Yanagi of Microsoft Game Studios for his help in putting this book together. Finally, massive thanks to Wiley's Tim Tate and Paul Gilchrist for their last-minute maneuverings!

How to Use This Book

This official *Dungeon Siege II* strategy guide was created with the full support of *Dungeon Siege II*'s developers and is packed with exclusive maps, stats, and strategies you won't find anywhere else.

Part 1, "Races and Classes," offers a strategic look at *Dungeon Siege II*'s race and class options. Selecting a race is your first game decision. Each race features a unique set of strengths and weaknesses and certain races are better suited for certain classes. This section includes an overview of the four primary classes with advantages and disadvantages presented for each. Use this section as a guide for race selection and pairing race with its best class to develop the most powerful character possible.

Part 2, "Character Development," provides in-depth analysis of combining *Dungeon Siege II*'s new class skills and powers to create specialized characters. Through careful skill selection, you can create a Melee class character focused on dual-wielding or develop a Combat Magic class character specializing in lightning magic. This section reveals several character templates to use as your skill selection guidelines to unlock *Dungeon Siege II*'s impressive new powers.

Part 3, "Combat Strategies and Pets," shifts focus from character development to combat. This section contains a wide array of combat strategies including exploiting monster weaknesses, using powers effectively, spell support, and equipment selection. This section also features a rundown of all available pets with tips on feeding, maturing, and getting the most out of your combat ally's benefits and bonuses.

Part 4 through 6, "Primary Quests Walkthrough," contain complete primary quest walkthroughs for all three Acts of *Dungeon Siege II*'s storyline. The walkthroughs feature detailed maps to guide your party to every quest location, optional area, teleporter, chant lectern, and shrine and include tips on equipment selection, resistances, and battle tips to help conquer every monster encounter and boss. Note that many of *Dungeon Siege II*'s monster locations are randomized so certain encounter specifics may differ slightly but the strategies for winning battles remain the same.

Part 7, "Secondary Quests Walkthrough," contains complete walkthroughs for all of *Dungeon Siege II*'s secondary quests. The walkthroughs provide instruction on how to initiate the quest and maps to guide you to the quest's location and through its solution.

Part 8, "Statistics," is a comprehensive reference section. It compiles the most important *Dungeon Siege II* into one section. You'll find statistics for all of the class skills and class powers, base weapons and armor, unique weapons and armor, set items, monsters, enchantments, reagents, chants, and spells.

Tip

Dungeon Siege II *features three game modes: Mercenary, Veteran, and Elite. Each mode is intended for certain character levels and you must complete one mode before unlocking the next. Mercenary mode is the game's initial mode and the one this strategy guide covers. Veteran and Elite quests remain the same, but monsters are much stronger and available equipment is much more impressive.*

: TABLE OF CONTENTS :

Nature-Magic Spells — 230

PART I:
RACES AND CLASSES

Character creation is the essence of a role-playing game. You're assuming the role of the game's main character—and you can mold that character to your specific wants and needs. In Dungeon Siege II, you decide the character's race, appearance, gender, and abilities. Character creation continues throughout the game as you gain new skills and powers.

This chapter covers Dungeon Siege II*'s four races and primary classes. You'll find suggestions on pairing race with class; a rundown of character attributes and how each impacts health, mana, and damage; and an overview of the primary classes, with advantages and disadvantages presented for each.*

Character Races

Deciding your character's race is your first choice before joining the Morden mercenary ranks in the Champions of the Second Age storyline. *Dungeon Siege II* features four distinct races; each offers unique statistics and appearance. Consider your choice carefully and base the decision on what type of character you plan to create. Certain races are better suited for certain classes, although no race limits your choice of classes, skills, or powers. And note that gender has no bearing on your character attributes or available classes, skills, or powers.

This section reveals *Dungeon Siege II*'s four race choices, their starting statistics, and suggestions for race–class pairings.

Human

- ◆ 2 unspent skill points
- ◆ +2 Strength
- ◆ +1 Dexterity
- ◆ +1 Intelligence
- ◆ +10% chance to find magic items

- ◆ Best class pairing: Any

The freedom to spend two points on skills of your choosing makes Human the most adaptable race. Instead of splitting skill points across classes like Dryads (Nature Magic and Ranged) and Elf (Melee and Combat Magic), selecting Human allows you to focus both skills points into the class discipline of your choice. A Human combat mage could focus both skill points on Devastation for increased combat-magic damage; a Human nature mage could focus both skills points on Aquatic Affinity for increased ice-magic damage and healing magic power (as well as unlock the Icicle Blast power); or a Human ranged fighter could assign both skill points to Critical Shot for added ranged weapon damage.

But what's gained in adaptability is lost in focus. Remaining Human statistics, while certainly positive, lack class-specific benefits. The Human doesn't possess the improved healing rate of the Half-Giant, great for a fighter, or the enhanced mana recovery of the Elf, excellent for a mage. The Humans' specific benefit is their increased chance to find magic items. Humans are born treasure hunters.

Dryad

- ◆ 1 point in Natural Bond (-6% to mana cost of spells, can harvest mana potions, Gravity Stone level 1)
- ◆ 1 point in Dodge (+4% chance to dodge melee or ranged attacks)
- ◆ -2 Strength
- ◆ +4 Dexterity
- ◆ +2 Intelligence
- ◆ +10% death-magic resistance
- ◆ Female only
- ◆ Best class pairing: Ranged, Nature Magic

A point in Natural Bond and Dodge skills makes the Dryad a "natural" choice for the Nature Magic or Ranged class, but these skills can benefit other classes as well. Natural Bond decreases the mana cost of all spells; this is a valuable mage skill even if you choose to switch to or multiclass Combat Magic. Natural Bond also grants the ability to harvest mana potions from mana bushes and is the prerequisite for the Gravity Stone power. Dodge increases your chance of avoiding melee or ranged attacks, which supports any class.

Even with this apparent skill versatility, other races provide stronger pairings. The Melee class should select the Half-Giant and his increased health regeneration, Fortitude skill, and Strength bonus. And the Elf's enhanced mana recovery, better Intelligence, and Brilliance skill point offer a stronger complement for combat mages.

The Dryad's Dexterity bonus, the strongest of any race, increases base ranged damage. The Dryad is the optimum choice for a ranged player; if you'd rather assign both skill points to Critical Shot (which grants the Take Aim power), Human would be a better match for the Ranged class.

Elf

- ◆ 1 point in Critical Strike (+8% chance to inflict a critical hit, Brutal Attack level 1)
- ◆ 1 point in Brilliance (+7% to maximum mana, Energy Orb level 1)
- ◆ +1 Dexterity
- ◆ +3 Intelligence
- ◆ +5% mana recovery
- ◆ Best class pairing: Combat Magic

The Elf offers points in a melee skill, Critical Strike, and a combat-magic skill, Brilliance. Remaining bonuses, though, are skewed strictly toward a mage class. The Elf lacks the Half-Giant's enhancements to Strength and health regeneration for the Melee class, as well as the Dryad's Dexterity bonus for the Ranged class. But the Elf features the best mage benefits of any race: the highest Intelligence bonus and an increased mana recovery rate.

Brilliance, which increases maximum mana, is a combat-magic skill but certainly aids any discipline should you decide to select the Elf for Nature Magic pairing. The Elf is the only race to start the game with two powers, Brutal Attack from the Critical Strike skill and Energy Orb from the Brilliance skill. A Human could gain a second power early depending on the skills chosen for its unspent points.

> **Developer Tip**
>
> *As a combat mage, stay true to one elemental tree: death (Grim Necromancy skill), Lightning (Amplified Lightning skill) or fire (Searing Flames skill). Spreading out your skill points will create a weaker mage in the end.*
> *—Jerry Pritchard, Tester*

Half-Giant

- ◆ 2 points in Fortitude (+10% to maximum health)
- ◆ +6 Strength
- ◆ -2 Dexterity
- ◆ +5% health regeneration
- ◆ Male only
- ◆ Best class pairing: Melee

The Half-Giant's statistics leave little doubt regarding its optimum class pairing. Increased health regeneration, increased maximum health, and a Strength bonus are ideal companions to the Melee class. Yet there are no limitations. You could groom your Half-Giant to be an ice mage, death mage, thrown weapons specialist—any discipline you desire—but the giant's statistics are paired best with close-quarters, hand-to-hand combat.

Reduced Dexterity weakens the Half-Giant as a Ranged option and the lack of an Intelligence bonus or any nature-magic or combat-magic skills gives other races the edge as superior mages. Strength provides a bonus to minimum and maximum melee damage and has the strongest impact on health. Increased health regeneration and two points in Fortitude further enhance the Half-Giant's role as a melee combatant. The downside is that the Half-Giant starts the game lacking an available power, but two points in Fortitude lay a foundation for Whirling Strike.

> **Developer Tip**
>
> If you choose to emphasize Melee class, coordinate your weapon choice with your skill and power selections. Notice that powers are specific to certain Melee subclasses (dual wield, sword and shield, two-handed). It helps to choose which style of melee you want to use early in the game, and then focus on the skills that get you the appropriate powers for your favorite weapon(s). —Chris Burns, Level Designer

Character Classes

Like its predecessor, *Dungeon Siege II* features four primary character classes: Melee, Ranged, Combat Magic, and Nature Magic. Also as in the first game, you'll learn by doing, guiding your character into a particular class. Improve the Melee class by fighting monsters with a melee weapon; improve the Ranged class by fighting monsters with a bow, crossbow, or thrown weapon; and improve Combat or Nature Magic by casting spells of the respective type. This section cov-

> **Tip**
>
> New to Dungeon Siege II are character skills and powers, which are used to further hone your character's class. Focus the Melee class on two-handed weapons or dual-wielding. A nature mage could concentrate on ice-magic spells, buff spells, or summoned creatures. See Part 2 for comprehensive tips on maximizing a character's potential with specific skill and power suggestions and examples.

ers the basics of all four primary classes and reveals strategic advantages and disadvantages for each.

Melee

The Melee class emphasizes hand-to-hand combat. To improve a melee character, wield a melee weapon and fight monsters at close range. Increasing the Melee class level increases your character's Strength at its highest rate, which provides the best base health reserve possible. Strength also impacts the Melee character's bonus to minimum and maximum melee weapon damage.

> **Tip**
>
> All Melee characters can equip a single, one-handed melee weapon. But to equip a shield, the Melee character must learn the Barricade skill; to equip a two-handed weapon, the Melee character must learn Overbear; and to equip dual one-handed weapons, the Melee character must select the Dual Wield skill. All of these skills are first available at melee level 5.

Through skills and powers, a Melee character can specialize in two-handed weapon combat, one-handed weapon and shield combat, or dual-wielding combat. See Part 2 for details on creating each type of specialized Melee character.

The following list below covers the primary advantages and disadvantages of the Melee class.

- ◆ **Highest base health of any class**: Strength has the largest impact on a character's base health reserve, and Melee characters boast the highest base Strength.
- ◆ **High armor rating**: Only the Melee class can equip the game's highest-rated armor offerings, which makes Melee characters the most durable.
- ◆ **Dependency on health potions**: Melee characters are usually the first into combat and therefore the first under attack from melee, ranged, or mage enemies. Keep your Melee character fully stocked with health potions.
- ◆ **Not easy to exploit enemy elemental weaknesses**: Many monsters are weak to specific elemental damage, such as ice or fire. Some melee weapons offer elemental damage, but not at the degree of a mage's spells.

Ranged

The Ranged class emphasizes long-range combat. Increase your Ranged class level by equipping a bow, crossbow, or thrown weapon. Building a ranged character's level primarily increases the Dexterity attribute at its highest rate, which has a moderate effect on health reserves and provides a bonus to minimum and maximum ranged weapon damage.

With specific skill and power selection, a Ranged character can specialize in bow and crossbow combat or thrown-weapon combat. See Part 2 for strategies for creating each type of specialized Ranged character. This following list covers the primary advantages and disadvantages of the Ranged class.

- **Maintain distance from enemy groups**: A Ranged character strikes from a distance (bow and crossbow range can be further increased through the Far Shot skill) and can assail enemies several times before being attacked.
- **Hit-and-run techniques**: A savvy Ranged character can employ hit-and-run attacks against slower enemies. Maintain a safe distance, attack, move, and repeat.
- **Decent armor and health rating**: Dexterity doesn't have as large an impact on health as Strength does. However, the Ranged class strikes a balance between the high health and armor rating availability of the Melee class and the low health and armor ratings of the mage classes.

- **Not easy to exploit enemy elemental weaknesses**: Many monsters are weak to specific elemental damage, such as ice or fire. Some ranged weapons offer elemental damage, but not at the degree of a mage's spells.

Combat Magic

Combat Magic emphasizes fire, lightning, and death-magic damage spells and curses. Increase your combat-magic level by equipping and casting combat-magic spells. Enhancing mage levels primarily increases the Intelligence attribute, which has the greatest affect on maximum mana reserves. Intelligence also determines the potency of most spells.

Through skill and power selection, a combat magic character can specialize in fire magic, lightning magic, or death magic (as well as curse spells and summoned creatures). See Part 2 for details on molding a powerful combat magic character.

This list covers the primary advantages and disadvantages of the Combat Magic class.

- **Dependency on mana**: Health potions are the lifeblood of fighters, mana potions are the lifeblood of mages. All spells require mana. Without it, a mage is little more than a party decoration.
- **Wide selection of elemental damage spells**: As the name suggests, combat magic is an offensive discipline and the combat mage has a variety of fire, lightning, and death-magic spells available.
- **Support party members through curses**: The combat mage can invoke curses on enemy monsters that decrease monster resistances, which in turn support other party attackers.
- **Low health and armor rating**: Both mage classes lack the high armor rating availability of the

Melee class; and high Intelligence, while having the greatest effect on mana reserves, also has the lowest impact on health reserves.

Nature Magic

Nature Magic emphasizes ice-magic damage, enchantment, heals, and summon creature spells. Raise your nature-magic level by equipping and using nature-magic spells. Like combat magic, increasing nature magic primarily boosts Intelligence, which has the greatest impact on maximum mana reserves and determines the potency of most spells.

Through your skill and power choices, a nature magic character can specialize in ice magic, enchantment spells, healing, or summon creatures. For additional strategies on crafting a formidable nature magic character, see Part 2.

Developer Tip

Nature mages are an excellent support class and I personally never leave town without one. A Nature mage specialized in the Feral Wrath skill and using the Wrath of the Bear spell to enchant the party is very effective—the spell increases critical hit chance. Give your Nature mage a Heal spell on autocast and your health potion bill plummets. I usually use a heal-over-time spell (Nourish) in autocast and an instant heal spell (Heal) in an active slot for emergencies.
—Sarah Boulian, Lead Level Designer

Character Attributes

All Dungeon Siege II characters have three primary attributes: Strength, Dexterity, and Intelligence. Guiding your character into a specific class shapes these attributes, and the attributes, in turn, shape other aspects of your character.

- **Strength:** *Every melee level gained raises your Strength by approximately three points (other stats rise one point). Strength is the largest factor in determining your character's maximum health reserve, and it adds a bonus to minimum and maximum melee-weapon damage. Strength has virtually no impact on a character's mana reserves.*
- **Dexterity:** *Every ranged level gained raises your Dexterity by approximately three points (other stats rise one point). Dexterity is the second largest factor in determining your character's maximum health reserve. Dexterity also adds a bonus to minimum and maximum ranged-weapon damage and has little effect on mana reserves.*
- **Intelligence:** *Every combat-magic or nature-magic level gained raises your Intelligence by approximately three points (other stats rise one point). Intelligence is overwhelmingly the largest factor in determining your character's maximum mana reserves and determines the effectiveness of mage spells. Intelligence has the smallest impact on maximum health.*

In Dungeon Siege II, attributes have no impact on your character's armor rating, which is determined entirely by gear and selected skills. Attributes also have no impact on a character's chance of scoring a hit.

The list below reveals formulas for determining character health and mana reserves, plus bonuses to minimum and maximum melee and ranged damage.

- **Health:** $[(Strength \times 0.5) + (Dexterity \times 0.39) + (Intelligence \times 0.23)] \times 5.0$
- **Mana:** $[(Strength \times 0.01) + (Dexterity \times 0.12) + (Intelligence \times 0.87)] \times 5.0$
- **Minimum Melee Damage Bonus:** $0.75 \times 0.2 \times Strength$
- **Maximum Melee Damage Bonus:** $1.25 \times 0.2 \times Strength$
- **Minimum Ranged Damage Bonus:** $0.75 \times 0.2 \times Dexterity$
- **Maximum Ranged Damage Bonus:** $1.25 \times 0.2 \times Dexterity$

This following list covers the primary advantages and disadvantages of the Nature Magic class.

◆ **Dependency on mana**: Nature mages require mana for all spells. Mana feeds the mage's ability to cast damage, enchantment, or healing spells, as well as summons. Maintain a stock of mana potions to keep your mages active.

◆ **Support party members through enchantments, heals, and summons**: Nature mages can serve primarily in a support role through a variety of enchantments (which include increasing resistances or improving health, mana, or power-recovery rate), heals, and creature summons.

◆ **Focus on ice elemental damage**: Nature-magic damage spells are limited to ice magic.

But through skills and powers, ice magic can freeze monsters in their tracks.

◆ **Low health and armor rating**: Both mage classes lack the high armor rating availability of the Melee class. High Intelligence, while having the greatest effect on mana reserves, also has the lowest impact on health reserves.

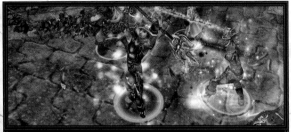

A nature mage can focus on attack through ice magic, or defense through enchantments and heals.

Character Classifications

Your character will carry a unique classification based on class level. A character with melee level 5 is a Soldier, but a character with melee and combat-magic level 5 is a Duelist. Table 1.1 reveals every possible character classification.

Table 1.1: Character Classifications

Class	Levels 1 to 4	Levels 5 to 10	Levels 11 to 19	Levels 20 to 49	Levels 50 to 99	Levels 100+
Melee	Squire	Soldier	Warrior	Knight	Champion	Grand Champion
Ranged	Bowyer	Archer	Marksman	Sharpshooter	Master Sharpshooter	Grandmaster Sharpshooter
Nature Magic	Apprentice	Theurgist	Magician	Grand Mage	Arch Mage	Supreme Arch Mage
Combat Magic	Savant	Hedge Wizard	Wizard	Sorcerer (Sorceress)	Grand Sorcerer (Grand Sorceress)	Grand High Sorcerer (Grand High Sorceress)
Melee, Ranged	Man-at-Arms (Woman-at-Arms)	Skirmisher	Raider	Campaigner	Crusader	Grand Crusader
Melee, Nature Magic	Friar	Curate	Druid	Preserver	Grand Preserver	Supreme Preserver
Melee, Combat Magic	Combatant	Duelist	Dragoon	Warlock (Warwitch)	Grand Warlock (Grand Warwitch)	Grand High Warlock (Grand High Warwitch)
Ranged, Nature Magic	Scout	Forester	Ranger	Warder (Wardess)	Arch Ward (Arch Wardess)	Supreme High Ward (Supreme High Wardess)
Ranged, Combat Magic	Jager	Conjurer	Channeler	Matross	Master Matross	Grandmaster Matross
Nature Magic, Combat Magic	Acolyte	Shaman	Scholar	Magus	Grand Magus	Grand High Magus
Melee, Ranged, Nature Magic	Cavalier	Marshal	Paladin	Templar	Arch Templar	Supreme Templar
Melee, Ranged, Combat Magic	Mercenary	Gladiator	Centurion	Myrmidon	Warlord (Warlady)	Warlord Noble (Warlady Noble)
Melee, Nature Magic, Combat Magic	Initiate	Mystic	Sage	Deacon (Deaconess)	Grand Deacon (Grand Deaconess)	Grand High Deacon (Grand High Deaconess)
Ranged, Nature Magic, Combat Magic	Adept	Conjurer	Thaumaturgist	Evoker	Senior Evoker	Lord Evoker (Lady Evoker)
Melee, Ranged, Nature Magic, Combat Magic	Freelance	Journeyman	Adventurer	Master	Grand Master	Grand High Siegemaster (Grand High Siegemistress)

Dungeon Siege II's new skills and powers expand the four classes—Melee, Ranged, Combat Magic, and Nature Magic—into an almost infinite number of subclasses and multiclasses. You receive a skill point for every character level gained and can spend that point on any available skill, provided you've met the prerequisites.

Although the options are virtually limitless, the skill and power system rewards planned, strategic selection. Focusing your skill choices on specific subclass paths can maximize your character's damage potential and the quantity and potency of unlocked powers. This part of the book provides guidance on skill and power selection and offers several specific examples to create unique and powerful Dungeon Siege II characters.

Skills and Powers

You'll finish the single-player Mercenary game around character level 40; adding skill points from character selection and rewards, expect to have between 43 and 49 to spend on dozens of skills and their levels. Careful selection is vital! Choosing skills indiscriminately will weaken your character in the long run; you may find you've spent a point on a skill you aren't using, or that careless spending has left you unable to unlock a power until much later in the game.

> **Tip**
>
> For additional subjective tips for all of Dungeon Siege II's skills and powers, see Part 8, "Statistics." The Class Skills and Class Power tables there also reveal complete statistics for every skill and power at every level.

You can spend skill points as soon as you acquire them, or save them until you reach a prerequisite for an even more valuable skill. For example, the melee skill Barricade requires melee level 5. Instead of spending the five skill points you acquired reaching *character* level 5, you could save them and place all five into Barricade upon reaching *melee* level 5. Your character will be at a disadvantage during the interval, but saving points and flooding more potent skills can pay off when you're able to meet power requirements earlier.

Character Templates

This section provides templates for sample character types. It includes suggestions for specific skills that lead to the potent powers for that character. Note that these character names aren't official; they're just our examples. Our allocation tables have matched skill point with character level. You will acquire additional skill points from quest rewards, so consider our tables development guidelines. Actual distribution may vary slightly, and thorough experimentation may yield even more powerful combinations.

In the skill-point allocation tables that follow, the first row refers to the default skills provided by race selection. Skills repeated in the same Assigned to Skill cell indicate you should spend all available points on that skill upon reaching that specific character level.

Knight (Melee)

Our sample Melee-class Knight fights with "sword and board," a weapon in one hand and a shield in the other. Offsetting the reduced damage of a single one-handed weapon (plus the fact that none of the Knight's best skill choices increase weapon damage) is the boost to the Armor rating. To put it simply, the Knight is a tank—a durable Melee-class character capable of soaking up enemy damage while other party members provide support with ranged weapons, damage spells, buffs, and heals.

Outfit the Knight with items that have modifiers that boost strength, health and health regeneration, resistances, and armor. To capitalize on the Knight's Barricade skill, save your best reagents to craft a magnificent shield (or save gold to purchase one).

Select the Half-Giant race and use the following skill and power selections for our sample level-36 Knight. This character build requires banking points to spend later, which will make stretches of the game more difficult but will net Provoke level 3 at its earliest point, melee level 36. After level 36, con-

tinue to feed Rebuke and consider Fortitude to add further to the Knight's durability.

The Knight's skill points and benefits:

- Fortitude level 2: +10% to maximum health
- Critical Strike level 1: +8% chance to inflict a critical hit
- Barricade level 10: +93% to Shield Armor, +14% chance to block melee and ranged attacks
- Toughness level 10: +18% to physical damage resistance
- Reinforced Armor level 10: +24.5% to Armor
- Rebuke level 5: 1.3 × melee-level damage, 1-second stun

Table 2.1: Knight Skill Point Allocation

Skill Point	Assigned to Skill
Half-Giant Race Selection	Fortitude, Fortitude
1	Critical Strike (unlocks Brutal Attack level 1)
2–4	—
5	Barricade, Barricade, Barricade, Barricade (unlocks Provoke level 1)
6-8	Barricade
9–11	—
12	Toughness, Toughness, Toughness, Toughness (unlocks Provoke level 2)
13	Barricade
14	Toughness
15	Barricade
16	Toughness
17	Barricade
18–21	Toughness
22–23	—
24	Reinforced Armor, Reinforced Armor, Reinforced Armor
25–31	Reinforced Armor
32–35	—
36	Rebuke, Rebuke, Rebuke, Rebuke, Rebuke (unlocks Provoke level 3)

Character Templates

Barbarian (Melee)

Our sample Barbarian is a Melee-class character focused on two-handed weapon skills and powers. Counter to the Knight, this two-handed-weapon powerhouse provides strong damage but at the expense of his Armor rating. A two-handed weapon skill (Smite) and power (Staggering Blow) offer the chance to stun monsters, which set your foes up for other party member attacks and powers.

Barbarians stress damage over defense.

The two-handed weapon is the Barbarian's most important piece of equipment. The Overbear skill in our sample character adds 38% to the two-handed weapon's damage. Equip the most potent weapon you can find, purchase, or craft. Remaining equipment should focus on boosting strength, health and health regeneration, resistances, and armor, one of the Barbarian's disadvantages.

Select the Half-Giant race and use the following skill and power selections for our sample level-36 Barbarian. After level 36, focus on either Toughness to boost armor and to reach Staggering Blow level 3, or Deadly Strike to boost critical-hit damage and to reach War Cry level 3.

The Barbarian's skill points and benefits:

- Fortitude level 2: +10% to maximum health
- Critical Strike level 12: +38% chance to inflict a critical hit
- Overbear level 10: +38% to two-handed weapon damage
- Toughness level 4: +9% physical damage resistance
- Smite level 8: +31% chance to stun with a two-handed weapon, 1.25-second stun duration
- Deadly Strike level 2: +242% critical hit damage

Table 2.2: Barbarian Skill Point Allocation

Skill Point	Assigned to Skill
Half-Giant Race Selection	Fortitude, Fortitude
1	Critical Strike (unlocks Brutal Attack level 1)
2–4	Critical Strike
5	Overbear (unlocks Staggering Blow level 1)
6	Critical Strike (unlocks Brutal Attack level 2)
7–10	Overbear
11–12	Critical Strike
13	Critical Strike (unlocks Brutal Attack level 3)
14–16	Toughness
17	Toughness (unlocks Staggering Blow level 2)
18–22	Overbear
23	Critical Strike
24	Smite (unlocks War Cry level 1)
25–27	Critical Strike
28–34	Smite
35	—
36	Deadly Strike, Deadly Strike (unlocks War Cry level 2)

Tip

Focus points into Critical Strike, Fortitude, and Reinforced Armor to unlock the Whirling Strike power. Whirling Strike is the only power that requires points into Fortitude, which means unlocking Whirling Strike delays the acquisition of other powers. Select a Half-Giant and mix points into Critical Strike and Fortitude to unlock Whirling Strike level 1 at character level 12. Start saving points as you approach level 24, the prerequisite for Reinforced Armor.

Hurricane (Melee)

Our Hurricane Melee class wields a one-handed weapon in each hand—dual-wielding. What the Hurricane lacks in armor and sheer power, he gains in speed. Selected skills are geared toward inflicting damage quickly and repeatedly. Alacrity increases melee attack speed and Fierce Renewal increases melee power recovery rate; both are essential to meeting the dual-wielding Hurricane's power requirements.

Items with modifiers that boost strength and damage are at a premium. Eschewing Fortitude for other skills means items that increase health and health regeneration and are also important. Look also for modifiers that increase your power recovery rate to further enhance the Hurricane's power.

Choose Half-Giant and use the following skill and power selections for our sample level-36 dual-wielding Hurricane. This character build requires banking points to spend later, which will make stretches of the game more difficult. After level 36, spend seven points in Deadly Strike and one in Alacrity to reach Waves of Force level 3, or spend them in Fierce Renewal and Deadly Strike to meet the requirement for Elemental Rage level 3.

The Hurricane's skill points and benefits:

- Fortitude level 2: +10% to maximum health
- Critical Strike level 10: +38% chance to inflict a critical hit
- Dual Wield level 10: +52% dual-wield damage
- Alacrity level 9: +14% melee attack speed
- Fierce Renewal level 6: +14% melee power recovery rate
- Deadly Strike level 1: +224% critical hit damage

Table 2.3: Hurricane Skill Point Allocation

Skill Point	Assigned to Skill
Half-Giant Race Selection	Fortitude, Fortitude
1	Critical Strike (unlocks Brutal Attack level 1)
2–4	—
5	Dual Wield, Dual Wield, Dual Wield, Dual Wield (unlocks Waves of Force level 1)
6	Dual Wield
7–8	Critical Strike
9–11	—

Skill Point	Assigned to Skill
12	Alacrity, Alacrity, Alacrity, Alacrity (unlocks Waves of Force level 2)
13–17	Dual Wield
18	Critical Strike
19–21	Critical Strike
22	Critical Strike (unlocks Brutal Attack level 3)
23	—
24	Fierce Renewal, Fierce Renewal
25–26	Critical Strike
27–30	Fierce Renewal
31–35	Alacrity
36	Deadly Strike (unlocks Elemental Rage level 2)

Ranger (Ranged)

The Ranger uses either a bow or crossbow as his primary weapon. Skill selections are focused completely on increasing the potency of the Ranger's weapon. Biting Arrow (prerequisite to equip a crossbow) increases damage and Far Shot increases range. The Ranger's greatest advantage is range. Keep your Ranger out of thick fighting and at his maximum range, dishing damage from afar.

The Ranger's specialized skills work well with both bow and crossbow.

Your bow or crossbow is the key; the Ranger's skills and powers are tied to the weapon's damage. Any bonuses should enhance dexterity (which applies a bonus to minimum and maximum damage), health and health regeneration, armor, and resistances. Save your best reagents to craft a formidable bow or crossbow, the Ranger's foundation.

(continued)

Character Templates

Select Human and use the following skill and power selections for our sample level-36 Ranger. Choosing Human allows you to reach Take Aim level 2 at character level 3, and Thunderous Shot level 2 at character level 13 because both of the Human's free points were placed in Critical Shot. After level 36, add four skill points to Mortal Wound and three to Biting Arrow to reach Thunderous Shot level 3. Then allocate points to Mortal Wound and Shockwave for Charged Shots level 2 and 3.

Developer Tip

I personally play a party of two or three Rangers, with one dabbling in Nature Magic for damage-increasing buffs such as Wrath of the Bear. A group of Rangers with buffs can safely deal strong damage while rarely taking damage. The only Ranged power I use is Thunderous Shot; it not only knocks back monsters, [but] briefly stuns them as well, allowing my Rangers ample time to turn the targets into pincushions of arrows. Along with the main hero, Deru and Taar make good allies. —Jerry Pritchard, Tester

The Ranger's skill points and benefits:

◆ Critical Shot level 10: +38% chance to inflict a critical hit

◆ Biting Arrow level 9: +36% bow and crossbow damage

◆ Far Shot level 8: +31% bow and crossbow range

◆ Shockwave level 8: +30% shockwave damage

◆ Penetrate level 1: +12% chance to penetrate

◆ Mortal Wound level 1: +224% bow and crossbow critical-hit damage

Table 2.4: Ranger Skill Point Allocation

Skill Point	Assigned to Skill
Human Race Selection	Critical Shot, Critical Shot (unlocks Take Aim level 1)
1–2	Critical Shot
3	Critical Shot (unlocks Take Aim level 2)
4	Critical Shot
5	Biting Arrow
6–12	Biting Arrow
13	Far Shot
14–17	Critical Shot
18–21	Far Shot
22–23	Biting Arrow
24–26	Shockwave
27	Shockwave (unlocks Charged Shots level 1)
28	Penetrate (unlocks Take Aim level 3)
29–32	Shockwave
33–35	Far Shot
36	Mortal Wound

Thrown Weapon Specialist (Ranged)

Thrown weaponry is the second major Ranged-class discipline. Thrown weapon firing rate and base damage are greater than for the bow and crossbow; furthermore, the thrown-weapon skills offer an additional increase to firing rate and a chance to cause more "bleed" damage. However, the thrown-weapon skills feature no additional increases to base weapon damage output.

None of the thrown-weapon powers require Far Shot since the increased firing rate means it's better to be closer to the target (thrown weaponry base range is shorter than the base range of bows and crossbows). Thrown Weapon Specialists should seek items that bolster dexterity, health and health generation, resistances, armor, and weapon damage, and use reagents to craft an impressive thrown weapon.

Choose Dryad for your race and then use the following skill and power selections for our sample level-36 Thrown Weapon Specialist. You could also build this character using a Human and place both unspent skill points into Critical Shot. After level 36, add points to Ricochet to cause any throw-weapon critical hit to ricochet into nearby enemies (also a prerequisite for Flurry level 2 and 3).

The Thrown Weapon Specialist's skill points and benefits:

◆ Natural Bond level 1: -6% mana cost of spells; can harvest mana potions

◆ Dodge level 1: +4% chance to dodge melee or ranged attacks

◆ Critical Shot level 8: +33.5% chance to inflict a critical hit

◆ Quick Draw level 10: +15% thrown-weapon firing rate

◆ Bleed level 8: +25% chance to cause bleed

◆ Penetrate level 6: +46% chance to penetrate

◆ Cunning Revival level 4: +10% ranged power recovery rate

(continued)

Table 2.5: Thrown Weapon Skill Point Allocation

Skill Point	Assigned to Skill
Dryad Race Selection	Natural Bond, Dodge (unlocks Gravity Stone level 1)
1	Critical Shot (Take Aim level 1)
2–4	—
5	Quick Draw, Quick Draw, Quick Draw, Quick Draw (unlocks Shrapnel Blast level 1)
6–8	Critical Shot
9	Critical Shot (Take Aim level 2)
10–11	Quick Draw
12–15	Bleed
16	Bleed (unlocks Shrapnel Blast level 2)
17–18	Critical Shot
19	Quick Draw
20	Bleed
21	Critical Shot
22	Quick Draw
23	Bleed
24	Penetrate (unlocks Take Aim level 3)
25–26	Quick Draw
27	Bleed
28–31	Penetrate
32	Penetrate (unlocks Shrapnel Blast level 3)
33–35	Cunning Revival
36	Cunning Revival (unlocks Flurry level 1)

Survivalist (Ranged)

Our Survivalist build uses the Ranged-class skills Survival and Dodge to meet the prerequisites for the Silence and Repulse powers. Silence is an area-effect power that prevents any monsters within its influence from casting spells; Repulse knocks monsters away from the user and temporarily stuns them.

Survival is a unique skill that increases the user's elemental resistances (except death). Astute equipment choices can push the user to near the max of 95% resistance to fire, ice, and lightning. The Dodge skill provides a chance to avoid melee or ranged attacks completely. Equip items that increase dexterity, health and health regeneration, resistances, and armor.

Our character build chooses the bow and crossbow over thrown weapons. You can follow the same

build with thrown weapons; replace Biting Arrow with Quick Draw and Far Shot with Bleed. Upon reaching level 36, select Ricochet instead of Mortal Wound and receive Repulse level 2 over Silence level 2. You can also put points in Dodge and Survival sooner to provide stronger defenses, but doing so would delay acquisition of the weapon powers (since Silence or Repulse level 2 can't be acquired until ranged level 36 at the earliest).

Choose the Dryad race (with +10% death resistance as its benefit) and use the following skill and power selections for our sample level-36 Survivalist. After level 36, bow and crossbow users should select Mortal Wound, Survival, and Dodge) to reach Silence level 3. Thrown weapon users should choose Ricochet, Survival, and Dodge to reach Repulse level 3.

The Survivalist's skill points and benefits:

- Natural Bond level 1: -6% mana cost of spells; can harvest mana potions

Developer Tip

Ranged and Nature Magic is a viable combination. Advance the character at an approximately 4:1 ratio of Ranged to Nature Magic levels. Place a low-level healing spell and low-level enchantment spell in your spellbook's autocast slot. Use Ice Bolt or other low-level Nature Magic damage spell when you want to level up in Nature Magic. —Matt Mahon, Level Designer

The Survivalist's primary powers are Silence and Repulse, which knocks monsters away from the caster and stuns them.

- Dodge level 10: +26% chance to dodge melee or ranged attacks
- Survival level 6: +35% to fire, ice, and lightning resistance; can harvest health potions
- Critical Shot level 8: +33.5% chance to inflict a critical hit
- Biting Arrow level 8: +33.5% bow and crossbow damage
- Far Shot level 1: +6% bow and crossbow range
- Penetrate level 3: +30% chance to penetrate
- Mortal Wound level 1: +224% bow and crossbow critical-hit damage

Table 2.6: Survivalist Skill Point Allocation

Skill Point	Assigned to Skill
Dryad Race Selection	Natural Bond, Dodge (unlocks Gravity Stone level 1)
1	Critical Shot (unlocks Take Aim level 1)
2–5	Dodge
6–7	Survival
8	Survival (unlocks Silence and Repulse level 1)
9	Biting Arrow (unlocks Thunderous Shot level 1)
10–16	Biting Arrow
17	Far Shot (unlocks Thunderous Shot level 2)
18–20	Critical Shot
21	Critical Shot (unlocks Take Aim level 2)
22–24	Critical Shot
25	Penetrate (unlocks Take Aim level 3)
26–28	Survival
29–30	Penetrate
31–35	Dodge
36	Mortal Wound (unlocks Silence level 2)

Fire Mage (Combat Magic)

Our Fire Mage is a Combat Magic–class character focused entirely on fire skills and powers. Searing Flames, which increases fire-magic and fire-power damage, and Ignite, which adds a chance to engulf monsters in damaging flame for a short duration, are the Fire Mage's primary skills. Increase Devastation, which increases general combat-magic damage, to meet requirements for the Flame Nexus power.

Choose equipment that increases intelligence, mana and mana regeneration, combat magic damage, resistances, and armor. Place the curse spell Dehydrate in your spellbook's autocast slot; Dehydrate weakens monsters to fire damage. And obviously the majority of your spellbook should be filled with fire-damage spells to gain maximum impact from the selected skills!

Select Elf and use the following skill and power selections for our sample level-36 Fire Mage. After level 36, place a point into Quickened Casting and dedicate eight to Arcane Fury, along with four more in Ignite and three in Searing Flames to reach Detonation level 3. Otherwise you could focus points solely in Quickened Casting and Arcane Fury to increase your firing rate and damage power exclusively.

The Fire Mage's skill points and benefits:

- Critical Strike level 1: +8% chance to inflict a critical hit
- Brilliance level 4: +28% to maximum mana
- Devastation level 12: +51% combat-magic damage
- Searing Flames level 13: +50% fire-magic and fire-power damage
- Ignite level 8: 20% chance to ignite

Table 2.7: Fire Mage Skill Point Allocation

Skill Point	Assigned to Skill
Elf Race Selection	Critical Strike, Brilliance (unlocks Brutal Attack and Energy Orb level 1)
1–2	Devastation
3–4	Brilliance
5	Searing Flames (unlocks Flame Nexus level 1)
6	Brilliance (unlocks Energy Orb level 2)
7	Searing Flames
8	Devastation
9	Searing Flames
10	Devastation
11	Searing Flames
12	Devastation (unlocks Flame Nexus level 2)
13	Devastation
14	Searing Flames
15	Devastation
16	Searing Flames
17	Devastation
18–19	Searing Flames
20–23	Devastation
24	Ignite (unlocks Detonation level 1)
25–27	Ignite
28	Ignite (unlocks Flame Nexus level 3)
29	Searing Flames
30	Ignite
31–32	Searing Flames
33	Searing Flames (unlocks Detonation level 2)
34	Searing Flames
35–36	Ignite

Death Mage (Combat Magic)

The Death Mage emphasizes the Grim Necromancy, Vampirism, and Debilitation combat-magic skills to increase the potency of death magic and curse spells and to unlock the Harvest Soul and Corrosive Eruption powers. Grim Necromancy isn't available until combat-magic level 12, which leaves the Death Mage underpowered through early levels. Equip items that increase intelligence, mana and mana regeneration, combat magic damage, resistances, and armor.

The Death Mage is a powerful blend of curses and elemental damage.

This character build requires banking points to spend later, which will make stretches of the game more difficult but does reward you with Harvest Soul as early as possible (and it'll be maxed before you reach combat-magic level 36). You can modify the build and increase Debilitation before Grim Necromancy to unlock Corrosive Eruption level 2 earlier, and Harvest Soul much later.

Select Human and use the following skill and power selections for our

sample level-36 Death Mage. We've selected Human to spend the free skill points on Devastation instead of the Elf's Brilliance and Critical Strike. You do sacrifice the Elf's natural 5% boost to mana recovery, but this benefit can be gained through equipment. After level 36, place points in Quickened Casting to unlock Arcane Fury, which increases power damage and is a prerequisite for maximizing Corrosive Eruption.

The Death Mage's skill points and benefits:

◆ Brilliance level 1: +7% to maximum mana

◆ Devastation level 10: +46.5% combat-magic damage

◆ Debilitation level 5: +77% curse-spell power; +102% curse-spell duration

◆ Grim Necromancy level 12: +48% death-magic and death-power damage

◆ Vampirism level 10: +18% death-magic damage added to health

Table 2.8: Death Mage Skill Point Allocation

Skill Point	Assigned to Skill
Human Race Selection	Devastation, Devastation
1–4	Devastation
5	Debilitation (unlocks Corrosive Eruption level 1)
6–7	Devastation
8–11	—
12	Grim Necromancy, Grim Necromancy, Grim Necromancy, Grim Necromancy, Grim Necromancy (unlocks Harvest Soul level 1)
13–15	Debilitation
16	Debilitation (unlocks Corrosive Eruption level 2)
17–19	Grim Necromancy
20	Devastation
21–23	—
24	Vampirism, Vampirism, Vampirism, Vampirism (unlocks Harvest Soul level 2)
25	Devastation
26–31	Vampirism
32–34	Grim Necromancy
35	Grim Necromancy (unlocks Harvest Soul level 3)
36	Brilliance (unlocks Energy Orb level 1)

Lightning Mage (Combat Magic)

Our Lightning Mage focuses skill points on Devastation and Amplified Lightning, which increases lightning magic and lightning-power damage (the mage's other specialty skill, Arcing, isn't available until combat-magic level 36). A mixture of Devastation and Amplified Lightning unlocks Chain Lightning and the ability to secure Gathered Bolt at combat-magic level 24. Lightning-damage spells drain mana quickly; spending points in Brilliance helps increase this mage's mana reserve. Further bolster the reserve with equipment that adds to mana and mana regeneration.

Other equipment should increase intelligence, combat-magic damage, resistances, and armor. Once available, equip the Drown curse in your spellbook's autocast slot; Drown weakens monsters to lightning damage (as well as ice). Lightning-damage spells will fill the majority of your spellbook to maximize the potential of your chosen skills.

Select Elf and use the following skill and power selections for our sample level-36 Lightning Mage. After level 36, start spending points in Arcing (after five, you meet the prerequisite for Chain Lightning level 3), which provides a chance for all lightning spells to arc and strike nearby enemies.

The Lightning Mage's skill points and benefits:

- Critical Strike level 1: +8% chance to inflict a critical hit
- Brilliance level 6: +44% to maximum mana
- Devastation level 12: +51% combat-magic damage
- Amplified Lightning level 12: +48% lightning-magic and lightning-power damage
- Quickened Casting level 6: +15.5% cast speed
- Arcane Fury level 1: +3% combat- and nature-magic power damage

Table 2.9: Lightning Mage Skill Point Allocation

Skill Point	Assigned to Skill
Elf Race Selection	Critical Strike, Brilliance (unlocks Brutal Attack and Energy Orb level 1)
1–4	Devastation
5	Amplified Lightning (unlocks Chain Lightning level 1)
6	Devastation
7–9	Amplified Lightning
10	Amplified Lightning (unlocks Chain Lightning level 2)
11–12	Brilliance
13	Brilliance (unlocks Energy Orb level 2)
14–16	Amplified Lightning
17–19	Devastation
20–23	Amplified Lightning
24	Quickened Casting (unlocks Gathered Bolt level 1)
25	Brilliance
26	Devastation
27	Brilliance
28–30	Devastation
31–35	Quickened Casting
36	Arcane Fury (unlocks Gathered Bolt level 2)

Ice Mage (Nature Magic)

Our Ice Mage is a Nature Magic–class character focused on the ice-magic damage skills Aquatic Affinity, Arctic Mastery, and Freezing. Aquatic Affinity also enhances healing magic spells. These three skills, combined with Natural Bond, unlock the ice-damage specialized powers Icicle Blast and Circle of Frost.

Freezing monsters in their tracks is a powerful ability. While frozen, monsters can't move, attack, or cast spells. Target frozen monsters with other attacks to eliminate them as quickly as possible. Any combat mages in the party should keep the curse spell Drown in their spellbook's autocast slot: Drown increases monsters' vulnerability to ice damage.

An Ice Mage's ability to freeze monsters can quickly turn the tide of battle.

Skill Point	Assigned to Skill
9	Arctic Mastery (unlocks Icicle Blast level 2)
10–12	Natural Bond
13	Natural Bond (unlocks Gravity Stone level 2)
14–18	Arctic Mastery
19–23	Aquatic Affinity
24	Freezing (unlocks Circle of Frost level 1)
25–30	Freezing
31	Freezing (unlocks Icicle Blast level 3)
32	Natural Bond (unlocks Circle of Frost level 2)
33–36	Freezing

Summoning Mage (Nature Magic)

The Summoning Mage is a Nature Magic–class character focused on improving the life span and damage output of a summon creature. At high levels, points are added to the Summon Bond skill, which creates a bond between mage and creature where a percentage of magic damage is absorbed by the creature. Specialized powers are Summon Provoke, which causes nearby monsters to focus their attacks completely on the summoned creature, and Aether Blast, which turns the summoned creature into an explosive device.

The weakness of the Summoning Mage is his lack of improvement to damage spells. To meet power requirements in our build, only two points are added to Aquatic Affinity, adding just 10% to ice-magic damage. Equip the mage with items that improve nature-magic damage to offset the weakness. Other modifiers should boost intelligence, mana and mana regeneration, resistances, and armor.

Select Dryad and use the following skill and power selections for our sample level-36 Summoning Mage. After level 36, add points to Summon Bond and Arcane Renewal to meet prerequisites for maximum levels of the Summon Provoke and Summon Bond powers. Consider also spending a point on Enveloping Embrace (perhaps early in the build) to unlock the Invulnerability power or to increase the power of your buffs, which can aid the summoned creature.

Choose Human and use the following skill and power selections for our sample level-36 Ice Mage. We've selected Human and placed both unspent skill points into Aquatic Affinity to unlock the Icicle Blast power immediately. Equip items that increase intelligence, mana and mana regeneration, nature-magic damage, resistances, and armor.

After level 36, continue to add points to Freezing to meet prerequisites for Circle of Frost level 3. You could also end this build with two points each in Arctic Mastery and Natural Bond, then secure the Freezing requirements for Circle of Frost level 3, which can be acquired at the 40th skill point.

The Ice Mage's skill points and benefits:

- Natural Bond level 8: -37% mana cost to spells; can harvest mana potions
- Aquatic Affinity level 10: +29% to ice-magic damage; +30% to healing magic
- Arctic Mastery level 12: +48% to ice-magic and ice-power damage
- Freezing level 8: +20% chance to freeze; +1.25 freeze duration

Table 2.10: Ice Mage Skill Point Allocation

Skill Point	Assigned to Skill
Human Race Selection	Aquatic Affinity, Aquatic Affinity (unlocks Icicle Blast level 1)
1	Natural Bond (unlocks Gravity Stone level 1)
2–4	Aquatic Affinity
5–8	Arctic Mastery

(continued)

Character Templates

The Summoning Mage focuses most of his skill choices on enhancing the health and damage potential of summoned creatures.

Table 2.11: Summoning Mage Skill Point Allocation

Skill Point	Assigned to Skill
Dryad Race Selection	Natural Bond, Dodge (unlocks Gravity Stone level 1)
1	Aquatic Affinity
2	Aquatic Affinity (unlocks Icicle Blast level 1)
3–4	Natural Bond
5–11	Summon Fortitude
12	Summon Might (unlocks Summon Provoke level 1)
13–14	Summon Might
15	Summon Might (unlocks Summon Provoke level 2)
16	Natural Bond
17	Natural Bond (unlocks Gravity Stone level 2)
18–19	Natural Bond
20–23	Summon Might
24	Arcane Renewal (unlocks Aether Blast level 1)
25–26	Summon Might
27–31	Arcane Renewal
32–34	Summon Fortitude
35	—
36	Summon Bond, Summon Bond (unlocks Aether Blast level 2)

The Summoning Mage's skill points and benefits:

◆ Dodge level 1: 4% chance to dodge melee and ranged attacks

◆ Natural Bond level 7: -34% mana cost of spells; can harvest mana potions

◆ Aquatic Affinity level 2: +10% ice-magic damage; +9% healing magic

◆ Summon Fortitude level 10: +76% summoned creature health

◆ Summon Might level 10: +115% summoned creature damage

◆ Arcane Renewal level 6: +14% combat- and nature-magic power recovery rate

◆ Summon Bond level 2: +20% of summoned creature damage transferred

Developer Tip

Do not place summoning spells in your mage's spellbook autocast slots. Summoning spells require a lot of mana to cast. Putting an expensive spell on autocast can drain your mana supply in the midst of combat! —Jerry Pritchard, Tester

Enchantment Mage (Nature Magic)

Our Enchantment Mage assigns skill points to Enveloping Embrace and Feral Wrath skills; both of these improve the power and duration of the nature-magic "buff" spells (spells that offer enhancements to the caster and allies).

The Enchantment Mage should keep a collection of buff spells in his spellbook and switch between them to counter monsters. For instance, if you're facing monsters with lightning attacks, put Spirit Embrace in the spellbook's autocast slot; when facing monsters weak to ice damage, put Wrath of Ice in the spellbook's autocast slot.

This is primarily a support character that lacks the damage output of other classes. But strategic use of

Developer Tip

Points added to Nurturing Gift and Aquatic Affinity skills improve the power of healing spells. Placing healing spells in autocast slots can autoheal party members and other players, but can drain your mana reserves very quickly, as the NPCs will autoheal very often. Keep buff spells in your autocast slot and a heal-over-time spell, such as Healing Rain or Nourish, in your active spell slots to cast during battles. —Jerry Pritchard, Tester

buff and healing spells makes other party members more powerful, in turn creating a stronger party overall. The Enchantment Mage may not receive the glory but arguably plays the most important role in party success. Equipment should boost intelligence, mana and mana regeneration, nature-magic damage, resistances, and armor.

Select Human and use the following skill and power selections for our sample level-36 Enchantment Mage. After level 36, add points to Freezing and Absorption to meet the requirements for Glacial Aura level 2.

The Enchantment Mage's skill points and benefits:

- ◆ Natural Bond level 4: -22% mana cost of spells; can harvest mana potions
- ◆ Aquatic Affinity level 2: +10% ice-magic damage; +9% healing magic
- ◆ Arctic Mastery level 1: +8% ice-magic and ice-power damage
- ◆ Enveloping Embrace level 6: +78% embrace-spell power; +114% embrace-spell duration
- ◆ Feral Wrath level 12: +124% wrath-spell power; +166% wrath-spell duration
- ◆ Nurturing Gift level 4: +30% healing magic
- ◆ Freezing level 8: +20% chance to freeze; +1.25-second freeze duration
- ◆ Absorption level 1: +14% magic damage absorbed; +8% of damage absorbed added to mana

Table 2.12: Enchantment Mage Skill Point Allocation

Skill Point	Skill
Human Race Selection	Aquatic Affinity, Aquatic Affinity (unlocks Icicle Blast level 1)
1	Natural Bond (unlocks Gravity Stone level 1)
2–4	Natural Bond
5	Enveloping Embrace (unlocks Invulnerability level 1)
6–10	Enveloping Embrace
11	Arctic Mastery
12–14	Nurturing Gift
15	Nurturing Gift (unlocks Invulnerability level 2)
16–23	Feral Wrath
24	Freezing (unlocks Glacial Aura level 1)
25–28	Feral Wrath
29–35	Freezing
36	Absorption

Character Templates

PART 3:
COMBAT STRATEGIES AND PETS

Taking advantage of race and class benefits and selecting specialized skills and powers creates impressive characters, but it's combining these elements in combat against Dungeon Siege II's *diverse collection of monsters that determines consistent game success. This section provides single- and multiplayer combat strategies, including several straight from the game's developers. You'll also find a rundown of available pets, and strategies for utilizing their abilities in combat.*

Combat Strategies

Combat is about maximizing damage per second. The higher your damage rate, the faster you can eliminate monsters—which means the shorter the amount of time the monsters have to harm you! You can maximize damage through skills and powers, covered in Part 2, as well as through keen equipment selection, support spells, character micromanagement, and effective power usage. The following combat strategies will maximize your party's effectiveness and minimize your enemy's.

◆ You can toggle your party between Rampage mode and Mirror mode. Rampage mode gives party members autonomy; members outside your control seek their own targets, spreading the party out. Select Rampage when faced with a group of weaker targets (such as Tharva, Grangeflies, Shambler Hatchlings and small tribes of Hak'u and Taclak). Rampage mode can eliminate multiple targets more quickly but leave party members more vulnerable if a strong beast enters the fray. Mirror mode keeps party members together and attacks are focused on a single enemy. Combining damage from the entire party can eliminate tough monsters quickly but may be overkill against weaker creatures.

◆ Each type of monster is unique. Some are slow, others are fast, and many feature specific resistances, weaknesses, and hatreds (take note of these characteristics in the monster's statistics at the top of the screen). Exploit them! Use fire damage and powers against monsters that are weak to fire, or have your ice-damage nature mage focus on party healing against monsters resistant to ice. Some monsters hate when characters use potions or powers. Have a durable Melee-class character use a potion to enrage that monster; lure the beast into other party attacks or powers.

◆ Notice what type of elemental damage a monster employs. For instance, the Hak'u mages inflict lightning damage, and Thrusks inflict fire damage. Adjust your resistances to counter specific monster types prevalent in a particular area.

> ### Developer Tip
>
> *If you're fighting slower-moving enemies (such as Rustguards, Vulks, or Rhinocks), try running circles around them to get them all to follow your party. Then aim carefully, and hit them with a power like Flame Nexus or Thunderous Shot that fires out in a cone to wipe them all out in one click! —Grant Roberts, Level Designer*

Keep high-resistance jewelry and pieces of armor in a town storage vault, and adjust equipment based on the area's monster population. Fill your equipment slots with items that provide as much resistance as possible to the elemental damage. With other items in storage, return to town and readjust your equipment as needed.

◆ A well-timed class power can devastate a monster group. *Well-timed* is the operative phrase here. The combat-magic power Gathered Bolt doesn't shock its targets instantaneously. Lightning effects appear on the ground along the target radius and after a second or two, the bolts shock anything within that radius. If in those one or two seconds, monsters move, Gathered Bolt will miss and the power will be wasted. You'll use a given power many times throughout your games; learn its direction and timing to inflict the greatest damage possible with each usage. Also, capitalize on powers that stun, freeze, or knock back enemies. Focus your attacks on immobilized enemies to inflict extra damage before they can retaliate.

◆ Equipment selection plays a huge role in combat success. Your equipment should enhance the advantages of your class. Melee characters should equip items that increase strength, health and health regeneration, armor, and damage; ranged characters should equip items that increase dexterity, health and health regeneration, armor, and damage; and mages should equip items that increase intelligence, mana and mana regeneration, and combat- or nature-magic damage. Use reagents and town enchanters to create powerful items tailored to your class.

◆ Use nature-magic enchantment spells or combat-magic curse spells to take advantage of your party's strengths and exploit monster weaknesses. For example, if there's an ice-damage-focused nature mage or a lightning-damage-focused combat mage in your party, the combat mage should place Drown (increases monster vulnerability to ice and lightning) in an autocast slot. Aquatic Embrace (which increases mana regeneration) and Wrath of Magic (which increases magic damage) are strong enchantments for mage-heavy parties, but are worthless to melee or ranged characters. Be prepared to swap autocast enchantment and curses depending on the monsters you're facing, and don't hesitate to cancel a current party enchantment to utilize a more potent buff better suited to the situation.

◆ Press the pause button when facing a challenging encounter. While the game is paused, you can't move but you also can't suffer damage. Plan your battle strategy. You may swap out equipment in your inventory, ready a devastating power, or adjust a mage's autocast spells.

Developer Tip

In multiplayer games, monsters don't drop more or less rewards. However, many multiplayer quest rewards drop separate items for each player. Players will see their name attached to a dropped item's name. Only that player's party can see and pick up that item. Also, allow gold sharing to evenly split collected gold; note that this will not split gold earned from selling items. In multiplayer, give class-specific rare, unique, and set items you can't use to other players that can. Share the wealth! —Jerry Pritchard, Tester

Developer Tip

If you were a fan of the slightly more automated Dungeon Siege control dynamic, or just prefer to let your fingers take a break, you can activate the same mechanics by choosing Selected Hero Attack Automation and Selected Hero Defend Automation from the Game tab of the Options menu. —Bert Bingham, Producer

Developer Tip

Make sure you always open a town portal before major boss fights—that way if you don't survive, you can easily get back to your tombstones and won't have to worry about respawned monsters chasing your armorless self halfway across Aranna! —Sarah Boulian, Lead Level Designer

Pets

During a single- or multiplayer game, you can recruit other characters to join your party, or purchase pets from one of the town pet shops. Pets are fixed-class party members; for example, you can't switch a pet from Melee to Combat Magic class. Other recruited party members' special skills are customizable, but pets' are not; because pet abilities are fixed, make your pet purchases based on how the pets' abilities will assist your party in the long run.

Combat Strategies

Pets are purchased as babies. To mature a pet, feed it! Pets eat inventory items like weapons, armor, potions, reagents, and jewelry. The type of inventory item you feed a pet determines the bonuses the pet receives upon reaching the next maturity level—the better the item (higher level, more modifiers, etc.), the faster the pet matures. The attribute bonuses the items bestow are the same as for regular party members, however; feed a pet melee weapons and armor to increase strength; ranged weapons and armor to increase dexterity; and mage weapons and armor to increase intelligence. Potions increase health or mana, and reagents and jewelry increase all attributes slightly.

Developer Tip

Standing on high ground (top of a staircase) can provide an advantageous angle for Ranged characters to rain down arrow death without suffering the impact of return fire from Ranged enemies like Hak'u Spearmasters or Windstone Archers. —Jerry Pritchard, Tester

In general, feed your pet items that enhance the pet's attributes and abilities. Melee pets should be fed melee equipment, while mage pets should be fed mage equipment. Maturing your pet is vital because the pet receives additional attribute and stat bonuses at each level, as well as upgrades to its attack and/or spell. Once a pet reaches Juvenile level, it receives its unique power (used like other class powers). When the pet reaches full maturity, it receives its Emanation, which provides a benefit to all party members within a specific radius around the pet.

Pack Mule

- ◆ **Availability**: Act I
- ◆ **Cost**: 300
- ◆ **Class**: Melee
- ◆ **Premium Food**: Melee Weapons, Melee Armor
- ◆ **Predetermined Maturity Bonuses**:
    - **Fledgling**: Health
    - **Juvenile**: Armor
    - **Adolescent**: Strength
    - **Young Adult**: Health
    - **Mature**: Strength

- ◆ **Attack**: A surprisingly potent kick attack. Kick at birth; Strong Kick at Juvenile; and Mighty Kick at Young Adult.
- ◆ **Power**: Staggering Kick—Enhances the Pack Mule's next attack that inflicts high damage and can stun up to four enemies for eight seconds. Lead with the Pack Mule and unleash the Staggering Kick once you're surrounded. Eliminate stunned enemies with the rest of your party's aid. Normal recharge.
- ◆ **Emanation**: Reveal Treasure—Opens all chests and boxes and breaks all containers in a four-meter radius. No direct benefit to the party other than saving time or revealing a container you may have missed.

The Pack Mule's primary benefit is its ability to carry more inventory than any other party member. The Pack Mule gains additional inventory space as it matures; when fully mature, the Pack Mule has five times the storage capacity of a regular character! You can use the Pack Mule to store treasures to trade or sell (or feed!) or to serve as potion storage to keep your fighters and mages stocked with health and

Tip

See the Pets section in Part 8, "Statistics," for specific stats on all pet food bonuses, predetermined maturity bonuses, and powers.

mana. Feed the Pack Mule melee weapons and armor to increase its strength and durability. Use the mule's durability to absorb monster damage, leaving other party members free to damage the monsters!

Scorpion Queen

- ◆ **Availability**: Act I
- ◆ **Cost**: 350
- ◆ **Class**: Ranged
- ◆ **Premium Food**: Ranged Weapons, Ranged Armor
- ◆ **Predetermined Maturity Bonuses**:
    - **Fledgling**: Dexterity
    - **Juvenile**: Armor
    - **Adolescent**: Dexterity
    - **Young Adult**: Health
    - **Mature**: Dexterity
- ◆ **Attack**: Lesser Scorpion Sting at birth; Scorpion Sting at Juvenile; Greater Scorpion Sting at

Young Adult. Shoots a deadly stinger at target enemy.

- ◆ **Power**: Explosive Sting—Area-of-effect explosive ranged attack. Fire into a group of monsters for maximum damage. Normal recharge.
- ◆ **Emanation**: Evasion Aura—Increases party's ability to dodge attacks in a four-meter radius. The emanation provides +20% chance to dodge attacks.

The Scorpion Queen is a Ranged-class pet and supports the party from long range with her stinger attack. Feed the Scorpion Queen ranged weapons and armor to increase dexterity (adding a bonus to her attack) and durability. Her ranged Explosive Sting power inflicts area-effect damage; launch the power against packed monster groups. Evasion Aura is an effective all-purpose enchantment, increasing the party's chance to dodge all attacks.

Ice Elemental

- ◆ **Availability**: Act I
- ◆ **Cost**: 500
- ◆ **Class**: Nature Magic
- ◆ **Premium Food**: Mage Weapons, Mage Armor
- ◆ **Predetermined Maturity Bonuses**:

  Fledgling: Mana, Ice Resistance

  Juvenile: Intelligence

  Adolescent: Armor, Ice Resistance

  Young Adult: Health, Ice Resistance

  Mature: Intelligence, Ice Resistance

- ◆ **Attack**: Lesser Icestrike at birth; Icestrike at Juvenile; Greater Icestrike at Young Adult. Throws a small ball of ice, which does damage and has a chance of freezing enemies it strikes.
- ◆ **Power**: Frost Aura—Damages and briefly freezes enemies in a two-meter radius around the pet. The power lasts for 20 seconds. Move the Ice Elemental through enemy ranks while other party members target frozen foes. Normal recharge.

Developer Tip

Because pets do not share in party experience and have their own progression, consider having only your hero supported by many pets as a party so he can take all the experience for himself. —Bert Bingham, Producer

- ◆ **Emanation**: Ice Resistance—Increases party ice resistance by 40% and mana regeneration by 150% within a four-meter radius.

The Ice Elemental is a strong Act I pet. Its Icestrike attack can exploit the Skath's weakness to ice; the Skath populate the Azunite Desert late in Act I. If matured and kept in the party during Act II, the Ice Elemental's Ice Resistance Emanation helps counter the Va'arth Iceball attacks. The Emanation also increases mana regeneration, which benefits mage-heavy parties. Feed the Ice Elemental mage weapons and armor to increase intelligence and durability.

Dire Wolf

- ◆ **Availability**: Act I (Complete the Dire Wolf secondary quest)
- ◆ **Cost**: 500
- ◆ **Class**: Melee
- ◆ **Premium Food**: Melee Weapons, Melee Armor
- ◆ **Predetermined Maturity Bonuses**:

  Fledgling: Strength

  Juvenile: Health

  Adolescent: Strength

  Young Adult: Armor

  Mature: Strength

- ◆ **Attack**: Bite at birth; Rending Bite at Juvenile; Devastating Bite at Young Adult. A vicious bite from powerful jaws.
- ◆ **Power**: Furious Howl—The Dire Wolf unleashes a damaging furious howl, a cone-shaped blast attack similar to Flame Nexus or Icicle Blast. Normal recharge.
- ◆ **Emanation**: Vicious Counter—Reflects 60% of physical damage back to the enemy for party members within a four-meter radius around the pet.

Unlock the Dire Wolf by completing the Dire Wolf Act I secondary quest (see Part 7). Enhance the Dire Wolf's Melee class by feeding the pet melee weapons and melee armor (and perhaps some health potions to increase health). Repel monsters ahead of the Dire Wolf with the Furious Howl power; the cone-shaped blast damages monsters in front of the pet. Vicious Counter reflects a percentage of all damage; it's a useful Emanation throughout the game.

Fire Elemental

- **Availability**: Act II
- **Cost**: 1,000
- **Class**: Combat Magic
- **Premium Food**: Mage Weapons, Mage Armor
- **Predetermined Maturity Bonuses**:

    Fledgling: Intelligence, Fire Resistance

    Juvenile: Mana

    Adolescent: Intelligence, Fire Resistance

    Young Adult: Health, Fire Resistance

    Mature: Mana, Fire Resistance

- **Attack**: Lesser Firestrike at birth; Firestrike at Juvenile; Greater Firestrike at Young Adult. Throws a small fireball that explodes on contact with an enemy, dealing fire damage to nearby enemies.
- **Power**: Inferno—Cone-shaped blast of fiery essence that inflicts fire damage per second against any enemies within the flames. Power lasts for five seconds. Normal recharge.
- **Emanation**: Fire Resistance—Increases party fire resistance by 40% and magic damage by 8% within a four-meter radius.

Think of the Fire Elemental as the Ice Elemental's warmer brother. Feed the Fire Elemental mage weapons and mage armor to increase intelligence and durability. The Firestrike attack and Inferno power aid against Act II's weak-to-fire adversaries, including Bracken, Lertisk, and Snow Va'arth. Mature the pet into Act III and receive its Fire Resistance Emanation benefit, a valuable counter to the damaging fire and magic attacks you'll face during the last act.

Dark Naiad

- **Availability**: Act II
- **Cost**: 1,375
- **Class**: Nature Magic
- **Premium Food**: Mage Weapons, Mage Armor
- **Predetermined Maturity Bonuses**:

    Fledgling: Intelligence

    Juvenile: Armor

    Adolescent: Mana

    Young Adult: Health

    Mature: Armor

- **Attack**: Duskbeam at birth. Damages target enemy with a beam of night energy.

- **Spell**: Lesser Fade Wounds at birth; Fade Wounds at Juvenile; Greater Fade Wounds at Young Adult. Soothing magic eases pain and closes wounds.
- **Power**: Arboreal Rejuvenation—Large dose of healing power for party members within a 10-meter radius. Perfect for rejuvenating the party quickly during a crowded battle or boss encounter. Normal recharge.
- **Emanation**: Regeneration—Increases party health-regeneration rate by 200% within a four-meter radius.

The Dark Naiad excels as party support. The pet includes the Lesser Fade Wounds healing spell (which upgrades as the Dark Naiad matures) for general battle use, the large-dosage Arboreal Rejuvenation healing power for emergencies during tougher encounters (keep the Dark Naiad close to your party), and the Regeneration Emanation, which increases the party health-regeneration rate.

> ### Tip
>
> *Complete the secondary quest The Aman'lu Arena (see Part 7) to unlock the Light Naiad, a variation of the Dark Naiad. Upon finishing the quest, you can purchase the pet from Daesthai at the arena. The Light Naiad costs the same and offers the same power and Emanation, but a stronger heal spell, Abolish Wounds.*

Mythrilhorn

- **Availability**: Act III, in Aman'lu (Finish the Mythrilhorn secondary quest)
- **Cost**: 1,750
- **Class**: Melee
- **Premium Food**: Melee Armor, Melee Weapons
- **Predetermined Maturity Bonuses**:

    Fledgling: Armor

    Juvenile: Health

    Adolescent: Armor

    Young Adult: Health

    Mature: Strength

- **Attack**: Lesser Claw Strike at birth; Claw Strike at Juvenile; Grievous Claw Strike at Young Adult. The Mythrilhorn's claws rake into enemies, enraging them.

- ◆ **Power**: Enrage—Provokes monsters within 10 meters to attack the Mythrilhorn. While monsters focus on the pet, obliterate the hostiles with party attacks or powers. Fast recharge.
- ◆ **Emanation**: Defense Aura—Increases party armor by 12% within a four-meter radius.

Unlock the Mythrilhorn pet by completing the Mythrilhorn secondary quest, which is initiated during Act II and solved during Act III (see Part 7). Feed the melee-based Mythrilhorn a diet of melee armor and melee weapons to boost strength and armor. Enrage is similar to the Melee-class power Provoke; the Mythrilhorn draws the attention of surrounding monsters. The Emanation Defense Aura is universal, boosting armor for all party members near the pet.

Necrolithid

- ◆ **Availability**: Act II
- ◆ **Cost**: 2,250
- ◆ **Class**: Combat Magic
- ◆ **Premium Food**: Mage Weapons, Mage Armor
- ◆ **Predetermined Maturity Bonuses**:
  - **Fledgling**: Intelligence, Death Resistance
  - **Juvenile**: Mana
  - **Adolescent**: Health, Death Resistance
  - **Young Adult**: Armor, Death Resistance
  - **Mature**: Health, Death Resistance
- ◆ **Attack**: Deathstrike at birth. Damages target enemy with a beam of concentrated death energy.
- ◆ **Spell**: Wasting at birth; Necrosis at Juvenile. Wasting and Necrosis increases monster vulnerability to nonmagical attacks. Dissolution at Young Adult adds vulnerability to ice and death magic. Curse increases with combat-magic level.
- ◆ **Power**: Decompose—Damages enemies within a three-meter radius with noxious gas. When infected enemies die, the decomposed bodies replenish party health (by a percentage of maximum enemy health). The power lasts for 20 seconds. Normal recharge.
- ◆ **Emanation**: Mana Steal—Party-member damage against monsters restores mana (radius of four meters). The emanation provides +10% mana steal.

The Necrolithid is a focused death mage with a trio of useful abilities. The pet's curse spell increases monster vulnerabilities and can be particularly deadly within some parties, specifically those with a high number of melee and ranged characters, an ice-damage-focused nature mage and a death-dam-

age-focused combat mage. Use Decompose against large monster groups as a one-two punch that will kill an enemy and heal your party. The Mana Steal Emanation aids mage-heavy parties.

Lap Dragon

- ◆ **Availability**: Act III
- ◆ **Cost**: 2,250
- ◆ **Class**: Nature Magic
- ◆ **Premium Food**: Mage Weapons, Mage Armor
- ◆ **Predetermined Maturity Bonuses**:
  - **Fledgling**: Armor
  - **Juvenile**: Intelligence
  - **Adolescent**: Mana
  - **Young Adult**: Health
  - **Mature**: Armor
- ◆ **Attack**: Dragon Breath at birth. Breathes an attack of natural force at target enemy. Dragon Fire at Adolescent. Spits a fireball that explodes on contact.
- ◆ **Spell**: Baby Dragon Scales at birth. Protects the party with immunity from curses. Dragon Scales at Juvenile adds increased lightning- and death-damage resistance. Infused Dragon Scales at Young Adult adds increased power-recharge rate.
- ◆ **Power**: Draconic Inspiration—Increases party-member power damage for 20 seconds. Time this power wisely and save it for encounters with a large enemy force or boss.
- ◆ **Emanation**: Dragon Vitality—Increases party-member strength, dexterity, and intelligence within a four-meter radius. Requires nature-magic level 41. Emanation increases with nature-magic level, providing +16 DEX, +9 INT, +10 STR at level 41 and steadily increasing to +34 DEX, +21 INT, +22 STR at level 100.

The Lap Dragon aids the party with a variety of enchantments. The Baby Dragon Scales spell protects the party from harmful curses; as the Lap Dragon gains maturity, the spell adds increased lightning- and death-damage resistance (countering Qatall in Act III), and eventually increased power-recharge rate. Draconic Inspiration is essentially an enchantment power—use it when faced with plentiful opposition to increase party-member damage. Dragon Vitality increases all attributes, obviously a benefit to any class type.

PART 4 – ACT I:
PRIMARY QUESTS WALKTHROUGH

The Morden have launched an assault on Western Greilyn Beach and are laying siege to a Dryad Shrine. You join your childhood friend Drevin in the Morden mercenary ranks, and you think questions of morality are irrelevant. But as the battle rages, a shocking event at the Dryad Shrine leaves loyalties shattered and futures unknown. In Act I, you must reconcile your role as a Morden mercenary with the imminent dangers facing the continent of Aranna.

Chapter 1–
The Siege of Greilyn Beach

This first quest serves as the *Dungeon Siege II* tutorial. Many of its tasks correlate to in-game instructions filed in your character's Handbook. Along with the learning process, The Siege of Greilyn Beach also begins your character's development. You'll end the quest at approximately level three; use the training to focus on your desired class. The quest tasks:

- Get your orders from Morden Lieutenant Jerind.

- Destroy a series of training dummies by using the following: a melee weapon, a ranged weapon, and a nature- or combat-magic spell.

- Get your orders from Morden Lieutenant Kargack.

- Destroy the Bracken Shell.

- Make your way to the front lines.

- Reinforce the troops on the other side of the tunnel.

Map Legend
- **IS** Incantation Shrine
- **MS** Mana Shrine
- **LS** Life Shrine
- **G** Ghostly Spirit
- **L** Chant Lectern
- **T** Teleporter

Western Greilyn Beach

Western Greilyn Beach

You begin the game on Greilyn Beach. Before going forward, search your landing vehicle for a chest containing some potions and items. Talk to Morden Supplier Vrang for attack tips and instructions on destroying nearby barrels for equipment (**1**). Speak with Morden Lieutenant Jerind (**2**) at the gate and receive your first orders. Proceed into the Morden combat training area and learn the basics of melee, ranged, and mage fighting (**3**). Speak with Morden Lieutenant Kargack at the tower.

Move through the open tower and battle the Dryad Bracken Defenders (weak to fire) then destroy the Bracken Shell (**4**). Slaughter the Bracken and Forest Golem ahead and find the path out of the trench to the east (**5**). Traverse the outer path and return to the trench, defeating Golems on the way. Open the gate and battle groups of Bracken and Mystic Protectors leading into the next trench (**6**).

Crush the Bracken as you proceed north through the trench. Collect the weapons and health potions in the infirmary (**7**). In a brief cut scene, Amren poses to attack you as you continue through the trench. Discover Ketril blocking the western path. Use Drevin's Brutal Attack power to aid in the battle. Continue west and battle more Ketril and Bracken (**8**). Encounter a large squad of enemies, including Bracken Defenders, Ketril, and Mystic Protectors, along the main path. Advance slowly; as enemies engage, focus your weapon or spell attacks on one creature at a time. Speak with Morden Archer Pulk (**9**) at the gate. You also automatically receive Drevin's Medallion at this time.

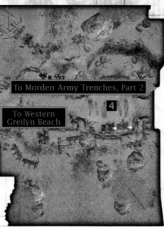

Morden Army Trenches

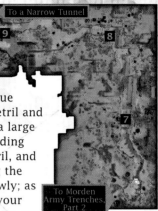

The Northern Trenches

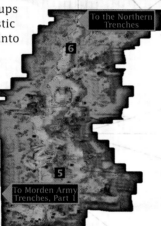

The Morden Army Trenches, Part 2

Grab the supplies within the Morden infirmary.

Drevin (Level-1 Friar) Profile

Utilize Drevin's Strength, Melee, and Critical Strike ratings by keeping him equipped with a melee weapon. Maintain melee focus by spending future skill points on Critical Strike. Drevin possesses a sharp intuition about the Morden and Dryad situation...perhaps there is something about Drevin's Medallion.

Strength: 13 ▪ Dexterity: 11 ▪ Intelligence: 11 ▪ Melee: 1 ▪ Ranged: 0 ▪ Nature Magic: 0 ▪ Combat Magic: 0 ▪ Health: 74/74 ▪ Mana: 59/59 ▪ Armor: 21 ▪ Skills: Fortitude, Level 1; Critical Strike, Level 1; Brilliance, Level 1 ▪ Power: Brutal Attack, Level 3

Chapter 1—The Siege of Greilyn Beach

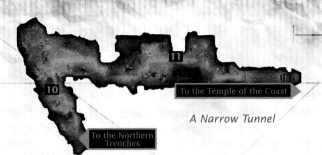

A Narrow Tunnel

The Temple of the Coast

Enter the cave to the north. Scattered enemies battle other Morden forces along the northwestern edge of the cavern. Focus your attention on the Infused Ketril, by far the most dangerous creature lurking here (**10**). Assist the Morden against Bracken and Ketril and continue east (**11**). Use Drevin's Brutal Attack against Ketril. Proceed through the exit and return outdoors to the Northern Trenches. Rendezvous with the mercenary forces just outside the temple (**12**); this triggers a cut-scene battle that concludes the quest...and Drevin's life.

Chapter 2—Prisoner of War

This is your first opportunity to explore the Dryad town of Eirulan, which is rich in non-player characters, shops, and secondary quests. Some areas are inaccessible until you've fully gained the trust of Prisoner Warden Celia (at the conclusion of the third primary quest). This section will outline the important town stops and guide you through your first stint in the jungle surrounding the Dryad town. Further details on all Eirulan secondary quests appear in Part 7, "Secondary Quests." The Prisoner of War tasks are as follows:

◆ Go to the merchant shops and ask for the Basket of Sharpening Stones.

◆ Bring the Sharpening Stones to the Dryad Outpost.

◆ Kill all of the Morden attackers and release the captured Dryads.

◆ Speak with Warden Celia at the Dryad Outpost.

Eirulan

Speak with the guard outside your cell. Talk to Warden Celia once she approaches; she asks you to proceed to the merchant shops to speak with Weaponsmith Duma and retrieve the Sharpening Stones. Once you have the Sharpening Stones, take them to the Dryad Outpost in the Northern Greilyn Jungle.

Before embarking on Celia's quest, take time to explore Eirulan. Some locations won't be available until you've completed the third primary quest and gained Celia's trust completely. You'll return to Eirulan throughout Act I to complete and receive several primary quests and to buy and sell equipment and potions. Also, the town is filled with potential party members, and non-player characters that offer story details and secondary quests. The secondary quests are entirely optional. You can follow the primary-quest path and ignore all secondary quests, but the optional tasks are worth completing for their rewards.

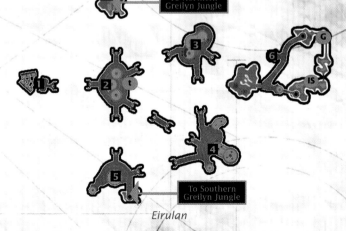

Eirulan

This section provides an overview of Eirulan and pinpoints important locations and characters. For more details, maps, and task solutions for all Eirulan secondary quests, see Part 7.

You enter Eirulan on the Prisoner's Terrace (**1**) on the western side of town. After speaking with the guard and Warden Celia, you're free to explore the town. Ride the trolley east to the Merchant Terrace.

Eirulan's Merchant Terrace (**2**) houses the Eirulan merchant shop, your one-stop equipment depot. Weaponsmith Duma sells weapons; Sen the Armorer deals in armor; Mage Elenu offers spells, potions, spell books, and jewelry; Arcanist Bernard sells reagents; and Enchantress Lumilla creates crafted items. Speak with Apprentice Telinu and offer your help to initiate The Armorer's Apprentice secondary quest. Discuss alchemy with Enchantress Lumilla to initiate the Lumilla's Salve secondary quest. Use the teleporter just outside of the merchant shop for your frequent trips between the Dryad town and other locations throughout the act. Necromancer Eranith, near the teleporter, resurrects slain party members. The north gate is on the Merchant Terrace north side; it's the entrance into the Northern Greilyn Jungle. Two potential party members hang out near the gate; speak with Lothar and Deru about joining your adventure.

Ride the trolley northeast from the shops to reach the Adventurers Terrace (**3**). Innkeeper Leni, on the tavern's second floor, manages recruited party members. She can also increase your maximum party size for a small fee. Soldier Jordhan, also upstairs, plays a role in the Lelani's Sorrow secondary quest. Talk with the Grizzled Bar Patron at the bar to initiate the Secrets of Xeria's Temple secondary quest.

Southeast from the Merchants Terrace and Adventurers Terrace is the Terrace of Wisdom (**4**), which contains the Great Hall and Eirulan's infirmary. The Terrace of Wisdom is blocked until you

Lothar (Level-3 Combatant) Profile

The Half-Giant Lothar offers a foundation of melee and combat magic, allowing you to follow either path to complement your main character. Lothar is skewed slightly toward melee but provides enough combat magic knowledge to assist immediately. Equip him with fire spells through the Greilyn jungles to counter the lightning-resistant Hak'u. Later in Act I, you may wish to switch off fire magic to counter the resistant Skath. Spend skills points on Devastation and then either Searing Flames or Amplified Lightning for fire and lightning-magic damage respectively (or hold off for Grim Necromancy for improved death-magic damage). These will supply the fire magic power Flame Nexus or the lightning magic power Chain Lightning, depending on your path.

Strength: 23 ▪ Dexterity: 11 ▪ Intelligence: 15 ▪ Melee: 2 ▪ Ranged: 0 ▪ Nature Magic: 0 ▪ Combat Magic: 1 ▪ Health: 106/106 ▪ Mana: 74/74 ▪ Armor: 1 ▪ Skills: Fortitude, Level 2; Critical Strike, Level 1; Devastation, Level 1 ▪ Power: Brutal Attack, Level 1

Deru (Level 3-Scout) Profile

Deru offers a combination of ranged skills and nature magic, and can be groomed to become a long-range force or follow specific nature mage skills to focus on damage, enchantments, summons, or healing. Deru's Natural Bond skill allows her to harvest mana potions from bushes. Since you can recruit Taar, a focused nature Mage, within a few quests, you may consider Deru for her Ranged class only or focus on a specific nature magic discipline that will be different from Taar's.

Strength: 11 ▪ Dexterity: 21 ▪ Intelligence: 17 ▪ Melee: 0 ▪ Ranged: 2 ▪ Nature Magic: 1 ▪ Combat Magic: 0 ▪ Health: 89/89 ▪ Mana: 88/88 ▪ Armor: 16 ▪ Skills: Critical Shot, Level 1; Dodge, Level 1; Natural Bond, Level 1 ▪ Powers: Gravity Stone, Level 1; Take Aim, Level 1

complete the third primary quest. Visit the Great Hall to find Taar, a party member to recruit later in Act I; Rokhar the Mage, who plays a role in the Dire Wolf secondary quest; and Historian Arisu if you want to hear additional backstory. Locate the Mothers of Eirulan and Tome of Smithing Lore Books inside; The Tome of Smithing is part of the secondary quest The Armorer's Apprentice.

Adjacent to the Great Hall, find the infirmary. Chat with Hesla inside to initiate the secondary quest The Hak'u. On the opposite side of the terrace, find Arianne's home; speak to her with Taar in your party to initiate the Taar's Investigation secondary quest.

South from the Merchants Terrace and southwest from the Terrace of Wisdom is the Terrace of Pets (**5**). The Terrace of Pets is blocked until you complete the third primary quest. Talk to Pet Seller Neda to acquire a pet and to initiate the Dire Wolf secondary quest. Visit a nearby home and speak with Lelani to initiate the Lelani's Sorrow secondary quest (which spans the entire game!). Ascend a ramp to the top of the pet shop to find Laenne's home. Talk to Laenne to initiate the Secrets of the Elven Shrine secondary quest.

The Terrace of the Falls (**6**) lies on the eastern side of Eirulan, accessible from the Adventurers Terrace. You can't visit the falls until you complete the third primary quest. Visit Fenella's home; she plays a role in the Lelani's Sorrow secondary quest. Move through her home to the lift and descend to the falls area. There's an Incantation Shrine here, as well as a ghostly spirit gazing at the magnificent waterfall. Cross the area to another lift and ascend. Locate Tamari in her home. Chat with her to initiate the secondary quest The Kithraya Hive.

> ### Tip
>
> *A ghostly spirit hangs out near the Eirulan falls. There are ghostly spirits scattered throughout Aranna—18 in all—and they're part of the Spirits of Aranna secondary quest initiated during Act II. You must first learn how to speak with the spirits. Talk to Mage Lyssanore once you reach Aman'lu to discover the secrets.*

Delivering the Sharpening Stones

Warden Celia has asked you to retrieve the Sharpening Stones from Weaponsmith Duma and to take the stones to the Dryad Outpost outside of town.

Proceed to the Merchants Terrace. Enter the merchant shop and speak with Weaponsmith Duma to learn that Duma's apprentice, Telinu, has the stones. Approach the weapon forge and speak with Telinu to recover a basketful of the Sharpening Stones.

Exit the merchant shop and speak with the Dryad Guard next to the north gate. With the Sharpening Stones acquired, you're allowed to proceed to the Dryad Outpost in the Northern Greilyn Jungle.

Retrieve the Sharpening Stones from the merchant shops to start on a path toward gaining Celia's trust.

To the Dryad Outpost

Northern Greilyn Jungle

Speak with Dryad Guard Jera (**7**) at the bottom of the lift. She provides escort to the Dryad Outpost. As you follow Jera, speak with Lirrit near the health and mana bushes, then Esselte (**8**) at the Incantation Shrine. Tell her you have learned no chant; she'll reveal the Lesser Chant of Fortification. Recite the chant on the shrine. Continue to follow the guard as you approach the Dryad Outpost just to the north.

The Dryad Guard Jera charges the Morden (**9**) who's guarding the Dryad prisoners...and pays with her life. Combat the Morden-Viir and Morden-Urg guards. Focus attacks on one enemy at a time to clear out the small garrison. Defeating the Morden nets the Morden Gate Key. Approach the captive Dryads (**10**) and use the key to free the prisoners. A freed prisoner vouches for your heroism and Warden Celia rewards your efforts with a new quest, the Dryad Outpost Gate Key for passage deeper into the jungle (**11**), an Eirulan Teleporter Activation Stone, and some new gear. Be sure to explore the tower (**12**) south of the Dryad Outpost for additional equipment (see the "Optional Area" sidebar).

Optional Area: Tower Dungeon with Four Sanctuary Doors

After descending the lift from Eirulan into the Northern Greilyn Jungle, move northwest through the Incantation Shrine to find a lone tower among the forest trees. Also reach the tower by exploring the jungle south from the Dryad Outpost. Enter the tower and descend the lift inside. Speak with Hanish (A). The bottom chamber offers four Sanctuary Doors—special locked doors that only certain classes can open. Only classes that have reached level three can open the Sanctuary Doors in this tower. If you recruited Lothar and Deru from Eirulan, you can open more doors. You can return after you've met the level requirement to open any remaining doors. Chests behind the locked doors contain random magical equipment generally suited for the class that accessed them. The dungeon also contains a lectern holding the Lesser Chant of Dexterity.

Chapter 3—The Morden Towers

The Morden Towers offers the first extended trip away from the comforts of Eirulan. Opposition includes the masses of Hak'u natives and the formidable Morden tower guards. Lightning resistance will help protect your party from Hak'u mage attacks; fire resistance will shield you from Morden mage blasts. We suggest at least one additional party member from Eirulan to tackle the jungle challenges, and return trips to Eirulan via Summon Town Portal to restock potions and buy and sell wares. Expect to be at level seven at the quest's completion. The Morden Towers tasks:

- ◆ Find and burn all four Morden towers.
- ◆ Return to Warden Celia in the Eirulan Prisoner's Terrace.
- ◆ Speak with Taar in the Eirulan Great Hall.

Northern Greilyn Jungle

Open the Dryad Outpost Gate (**1**) using the key from Warden Celia. Cross the wooden bridge heading north. Search the small camp to the east (**2**) for gold and supplies. Discover a tribe of Hak'u as you move north (**3**) along the forest path. Repel their attacks and search two western alcoves (**4**) to find statues that reveal hidden chests (the second also contains mana bushes). Speak with the Morden-Viir Thug Leader Greknev at the north gate (**5**).

Northern Greilyn Jungle, Part 1

The Morden guard welcomes you back and provides the password ("Chaba") for reporting to the tower to the north (**8**). Along the way, face more Hak'u. Search a western path to encounter a Hak'u

miniboss and supporting minions. The path leads into a camp on a hill.

Speak with the Morden Captain at the tower. Tell him the password—though it really doesn't matter because the Morden are alerted to your deception. Counterattack the Morden defending the first tower. Break the cage to the tower's right and free Nen (**9**). She provides instructions on how to burn down the Morden tower. Use the broken cage to recover a Cage Fragment. Equip the Cage Fragment and set it on fire using the campfire left of the tower. Use your newly created torch on the tower to burn the structure to the ground.

> **Tip**
>
> Before moving through the gate and approaching the first Morden tower, ascend hills on the eastern side of the path to encounter more Hak'u (**6**) and locate a small camp (**7**). The extra exploration nets additional experience and equipment.

Proceed north through the tower debris and battle more forest beasts (**10**). Search the ruins on the western side of the path for chant lecterns, holding the Lesser Chant of Strength and Lesser Chant of Intelligence; there's a teleporter on the eastern side to activate. Ascend the western hill and search the tower (**11**); press a switch inside to reveal a hidden chest. Cross the small bridge and ascend a hill to spot Morain battling a Hak'u; this sequence is part of the secondary quest called The Hak'u (speak with Morain for further details, and see Part 7). The Hak'u's escape results in the destruction of the bridge to the south (**12**). There's a Life Shrine between the first and second

Northern Greilyn Jungle, Part 2

Morden towers, just north of the broken bridge. Use the shrine to heal your party's wounds.

Ignore the southern route and continue west. Battle a squad of Morden (**13**) near an Incantation Shrine. Invoke a chant before moving south toward the second Morden tower. A large squad defends the second tower. Burn the tower (**14**) using the same method as before.

Resume your course south. Battle assorted Morden, Terrak, Boarbeasts, and Gila. Search a small camp to the east (**15**). A narrow path west of the main road leads to a waterfall. Walk behind the waterfall to enter a tranquil cave. Follow the main path east and find the third Morden tower (**16**). Defenders include a Morden miniboss—the Grunt Captain. Defeat all defenders and burn down the third tower using the same torch method as before. The northern route from the third tower ends at the broken bridge (**17**). Move through the debris and head south. Find a side route east that offers some containers to search (**18**).

Burn the Morden towers to the ground!

The Hak'u

Although relatively weak when faced alone, the true strength of the Hak'u lies in their numbers. Expect to face large groups that include a mix of mages, melee fighters, and ranged fighters. Hak'u are lightning-resistant, so combat mages should switch to fire or death magic for better results. You'll face Hak'u Hunters, Skinners, Shamans, and Drummers early in the act then battle their tougher counterparts, the Hak'u Spearmasters, Slayers, Witch Doctors, and Signalers later. The Hak'u Drummers and Signalers can resurrect fallen comrades, so target them quickly. The Hak'u mages cast lightning magic, so increase your resistance to it. Concentrate attacks on the Hak'u Shaman and the Hak'u Witch Doctor to avoid their Summon Raptor and Blind spells.

Optional Area: A Tranquil Cave

A gorgeous waterfall in the Northern Greilyn Jungle conceals a hidden, tranquil cave. Explore the cave for its plentiful containers, which hopefully hold some precious loot. A ghostly spirit (A) haunts the cave. You can't understand any of the spirits until you've completed the A Dark Ohm secondary quest in Act II. Locate a lectern (B) that holds a mysterious chant; it's the Lesser Random Item chant.

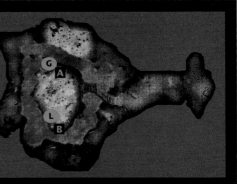

Morden

You begin as a mercenary working alongside the Morden, but by the second primary quest you're trying to earn your freedom from the Dryads by battling the Morden! You'll encounter Morden forces throughout the Greilyn Jungle that surrounds Eirulan. The Morden-Urg are the lowest caste of Morden and the weakest adversaries. You'll encounter the melee-specialist Urg Thugs, ranged Urg Scavengers, and the mage Urg Prodigies (using fire magic). The Morden-Viir are the common caste and much tougher than their lesser kind. The Viir Grunts use shield and sword in melee combat, the Viir Spearmen toss spears at range, and the Viir Recruits use crossbows. The Morden-Gral are the mage class; these spellcasters wield fire-damage spells and will mend wounds with healing spells. Eliminate the mages on sight to prevent their aid. In later Acts, you'll face new and more impressive Morden classes.

Western Greilyn Jungle

Fight groups that could include Maguars, Gorgaks, Boarbeasts, and Morden squads as you move south. A path west (**19**) leads to The Hak'u Caves that are part of the secondary quest The Hak'u. Proceed south along the main route and find health bushes on the western side and a populated Hak'u camp (**20**) on the eastern side. There's an Incantation Shrine to the west just before you reach the fourth Morden tower (**21**), found to the south. Lure the minibosses away from their support forces before engaging. Burn down the tower.

Western Greilyn Jungle

You've completed the main portion of the quest and must return to Warden Celia with the news. Cross the bridge to the west and

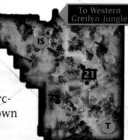

Fourth Morden Tower

use the teleporter to Eirulan. Find Warden Celia on the Prisoner's Terrace on the western side of town. Speak with her to receive your reward: the removal of the Ring of Submission and the recovery of your goods, including Drevin's Medallion. She tells you to speak with Taar in the Great Hall. She removes the ring and returns your equipment...but also bears bad news. You were bitten during your battles and are now infected with the plague that ravages Greilyn Jungle.

Chapter 4—The Plague

Using the teleporter to reach the Western Greilyn Jungle makes this a rather short quest and the first that delves into a significant underground dungeon. Increase lightning resistance to help protect you from the plentiful Hak'u mages, and use weapons and spells with fire, ice, or death elemental magic to counter the Hak'u resistance to lightning damage. Expect to reach level nine by the quest's completion. Perform the following tasks to complete this primary quest:

- ◆ Find the Ancient Elven Shrine.

- ◆ Locate the Elven Fountain and fill the Empty Vial with water from it.

- ◆ Report back to Taar in the Eirulan Great Hall.

Western Greilyn Jungle

Western Greilyn Jungle

Use the Eirulan teleporter to return to the Western Greilyn Jungle (**1**). Battle Gorgaks and Boarbeasts. Follow the main road south until you reach a Dryad gate (**2**). The gate was previously locked, but since you are no longer a prisoner, you're free to explore what lies beyond. Take time to explore the Hak'u camps to the west (**3**).

There's an Incantation Shrine and the Lesser Chant of Mage Health lectern on the northern side. The western ruins contain another lectern holding the Lesser Chant of Ranger Health, a ghostly spirit

Locate the Ancient Elven Shrine within the Western Greilyn Jungle. The path to the shrine was previously blocked.

(part of the Spirits of Aranna secondary quest in Act II) and the Hak'u Usurper's hideout (part of the secondary quest The Hak'u, Part II). The southern side of the ruins contains the Lesser Chant of Casting lectern. The gate guard reveals that the shrine is just ahead. Assist the Dryad against the beasts gathered near the gate. Pick up the Lesser Chant of Fighter Health from the lectern at the gate before exiting south.

Continue along the winding road and battle assorted beasts that could include Gorgak, Maguar, and Hak'u forces. Find a patch of mana bushes (**4**) on the northern edge of the road. Proceed along the main road as it winds southeast and find the entrance into the Ancient Elven Shrine (**5**) at the end. Defeat the Hak'u Rhythm Drummer and his minions; be cautious of the drummer's ability to resurrect his fallen allies. Open the door and enter the shrine.

The Ancient Elven Shrine

Follow the main hall toward a Sanctuary Door (**6**); only a party member at ranged level six can open it. Proceed through the adjacent door and find a War Pedestal to recharge powers (**7**). Open the door at the hall's back end to locate the lift (**8**). Ride it into the depths of the shrine.

An Ancient Elven Shrine, Upper Floor

Battle the mixed Hak'u forces at the next junction (**10**), including a mini-boss. Search the eastern room for supplies. The next hall splits south and east. Additional Hak'u (**11**) populate the eastern room; the main path resumes to the south. Find a Sanctuary Door (**12**) on the western side of the next chamber; the lock requires nature magic level six. Search the opposite room for additional treasure.

Tip

*The switch at the bottom of the lift in the Ancient Elven Shrine (**9**) opens a hidden room that's part of the secondary quest Secrets of the Elven Shrine. You can bypass this optional room if you're sticking to the primary quest. For more information, see Part 7.*

A magical lock protects the door in the southern chamber (**13**). To break the spell, defeat all Hak'u present, which includes tougher minibosses. Eliminate the mages quickly to avoid summons and spells and use your powers on tight enemy groups. Proceed inside the final chamber that includes the Elven Fountain at its center (**14**). Defeat the Hak'u Witch Doctors that populate the room. Proceed to the fountain and use it to automatically fill your empty vial with healing water and receive the Filled Vial. Search the northwestern corner of the chamber for a lectern holding the Lesser Chant of Prosperity.

Proceed through the exit door (**15**) to the east—the room contains a teleporter that returns you to Eirulan. Make your way to the Great Hall and speak with Taar. She tells you about the infected Dryads living in exile and asks you to bring the healing water to their colony. Taar also offers to be your guide and join your party.

An Ancient Elven Shrine, Lower Floor

Use the fountain to recover the powers of the Elven healing water.

Chapter 5—The Dryad Exile Colony

This primary quest opens Eirulan's southern gate for the first time. Hak'u dominate the jungles, so prepare lightning resistance and non-lightning weapons and spells. The next quest begins away from Eirulan, so prepare for return trips to the Dryad town for more potions and better equipment. A wise use of the gold you've collected includes increasing your party size to the maximum and recruiting any remaining NPCs in Eirulan or hiring a pet. You should reach level 10 by the end of this quest. The chapter's tasks:

- ◆ Find the Dryad Exile Colony.
- ◆ Save the old man.

Taar (Level-9 Theurgist) Profile

You can recruit Taar after completing The Plague primary quest. Taar's class statistics are focused completely on nature magic. Even if you're already using Deru as a nature mage you can recruit Taar to focus on a different discipline. Spend her unused skill points to focus on enhancing ice spells, party healing, summoning, or enchantment spells. You must have Taar in your party to initiate the Taar's Investigation secondary quest.

Strength: 17 ▪ Dexterity: 23 ▪ Intelligence: 39 ▪ Melee: 0 ▪ Ranged: 0 ▪ Nature Magic: 9 ▪ Combat Magic: 0 ▪ Health: 134/134 ▪ Mana: 187/187 ▪ Armor: 23 ▪ Skills: Aquatic Affinity, Level 1; Dodge, Level 1; Natural Bond, Level 2 ▪ Power: Gravity Stone, Level 1

Southern Greilyn Jungle

Southern Greilyn Jungle

Exit Eirulan through the south gate. Descend on the lift (**1**) and advance south carefully to reach the Hak'u camps (**2**). Searching farther south reveals the entrance to the Dark, Bone-Filled Cave (**3**) that's part of the Taar's Investigation secondary quest. Resume an eastern course along the main road and combat the plentiful Hak'u and Raptors scattered throughout the jungle.

Ascend the hills to the east and locate another small Hak'u camp (**4**). Harvest mana potions from the bushes north of the camp (**5**). The main path winds south and the jungle's inhabitants become fiercer; expect to face Rhinock (weak to death magic) along with the squads of Hak'u Slayers. Although you can stick to the main road as it continues east, search the southern forest for large squads of Hak'u and two secret areas: abandoned ruins (**6**), part of the secondary quest Finala's Contempt (see Part 7), and an optional area, a small cave (**7**).

Proceed east and battle Hak'u Slayers and Vulk (weak to death magic) supported by Hak'u Witch Doctors (and their summons). Utilize the Mana

Shrine on the road's north side and find health bushes behind ruins on the southern side (**8**). Activate the teleporter ahead. The road ends at an amphitheater called Razka's Ruins (**9**). Squads of Morden-Viir and Hak'u defend the ruins. Don't advance quickly into the amphitheater. Use the height advantage gained from remaining along the sides of the amphitheater to pummel enemies below. Remain on the outskirts and combat small enemy groups as you work through the ruins and continue along the eastern route into the Eastern Greilyn Jungle.

> ### Tip
>
> *Descend the lift at the center of Razka's Ruins to discover a locked door. To open this door you must have Deru in your party and activate the secondary quest Deru's Treasure Hunt during Act II. For a complete walkthrough, see Part 7.*

Eastern Greilyn Jungle

Battle Hak'u in their small camps (**10**). A northern path leads to additional camps and a small bridge to a small cave (**11**). A side path south off the main road leads to another optional cave (**12**). Check a second northern side path to find a curious circle of mushrooms (**13**). This location is part of the secondary quest Amren's

Eastern Greilyn Jungle

Optional Area: A Small Cave

*Explore a couple of small side areas south of the road that runs through Southern Greilyn Jungle. The cave is rather small, but it's worth the side trip for potential loot and the extra experience. Encounter a gang of Raptors supported by a Hak'u Witch Doctor miniboss (**A**). Eliminate the Hak'u and their assorted beasts that patrol the dwelling, then raid the containers for loot.*

Vision, initiated during Act II. Search the chest and containers north of the mushrooms.

The main path continues east toward a small camp (**14**) that contains a mix of forest minions, including Hak'u, Shard Souls, and possibly a Rhinock miniboss. The road winds south. Harvest health potions from the bushes on the road's western side (**15**). Battle the Vulk, Plagued Bracken, Plagued Hak'u, and other jungle inhabitants as you head south along the main path. Search the tower (**16**) on the eastern side of the road. Descend the lift inside to enter a small underground room that holds treasure and a few monsters, including a Hak'u miniboss.

Save the old man. He's under attack from Dryads infected by the plague.

The Dryad Exile Colony (**17**) is southwest of the tower. You'll spot an Azunite Scholar under attack from plagued Dryads; the old man is casting healing spells to keep himself alive. Quickly attack the Dryads to save the old man. After clearing the camp, speak with the Azunite Scholar. You learn the Dryad Exile Colony is now just a cemetery. The old man clears the blocked path and ushers in the next quest.

Chapter 6—Leaving Greilyn Isle

This quest is a long, challenging journey through jungle and caves. You aren't required to visit Eirulan during the quest, but it's wise to use a teleporter or spell to return and bolster your potion supply or shop for improved armaments. The lengthy quest offers time to further focus your party members' class, skills, and powers. You should be approximately level 14 upon completing the following Leaving Greilyn Isle tasks:

- Locate the Kithraya Caverns.
- Look for survivors from Vix's squad.
- Investigate Eastern Greilyn Beach. Destroy the Shard. Use the portal to leave Greilyn Isle.
- Talk to Captain Suzor.

Optional Areas: Small Caves

The small cave on the northern side of the main road contains groups of Hak'u (A) guarding an exit that leads into Rokhar's Rift Site (B), which is part of the secondary quest Dire Wolf. Part 7 offers additional information. The small cave on the southern side of the path contains a scattered squad of enemies, a possible miniboss (C), and potential loot.

Eastern Greilyn Jungle

Leaving the Dryad Exile Colony

The quest begins at what's left of the Dryad Exile Colony (**1**). The Azunite Scholar clears the eastern route; however, before you explore that path, consider the optional path to the southwest. Follow the road and battle through Plagued Forest Golems. You'll discover an Incantation Shrine, mana bushes (**2**), and a small cave (**3**) that's part of the secondary quest The Hak'u, Part 2.

The primary quest path leads east. Expect to encounter Scorpions and Plagued Forest Golems (**4**) on the road. Eventually you'll face additional Plagued Dryads; the Sentinels use melee attacks while the Dryad Guardians attack from range. The Hak'u also crowd the jungle path in abundance. Search a small camp (**5**) on the southern side of the road for treasure and find more crates and containers in an abandoned tower (**6**) on the northern side. After ascending a small hill, activate the teleporter to return to Eirulan if needed. Farther east, you'll find the forest beasts have

overrun several Morden camps (**7**). Comb the area for supplies as you continue the trek through the jungle.

The path splits just beyond the ravaged camps. Some ruins lie to the east while a narrow wooden bridge connects to another path headed south. Advance cautiously into the ruins; monsters heavily populate the area. In the eastern ruins find mana bushes (**8**) and several containers and crates around a locked tower (**9**). There's also an entrance to an underground shelter (**10**) for optional exploration. After clearing the area of Hak'u and other forces, cross the bridge to the south (**11**), and clear out Hak'u camps until reaching the entrance to the Upper Kithraya Caverns, on the primary quest path, in the southern corner (**12**).

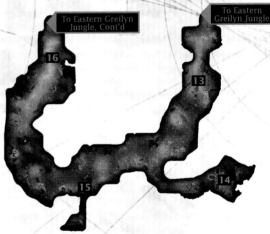

> ### Tip
>
> *The underground shelter is home to Feldwyr the Blacksmith. Exploring it is completely optional and is part of the Feldwyr the Blacksmith secondary quest. See Part 7 for a map and the complete solution to the quest.*

The Upper Kithraya Caverns

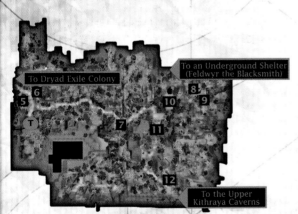

Eastern Greilyn Jungle, Cont'd

The Upper Kithraya Caverns, Part 1

Push south into the cavern (**13**) and battle Plagued Hak'u and Dark Orthrac. Work slowly south and search an alcove in the southeastern corner (**14**) to discover a gang of Plagued Hak'u and a Dark Orthrac guarding chests and assorted treasure.

Use magic or ranged attacks against the Orthrac and focus your melee characters on other targets. Clean the area of treasure.

Proceed west and encounter a second alcove along the southern edge of the cavern (**15**); the small area hides additional containers to search. Clear out the cavern and exit through the north opening (**16**) to return to the jungle.

Eastern Greilyn Jungle

Groups of Plagued Dryad and Hak'u greet your party upon exiting the cavern (**17**). Proceed along the main path to the west. Speak with Vix (**18**) inside the ruined outpost; he requests your aid in finding his infected companions. If there's room, Vix can also join your party. Before leaving the area, grab the Lore Book near Vix, the Lesser Chant of Ranged Awareness and Lesser Chant of Magic Awareness from the lecterns, and gather health potions from the bushes north of the outpost. Continue west along the main road to find the entrance (**19**) to the Kithraya Caverns as the path turns south.

Eastern Greilyn Jungle, Cont'd

The Upper Kithraya Caverns

Advance south into the Kithraya Caverns. Expect to face plagued groups of Carver Bats, Boggrots, Larvax, and Veesh as you descend deeper into the cave (**20**). Search the cavern's edge for containers holding potential treasures. The largest group of enemies patrols where the path forks (**21**). Hak'u and Kurtle support a squad of Morden Grunts.

Navigate the cavern carefully south. As you near the southern edge of this section, beware of Kurtle, Carver Bats, and Larvax groups (**22**) as you near the next section of the upper caverns.

The Upper Kithraya Caverns, Part 2

Plagued creatures populate the Kithraya Caverns.

Vix (Level-12 Marksman) Profile

Vix is an experienced marksman and focused completely on the ranged skill. His Critical Shot skill lays the foundation for bow, crossbow, or thrown-weapon ranged disciplines. Vix does come equipped with Quick Draw level 1, the prerequisite for thrown weapons; consider that path to capitalize on the free skill selection. You must have Vix in your party to initiate the Vix's Vengeance secondary quest.

Strength: 24 ▪ Dexterity: 47 ▪ Intelligence: 23 ▪ Melee: 0 ▪ Ranged: 12 ▪ Nature Magic: 0 ▪ Combat Magic: 0 ▪ Health: 178/178 ▪ Mana: 129/129 ▪ Armor: 58 ▪ Skills: Critical Shot, Level 2; Dodge, Level 2; Quick Draw, Level 1 ▪ Powers: Take Aim, Level 1; Shrapnel Blast Level 1

Search a small camp in a northern alcove (**23**) for a collection of crates and containers holding potential loot. Farther south you'll find Trasak. Weaken these life leechers with long-range attacks before sending in your own melee characters (death resistance also helps). Locate a broken lift (**24**) on the western side of the cavern (see the tip for details on the lift mechanism). There are two southern exits to this portion of the caverns. The western exit (**25**) is just south of the broken lift and leads to a dead end featuring an abandoned tower, with a nasty Boggrot surprise on the lift, and a squad of Trasak. The eastern exit (**26**) is the primary quest path and leads past a Life Shrine, then outside to a teleporter.

The Upper Kithraya Caverns, Part 3

Tip

A broken lift in this section of the Upper Kithraya Caverns leads to a hidden Morden intelligence camp. To use the lift, you must have a party member who can fix things. Return to the lift later in the game with Finala in your party to repair the lever. This area is part of the Finala's Contempt secondary quest covered in Part 7.

The Kithraya Valley

The exit from the Upper Kithraya Caverns on the western side leads to an abandoned tower (**27**). The main quest path extends from the caverns' eastern exit. Activate the teleporter as you follow the road south. Take a moment to harvest mana potions from the bushes (**28**) just southwest of the teleporter.

The Kithraya Valley

Continue south along the road; Boggrots hatch from eggs and ambush your party where the road bends east (**29**). Battle the Boggrots as you proceed. Advance into the cavern entrance (**30**) after clearing the path.

Lower Kithraya Caverns

Greater dangers lurk within the Lower Kithraya Caverns. The creatures are much tougher and more durable than your earlier foes; avoid battling a creature with near infinite health by slaughtering any Maltratar first—they cast healing spells on their allies. Approach all large egg sacs carefully; most sprout Boggrots and Larvax. Search the smaller egg sacs for treasure; strike a sac to release its contents.

Lower Kithraya Caverns

Crush the Maltratar and Gantis near the entrance and approach the eggs along the eastern wall (**31**). Combat the Boggrots that emerge. Search the small egg sacs in the eastern alcove (**32**) for loot. Follow the cavern northeast and face Boggrots escorting a Dark Orthrac as you near the passage (**33**) into the next section of the lower caverns.

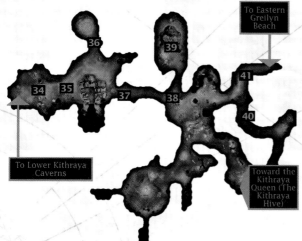

Lower Kithraya Caverns, Cont'd

A brief cut scene reveals a Kurtle perishing at the hands of the cavern's poisonous spouts—avoid those spouts or suffer damage. Encounter a group of Shard Souls and Trasak near the northern edge (**34**). Lure enemies away from the cavern edge; egg sacs there sprout Larvax. Advance carefully east; the density and ferocity of creatures increases the farther you move into the cavern. Eliminate the minions around the gaping hole in the cavern floor (**35**).

Explore an alcove to the north (**36**). A Maltratar Overlord protects the entrance; defeat the beast to make the nearby wall crumble, revealing an alcove with more monsters and potential treasure. Resume course east and dispatch another Maltratar Overlord (**37**). Defeating the creature crumbles a wall that blocks the primary quest path east. Proceed through the narrow tunnel until you enter the open chamber and discover Vix's companions (**38**).

You're told that there's something horrible near the beach...but that's all that Vix's comrades can reveal before Shard Souls infect them. Eliminate Vix's former friends, the Plagued Windstone

Soldiers. Explore a tunnel to the north (**39**) that contains Maltratar and Gantis Workers. Farther east, the path splits north and south. The southern path (**40**) is optional and part of the secondary quest The Kithraya Hive (see Part 7 for a map and solution). Follow the northern route (**41**) to remain on the primary quest path. Exit the caverns and emerge close to the beach—and near your way off of Greilyn Isle.

Eastern Greilyn Beach

A huge battle awaits your party soon after you exit the Lower Kithraya Caverns. Follow the road east and spot the gigantic Shard blocking the path (**42**). Eliminate the Shard Souls then focus your attack on the Shard itself.

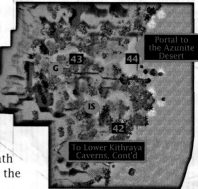

Eastern Greilyn Beach

Proceed along the road as it winds toward the beach. Pass and utilize an Incantation Shrine and locate health bushes (**43**) on the road's southern side. Harvest potions with a ranged character's Survival skill. Gather the goods and move east toward the beach. Speak with the Azunite Scholar (**44**). After the conversation, enter the activated portal to teleport to the Azunite Desert. Once there, speak with Captain Suzor to complete the quest.

Chapter 7—Secrets of the Azunite Desert

You've escaped the jungle at last and can now explore the arid Azunite Desert. You can return to Eirulan at any time using a teleporter or spell. The menacing Skath populate this region. Increase your fire resistance to counter their spell attacks and utilize a nature mage proficient in ice magic to exploit the weakness of the Skaths and many other desert creatures. After this quest you should reach approximately level 15. Tasks in the Secrets of the Azunite Desert are as follows:

- ◆ Find the Stela of Blindness Stela of Life, Stela of Death, and Stela of Sight.
- ◆ Place the four Stelae and learn the location of the Lost Vault of the Azunites.

Azunite Desert

You arrive through the portal (**1**) inside the desert outpost. There's a teleporter just west of your start position; activate it to retain your connection to Eirulan and the surrounding jungles. Speak with Captain Suzor (**2**) inside the outpost. After the conversation, Captain Suzor opens a gate (**3**) east of the outpost.

To Azunite Desert, Cont'd

To a Ruined Crypt (A Family Heirloom)

Azunite Desert

Search the base interior for supplies. Soldier Balamar hangs out inside; he's part of the Lelani's Sorrow secondary quest. Proceed through the gate east of the outpost. Battle packs of Sand Reapers and Thrusk (**7**) in the eastern corner. Thrusk fire ranged attacks; avoid prolonged confrontations with melee-based Sand Reapers when Thrusk are peppering your party from long range. Locate the first Skath camp to the north (**8**). Speak with the Skath. No matter what conversational path you pursue, the end result is the same: combat! Kill the Skath Zealots and Devoted Skath Avenger Stelae Guardian (resistant to fire) and recover the Stela of Blindness.

Proceed west from the first Skath camp and move under the damaged bridge. Find the second camp (**9**) in the western alcove. Crush the Skath Zealots, Skath Cats, and Devoted Skath Zealot Stelae Guardian and recover the Stela of Life. Pillage the camp of its supplies (**10**). Return to the first camp and proceed north. Descend a lift inside a tower on the hill (**11**), Master Thestrin, at the bottom, triggers the A Family Heirloom secondary quest (see Part 7).

Tip

*Before heading off to battle the Skath, search areas around the outpost for additional combat and treasure opportunities. Hyenas, Thrusk, and Sand Reapers (these creatures leap into battle, so be ready to counterattack) lurk north (**4**) of the desert outpost. Explore west of the outpost to find a tower (**5**) that features a melee Sanctuary Door (level 13). Look south and southeast from the outpost to find more monsters lurking around a dry river bed. There's also a ruined crypt (**6**) that's part of the A Family Heirloom secondary quest.*

The Skath

The Skath are a hyena-like bipedal race that guards the four Stelae you require to unlock the secrets within the inner chamber of the Ancient Azunite Shrine. You'll encounter the Skath throughout the desert until your eventual approach toward Windstone Fortress. Skath are resistant to fire magic but weak to ice magic. Combat mages may be better served using lightning or death spells or curses to harm Skath while nature mages focus on ice spells and healing allies. Skath Zealots use two-handed bone axes in their melee attacks, Skath Avengers employ thrown axes at long range, and Skath Disciples rely on fire-magic attacks and an assortment of spells, including Dehydrate and Summon Ironhorn. Dehydrate will make your party more susceptible to melee and fire damage—not coincidentally the damage spell of the Skath mages. Bolster your fire resistances before venturing into the desert. Tougher Skath Stelae Guardians protect the Stelae; these minibosses feature increased statistics.

Speak with Captain Suzor to learn the location of the four Stelae.

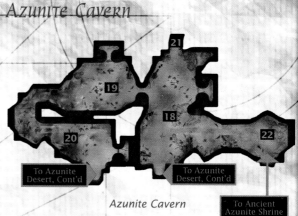

Azunite Cavern

To Azunite Desert, Cont'd

To Azunite Desert, Cont'd

To Ancient Azunite Shrine

Ascend to the top of the ridge. You're on the other side of the damaged bridge. Enemies abound, including a Giant Thrusk Channeler (weak to ice, resistant to fire) bursting from the ground. Use the nearby Mana Shrine for assistance against the large force and stick to the side to avoid getting surrounded. Locate the third Skath camp (**12**) on the bridge. Defeat the Skath Zealots and Devoted Skath Zealot Stelae Guardian to recover the Stela of Death. Battle Sand Reapers, Giant Thrusk, and Hyenas (**13**) as you proceed north.

Battle the Scorpions (**14**). Before the cave entrance, search the western corner for the fourth Skath camp (**15**). This is a challenging fight against multiple Zealots and Avengers and a Devoted Skath Disciple

Azunite Desert, Cont'd

Stelae Guardian. The Stelae Guardian summons an Ironhorn. Recover the Stela of Sight. The cave to the north has two entrances, one on the eastern side, guarded by a King Scorpion (**16**), and a second on the western side (**17**). The primary quest path is through the eastern side; explore the western side for optional battles against Skath.

The Azunite Cavern contains large Skath groups (**18**). A cage on the eastern edge of the cavern contains Skath Cats. Explore the western side (**19**) to discover more mixed groups of Skath; another cage on the northern side also holds Skath Cats. The far western side of the cavern is separated from your current location. Use the western entrance from the previous area to explore this optional area (**20**) for experience and treasures. A northern exit (**21**) leads to a dead end that offers more battles. Follow the primary quest path to the east (**22**), out of the cavern, and into the hidden shrine. Combat the Skath and Thrusk that guard the passage.

Tip

Search the dead-end area north of the Azunite Cavern to enter a small canyon. East of the entrance, find a skeleton holding a note that refers to buried treasure! Look along the northeastern edge of the short area for a sand pile. Click on the sand pile to reveal the so-called "treasure." This optional area also contains Skath and a Skath Cat miniboss.

An Ancient Azunite Shrine

Use the bas relief on the southern wall to expose a small treasure room (**23**) that also holds the Lesser Chant of Purity lectern. Open the door to the east and battle the Twisted Shails (resistant to death magic) in the next room. The room (**24**) also contains a War Pedestal near the entrance. Follow the halls east then south. Search room edges (**25**) for treasure.

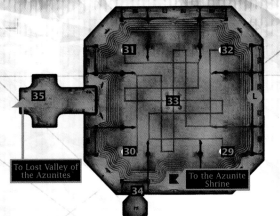

An Ancient Azunite Shrine

A southern room contains a large treasure chest in its center (**26**). It's a trap! If you open the chest, Twisted Shails emerge from side chambers. Open the smaller chests first to open the side rooms one at a time and leave the large center chest for last. A western side room contains a lectern with a mysterious chant, the Lesser Chant of Summon Enemies

One chest in the southeast corner is more than meets the eye! It's a Mimic and it attacks! Defeat the wide-jawed chest for its ample treasure contents. Continue south to the lift (**27**). Descend one floor and then another (**28**) to reach the bottom chamber.

The Inner Chamber of the Ancient Azunite Shrine

The inner chamber contains four sockets, one for each of the four Stelae. Place the Stelae in the following locations:

Inner Chamber

- ◆ Stela of Life—green socket (**29**)
- ◆ Stelaof Sight— yellow socket (**30**)
- ◆ Stela of Death—purple socket (**31**)
- ◆ Stela of Blindness—red socket (**32**)

Once all Stelae are in place, new items appear on the pedestal (**33**) in the chamber's center. Pick up the Map to the Lost Azunite Shrine and the Silver Mirror. Recovering these items opens the exit. Before leaving, open the level-13 ranged Sanctuary Door on the southern side of the chamber (**34**). Recover the Lesser Chant of Melee Awareness from the lectern on the east side. Exit the chamber through the west route (**35**). Ascend two lifts until you return outdoors.

Place the Stelae in their respective sockets to complete the quest and recover an important map.

Chapter 7—Secrets of the Azunite Desert

Chapter 8—The Lost Azunite Artifact

Placing the four Stelae provided a map that revealed the location of the lost Azunite vault. Your journey across the desert continues. Your primary foes are still the armies of Skath. Reaching the vault and recovering the weapon should place you near level 17. The tasks to complete in The Lost Azunite Artifact:

- Find the Lost Vault of the Azunites.
- Retrieve the Azunite weapon.
- Talk to the Elven spirit in the Lost Vault of the Azunites.

The Lost Valley of the Azunites

Exit the inner chamber (**1**) and emerge outdoors. The primary quest path is to the north; however, search the southern corner for an Incantation Shrine, ghostly spirit, health bushes (**2**), and a Skath camp (**3**) for additional experience. Checking the far southern edge reveals the entrance (**4**) to the Cavern of the Phoenix, part of Kalrathian Nexus secondary quest initiated during Act III. Return north and proceed northeast from your start position. Battle mixed groups of Skath and Ironhorns among the ruins (**5**) along the main path as it winds north. Search the debris (**6**) for crates and other containers holding possible loot.

Search the eastern edge of the lost valley for an abandoned tower (**7**) holding a couple of chests. Activate the teleporter to the north. Combat Blastwings and Skath to the east (**8**). Proceed farther east (**9**) and encounter a larger enemy force likely consisting of Blastwings, Ironhorns, and Iraca (**10**).

The Lost
Valley of the Azunites

Follow the path north and find mana bushes on the eastern side (**11**). Stock up because a series of tough Skath camps (**12**) protects the primary quest path. Using ice damage (ideally), defeat groups that could include Skath, Skath Cats, and Iraca. Reach the northwestern corner of the valley to reach the entrance (**13**) into an Azunite cavern.

> **Tip**
>
> *Some Lost Elven Ruins on the eastern side of the path are part of the Arinth the Mad secondary quest, which can be activated during Act II (see Part 7). The dungeon leads to a prison holding Arinth the Mad. The question is, do you free him or not?*

An Azunite Cavern

Utilize the Life Shrine just west of the cavern entrance to mend any party wounds before engaging the tough Skath and Thrusk (**14**) south of the shrine. Proceed south through the cavern and spot a pack of Scrub Boars beyond a narrow rock bridge (**15**). It's a dangerous bottleneck; lure enemies onto the bridge and bombard them with area-effect damage. Reach the cavern's southern side (**16**), and combat mixed monster forces before exiting the cavern through the western passage.

An Azunite Cavern

A Small Canyon

The Azunite Desert

Proceed west. Defeat the defenders at the bridge (**17**). Cross the narrow bridge. Harvest health potions from the bushes (**18**) then advance toward the next cavern entrance on the western side of this short area, which overlooks the area with the skeleton and his "treasure" in the valley below.

An Azunite Cavern

Mixed groups of Skath and Plagued Skath—stronger than their earlier counterparts—patrol this Azunite cavern. Search the ruins near the entrance for supplies before proceeding along the narrow path headed north (**19**). Lure the Skath into your attacks and remain at long range for as long as possible. A larger Skath camp lies to the north. Focus your efforts on the Plagued Devoted Skath Zealot, then combat the remaining Skath

Azunite Cavern with Mirror Puzzle

and Plagued Skath in the area. The bridge to the north isn't connected (**20**). Locate the button on the ruins to activate the bridge mechanism and connect the path. Proceed north and combat any Skath nearby.

There's a second bridge to the east; use a lever near the bridge (**22**) to connect the platform, allowing your party to cross. Continue east and eliminate any Skath in your path. You could also have traversed the cavern's central path (and can return there, as well) and face other Skath and Shard Souls. Your primary quest goal waits in the far eastern corner of the chamber.

Tip

There's a breakable rock within the ruins north (**21**) of the mechanical bridge. Break the rock with any weapon or spell to expose a button underneath. Press the button to raise the lift. Descend into a small chamber that contains a locked door. This area is part of the secondary quest *The Legendary Mace of Agarrus*, activated during Act III.

The eastern side contains a series of statues and mirrors (**23**). You have a Silver Mirror in your possession. Move to east side of the area and find the statue with no mirror. Click on the statue to fix your mirror in place. Your goal is to rotate the mirrors so the beam of light reaches the jewel in the rock in the center of the area. Here's how:

Rotate the mirrors so the beam of light hits the gem on the cave wall.

- Start with the mirror you just placed. Rotate that statue so the mirror points northwest—the beam of light shines north.

- Move north to the next statue. Rotate this statue so the mirror points southwest—the beam of light points west.

- Move to the statue to the far west. Rotate the statue so the mirror points southeast—the beam of light points south.

- Move south to the next statue. Rotate this statue so the mirror points northeast—the beam of light points east.

- Move east to the next statue. Rotate the statue so the mirror angles northwest—the beam of light shines north.

- Move north to the next statue (there are two statues close together). Rotate the eastern statue so the mirror points southeast—the beam of light points east.

- Move to the adjacent statue (the other one of the two statues close together) and rotate the closest statue so the mirror points southwest—the beam of light shines south.

- Adjust the middle statue (nearest the jewel in the rock and the gold star on the map) so the beam of light points east at the jewel.

The completed mirror puzzle opens a new passage.

Lost Vault of the Azunites

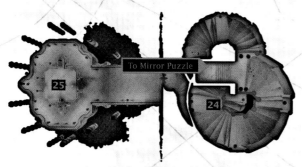

Lost Vault of the Azunites

Descend the spiral staircase (**24**) to the vault at the bottom. Approach the pedestal in the vault's center (**25**) and pick up the Azunite Artifact. Speak with the Elven spirit. The Ancestor of the

Azunites appears and provides your next quest. Open the big chest for your reward. You need to find a hidden vault in the Windstone Fortress to power the artifact.

Chapter 9—Windstone Fortress

The Ancestor of the Azunites instructs you to take the artifact to Windstone Fortress. The plague reaches even there and the fortress is overrun by infected soldiers. Increase physical resistances to counter the Windstone Soldiers and Archers, death resistance to counter the Windstone Mages, and lightning resistance to counter the horde of Fellspine at the quest's conclusion. You should approach level 19 at the completion of this quest. The tasks for Windstone Fortress:

- Begin the journey to Windstone Fortress by speaking to the Azunite Ancestor.

- Take the Azunite Artifact to Windstone Fortress.

- Find the person in command.

- Enter the Windstone Fortress Outer Vault. Find the Windstone Fortress Inner Vault Key.

- Enter the Windstone Fortress Inner Vault. Activate the Azunite Artifact.

- Bring the Activated Azunite Artifact back to Captain Dathry.

- Enter the Temple of Xeria.

Retrace your steps up the spiral staircase and find the Ancestor waiting for you on the northern side of the chamber. Speak with him again, and he'll open a northern passage. Exit through it.

The Cliffs of Azunai

Proceed east along the road and activate the teleporter on the path's southern side. Continue east along the path and encounter a mixed force that could include Blastwings, Skitters, and Ironhorns. Follow the road to its end to discover mana bushes (**1**). Follow the primary quest path into the cave entrance (**2**) on the southern side of the road just before the mana bushes.

The Cliffs of Azunai

The Cliffs of Azunai

Isteru's Caverns

Isteru's Caverns

Advance south into the caverns. Battle the hordes of Skath near the eastern ramp (**3**). There's an optional area to the southwest. Battle Skath guards near a War Pedestal. Proceed up the spiral staircase and enter the southern room that contains two circular valves (**4**). Use each valve to open an adjacent treasure room. Lower the lift using the nearby button. It leads to an Ancient Elven Reliquary, part of the Arinth's Legendary Staff secondary quest, initiated in Act III (see Part 7). There's an Incantation Shrine east of these rooms.

You'll encounter more and more Plagued Windstone troops as you near the fortress.

Proceed to the northeastern section (**5**) and find the exit back to the Cliffs of Azunai. Battle assorted beasts just north of the cavern exit (**6**). Move east and then south to reenter Isteru's Caverns (**7**). Combat mixed groups of Skath (**8**) and other creatures and advance east then north up the ramp and through the cavern exit (**9**).

Crush groups of Plagued Windstone troops and other minions upon returning to the cliffs (**10**). Eliminate the forces around the small camps and move north to the narrow bridge (**11**). Cross the bridge and move northwest to find the teleporter. Search the alcove north of the teleporter and find health bushes (**12**). An optional alcove lies east. Find a small camp (**13**) and expect to face Plagued Windstone troops, Blastwings, or other mixed monster groups. There's an Incantation Shrine at the end of the eastern path. Proceed west from the teleporter and find the entrance (**14**) to the tunnels on the northern side of the road.

The Windstone Tunnels

Expect to face more squads (**15**) of Plagued Windstone troops inside the tunnels, including Plagued Windstone Mages and their summoned creatures. Search for an exit to a cliff (**16**) just west of the tunnel entrance to battle additional monsters and find treasure. Advance north through the short cavern and exit through the opening in the northwestern (**17**) corner.

Windstone Fortress, Part I

Dense armies of Plagued Windstone troops block the route toward the Windstone Fortress, which lies north along this main route (**18**). Work your way north and eliminate the infected troops and assorted monsters. Expect to face a Kragen mini-boss (**19**). Continue north until you reach the fortress entrance (**20**). The door won't budge. Turn east and spot a secondary entrance (**21**). You must battle through infected troops within the western gatehouse to reach your goal.

Western Windstone Fortress Gatehouse

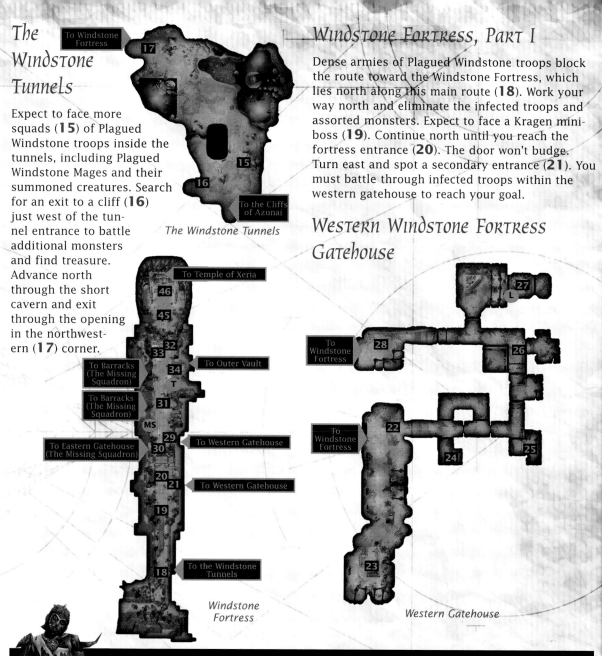

The Windstone Tunnels

Windstone Fortress

Western Gatehouse

Plagued Windstone Soldiers

Windstone Fortress has been plagued and legions of the best troops were instantly transformed into strengthened, corrupted mockeries of their former selves. The Windstone Soldiers use melee attacks; the Windstone Archers fire from long range with their bows; and the Windstone Mages cast spells. Windstone Mages cast Grave Beam, a death-magic damage spell, Infect, which lowers your death resistance, and Summon Twisted Shail. Increase death resistance to counter the mages.

The Plagued Windstone troops command the western gatehouse. Squads of mixed Windstone forces guard the entrance (**22**). Search an optional area to the south and find more infected troops and a War Pedestal (**23**). The primary path is up the stairs east of the gatehouse entrance. Use powers to help clear out the soldiers guarding the top of the stairs.

Follow the hall east. Search the treasure room in the southeastern corner (**25**), which could contain a Mimic. Head north and search side rooms for more infected troops and other enemies. There's a level-17 melee Sanctuary Door (**26**) at the northeast corner. Grab the nearby Lore Book and move east. Find another optional area through the door along the northern wall. A horde of plagued troops lurks inside. Reach the statue (**27**) to the east; press a button near the statue to open a hidden room. Find the Lesser Chant of Mage Skill in the same room as the statue. Complete the gatehouse through the western exit (**28**). You return to Windstone Fortress on the other side of the locked door.

> **Tip**
>
> *After ascending the stairs east of the entrance, search the first room on your right side (along the southern wall) to find Private Banos (**24**). He requests an escort back to the captain and reports that a few of his fellow soldiers are trapped within the fortress. Speaking with Private Banos instigates the secondary quest The Missing Squadron. See Part 7 for a full map and solution.*

Windstone Fortress, Part II

Return to the main road (**29**). There's an entrance to an optional area east of the main road (**30**). It's part of the secondary quest The Missing Squadron. Use the Mana Shrine on the left side of the road as you advance north. Eliminate any infected troops (**31**) blocking the path.

Activate the teleporter on the right side of the road. Speak with Captain Dathry (**32**) at the northern end. He provides the first key, the Windstone Fortress Outer Vault Key, but you must find the second. After the conversation, speak with Sartan, the Half-Giant in the hole (**33**). Complete the secondary quest The Imprisoned Half-Giant to release Sartan, and you can add him to your party. Enter the vault (**34**) east of the captain.

Windstone Fortress Outer Vault

Outer and Inner Vaults

To Windstone Fortress

Sartan (Level-19 Warrior) Profile

Sartan is a mighty Half-Giant and proficient in melee combat. If you previously recruited Lothar and trained him in combat magic, then Sartan is likely the first melee-based addition to your party. Sartan's strength and durability create a potent frontline warrior. Focus unused skill points on Barricade (shields), Dual Wield (two one-handed weapons), or Overbear (two-handed weapons). Decide based on your most valuable equipment and choose the skills and powers that enhance your armaments. You're also eight skill point selections away from adding the Whirling Strike power if you choose that direction. You must have Sartan in your party to initiate the Sartan's Suspicion secondary quest.

Strength: 74 ▪ Dexterity: 27 ▪ Intelligence: 29 ▪ Melee: 19 ▪ Ranged: 0 ▪ Nature Magic: 0 ▪ Combat Magic: 0 ▪ Health: 323/323 ▪ Mana: 148/148 ▪ Armor: 58 ▪ Skills: Critical Strike, Level 2; Fortitude, Level 4; Toughness, Level 1 ▪ Power: Brutal Attack, Level 1

Find the outer vault lock (**35**). Click the lock to automatically use the key provided by Captain Dathry. Defeat the Plagued Windstone forces inside the outer vault and follow the hall north. Locate the Yellow Sight Hexahedrons in the pile at the north edge (**36**) of the hall. Pick up one and place it in the empty socket (**37**) near the locked door to the east. The passage opens.

The next room features exits to the north and south. The optional room lies to the north; explore there for additional battles that'll earn you experience and possible loot. Search the southern room for a pile (**38**) of Green Life Hexahedrons. Pick up two and return to the closed door to the east. Place one hexahedron in each socket (**39**) to open the next passage.

Use the artifact on the Font of Azunite Fire to activate the weapon.

In the next chamber, search north (**40**) for more infected soldiers led by Lieutenant Namyek; he holds the key to the inner vault. Defeat the plagued troops and their leader and recover the key. Check the southern section for a pile (**41**) of Red Blindness Hexahedrons. Pick up two and return to the closed door. Place one hexahedron in each socket (**42**) to open the passage.

Windstone Fortress Inner Vault

Approach the inner vault lock and click it to automatically use the key recovered from the infected Namyek. Inside the next chamber, move south and defeat the enemies around the Font

of Azunite Fire (**43**). After clearing the area, use the font to receive the Activated Azunite Artifact and gather a reward from the big chest. Return to Captain Dathry.

Windstone Fortress, Part III

Speak with Captain Dathry with the Activated Azunite Artifact in inventory. The time has come to advance to the Temple of Xeria! The troops detonate explosives to clear the blocked passage to the north. Advance through and combat the horde (**45**) of Fellspine; the creatures are resistant to lightning, so use other elemental attacks. After clearing the area, proceed inside the temple (**46**).

> **Tip**
>
> There's a secret chamber (**44**) inside the Windstone Fortress Inner Vault, but you'll need the Dusty Vault Key. Complete the Missing Squadron secondary quest to acquire the Dusty Vault Key. Use the key to open the door in the back of the inner vault. See Part 7 for details on solving the room's puzzle.

Chapter 10—The Temple of Xeria

The last battle of Act I is at hand. There's one more teleporter inside the temple, which should be used before venturing onward and facing the act's final boss. Complete Chapter 10 to approach level 20 as you enter Act II. Your tasks for The Temple of Xeria are as follows:

- ◆ Clear out the Temple of Xeria.
- ◆ Place the Azunite Artifact on the Azunite Statue.
- ◆ Find the Shard.
- ◆ Destroy the Giant Trilisk in the Temple Courtyard.
- ◆ Destroy the Shard.

The Temple of Xeria

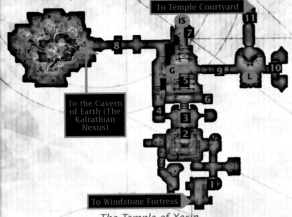

The Temple of Xeria

Place the artifact on this statue to eradicate the enemies from the temple.

Proceed into the temple and battle hordes of Fellspine. Locate the door in the northeast corner (**1**) of the initial room. Continue north. Searching the eastern room reveals nothing. Find the door in the northwestern corner and enter. The next chamber contains two sockets in its recessed center, and a pile of stones in the southeastern corner. Proceed through the northern doors (**2**).

> **Tip**
>
> The sockets and stones in the Temple of Xeria are part of the Secrets of Xeria's Temple secondary quest. Solving the sockets puzzle is entirely optional but will net you gold and equipment. See Part 7 for a complete map and solution for the side quest.

Mixed groups of Plagued Windstone troops guard the northern room (**3**). Your first task is to clear out the temple. There's a statue in the room, as well as doors leading out to the north; however, magic protects both the statue and the doors. You must clear out the plagued troops to release the magic. Defeat all enemies inside the room. There are War Pedestals to aid your party. Search the western corner of the room and open the door (**4**) to reveal additional troops. Defeat all enemies present to complete the task and release the magic.

With the temple cleared, approach the statue. Click on it to use the Activated Azunite Artifact. The resulting magical explosion clears the northern section of the temple. Advance through the doors to the north and search the corpses scattered throughout the next room (**5**). Ascend a staircase on the room's southeastern side to find a statue that's also a switch (**6**). Use it to expose a room containing a lift to hidden treasure. Return to the main chamber, pick up the Lore Books, and then proceed to the far northern side of the hall to find an Incantation Shrine.

From the main room, proceed through the eastern (**9**) hallway. Find the teleporter on the southern side and activate it. Continue east to find a couple of Sanctuary Doors (**10**). You'll need combat magic or nature magic level 17 to open the doors. Go north from the teleporter to find the temple exit (**11**). Ascend the stairs and enter the next section.

> **Tip**
>
> A statue switch (**7**) near the Incantation Shrine opens a secret passage to the west. Follow this passage to the Cavern of Earth (**8**). This cavern is part of the secondary quest The Kalrathian Nexus, which can be activated during Act II (see Part 7).

The Temple Courtyard

The Temple Courtyard

The stone barrier offers protection against the Trilisk's attack.

Something horrific waits at the northern end of the courtyard. It's no coincidence that there's a teleporter nearby. Use it to return to Eirulan if necessary and restock your potions or upgrade your equipment—a huge battle is about to begin. Walk north to encounter the Giant Trilisk (**12**) guarding the Shard you've been tasked to destroy.

The Trilisk is a mammoth three-headed serpent. It can attack with each head or combine all three for a different, and extremely potent, attack. The beast's tail is also a formidable weapon. A stone wall (**13**) provides cover against the Trilisk's primary attack: gas from the serpents' mouths. Watch the Trilisk's heads; when one of the mouths opens, retreat behind the stone wall to avoid damage. The tail jams the courtyard floor and can damage nearby party members. When the tail begins to sparkle, retreat your party quickly and take cover behind the wall.

Eliminating the Shard requires much less effort. Simply attack it until it explodes. Proceed to the portal (**15**) and usher your party inside to travel to Aman'lu and Act II.

Your first target should be the Trilisk's middle head, Vitalis, which can cast Heal to mend damage you've inflicted on the other heads, Malac and Brune. It's vital that you eliminate the middle head first! Find a War Pedestal in the northwest and northeast corners of the courtyard to recharge powers. Use a hit-and-run technique; blast a Trilisk's head then retreat behind the barrier when the beast attacks. Slice off all three heads to slay the Giant Trilisk and gain access to the Shard (**14**).

PART 5 – ACT II
PRIMARY QUESTS WALKTHROUGH

Fresh from the victory over the Giant Trilisk assaulting Windstone Fortress, the party uses a portal to reach the Elven town of Aman'lu. Prior to your arrival, Valdis unleashed his fury on the defenseless town, and Aman'lu burns with unquenchable magical fire. In Act II you'll help a former acquaintance, Aman'lu's town engineer Finala, find a way to douse the devastating fires; track a resistance leader into the domain of the Vai'kesh to recover the Aegis of Death; and assist Snowbrook Haven in its battle against Valdis's massive Morden army.

Chapter 1—The Town of Aman'lu

This first quest of Act II is short and simple, providing an introduction to the town of Aman'lu. There's no time limit in which to complete the quest, though routes out of town are blocked until you speak with Celeb'hel. Take the opportunity to explore the new town, shop for better equipment, and initiate secondary quests. There is only one task for this quest:

◆ Speak with Celeb'hel the Elder in Alt'orn Hall in the town of Aman'lu.

You arrive in what's left of Aman'lu via portal (**1**). Proceed east to the town's teleporter then turn north to Alt'orn Hall (**2**). Enter and speak with Celeb'hel the Elder. He provides information on an important caravan that left town to the south. But the bridge there is broken. Finala, the town's engineer, could fix the bridge but she's traveling north toward Elen'lu Isles.

Celeb'hel provides the Aman'lu Teleporter Activation Stone (activate the Aman'lu teleporter before leaving town) and opens the north gate.

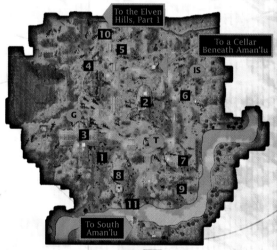

Aman'lu

He also tells you to visit your late best friend Drevin's childhood home here in town. Before leaving, grab the Lore Book and speak with Historian Bidelia for backstory.

Touring the Town of Aman'lu

Take the opportunity to completely explore the Elf town. You'll return to Aman'lu throughout this act to shop for new equipment, switch party members, and participate in secondary quests. See Part 7, "Secondary Quests," for complete information on Act II's optional side quests.

Start at the Aman'lu teleporter. Necromancer Kerion stands nearby and can resurrect party corpses for a fee. Find the Aman'lu Tavern and Inn (**3**) west of the teleporter. Speak with Barkeeper Drudwyn to initiate the secondary quest The Aman'lu Arena and chat with Athelas to initiate the A Family Heirloom, Part 2 secondary quest if you completed part 1 during Act I. Find Amren at the bar and recruit his ranged skills into your party if you need a sharpshooter. Talk with Roland

with Lothar in your party to initiate the Lothar's Innocence secondary quest.

Locate Innkeeper Odelina near the Aman'lu bar. She manages your party members. Any members you've disbanded appear here. Use her to increase the size of your party or to switch out recruited party members. Before leaving the tavern, search the upper floor for a Lore Book.

Locate the Aman'lu Armory (**4**) north of the tavern. Talk with Weaponsmith Derowen to shop for new weapons. Speak to Armorer Leodegan inside for armor and to Blacksmith Apprentice Fyrndolf, friend of Feldwyr from the Act 1 secondary quest Feldwyr the Blacksmith, to complete that task. Grab a Lore Book inside the armory.

Continue north and find Drianjul's Home (**5**). She's Drevin's sister and has a letter for you. Just north of Drianjul, find the home of Ithir'renne the Fletcher; she has an Aman'lu Orchid that's part of the Lelani's Sorrow secondary quest. East of Drianjul, enter the home of Tywlis the Mage. Speak with Tywlis to initiate the Tywlis' Broken Staff secondary quest. Grab the Lore Book inside the house before leaving. Search below Tywlis's home for a cellar beneath Aman'lu.

Move east and find an Incantation Shrine. Just south, find a collection of Aman'lu warriors (**6**). Eumenidie initiates the Viperclaw secondary quest. Procure two Lore Books in the house to the south. Speak with Eolanda the Combat Mage inside

Visit the Aman'lu Tavern and Inn to recruit a new party member or speak with the patrons.

Amren (Level-20 Sharpshooter) Profile

Amren's focused Ranged class offers impressive long-range support for your party. Six skill points have already been placed in Critical Shot, which increases Amren's chance of scoring a critical hit to over 28%. Allocate your skill points depending on your best weapon offering. Focus Amren with a bow or crossbow or choose thrown weapons. Both power options require plenty of Critical Shot, so you're well on the way to unlocking decent ranged powers. You'll need Amren in your party to initiate and complete the Amren's Vision secondary quest. Solving the quest nets a unique bow, Virtuous Rebellion, so it may be wise to focus Amren's skills in bow improvements and then equip the bow at the quest's completion.

Strength: 30 ▪ Dexterity: 92 ▪ Intelligence: 33 ▪ Melee: 0 ▪ Ranged: 20 ▪ Nature Magic: 0 ▪ Combat Magic: 0 ▪ Health: 292/292 ▪ Mana: 214/214 ▪ Armor: 65 ▪ Skills: Critical Shot, Level 6; Biting Arrow, Level 2; Survival, Level 2; Brilliance, Level 1; Critical Strike, Level 1 ▪ Powers: Brutal Attack, Level 1; Energy Orb, Level 1; Take Aim, Level 1; Thunderous Shot, Level 1

Optional Area: A Cellar Beneath Aman'lu

Descend into the cellar beneath Tywlis the Mage's home. Search the cellar for items as you move west across the bridge. Spot the ghostly spirit (A) on the level below. Cross the bridge and find an Incantation Shrine in the southern room. A button (B) in the adjacent hall opens a northern passage. Follow the passage to reach the lower level and the ghostly spirit haunting the cellar. To learn how to speak with this ghostly spirit and the others scattered throughout the game, speak with Mage Lyssanore in the Aman'lu Magic Shop and complete the A Dark Ohm secondary quest.

the house to start the Arinth's Legendary Staff secondary quest and to receive another Lore Book.

Visit the Aman'lu Pet Shop (**7**) to the south. Galeron the Pet Seller can begin the Mythrilhorn secondary quest. Search the house south of the pet shop to find an intriguing stone, which starts the Mark of the Assassin secondary quest.

Move east toward the portal and into the Aman'lu Magic Shop (**8**). Talk to Mage Lyssanore inside for magic items. Ask her about talking to spirits to initiate the A Dark Ohm secondary quest. This is an important secondary quest that rewards you with the chant that grants the ability to speak with the dead. Enchanter Khailen enchants items, and Arcanist Agrand sells reagents. Recover a couple of Lore Books on the shop's second floor. Locate Prospector Albain in the southeast corner near the river (**9**). He starts Deru's special secondary quest, Deru's Treasure Hunt (Deru must be in your party).

The primary quest directs you toward Aman'lu's northern gate (**10**). Later you'll find Finala at the southern bridge (**11**) to continue other primary quests.

Chapter 2—Finala and the Broken Bridge

Finala isn't far from town—a short trip north through the Elven Hills. Increase lightning resistance to counter the hills' Vasps and ice resistance

to counter the Forest Va'arths. Equip weapons and spells that inflict fire damage to exploit the Forest Va'arths' weaknesses. The Tharva that populate the hills are plentiful but aren't particularly tough except in large numbers. Employ area-effect powers against grouped Tharva or save your best attacks for the tougher Kurgan and Va'arth packs. The tasks for this quest are as follows:

◆ Find Finala, the town's engineer, in the hills north of Aman'lu.

◆ Convince Finala to return to Aman'lu and repair the broken bridge.

The Elven Hills

The Elven Hills, Part 1

Va'arth

The Va'arth were enslaved centuries ago by a long-vanished civilization. Chains of metal decorate the Va'arth soldiers as a reminder of their past oppression. You'll encounter the Forest Va'arth throughout the hills and Vai'lutra Forest surrounding Aman'lu. Snow Va'arths reside in the frigid mountains of Snowbrook. The Brute and tougher Barbarian wield mammoth clubs for their melee attacks; the Cannoneer and stronger Bombadier launch cannonballs as their ranged attack; and the Frostcrusher and more-dominant Avalancher use ice-magic attacks against their prey. The Va'arth spellcasters also cast Drown (to alter your ice resistance) and Wrath of Ice (altering ally freeze chance). The melee Va'arth can cast Summon Uhn Blaster and Wrath of the Bear (altering ally melee damage and critical-hit chance) and ranged Va'arth can cast Summon Rugged Snow Kurgan. All Va'arth are resistant to ice-magic damage and weak to fire attacks. The Va'arth are strong foes and it's wise to focus a strong power, particularly flame-based, on any approaching group before engaging the supporting minions.

Exit Aman'lu through the north gate. Expect to encounter scattered groups of Kurgan, Tharva, Taclak, Vasps, and Forest Va'arths along the main road (**1**). Search east and west of the main path for additional creatures; the western side includes a small farm (**2**) overrun by Kurgan. Instead of heading east across the bridge, move northwest, kill defending enemies, and loot a hut (**3**). Find mana bushes to harvest east of the hut.

Cross the bridge (**4**) eastward and keep heading northeast. Prepare for swarming Tharva when checking huts along the road. Ascend the steps

(**5**) and remain on the main road as it bends west. Expect to encounter a Forest Va'arth miniboss nearby. Once the road bends north search the western corner for health bushes (**6**).

Advance north. Find a Life Shrine on the west side and a ruined home overrun by Taclak on the east side (**7**). Explore the home's cellar for treasures. Continue north and find Finala (**8**). She's hoping to discover a way to put out the Aman'lu fires. Finala hands over a diagram of the Elen'lu Prism Diagram and a Bridge Activation Crystal.

Chapter 3—The Elen'lu Isles

The Elen'lu Isles are a series of islands and bridges. Finala's Bridge Activation Crystal permits you access to adjacent islands. You'll comb the islands in search of four prisms held by Taclak minibosses, then replace each prism in a beam-focusing device. Taclak are primary enemies during this quest. Area-effect spells and powers provide a hearty counter against tribes of Taclak. Complete the task and Finala, a capable combat mage, can join your party. The quest tasks:

◆ Travel to the Elen'lu Isles.

◆ Find and replace the prism's four small Refractor Crystals. Find the prism's large Refractor Crystal and activate the prism.

◆ Return to Aman'lu and speak with Finala.

Find Finala at the northern edge of the Elven Hills. She's the only person who can fix Aman'lu's southern bridge.

location. The main path crosses a bridge (**6**) to the east. You can also search the far western corner of the forest to find an optional area, a damp cave (**7**).

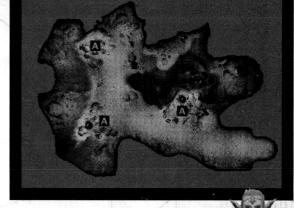

Optional Area: A Damp Cave

*Search the Damp Cave within the Vai'lutra Forest to discover three Taclak camps (**A**). Expect to battle mixed groups of Taclak Trackers and Bashers. Support any of your melee characters with area-effect spells and powers to combat the large number of Taclak guarding their abode. Search the camps for gold or useful loot before returning to the Vai'lutra Forest.*

Finala returns to Aman'lu. Continue north (**1**) and battle groups of Taclak, Kurgan, Vasps, Forest Va'arth, Taugrim, and Tharva throughout the hills. Follow the main road and activate the teleporter on the western side. Harvest mana potions from the bushes in the northeast corner (**2**) just before the main path turns east.

A large force of hill beasts (**3**) guards the main road before it turns north into the Vai'lutra Forest. Search the alcove southeast of the main road and harvest health potions from the bushes (**4**). Use the main road and head north into the Northern Vai'lutra Forest.

The Elven Hills, Part 2

Northern Vai'lutra Forest

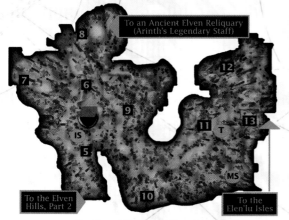

Northern Vai'lutra Forest

Continue north on the main road. Be prepared for a Taclak ambush (**5**) near an Incantation Shrine. At the shrine, you can take a shortcut east or follow the main road; both paths end up at the same

Cross the bridge to the east. Harvest health potions from bushes north of the main road. Continue on the road south. Search Taclak camps (**9**) for equipment and gold. Explore an abandoned tower (**10**) on the southern edge of the primary path. Press a button inside the tower to reveal a hidden chest. Plentiful groups of Taclak, Forest Va'arths, and other forest beasts guard the route northeast. Check the southeastern corner for a Mana

Tip

*Before crossing the short bridge, search the far northern corner of the forest to discover the entrance into An Ancient Elven Reliquary. Taclak and a miniboss defend it. This dungeon is part of the Arinth's Legendary Staff secondary quest. Find it by navigating through the dense forest northeast of the entrance to a damp cave (**8**). For a full solution and maps, see Part 7.*

Shrine to aid your casters. You can also find mana bushes to harvest (**11**) on the western side and a teleporter on the eastern side.

Before following the main road east, explore the far north edge and find an abandoned tower (**12**) with a few containers. Follow the primary quest path into the Temple of Istaura and Isteru (**13**) on the eastern side. The road leads directly into the Elen'lu Isles.

The Elen'lu Isles

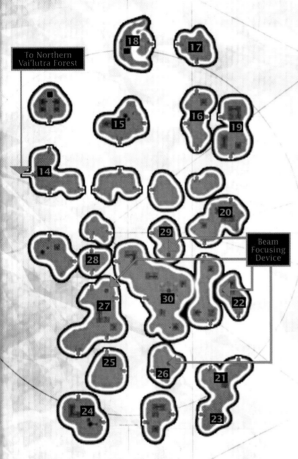

The Elen'lu Isles

You begin on the western side (**14**) of the isles. As you walk onto the first platform, a brief cut scene reveals the isle layout. Defeat the Taclak miniboss here to recover the first small Prism Refractor Crystal. Your goal here: follow the path to traverse isles, reach and defeat Taclak minibosses, recover crystals, and find all the beam-focusing devices.

From the start location, enable and cross the bridges in the following order: eastern, northern (with the small campsite) (**15**), eastern (**16**). If you wish to take a quick detour to a side dungeon, enable and cross the northern bridge (**17**) then the western bridge (**18**) to find the entrance. Expect Taclak to leap onto the isles and engage.

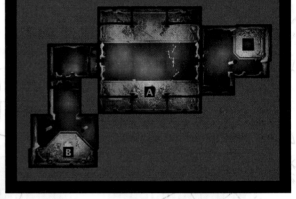

Optional Area: Elen'lu Isles Dungeon

The dungeon on the northwest corner of the Elen'lu Isles is completely optional and doesn't house a Prism Refractor Crystal. Use the War Pedestal (A) to recharge a power for use against the Taclak miniboss (B). Search the rooms for chests and equipment. You can exit on the opposite side of the dungeon to arrive on an otherwise inaccessible isle.

The primary path is eastward. Enable the east bridge and cross. Defeat the Taclak miniboss there (**19**) and recover the second small Prism Refractor Crystal. Enable the southern bridge and cross (**20**). Continue across two bridges to the south (**21**), then use the northeast bridge on this same isle and cross to a beam-focusing device (**22**). Place a prism in the device and ensure its beam shines on the isle center—to the west.

Return south and reach the far southwestern island (**23**). At its southern point, find mana bushes to harvest potions. Activate the next two west bridges and cross (**24**). Combat the Taclak miniboss and recover the third small Prism Refractor Crystal. Use the north bridge and cross, then take the southern bridge (**25**) on the same isle. Enable the east bridge and cross to another beam-focusing device (**26**). Place a prism inside the device and ensure the beam points north.

Recover four small prisms and place each one in a separate beam-focusing device.

Return west and cross the bridge north to the third beam-focusing device (**27**). Place a prism inside and ensure the beam aims east toward the isle center. Activate and cross the bridge to the north. Kill the Taclak miniboss (**28**) and recover the fourth and final small Prism Refractor Crystal. Enable and cross the northern then the eastern bridge to find the last beam-focusing device; place the prism inside (**29**) and make sure the beam points south.

Move to the western beam-focusing device (marked **27** on the map) and cross the eastern bridge to the central structure (**30**). Defeat the Taclak miniboss protecting the structure to recover the large prism crystal. Place it in the central beam-focusing device on top of the structure to complete the task. Taclak appear everywhere! Fight the defenders or summon a teleporter to Aman'lu. You can also retrace your steps to the Northern Vai'lutra Forest teleporter.

Once in Aman'lu, find Finala near the southern bridge. She repairs the broken bridge, initiates the next quest, and can join your party!

Chapter 4—The Royal Caravan

South Aman'lu stretches through the Vai'lutra Forest and into Vai'kesh territory where the caravan and Princess Evangeline might be found. Taclak still crowd the forest path and fight alongside Kurgan, Bracken, and Forest Va'arth. Explore several side caves for additional loot and combat opportunities. Prepare for battle against the Vai'kesh by enhancing lighting damage and spells. This quest's tasks include the following:

- ◆ Locate the caravan.
- ◆ Find the Vai'kesh Sanctuary. Find the leader of the Vai'kesh.
- ◆ Find the Aegis of Death.

Finala (Level-22 Sorceress) Profile

Finala has centered training on Combat-Magic and could provide valuable curses, summons, or damage spells. Lightning magic is a capable counter against the Vai'kesh, and fire provides power for the snowy landscape that envelops the latter portion of the second act. Consider spending Finala's skill points on Amplified Lightning to increase lightning-magic damage or Searing Flames to enhance fire-magic damage, as well as Brilliance and Devastation to increase mana capacity and enhance all combat-magic damage. Focus points on one of the other and acquire the Combat-Mage powers Flame Nexus and Detonation (for a fire mage) or Chain Lightning and Gathered Bolt (for a lightning mage). You need Finala in your party to initiate and complete the Finala's Contempt secondary quest.

Strength: 32 ▪ **Dexterity: 33** ▪ **Intelligence: 81** ▪ **Melee: 0** ▪ **Ranged: 0** ▪ **Nature Magic: 0** ▪ **Combat Magic: 22** ▪ **Health: 265/265** ▪ **Mana: 471/471** ▪ **Armor: 15** ▪ **Skills: Devastation, Level 2; Brilliance, Level 2; Critical Strike, Level 1; Debilitation, Level 1** ▪ **Powers: Energy Orb, Level 1; Corrosive Eruption, Level 1; Brutal Attack, Level 1**

South Aman'lu

Cross the repaired southern bridge. Enter the house on the eastern side (**1**) and speak with Eldoriath Wilwarin. You'll receive The Guard's Report Lore Book if you accept the Servant's Haunt secondary quest. Check the house on the western side (**2**) and speak with Alar'ithil. He has a bottle of Elven Water that's part of the Lelani's Sorrow secondary quest. Grab the Lore Book from his home before exiting. Resume your path south into the Southern Vai'lutra Forest.

Southern Vai'lutra Forest

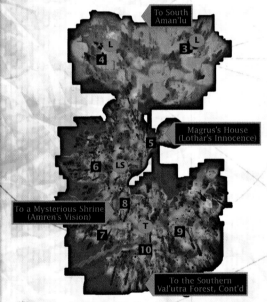

Southern Vai'lutra Forest

Expect to battle Rotten Bracken, Vasps, Rugged Kurgan, Tharva, Forest Va'arths and Taclak throughout the forest. Rotten Bracken are weak to fire; equip weapons or spells that inflict fire damage to counter them. Search the eastern (**3**) side of the main path and check an overrun farm

for loot and a lectern with the Chant of Strength. The western (**4**) side contains a farm infested with Taclak. The home contains two lecterns with the Chant of Dexterity and Chant of Intelligence.

Continue south through the forest. Find an eastern path and discover Magrus' House (**5**) in a small clearing—part of the Lothar's Innocence secondary quest. Use the Life Shrine south of the hidden path. On the opposite side, harvest potions from the mana bushes (**6**). Battle the Taclak that ambush from under logs and then search their camps. Locate a tower (**7**) in the southwestern corner before the path turns east. A button inside reveals a lift.

Tip

Before crossing the bridge in the Southern Vai'lutra Forest, locate a path behind the teleporter and follow it to a curious mushroom formation (**8**). This location is part of the Amren's Vision secondary quest.

Activate the area's teleporter. The primary path runs across a southern bridge. Before crossing, explore an eastern alcove to discover Taclak camps, health bushes, and a gorgeous waterfall view (**9**). Continue on the primary route across the bridge (**10**) and into the next section.

Locate a path west of the main road to discover an entrance to an optional area (**11**), a small cave. Battle groups of forest beasts (Taugrim, Kurgan, etc.) and ambushing Taclak near the camps to the south (**12**). You'll also encounter Sangor, Fettershin, and Rotten Bracken (weak to fire) as you continue deeper into the forest. Search east for health

Southern Vai'lutra Forest, Cont'd

Optional Area: Small Caves

Expect to battle hordes of Forest Va'arth within the western small cave (A). Clear out the recessed area (B) and ascend the rock bridge. Discover Magrus (C) hanging around (part of the Lothar's Innocence secondary quest) and continue to the far southeastern corner to discover a cave exit (D) into the Southern Vai'lutra Forest.

The eastern small cave offers similar opposition. Combat plentiful Forest Va'arth in the lower section (E) around a camp. Discover another camp (F) in the southeastern corner. Both side areas are small but offer additional battle opportunities and potential loot.

A Small Cave (West)　　　　　**A Small Cave (East)**

bushes (**13**) and another small cave (**14**), northeast of the bushes.

The road continues south into a heavily guarded Taclak camp (**15**) before bending west. Discover the large structure and lift in the clearing (**16**); this is the Levreth Estate and part of the Servant's Haunt secondary quest. Locate the teleporter ahead and find the caravan (**17**) nearby. Speak with the wounded driver, Mylindril. Princess Evangeline and the Aegis of Death are missing!

Search west of the caravan for an Incantation Shrine. Resume a southern course on the main road and battle forest beasts near a campsite (**18**). Explore southeast from the main road and find an abandoned tower (**19**) that leads into an optional area, a flooded chamber. Use the button inside the tower to reveal a hidden chest. Harvest mana potions from the bushes north of the tower. Follow the primary path south into Vai'kesh territory.

You find what's left of the caravan in South Vai'kesh Forest...but no sign of the princess or the Aegis.

Optional Area: A Flooded Chamber

Descend the abandoned tower in the Southern Vai'lutra Forest and enter a small flooded chamber. There's a War Pedestal in the initial room (A) to aid your battle against the chamber's inhabitants, including a miniboss. Find a hidden lamp switch (B) on the western wall to open an adjacent large treasure room (C) containing a lectern with a mysterious chant (Random Item). Pillage all containers before using the lift to return to the forest.

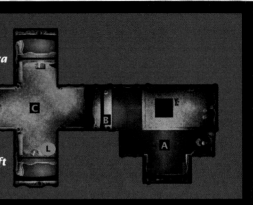

The Vai'kesh Forest

The Vai'kesh Forest

Battle the Bracken, Fettershin, Naldrun (resistant to lightning), and Thrine throughout this forest area. The Naldrun employ vicious lightning attacks, so bolster your resistance to counter. Harvest health potions from the bushes (**20**) alongside the road if you have a party member with the Survival skill. Follow the road east to a closed gate. Attempt to open the gate and speak with the Vai'kesh Fanatic Neophyte (**21**) standing guard.

Developer Tip

To maximize the humor factor, try different combinations of party characters. My favorites are boisterous Deru with headstrong Vix, who can't really stand each other, and overbearing Sartan with any female character, which is really an ongoing one-way conversation about how great he is. Third place would have to be Vix and Finala. He constantly trips over himself when talking with her. —Bert Bingham, Producer

Take the north path and find the entrance into the Vai'kesh Sanctuary. Speak with the Vai'kesh Zealot Neophyte (**22**). You can choose how to address the Vai'kesh; the resulting encounter inside the sanctuary plays differently depending on your selection:

- Play nice with the Vai'kesh Zealot Neophyte and you're free to enter the Vai'kesh Sanctuary without incident. Locate the leader inside and speak with him. However, the conversation turns sour and the Vai'kesh attack as the leader flees.

- Be aggressive with the Vai'kesh Zealot Neophyte and the Vai'kesh leader is warned of your arrival. The Vai'kesh immediately attack while the leader flees the area.

Regardless of the stance you choose, ensure your party members have full health and mana before entering the sanctuary.

The Vai'kesh Sanctuary

If you entered the sanctuary on good terms, speak with the Vai'kesh leader (**23**) before chaos ensues and the leader flees out of the chamber's eastern side. An aggressive entrance sends the leader out of the eastern side

The Vai'kesh Sanctuary— The Vai'kesh Leader

immediately. Either way, a battle ensues against the sanctuary's defenders.

Chapter 5—The Vai'kesh and the Aegis of Death

This quest is a long chase through Vai'kesh territory ending with a couple of challenging boss battles. Your principal adversaries throughout the quest will be the Vai'kesh, which are particularly vulnerable to lightning damage and heavily resistant to death magic. Increase your own death-magic resistance to counter the Vai'kesh spellcasters. Return to Aman'lu via teleporter or spell to restock potions or adjust equipment. Quest tasks are as follows:

- ◆ Follow the Vai'kesh Prophet.

- ◆ Defeat the Vai'kesh Prophet and his followers.

- ◆ Find the Aegis of Death.

- ◆ Defeat the Knotted Shambler. Claim the Aegis of Death.

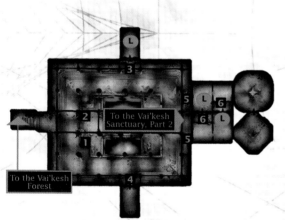

The Vai'kesh Sanctuary, Part 1

You must defeat all Vai'kesh in the initial chamber before you can pursue the Vai'kesh Prophet leader through the eastern exit. The Vai'kesh quickly surround your party. Retreat off the catwalk and allow enemies to funnel toward you. Blast groups of Vai'kesh with powers and area-effect spells. Use nearby War Pedestals to recharge powers; there is a pedestal (**1**) in each back corner (**2**) along the bottom of the chamber.

Open a ranged Sanctuary Door (**3**) on the northern side of the room (a Chant of Ranger Power lectern is also in the room) and a nature-magic Sanctuary Door (**4**), both level 22, on the southern side. Activate buttons (**5**) on the upper catwalk to open a couple of treasure rooms (**6**) containing lecterns with the Chant of Fighter Power and Chant of Mage Power. A torch in the northern room opens another hidden treasure room; a button in the southern room opens yet another. The room on the right may contain a Mimic. Upon clearing the area, proceed east through the opened passage in the chamber's lower area.

The Vai'kesh leader isn't going to give up the Aegis easily.

The Vai'kesh

Some of Aman'lu's greatest mages became enthralled by the Aegis of Death's power. Unable to control the darkest of death magic, these sorcerers were consumed by their lust for power and eventually exiled into the forest by Aman'lu's elders. These dark Elves became the Vai'kesh, or "evil spirits." You'll battle the Vai'kesh throughout their forest, caves, and sanctuary that comprise Act II's fifth quest. Face off against Zealots, melee warriors that dual-wield sabers; Fanatics, which employ long-range bows; and Seers, casting their Soul Lance, Life Embrace (increases ally health recovery), Heal, and Summon Feaster spells. The An'tul ("elite" or "master") Vai'kesh are stronger and typically surrounded by Vai'kesh Diabolists that regenerate the An'tul's health and power. Defeat the Diabolists on sight to prevent the An'tul from regaining their strength. The An'tul melee and ranged versions can also cast Life Embrace on their allies. All Vai'kesh are highly resistant to death magic and weak against lightning damage.

Spot the lectern south of the entrance; grab the Chant of Casting. Battle the Vai'kesh and surrounding support forces (**7**). Loot their treasures before exiting east.

The Vai'kesh Sanctuary, Part 2

Open the door and ascend the staircase. Find a War Pedestal in the next room's eastern corner (**8**). Recharge a power for aid in battling the Vai'kesh within the room. Grab the Lore Book off the bench on the next staircase. The next room (**9**) offers another War Pedestal. Continue west (**10**) and return to the Vai'kesh Forest.

Encounter mixed groups of Vai'kesh outside the sanctuary. During the fight, utilize the Life Shrine

west of the sanctuary exit. Harvest potions from the mana bushes (**11**) along the main road. Follow the path south. Cross the narrow bridge (**12**) and find a teleporter at the southern edge of the forest.

The Vai'kesh Forest, Part 2

Activate the teleporter and use it if you need to return to Aman'lu.

A Large Vai'kesh Cavern

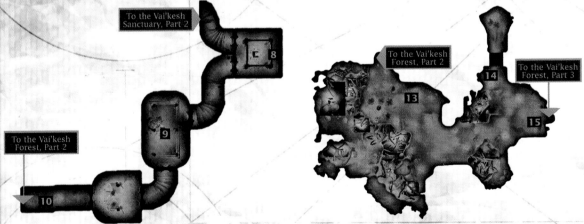

The Vai'kesh Sanctuary, Part 3

A Large Vai'kesh Cavern

Battle mixed groups of Vai'kesh forces (**13**) around a campsite just south of the cavern entrance. Advance southeast then east into the second half of the cavern. Before exiting, search an alcove to the north for a lever (**14**) that opens a treasure room on the northern side of the cave wall. Resume course east and locate the exit (**15**) into the Vai'kesh Forest.

The Vai'kesh Forest

The Vai'kesh Forest, Part 3

Defeat groups of Vai'kesh and support units around the teleporter. Search south for health bushes, a Life Shrine, and an entrance into a small Vai'kesh prison (**16**), part of the secondary quest A Family Heirloom, Part 2. Follow the main path northeast. You encounter the Vai'kesh Prophet (**17**) but he makes another escape, this time across a chasm to the east. Defeat the Vai'kesh that attack. A small Vai'kesh cave north (**18**) of the main path is part of the A Dark Ohm secondary quest.

Cross the bridge east in pursuit of the Vai'kesh Prophet. At the fork, search north for an Incantation Shrine and a group of mana bushes (**19**). Follow the main path east and move over another bridge that heads south. Immediately after crossing the bridge, explore the western route to discover a hidden cave (**20**) that's part of the Evangeline's Folly secondary quest. Proceed along the forest path to the southern corner to discover an optional area, a small Vai'kesh cave (**21**).

Optional Area: A Small Vai'kesh Cave

There are several small caves throughout the Vai'kesh Forest and Arinth's Ravine, an area connected to the vast forest. Most are included in Act II secondary quests. One small cave on the southern tip of the Vai'kesh Forest is completely optional. This Vai'kesh cave features an An'tul Vai'kesh and supporting Diabolists on the western side (**A**) near a small camp. Eliminate Diabolists to prevent the An'tul from regaining health. After the battle, loot the camp for its supplies.

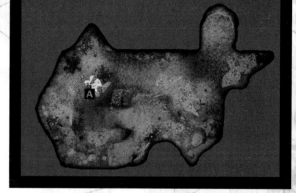

The path bends east. Check an abandoned tower in the southeastern corner (**22**). Push a button inside to reveal a hidden chest. Remain on the main path as it extends east (**23**) and into Arinth's Ravine.

Arinth's Ravine

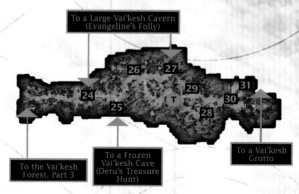

Arinth's Ravine

Arinth's Ravine is a narrow stretch of road running west to east. Expect to encounter mixed groups of Vai'kesh and assorted forest beasts (Sangor, Bracken, Fettershin, etc.) throughout the area. Check a side route to the north and discover a large Vai'kesh cavern (**24**) that's part of the Evangeline's Folly secondary quest. Traverse the bridge and battle the Vai'kesh miniboss and Diabolists. Find another side path, this time to the south, and locate a frozen Vai'kesh cave (**25**) used in the Deru's Treasure Hunt secondary quest.

Check an abandoned tower on the northern side of the road (**26**) for containers and equipment. Approach a bridge on the southern side of the main road. Before your party can confront the Vai'kesh leader, he flees again deeper into Arinth's Ravine. He calls upon a large group of mixed Vai'kesh to defend the bridge. Counter the Vai'kesh with area-effect powers, ideally employing lightning damage to exploit their weakness. Before following the prophet, search the eastern alcove (**27**) for a camp and another side dungeon. It's a large Vai'kesh cavern and part of the Evangeline's Folly secondary quest.

Proceed across the bridge. Stay on the main road to the east and find the teleporter to the east. You can cross a second bridge east or take a southern route and find a group of health bushes (**28**). Both paths connect at the same location. North of the bridge, find some mana bushes (**29**).

You catch the Vai'kesh Prophet (**30**) east of the bridge near a couple of cavern entrances. These entrances remain locked until you defeat the Vai'kesh Prophet and his escort. Exploit the Vai'kesh's weakness to lightning. Support your melee attackers with powers, buff, and area-effect spells. Face the Prophet again after you've knocked him off his mount. Crush the Prophet then finish off the supporting Zealots.

The Vai'kesh Prophet didn't have the Aegis of Death. With the cavern entrances unlocked, check the northern cavern, a large Vai'kesh cavern, for an Incantation Shrine and reward chests. Follow the primary quest path into the eastern entrance (**31**), a Vai'kesh Grotto.

A Vai'kesh Grotto

Follow the cavern path north. The cavern splits into three paths. Northern and eastern routes lead to dead-end alcoves with treasure (and a ghostly spirit). Find the primary quest path southeast. Cross the bridge in the southeastern corner of the grotto (**32**) and spot the Aegis of Death (**33**) held inside a large chamber. The Vai'kesh have corrupted a tree into the form of a Knotted Shambler and enchanted it to guard the Aegis. The Aegis remains locked in place until you defeat the beast (**34**).

A Vai'kesh Grotto

The Knotted Shambler begins the fight with leaf armor. When you damage the armor, it begins to fall off; the leaf armor turns into Shambler Hatchlings that attack you (the Hatchlings are plentiful but not strong attackers). After the Knotted Shambler is stripped of leaf armor, you can begin inflicting damage. After sustaining damage, the Knotted Shambler folds itself into a cocoon state (during which time he's invulnerable) and summons nearby Shambler Hatchlings to regenerate the armor.

Developer Tip

When Shambler Hatchlings flood the area, switch your party to Rampage Mode so the party members will spread and attack individual hatchlings quickly. Trying to attack individual leaves in Mirror Mode is much too slow, which leads to armor regeneration and likely damage from the Knotted Shambler's attacks.
—John Cutter, Designer

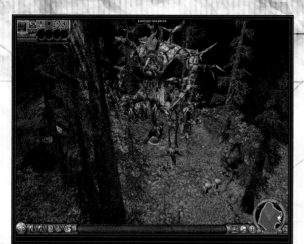

Eliminate the Leaf Generators that release hatchlings capable of regenerating the Knotted Shambler's armor.

Leaf Generators scattered around the cavern release additional Shambler Hatchlings. Prevent the Knotted Shambler from regenerating armor by eliminating the Shambler Hatchlings that have fallen from the Knotted Shambler and, more importantly, the Leaf Generators that release them.

Search for the Leaf Generators during the battle's early stage and destroy them all before focusing your attacks on the Knotted Shambler. To aid in the battle, locate a War Pedestal on the cave's eastern side and use it to recharge your most devastating power. Once the Leaf Generators are gone, the number of Hatchlings available to the Knotted Shambler decreases dramatically. Concentrate all powers and attacks to destroy the formidable tree. The Knotted

Shambler is weak against fire damage. Upon conquering the boss, you release the magic that locks the Aegis of Death.

Grab the Aegis. An exit opens (**35**) and the Azunite Scholar rewards your fine work. Follow the scholar to a portal, and enter the portal to initiate the next primary quest.

Chapter 6—Princess Evangeline

You've reached the mountains around Snowbrook. Various snow monsters (many resistant to ice magic) support the Undead Azunites (resistant to death and lightning magic) that heavily populate the frigid landscape and the various tombs within. Strengthen your party's ability to inflict fire damage and increase ice and death resistances to counter the area's monsters. A hefty lightning resistance will also help against the Dark Wizard encountered at the quest's conclusion. This quest's tasks include the following:

- ◆ Enter the Azunite Burial Grounds.
- ◆ Look for death masks of Champion Rahvan's brothers.
- ◆ Enter the Azunite Catacombs.
- ◆ Find and rescue Princess Evangeline.

Optional Area: A Frozen Crypt

The frozen tomb closest to the area's portal is an entirely optional side dungeon. There are no quest items inside, only possible loot and additional combat chances. Find a War Pedestal in the tomb's center (A) to recharge a power. Investigate the southeastern corner of the crypt to discover a statue switch (B). Use the statue to open a hidden treasure room to the south; it contains a lectern with the Chant of Master Self Awareness.

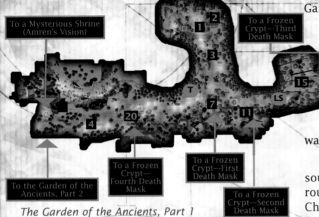

The Garden of the Ancients, Part 1

Continue southwest into the next section of the Garden of the Ancients (part 2). The monster population is impressive. Attempt to engage small groups of enemies instead of charging into the belly of the beast and forcing your party to fight more than they're capable of handling. Expect to encounter Grangeflies, Lertisk, Flaypicks, and Snow Va'arths. Work your way southwest to the teleporter; then activate and use it as a gateway to Aman'lu during the fight if needed.

The entrance you're seeking is south of the teleporter. Clear surrounding beasts then speak with Champion Rahvan (**6**), who's standing guard at the burial grounds entrance. Rahvan won't open the passage until you retrieve death masks of Rahvan's three brothers from within tombs in the previous area of the Garden of the Ancients (part 1). Backtrack, or use the teleporter to travel quickly.

> **Tip**
>
> *The southern section of the Garden of the Ancients, Part 2 isn't accessible from here. You'll find a passage to the southern area via the Azunite Burial Grounds. Check in that section for a map of the area, which is littered with structures and towers containing treasure, a couple Chant Lecterns, and a ghostly spirit.*

The tombs can be searched in any order. For the purposes of this walkthrough, approach the tomb entrance (**7**) just south of the teleporter. Descend the steps into the frozen tomb.

You arrive via portal (**1**) into a snow-covered landscape. Expect to face Snow Va'arth, Grangeflies, Snow Kurgan, and Undead Azunites throughout the area. Check the structure east of the portal and find an entrance into an optional dungeon (**2**), a frozen crypt.

Move south from the area's start position. Search a small structure (**3**) and loot its contents. Harvest health potions from bushes on the opposite side. The path forks west and the east at the southern tip of the main road. Ignore the eastern side initially and proceed west. Find the area's teleporter and use it to return to warmer Aman'lu to adjust equipment or party members as desired. Harvest mana potions from bushes just west of the teleporter.

As you move through the area, you'll discover entrances to other tombs. Ignore them for now; though many of these tombs are involved in the area's primary quest, you should find the burial grounds entrance first. The area's fierce beasts protect the western route (**4**). Locate a hidden path northwest and discover an entrance (**5**) into an underground chamber, part of the Amren's Vision side quest.

> **Tip**
>
> *Explore the northern side of the snowy hills near the curious mushroom formation that's part of Amren's secondary quest, and look in the valley below to see a Morden army moving toward an unknown destination. Perhaps Princess Evangeline can shed some light on this development.*

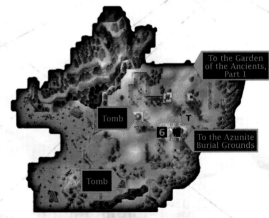

The Garden of the Ancients, Part 2

Rahvan blocks access to the burial grounds... but he'll let you pass for a favor.

Undead Azunites

Many brave souls searched for the lost treasures of the Azunites and never returned. Or so it was thought. The ghastly truth, however, is that those brave souls returned from the dead and were charged with protecting the ancient Azunite artifacts and shrines from outsiders. The Undead Azunites defend the areas around Snowbrook Haven, including the Garden of the Ancients and the frozen crypts harboring Rahvan's death masks. Undead Azunites are resistant to lightning and death magic; employ weapons or spells that inflict fire or ice damage to avoid the Undead Azunites' specific counter. The melee-based Undead Soldiers wield swords; the ranged Undead Archers fire with their bows; and the magic-based Undead Mages cast the death-magic spell Leech Life—which drains your health and replenishes the mage's health—and Summon Bone Minion to support their fellow warriors. Mage groups are particularly deadly: they're able to drain the life of a party member quickly and even resurrect their comrades. Eliminate Undead Mages first to avoid their spells and summons. Soldiers are the most durable. Use freeze spells and powers to stop the Undead Soldiers in their tracks and bombard them with fire or ice damage.

A Frozen Crypt—First Death Mask

Locate the Champion's Death Mask on top of a sarcophagus south of the entrance in the crypt's center (**8**). If possible, reach the War Pedestal in the southwest corner of the crypt's center (**9**) and use it to aid in the battle against the chamber's enemies.

Expect to encounter other enemies lingering in the tomb's treasure rooms.

A Frozen Crypt—First Death Mask

Locate buttons (**10**) on the western, eastern, and southern tomb walls. Press the buttons to reveal adjacent treasure rooms. Tread carefully in the western and eastern treasure rooms and avoid the traps (the projectiles damage enemies, as well). After retrieving the first death mask, return outside to the Garden of the Ancients (part 1).

Proceed to the east. Bypass the northern path (it returns toward the portal) and find the next tomb (**11**) on the southern side. Pillage a nearby structure for equipment before entering the tomb.

A Frozen Crypt— Second Death Mask

Move south into the second frozen crypt. Expect to find groups of Undead Azunite, Lertisk,

A Frozen Crypt—Second Death Mask

and Grangeflies guarding the central chamber, which houses the second Champion's Death Mask (**12**) on one of the sarcophagi. To aid in battle, use one or more of the four War Pedestals positioned in the chamber's four corners.

Continue east along the snowy path, where you'll find a Life Shrine. Stick close to the shrine as you battle the beasts in the alcove that houses the third frozen crypt. Search structures near the tomb entrance for equipment, then descend the east steps (**15**).

Tip

Find a button on each of the western, eastern, and southern tomb walls (**13**). Press each button to open an adjacent treasure room (which may also contain more monsters). The eastern treasure room also offers a combat-magic Sanctuary Door (level 25) on its southern side (**14**). After recovering the death mask and exploring the area, return to the Garden of the Ancients (part 1) to find the next frozen crypt.

A Frozen Crypt—Third Death Mask

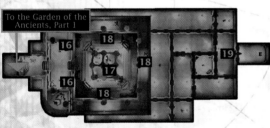

A Frozen Crypt—Third Death Mask

Expect to face similar beasts in this third crypt. After descending the second staircase, find a couple of War Pedestals to aid your fight (**16**).

Find the third Champion's Death Mask (**17**) in the center of the large chamber defended by an Undead miniboss. Locate buttons (**18**) on the northern, southern, and eastern walls. The buttons open new halls. Move cautiously through the opened halls to avoid projectile traps. Explore the northern hall and use the statue switch there to gain access to a nature magic Sanctuary Door (level 25) along the eastern wall (**19**). Use statue switches in the northern and western halls to gain

access to another treasure area. Return to the Garden of the Ancients (part 1).

Proceed west past the teleporter and find an entrance to a fourth frozen tomb (**20**) on the southern side of the main path.

A Frozen Crypt—Fourth Death Mask (Optional)

You can recover the death masks in any order. And since you need only three to complete the primary quest task, retrieving a fourth is entirely optional (it initiates the Rahvan's Curse secondary quest). For the purposes of this walkthrough, we've chosen this frozen crypt as the optional fourth. However, since you may visit this crypt third instead of fourth, we've included it in the primary quest walkthrough.

A Frozen Crypt— Fourth Death Mask (Optional)

Defeat the beasts in the crypt's central chamber. Locate the Champion's Death Mask (**21**) among the sarcophagi. There's also a center War Pedestal to assist in the battle against the mask's defenders. Look for buttons (**22**) on the western, eastern, and southern walls to reveal hidden treasure rooms.

Return to the Garden of the Ancients (part 1) and move southwest into the adjacent section (part 2). Return to Champion Rahvan, still at his post in front of the burial grounds. Speak with Rahvan with at least three Champion's Death Masks in your inventory; he opens the passage into the burial grounds.

Azunite Burial Grounds

Descend the steps into the burial grounds. Undead Azunites are your primary foes throughout this dungeon; use fire or ice damage (avoid weapons and spells that inflict lightning or death damage). Find the door on the northeast section. Traverse the stairwell to the next chamber and defeat the enemies gathered inside. The room (**23**) contains a ranged Sanctuary Door (level 25) and a War Pedestal to recharge a power.

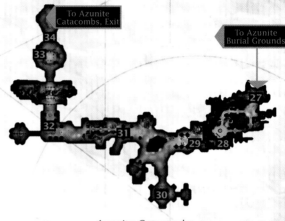

Azunite Burial Grounds

Move south into a large, open area filled with undead and other supporting minions. There are essentially two routes here: You can remain on the upper catwalk and continue along the path to the south or search a lower region to the west that bends to the southwest and reconnects to the upper path. Both routes are crowded with undead. Look on the northeast side of the upper catwalk (**24**) for a War Pedestal. The lower, western side also contains a War Pedestal (**25**). Search the ridge south of this War Pedestal for a lectern hidden in the corner along the wall. It contains the Chaotic Chant of Might.

At the steps where the two paths connect, take note of the Azunite floor symbols (**26**) and, most importantly, the order from left to right: Death, Blindness, Sight, and Life. Follow the primary quest path south. Beware of the projectile traps positioned on either side of the upper catwalk. Work your way to the southern corner to find the area's teleporter. Use it if necessary before proceeding into the catacombs.

Azunite Catacombs

Azunite Catacombs

Cross the narrow bridge south. The path forks west and south (**27**). Both routes connect at the same location and contain various projectile traps—tread carefully to avoid them. Advance to the western side and discover a locking mechanism adorned with Azunite symbols (**28**). You

Optional Area: The Garden of the Ancients, Secret Area

An exit on the far western side of the Azunite Burial Grounds leads into the southern area of the Garden of the Ancients (part 2). This area is accessible only through the burial grounds. Mixed groups of the garden's beasts (Snow Va'arth, Grangeflies, Snow Kurgan) protect the tombs throughout this southern area. Locate a Life Shrine south of the area's entrance and an Incantation Shrine to the north. The northern end also features a tower (A). Use a lift inside of the tower to reach the top and find a couple of lecterns with the Chant of Melee Awareness and Chant of Ranged Awareness. Explore the eastern elevation to discover a ghostly spirit (B) haunting the tombs.

must rotate the mechanism to match the Azunite symbols shown on the catwalk in the previous area to unlock the adjacent lift. From left to right, rotate the locking mechanism to match: Death, Blindness, Sight, and Life. Use the lift.

Make the lock mechanism match the symbols' order to activate the nearby lift.

Be ready to counter the enemies at the bottom of the lift. Recharge a power at the War Pedestal in the western room's center (**29**). Continue west to a fork in the path. The southern route is a small side alcove. Defeat the undead lurking along the path and use the War Pedestal to aid in the fight. Pillage containers (**30**) scattered around the southernmost end of the chamber. This location also harbors a secret chamber containing Letiso the Lich from the Rahvan's Curse secondary quest.

The primary quest path leads west. Before the narrow bridge, explore a southern alcove for more containers. Beware of traps while crossing the bridge (**31**). Move cautiously into the next area; projectile traps cover the room almost completely. Lure enemies away from traps to defeat them, then cross the room (**32**) carefully. A heavily trapped western alcove offers potential loot. Move north and spot Princess Evangeline (**33**).

The Dark Wizard of Valdis holds Princess Evangeline captive. The Dark Wizard can summon three towering Undead Azunite Soldiers (resistant to death magic) during the battle. Counter the summons with lightning damage (you can also lure them into the Dark Wizard's lightning elemental attack, the circles that show up at the feet of the party members, for big damage).

The Dark Wizard also invokes a large crystal that attacks the party with lightning damage. When the large crystal appears, small versions appear over the heads of the party members. The smaller crystals follow the party wherever they go. The large crystal delivers a lightning attack to the smaller crystals that deliver it to the party members. Prevent the attack by destroying the large crystal on sight!

The Dark Wizard can also summon three smaller crystals that serve to protect the Dark Wizard from all attacks. You must destroy all three smaller crystals to inflict damage.

Utilize your powers carefully; the Dark Wizard has the ability to teleport around the battle area, providing a difficult target. Line up your powers

Evangeline (Level-29 Knight) Profile

Don't let the "Princess" title fool you: Evangeline is quite a fighter! Eva's trained exclusively in melee skills and could provide the brute force you need to survive the siege of Snowbrook Haven. You could spend her remaining skill points depending on your best available equipment, a great shield, a two-handed weapon, or a couple potent one-handed weapons. Take note that Eva does already have a skill point in Dual Wield, so you'll pick up a free point if you choose that development path. You need Eva in your party to initiate and complete the Evangeline's Folly secondary quest.

Strength: 112 ▪ Dexterity: 40 ▪ Intelligence: 40 ▪ Melee: 29 ▪ Ranged: 0 ▪ Nature Magic: 0 ▪ Combat Magic: 0 ▪ Health: 499/499 ▪ Mana: 205/205 ▪ Armor: 116 ▪ Skills: Critical Strike, Level 5; Fortitude, Level 3; Toughness, Level 2; Dual Wield, Level 1 ▪ Powers: Brutal Attack, Level 2; Waves of Force, Level 1

carefully to ensure a solid hit. Locate a couple of War Pedestals in the room's back corner to recharge your most potent powers. The Dark Wizard can also cast System Shock, which knocks the party back, lowers armor, and Blinds the party (making melee and ranged attacks miss more often).

At the battle's conclusion, speak with Princess Evangeline. Follow her and accept her into your party if you wish before proceeding into the northern chamber and ascending on the lift (**34**).

Chapter 7—The Siege of Snowbrook Haven, Part 1

Morden forces have surrounded Snowbrook Haven. You'll encounter soldiers, crossbowmen, and lancers as you near the outskirts of the area and infiltrate the castle through its rear entrance. Complete the following tasks in this chapter:

- ◆ Enter Snowbrook Haven through the servant's quarters.
- ◆ Find the throne room and acquire the Display Case Key.
- ◆ Locate the Snowbrook Haven Commander.

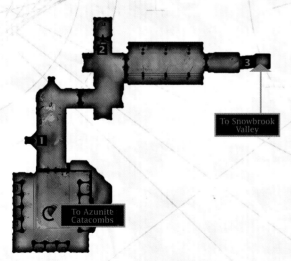

Azunite Catacombs, Exit

You begin the quest in an upper section of the Azunite Catacombs. Proceed north and defeat the enemies around the lift. Ascend the lift and be ready for a fight. You're quickly surrounded. Employ area-effect powers against enemy groupings. Move to the side of the room and face oncoming attackers. Continue north and recharge a power at a War Pedestal in the left corner of the adjacent room (**1**). There's a level-26 nature magic Sanctuary Door on the room's northern side (**2**). Proceed east and out of the catacombs (**3**).

Snowbrook Valley

Snowbrook Valley

Exit the catacombs and head north. Expect to battle Snow Kurgan, Grangeflies, Snow Va'arth, and Undead Azunites within the valley (**4**). Find the area's teleporter to the north. Check the northeast to uncover a Life Shrine. Look east to spot the Morden continuing to mass their army.

Follow the main path west. Harvest potions from the health bushes (**5**) alongside the road. The main path weaves southwest into a camp (**6**) filled with Grangeflies, Armored Lertisk, Undead Azunites, and Snow Va'arth. Cross the bridge west. Locate an entrance (**7**) to a frigid cave in a southern alcove after the bridge.

Optional Area: A Frigid Cave

There are two entrances into the frigid cave, one in Snowbrook Valley and a second at the border of the Snowbrook Foothills. The valley entrance is fairly barren; there's a lift station but the mechanism is lowered and there's no way to raise the platform. Find a Rainbow Trinket (A) just east of the entrance. Deliver it to Tywlis to complete the Tywlis' Broken Staff secondary quest. Enter from the Snowbrook Foothills (B) and use the lift (C) to descend to the lower floor. The eastern room contains a couple of War Pedestals (D) to recharge your powers. Move to the northwest room (which contains the lift to the valley entrance). Press a button (E) to open a western treasure room. Another button (F) in this room exposes another treasure room (G) adjacent to the other lift.

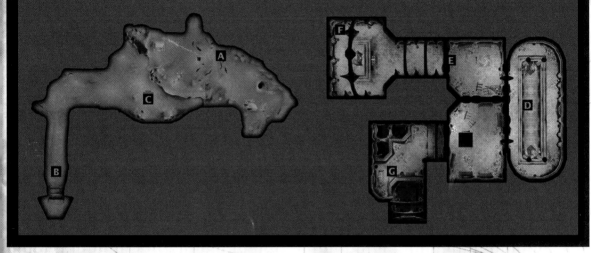

Combat assorted valley beasts along the road as the path bends north. Check an abandoned tower (**8**) on the northern edge. Ascend a lift inside to reach a chest and a lectern with the Chant of Magic Awareness at the tower's peak.

The bridge to the west is impassable (**10**) but there's an Incantation Shrine nearby. Loot the containers in the area before venturing south. Battle enemies on the ramp and harvest mana potions from bushes (**11**) at the top. Proceed south. An eastern path leads to another entrance into the frigid cave (**12**). Continue south into the Snowbrook Foothills.

Tip

*Find a path northeast of the abandoned tower and discover an unusual marking on the snowy ground (**9**). It's a lift into an Ancient Elven Reliquary. This dungeon is part of the Arinth's Legendary Staff secondary quest.*

Snowbrook Foothills

Snowbrook Foothills

Snowbrook Foothills is littered with entrances to and exits from a large underground series of caverns and ducts called the Snowbrook Grotto.

Optional Area: A Snowbrook Grotto

This walkthrough assumes you entered the grotto through the first available entrance just west of the primary quest path in Snowbrook Hills. Expect to battle Snow Va'arth, Armored Lertisks, and Undead Azunites throughout the tunnels. Follow the winding path east until the path forks (A). Find containers to the northeast. Proceed south. At the next fork (B), the western path leads outside to the foothills. Advance south and locate some containers on an upper ledge (C) guarded by mixed groups of snow beasts. The primary path forks southwest and northwest; both converge at the western end. Spot a staircase (D) along the northwestern route that leads to a locked door— part of the Legendary Mace of Agarrus secondary quest. The staircase also contains two lecterns with the Chant of Magic Skill and the Chant of Melee Skill.

Continue west into the next section of the grotto. Traverse a rock bridge (E) south and rummage through a collection of containers. Combat the grotto's beasts to the west. When you reach the fork, the northern route (F) returns to the foothills. Search south for some containers on a narrow ledge. The path forks again just to the west (G). The northern path leads to a foothills exit. Proceed to the northwest to continue through the grotto. Find the final exit (H) to the grotto in the northwest corner.

A Snowbrook Grotto, Part 1

A Snowbrook Grotto, Part 2

Although the area is almost entirely optional, it does factor into the secondary quest, the Legendary Mace of Agarrus, initiated during Act III (see Part 7 for details). Locate an entrance (13) into the grotto just west of the primary path. Another entrance lies southeast (14) of the road. Activate the teleporter along the main route and return to Aman'lu if necessary.

The road through Snowbrook Foothills weaves west then northwest. There are several entrances into the optional underground Snowbrook Grotto area. Find them along the southern (15, 16) and western (17) edges of the primary path. Harvest mana potions from bushes where the main path

bends north. Check a structure (18) on the northern side of the road for possible treasure and a Lectern with the Chant of Ranged Skill. The northwest corner extends to a bridge (19). Cross it into Snowbrook Mountain.

Snowbrook Mountain

Find the mountain's teleporter north of the area entrance. A group of bushes nearby can be used to harvest health potions. Follow the road west as it bends north; defeat various snow beasts and undead minions along the route.

Snowbrook Mountain

As you get closer to Snowbrook Haven, you begin to encounter Morden (**20**) near their camps. Expect to battle undead alongside Morden forces: Morden-Viir Soldiers and Lancers are resistant to melee attacks but weak against magic, and Morden-Viir Crossbowmen are resistant to ranged attacks but weak against melee damage. Loot an abandoned structure (**21**) just north of the camp. The path bends east to a force of Morden and Va'arth defending the passage (**22**). Explore a southern alcove to find mana bushes.

Remain on the main path and follow it east, then south, then southwest. As you near the Morden camps (**23**) along the castle's outskirts, a cut scene interrupts the action. Snowbrook Haven is under siege! Defeat the Morden forces and assorted beasts lurking in the camps. Locate the teleporter to the southwest. Use the Life Shrine before descending the steps (**24**) into Snowbrook Haven.

The Snowbrook Haven Servants' Quarters

Mixed groups of Morden and lumbering Klask have overrun the haven's living quarters. West (**25**) of the entry point, find a War Pedestal for recharging a power. Expect to encounter Morden-Gral Igniters within the quarters; these magic-users provide spell support for their Morden allies. Counter the casters on sight, ideally with ranged weaponry. Locate the door west and follow the route north.

A large Morden force (including a possible miniboss) guards the next chamber (**26**). Additional Morden will emerge from side rooms. Lure the Morden into the doorway choke point and blast enemy groups with area-effect powers while keeping your frontline party members healed. Recharge powers from the War Pedestals flanking the entrance. Check side rooms for lingering Morden and treasure.

There's an Incantation Shrine in a room in the northwest corner. Search the armor stands and weapon racks surrounding the shrine. Go east up the stairs then follow a path north or proceed west. The northern path leads to the Cavern of Frost (**28**), which is part of the Kalrathian Nexus secondary quest initiated during Act III. Instead, go south. A side room contains Morden, a ghostly spirit, and a Lectern with a mysterious chant, Chant of Summon Friends. Cross the catwalk that stretches over the previously explored room. Use the War Pedestal (**29**) and grab the Lore Book off of the floor. Ascend the staircase and defeat the Morden and Klask guarding the lift (**30**).

The Snowbrook Haven Servants' Quarters

Tip

There's a melee Sanctuary Door on the western wall (**27**) inside the Snowbrook Haven living quarters. To open the Sanctuary Door, a party member must have at least level-29 melee skill.

To the Snowbrook Haven
Servants' Quarters

30   31   32   33   34

*The Snowbrook Haven Living
Quarters*

36   35

To the Snowbrook
Haven Courtyard

long-range powers, spells, or ranged attacks. Defeating the group opens the eastern exit.

Lure the Morden in the next room (**33**) into the doorway and blast them with powers. The next room to the east contains a War Pedestal. Search a northern icy cavern in the same room for additional battles and containers. Activate the teleporter in the next room. Open a level-29 combat magic Sanctuary Door (**34**) before proceeding south. Locate another lift in the southeastern room (**35**). Utilize a couple of War Pedestals in the room to recharge powers. Before riding the lift, explore the western area (**36**) for more chests and combat opportunities. A button in the adjacent room lowers center walls, exposing more treasure. Ascend the lift and crush the Morden at the top. Exit the door into the castle courtyard.

The Snowbrook Haven Courtyard

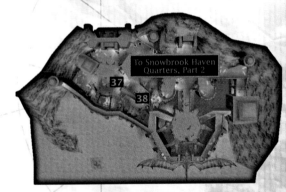

To Snowbrook Haven
Quarters, Part 2

37

38

The Snowbrook Haven Courtyard, Part 1

The throne hides a compartment containing the key to the Aegis display case.

Use the lift and blast anything waiting at the bottom. The southern alcove contains a Lectern with a mysterious chant, the Chant of Summon Enemies. There's a War Pedestal (**31**) to the east to assist against the Morden forces defending the room. North and south exits lead to stairwells that connect to the throne room. Approach the throne (**32**) and move it to find the hidden key to the display case. Grab the key, which activates the Rustguards. These enemies must die before you can move onward. The sluggish Rustguards are easy to outmaneuver; keep your distance and bombard the guards with

Exit the living quarters into a huge battle between Snowbrook Haven soldiers and Morden forces (**37**). Combat Morden troops alongside the haven's troops before ascending a staircase just southeast of your entry point. Find the commander (**38**) at the top—she's currently under siege from Brall. Speak with her to complete the quest.

Chapter 8—The Siege of Snowbrook Haven, Part 2

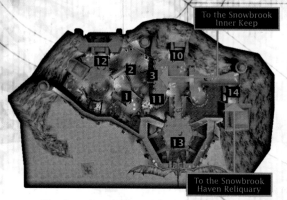

To the Snowbrook
Inner Keep

To the Snowbrook
Haven Reliquary

The Snowbrook Haven Courtyard, Part 2

Valdis has brought one of his dragons to attack Snowbrook Haven! This is the last quest in the second act. Bolster your party's fire resistance as much as possible to counter the dragon's scorching attacks.

- Destroy the Brall on top of the Snowbrook Haven Inner Keep.

- Meet the commander at the North Gate. Destroy the Morden enemies that have broken through the north gate.

- Defeat the dragon. Report to the commander.

- Retrieve the Aegis of Blindness.

- Kill the dragon. Escape from Snowbrook Haven.

- Travel to the town of Kalrathia and speak with the Town Lord there.

The quest begins at the commander (**1**). Descend the staircase and move to the eastern side. Defeat any remaining Klask or Morden forces. There's a War

Tip

Search the dining hall in the room underneath the commander's position. Find and speak with Soldier Kiernan inside. He has a Morden Head on a Pike he'd be willing to give up if you have something that might change his luck. Kiernan is part of the secondary quest Lelani's Sorrow that starts in Act I and spans the entire game (see Part 7).

Pedestal (**2**) to recharge a power. The entrance into the inner keep is just ahead (**3**). The lift to the right is currently unusable.

The Snowbrook Inner Keep

To reach the creatures on top of the keep, your party must ascend the keep's interior and battle plenty of Morden and Klask defenders along the way (including minibosses). Ascend the stairs and open the heavily defended room to the east (**4**). Exit the room east toward another staircase. Use the War Pedestal (**5**) at the foot of the stairs. Clear the top room of Morden (**6**).

To the Snowbrook Inner
Keep, Middle Floor

To the Snowbrook
Haven Courtyard

*The Snowbrook Inner Keep,
Lower Floor*

Exit the room east to another staircase (**7**). At the top of the stairs, use a nature War Pedestal on the far western side (**8**). There are exits to the north and south. Search the northern side for barracks containing treasure. Proceed south (**9**) and exit to the top (**10**). Help the Snowbrook Haven defenders defeat nearby enemies. Recharge powers with a couple of War Pedestals to the south. Crush the Brall (**11**) that are hurling projectiles at the Snowbrook troops below. After the battle, meet the commander at the north gate (**12**).

To the Snowbrook
Inner Keep, Upper
Floor

To the Snowbrook
Inner Keep, Lower
Floor

*The Snowbrook Inner Keep,
Middle Floor*

To the
Snowbrook
Inner Keep,
Middle Floor

To the Snowbrook
Haven Courtyard

*The Snowbrook Inner
Keep, Upper Floor*

Instead of returning through the keep, use the lift on the left. Go west to the north gate and find the commander and her escort waiting. During the conversation, a gang of Morden bust through the north gate. Retreat from the chaos so you can target the Morden attacking your party. Bombard a packed group of Morden with your area-effect powers. Crush all Morden to complete the task. Afterward, speak with the commander again to receive your new objective: defeat the dragon!

ers above the tower, move around quickly to avoid the rain of fireballs. When Talon latches onto the tower, point the ballista at Talon then use the weapon to fire and wound the beast. Repeat until Talon is defeated.

Report to the commander—she's north of your current position. She provides the key to the Snowbrook Haven reliquary. After the conversation, Shard Souls appear and infect the commander and her escort. Defeat the infected group. Scamper east from her position. Defeat the Morden and Klask guarding the reliquary entrance (**14**).

Developer Tip

The Durvla siege bugs launched into battle by the Morden are weak against fire attacks. Exploit this weakness by luring the Durvla into Talon's fiery attacks! This will help kill them in a hurry. —John Cutter, Designer

Operate the ballista on the keep's tower to defeat Talon the mighty Dragon. High fire resistance will certainly help!

Return to the lift and ride to the top of the keep. Once there, go east then south to find Talon, the Morden's dragon (**13**) attacking the keep's southern tower. The dragon uses plenty of fire-based attacks. Beef up your party's fire resistances before the battle. To defeat the dragon you must use the ballista, which you can rotate left and right using the ground controls. You must hit the dragon eight times to defeat it.

Neither the controls nor the ballista will budge if Talon's fire scorches them; wait for the flames to subside before trying to rotate or fire the ballista. The Morden army surrounding Snowbrook Haven catapult Durvla onto the tower to help defend Talon. Defeat the Durvla on sight and then resume the attack against Talon. When the dragon hov-

The Snowbrook Haven Reliquary

Descend the stairs and find the relic vault (**15**). Grab the Aegis of Blindness from the vault and loot the big chest. Resume course east into the next hall. Talon, the battered and bloody dragon, bursts through the wall (**16**) and blocks the route. Defeat the dragon for the last time using everything in your arsenal. After the battle, find the Azunite Scholar to the southeast (**17**). Speak with him and receive the Kalrathia Teleporter Activation Stone. Move southeast and collect the Chant of Greater Dexterity, Chant of Greater Intelligence, and Chant of Greater Strength from the Lecterns. Activate the nearby teleporter and use it to transport your party to Kalrathia and the third act. Once there, go into Kalrathia Hall and speak with Lord Kalrathia to officially complete this quest.

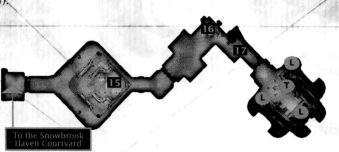

To the Snowbrook Haven Courtyard

The Snowbrook Haven Reliquary

:PART 6 – ACT III:
PRIMARY QUESTS WALKTHROUGH

After defeating Talon, Valdis's mighty dragon, your party transports to Kalrathia, a once-proud town currently occupied by Morden oppressors. Kalrathia may possess a piece of the Aegis Shield but until you loosen the Morden's tight grip, the piece of the Aegis shield remains safe and hidden. In Act III, you'll spark a rebellion in Kalrathia, traverse desert and cave to find the Dark Wizards, discover the mystery of the Agallan chamber beneath Kalrathia, and ascend Zaramoth's Horns in a final confrontation with Valdis.

Chapter 1—Restore Kalrathia's Water

Find the Town Lord in Kalrathia Hall on the eastern side of town. Speak with him to begin Act III. Before leaving town, use the opportunity to visit the Kalrathian shops and speak with the townsfolk to initiate various secondary quests. Increase lightning- and death-magic resistance to counter the Mucrim and Korven that inhabit The Northern Plain of Tears, a long stretch of desert that leads to the quest's goal, a heavily guarded cistern. The intended level for this quest is 33. These are your quest tasks:

◆ Follow the aqueduct to its source. Defeat the Ganth.

◆ Restore Kalrathia's water.

◆ Return to Lord Kalrathia in the great hall.

The Town of Kalrathia

You arrive in the Morden-occupied town of Kalrathia via teleporter. Take the opportunity to search the town before venturing off on the act's

Map Legend

IS Incantation Shrine
MS Mana Shrine
LS Life Shrine
G Ghostly Spirit
L Chant Lectern
T Teleporter

The Town of Kalrathia

first primary quest. Necromancer Finas, near the teleporter, resurrects slain party members. Move north and visit the Kalrathia Pet Shop (**1**). Speak with Pet Seller Brigid to shop for a new pet.

From the pet shop, check east to find Nora, the nature mage (**2**). Speak with her to initiate the secondary quest The Kalrathian Nexus. Around the corner, find Berseba, who initiates the secondary quest The Legendary Mace of Agarrus. Ascend the staircases and find Telgrey the Scholar in a small house; speak with him to initiate the Lord of Aranna secondary quest. Cross the planks and reach the northern rampart to find Nalus (**3**), who has a Bundle of Harpy Feathers he's willing to part with; Nalus is part of the Lelani's Sorrow secondary quest initiated during Act I. Search the nearby dome interior for a Lore Book.

Explore the eastern side to find Kalrathia Hall (**4**). Inside, Historian Leontia provides additional backstory and initiates the Dwarven Song of Ore secondary quest. Speak with Lord Kalrathia to officially complete Act II and begin the first primary quest in Act III.

Find the Kalrathia Tavern and Inn (**5**) in the south. Chat with Kevarre the Explorer to initiate the secondary quest The Lost Jewels of Soranith. Khartos the Strong stands here; he's part of Act II's Mythrilhorn secondary quest. And, with Sartan in your party, speak with Feltan the Drunkard to initiate the Sartan's Suspicion secondary quest. Talk to Innkeeper Angus on the upper floor for party management. Merchant Kendril is staying at the inn; he's part of Act II's Mark of the Assassin secondary quest. Move behind Barkeep Amina to find a Lore Book on the shelf and to discover a lift into an optional dungeon.

West of the tavern, shop for weapons and armor at the Kalrathian Armory (**6**) and potions, spells, and jewelry at the Kalrathian Magic Shop (**7**). In the armory, Blacksmith Volkor peddles weapons and Armorer Bertin carries armor. Chat with Mage Boden in the magic shop to initiate the secondary quest The Mage's Apprentice. Enchantress Valeria will help you craft items, and Arcanist Bianca sells reagents.

After exploring Kalrathia thoroughly, exit through the north gate (**8**) toward the Northern Plain of Tears; there's an Incantation Shrine outside the gate. The town's eastern exit (**9**) remains closed until later in Act III.

The Northern Plain of Tears

The Northern Plain of Tears

Spot the Kalrathia aqueduct running along the plain's western edge. Expect to battle squads of new beasts (**10**), including Mercrus (cast Steal Magic) and Borga, Korven Boneslayers and Korven Blightwalkers (both resistant to death magic), and Mucrim and Mucrim Shockers. Follow the main path north. Discover mana bushes (**11**) in an eastern campsite across from a button (**12**) near ruins; press the button to activate a lift into an optional dungeon of crumbling ruins.

Optional Area: A Cellar beneath Kalrathia

Pull a lever (A) on the southern wall to discover a second lift station (B). Descend deeper into the cellar. Search the eastern room to discover a Lore Book (C). Find Kalrathian rebels in the southern room (D). Speak with them to learn more about the Kalrathians' current fate at the hands of the Morden.

The road forks north and east. Find the area's teleporter north near a group of health bushes (**13**). Search the eastern path to discover an entrance to a mysterious vault (**14**), part of the secondary quest The Lost Jewels of Soranith, and an entrance to a magical oasis (**15**), part of the Deru's Treasure Hunt secondary quest. Proceed northeast before reaching the teleporter and locate Khartos' Rift Site (**16**), part of the Mythrilhorn secondary quest. See Part 7 for complete maps and solutions to these secondary quests.

The main route bends west at the teleporter. Stand on the Life Shrine to mend party wounds before the battle against Mercrus, Mucrim, Orthrac, Korven, and other minions guarding the north path (**17**). The entrance into the water chapel waits at the path's end.

The Water Chapel

A menacing and quite formidable Ganth guards the cistern. The Ganth is resistant to fire, lightning, and death damage. It's also immune to knockback and stun effects. The Ganth employs a special attack (50% chance of happening) with which it can heal itself. If the attack strikes a party member, the amount healed is even greater. Defeat the Ganth (**18**) to gain access to the aqueduct's source and the means to restore Kalrathia's water. Unleash all powers, spells, and attacks on the Ganth. Have nature mages cast heal spells to mend wounds on your melee characters; have curse spells on

autocast to weaken the Ganth to your most powerful elemental attacks; and summon creatures to aid in the battle against this powerful foe. After the battle, exit the Water Chapel to the north.

The powerful but sluggish Ganth defends the cistern. Keep your distance with long-range attacks.

The Water Chapel

The Chapel Courtyard

The Chapel Courtyard

Emerge from the Water Chapel (**19**) and spot the cistern to the northwest. Defeat a staggering number of defenders in the area, which could include Korven, Mucrim, Borga, and a miniboss. Retreat into the Water Chapel if necessary. Maximize damage by focusing area-effect powers on packed enemy groups. Harvest potions from the health bushes (**20**) north of the Water Chapel exit. Rotate the cistern's valve (**21**) to restore Kalrathia's water and complete the quest's primary objective. Locate a switch on a rock on the northwest side of the aqueduct; it reveals a hidden treasure compartment. Return to Kalrathia via the teleporter on the courtyard's west side, and speak with the lord.

Chapter 2— The Morden Chief

Make the long journey to reach the Morden city of Darthrul. Through the Eastern Plain of Tears and the Ruins of Okaym, expect to encounter beasts similar to the ones in the northern plain. Varied types of Morden defend Darthrul with ferocity. Increase resistance against physical damage to counter Impalers, Piercers, Scrappers, and Marksmen within the city and boost fire resistance to counter the Morden-Durvla and Morden-Gral Despoiler damage spells. The intended level for this quest is 33. The quest's tasks are the following:

◆ Enter the Morden city of Darthrul.

◆ Gain access to the Morden Chief's audience chamber.

◆ Speak to and defeat the Morden Chief.

◆ Bring the head of the Morden Chief back to Lord Kalrathia.

You're tasked with visiting a nearby Morden city and distracting the Morden Chief long enough for the Kalrathians to rebuild their defenses and rebel against their oppressors. Exit Kalrathia through the eastern gate.

The Eastern Plain of Tears

Expect to battle groups of Korven, Mucrim, Iraca (weak to ice, resistant to fire), Skeen (inflict fire damage), and Bortusk along the eastern plains. Search a northern side route off the main path to find the entrance to a hidden cave (**1**). It's part of the secondary quest The Kalrathian Nexus. A southern outcropping holds a lever that reveals a

hidden chest. Harvest potions from health bushes to the east (**2**).

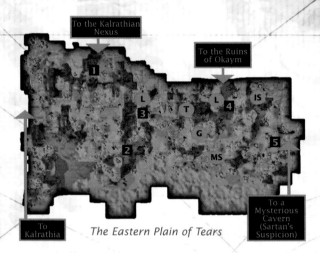

The Eastern Plain of Tears

Search an abandoned tower (**3**) along the main road for treasure and a lectern containing the Greater Chant of Mage Health. Activate the teleporter to the east and locate a Mana Shrine to the south. The road bends northward. Harvest the mana bushes (**4**) and collect potions; search an adjacent tower for treasure and a lectern containing the Greater Chant of Ranger Health. Locate an Incantation Shrine east of the main road; Korven, Borga, and Mucrim likely crowd the optional eastern rock paths. In the southeastern corner, find an entrance into a mysterious cavern (**5**). It's part of the Sartan's Suspicion secondary quest. The main road extends north into the next area.

The Ruins of Okaym

Investigate an abandoned tower (**6**) on the road's western edge and find treasure and a lectern with the Greater Chant of Fighter Health. Expect to face a host of the plains' minions, including Shaggrots, Borga, Bortusk, and Korven. Follow a path northwest of the primary route to discover a curious circle of mushrooms (**7**). It's part of the Amren's Vision secondary quest. Continue along the main route east. Harvest potions from the mana bushes (**8**) then enter an optional dungeon (**9**) on the east side. It's a large abandoned shelter.

To Some Ancient Ruins (The Mage's Apprentice)

To Darthrul

15

14

IS

13

12

11 10

T

9

8

7

To a Morden Arsenal (Sartan's Suspicion)

L 6

To a Mysterious Shrine (Amren's Vision)

To the Eastern Plain of Tears

The Ruins of Okaym

A building (**10**) on the road's northern side contains a nature magic Sanctuary Door (level 30). Activate the area's teleporter just west. On the opposite side of the road, find a War Pedestal (**11**) to recharge a power. Explore a side route that leads far west of the main path and discover an entrance (**12**) into a Morden arsenal; it's part of the Sartan's Suspicion secondary quest.

Continue north from the area's teleporter. Invoke a chant on the Incantation Shrine. Nearby health bushes (**13**) can be harvested for potions. Journey to the northern end of these outskirts and find the entrance to Darthrul (**14**). Before entering, search west of the bridge to find some ancient ruins (**15**); they're part of the secondary quest The Mage's Apprentice.

Optional Area: A Large Abandoned Shelter

*Locate the lift (**A**) in the initial room of the large abandoned shelter. Go through the door to the east. Defeat Korven protecting an Azunite Stone of Life (**B**). Grab a stone and exit east and into the shelter's primary chamber (**C**). Here you must place the Azunite Stones on their correct stands; doing so creates a symbol of light that opens a hidden treasure room. Place the Azunite Stone of Life on its stand (the living tree). Search the northern area and find the Golden Chalice on the western side (**D**). Grabbing the chalice opens a new passage. Follow the hall counter-clockwise around the northern edge. A couple of buttons along the northern and western walls open hidden treasure rooms. The final room on the southwestern side contains the Azunite Stone of Death (**E**). Grab it and return to the main chamber. Place the stone on its stand (the dead tree).*

*Exit the main chamber south and explore the cave. Traverse the cavern to the eastern alcove and locate the Azunite Stone of Sight (**F**). Move through the cavern's western side and into a series of rooms, one of which holds the Azunite Stone of Blindness (**G**). Return to the main chamber and place both Azunite Stones on their stands (Sight on the open eye and Blindness on the closed eye). This completes the puzzle; an eastern chamber (**H**) opens. Defeat the Korven and the miniboss guarding the treasure and lecterns that hold the Greater Chant of Ranger Power and the Greater Chant of Mage Power.*

The City of Darthrul

To a Cellar Beneath Darthrul (The Morden Riders)

23

22

20

21

17

19

T

G

16

18

IS

24

25

To the Ruins of Okaym

To the Morden Riders

The City of Darthrul

Savants; and Morden-Durvla Butchers, Enforcers, and Purifiers comprise the defensive forces. Morden Patrol Leaders and Lieutenants maintain the district keys; approach Darthrul's center courtyard to encounter the first Morden leader. Defeat the miniboss and his escort to recover the key to the District of the Sword. Darthrul's teleporter is on the northwest side of the courtyard.

Morden-Durvla

A separate caste of Morden helps defend the city of Darthrul. Morden-Durvla are defenders of Morden cities. These large, four-legged creatures are fused together from both Morden flesh and Durvla shells; the combination creates a highly armored menace. The Morden-Durvla Butchers, the foot soldiers wielding massive staffs, can cast Wrath of the Bear (increases chance of critical hits); the Morden-Durvla Enforcers, armed with giant axes, can cast Dehydrate (increasing the party's weakness to fire); and the Morden-Durvla Purifiers, the caste's spell casters, are resistant to fire damage and can cast Wrath of Magic (alters magic damage), Fireball, and Plasma Globes.

More formidable Morden-Urg, Morden-Viir, and Morden-Gral also populate Darthrul. Urg Scrappers use melee weapons; Urg Marksmen attack with ranged weapons; and Urg Savants cast spells, including Embers, Leech Life, and Heal. Morden-Viir Rippers carry massive swords and shields; the Morden-Viir Impalers use spears; and the Morden-Viir Piercers are armed with crossbows. Finally, the Morden-Gral Despoilers utilize fire magic for their primary attack.

Speak with the Morden guard at the entrance. The conversation ends poorly—you must fight your way to the Morden Chief's audience chamber!

Darthrul is split into five districts: the District of the Crossbow (southwest), the District of the Lance (northwest), the District of the Sword (northeast), the District of the Shield (southeast), and the District of the Chief (far north). You must recover keys—held by Morden minibosses—in order to explore the districts and reach the Morden Chief's audience chamber.

Move north into the center of Darthrul (**16**). You're heavily outnumbered on the Morden's own turf. Morden-Viir Impalers, Rippers, and Piercers; Morden-Gral Despoilers; Morden-Urg Scrappers, Marksmen, and

Tip

Darthrul's District of the Shield is entirely optional. Exploring it is necessary for completing the secondary quest The Morden Riders (see Part 7 for more details). Recover the key to the District of the Shield by defeating the Morden Lieutenant who occupies the cellar beneath Darthrul.

Battle toward the northeast section of Darthrul and find the entrance to the District of the Sword (**17**). Enter and locate the Morden Lieutenant in this section; recharge a power at the nearby War Pedestal. Defeat the lieutenant and his guards to recover the key to the District of the Crossbow. Loot the area before returning through the Darthrul courtyard and to the southwest section of the city.

Enter the District of the Crossbow (**18**). Utilize an Incantation Shrine and a War Pedestal on the southern side to aid your efforts against the Morden Lieutenant. Crush the miniboss and his escort. Collect the key to the District of the Lance. Exit through the north door and enter the District of the Lance (**19**) in Darthrul's north-west quadrant.

Defeat the third Morden Lieutenant patrolling this north-western district. Use a nearby War Pedestal (**20**) to recharge a power. Recover the key to the District of the Chief. Before exiting east, search an alcove west of the pedestal (**21**) for an entrance to a cellar beneath Darthrul, part of the Morden Riders secondary quest.

> ### Tip
>
> *Each of the three Darthrul districts contains a locked supply room. These rooms are part of the secondary quest The Morden Riders. The riders are east of Darthrul in a desert canyon and possess the supply-room keys. Help them out to gain access to ruins with extra treasure. For more details, see Part 7.*

Unleash a devastating power on the Morden Chief and his bodyguards.

Find the District of the Chief in the northern (**22**) section of Darthrul. On the western wall, open a ranged Sanctuary Door (level 32) to gain access to hidden loot. Eliminate Morden defending the northern door. Follow the path and locate the Morden Chief (**23**) in the far chamber; Menacing Morden-Durvla bodyguards flank the chief. Speak with the chief. The brief discussion ends in battle. Retreat from the small chamber and lure enemies away from their group. Eliminate the Morden Chief to complete the task and receive the chief's head.

Before leaving Darthrul via teleporter, search rooms for unopened chests, and other containers for loot. Return to Kalrathia when ready. Enter Kalrathia Hall and speak with the lord. Show him the head of the Morden Chief as proof of the leader's death. The time for rebellion has come!

Chapter 3—The Kalrathian Rebellion

The Morden Chief's death inspires the Kalrathian townspeople to take up arms against their occupiers. This quest takes place completely in Kalrathia, and its principal objective is as straightforward as they come! A counter at the bottom of the screen reveals how many Morden remain. This quest is intended for level-35 characters. Quest tasks are as follows:

- Defeat all the Morden in the town of Kalrathia.
- Report to Tehruth.

Follow Tehruth out of Kalrathia Hall and engage the Morden forces. You'll spot other townspeople engaged in battle. Work your way through Kalrathia's entire lower section. Move slowly and engage small Morden squads one at a time. Use long-range attacks to blast Morden engaged against Kalrathian rebels. Advance up staircases throughout Kalrathia and clear Morden forces from the upper ramparts. The quest ends only after you've eliminated every single Morden.

After clearing Kalrathia, return to Kalrathia Hall and find Tehruth inside. Speak with him to complete the quest. You receive the Aegis of Sight from Lord Kalrathia. He claims the Dark Wizards have the final Aegis piece. You also receive the Morden-Viir Teleporter Activation Stone; the Kalrathia teleporter will now transport you to the Southern Desert of Kaderak.

Chapter 4—The Mines of Kaderak, Part 1

Four mystical statues use magic to envelop the entrance into the Mines of Kaderak. You must destroy all four statues to break the magic and expose the entrance into the mines. Find the statues and the mine entrance just north of the southern teleporter. The Desert of Kaderak is a large map and offers optional exploration to the far west, east, and north of the mine entrance. This quest is intended for level-35 characters. Tasks for this quest are as follows:

- ◆ Travel to the Desert of Kaderak.
- ◆ Destroy all four protective statues.
- ◆ Enter the Mines of Kaderak.

The Desert of Kaderak

The Desert of Kaderak

You arrive on the southern side of the desert via the Kalrathian teleporter. Proceed northeast, cross the hills, and reach the center structure—it's the statue-protected and monster-guarded entrance to the mines. Clear the Blastwings, Morden, and other beasts around this southern ridge. Approach and destroy the first statue (**1**).

Proceed around the eastern side of the center structure. Harvest potions from the mana bushes along the ridge (**2**). Explore ruins to the distant east for additional battles and treasure. Defeat the monsters around the second statue, which lies east of the center structure. Approach and destroy the second statue protecting the mine entrance. Find a War Pedestal to the north (**3**) to recharge a power.

There's a lot of territory to explore on the northern side of the desert. Traverse the hills north and uncover various desert beasts around camps and ruins (**4**). Find the desert's northern teleporter among the ruins. Harvest mana potions (**5**) from bushes. A steep hill contains a broken lift at its peak. Once repaired, the lift descends into a large Morden intelligence camp, which is part of the Finala's Contempt secondary quest.

Magic protects the entrance to the mines. Destroy the statues to gain access to the lift.

Return to the protected mine entrance and destroy the third statue, which stands on the entrance's northern side (**6**). Continue counter-clockwise around the center structure. Search ruins to the distant west to uncover a couple lecterns (**7**) that hold the Chant of Greater Ranged Awareness and Chant of Greater Melee Awareness. The western ridge along the center structure offers health bushes (**8**). Destroy the fourth and final statue on the western side of the mine entrance. Destroying all four statues exposes the mine entrance. Stand on the lift and use the lever to descend into the Mines of Kaderak.

Chapter 5—The Mines of Kaderak, Part 2

The search for the Dark Wizards and the Aegis of Life takes you through the dangerously populated Mines of Kaderak. Your primary opposition includes the Uhn, a race of miners hired to unearth the Crystal Shards plaguing the lands of Aranna, and the Morden overseeing the Uhn's progress. Before venturing into the mines, increase fire resistance to counter Uhn Scorchers and increase lightning resistance (though fire and ice are important as well) for the battle against the Dark Wizards. This quest is intended for level-35 characters. Quest tasks are as follows:

◆ Destroy the Giant Shard Cluster.

◆ Find and destroy the Dark Wizards.

◆ Recover the Aegis of Life and return to Lord Kalrathia.

The Upper Mines of Kaderak, Part 1

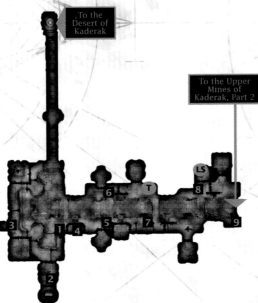

The Upper Mines of Kaderak, Part 1

You must use a series of levers to move an explosive-laden mine cart into a Giant Shard Cluster; the collision destroys the Shard and opens access to the lower mines. Morden, Crawn, Traglok, Feasters, Impus, Shard Souls, and Uhn populate the Mines of Kaderak. Move south from the lift. Explore a southern staircase (**1**) to search optional areas. The southern corner contains a lever (**2**) that opens a treasure room; this room contains an Ancient Dwarven Chest that's part of the Mark of the Assassin secondary quest. Continue along the western edge. Find a ranged Sanctuary Door (level 33) on the western wall (**3**).

Move east through the passage (**4**) on the southern side. Find a War Pedestal to recharge a power (**5**). Traverse north across the bridge. Pull another lever (**6**) to shift the mine cart closer to the Shard. The lever also opens the eastern passage. Locate the teleporter and search side rooms along the northern wall for loot.

Move south across the bridge and pull a lever (**7**) that moves the mine cart and opens the eastern door. Loot a southern chamber of its treasure. Find a War Pedestal across the bridge (**8**). Use the Life Shrine in the northern room then pull the nearby lever to move the cart. Continue east into the mines. The next room on the northern side contains an Ancient Dwarven Chest that's part of the Dwarven Song of Ore secondary quest. Traverse the bridge to the southern side. Pull a lever (**9**) to send the cart toward the Shard and open access east.

The Upper Mines of Kaderak, Part 2

The Upper Mines of Kaderak, Part 2

(**16**) to discover a combat magic Sanctuary Door (level 33). The western barracks contains a lever; pull it to reveal a hidden treasure room that holds the third Ancient Dwarven Chest, part of the Dwarven Song of Ore secondary quest. Return to the center of the mines. Explore the eastern side for monsters and treasure, then descend on the lift (**17**). Proceed north into the lower mines.

The Lower Mines of Kaderak

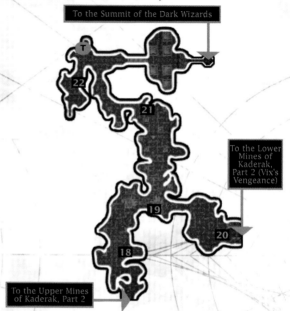

The Lower Mines of Kaderak

Pull another lever to move the cart (**10**). Continue east and blast groups of Uhn and other mine beasts. Explore a southern room for treasure. Traverse the bridge going north and find the mines' second teleporter. Pull the nearby lever (**11**). Ascend the stairs into the northern section. Follow the path west to discover a hallway containing a ghostly spirit and the second Ancient Dwarven Chest (**12**), part of the Dwarven Song of Ore secondary quest. Find an Incantation Shrine on the eastern side of the high bridge. Follow the lower route east toward the mine's center section.

Cross the bridge going south. Search the southern rooms for a lectern containing the Greater Chant of Magic Awareness. Pull the lever (**13**) to move the mine cart and open the eastern route. Defeat the monsters guarding the final lever (**14**). Pull the last lever to send the mine cart into the Shard cluster (**15**). Explore the southern section

Expect to face a similar set of beasts to those you battled in the upper mines: mixed groups of Morden, Uhn, Feasters, and Crawn. Follow the path north. Target a War Pedestal along the east-

---

Uhn

The Morden have enslaved a race known as the Uhn and are exploiting the Uhn's love for creating vast underground tunnels. The Morden force the Uhn to dig out the Crystal Shards that plague the world. Constant exposure to the crystals has turned the Uhn vicious and ready to defend their territory against any intruders. The Uhn Miners attack with the same pickaxes used to unearth the crystals; Uhn Blasters toss explosive grenades; and Uhn Scorchers inflict fire damage and cast Punishing Fire (reflects damage). The Uhn's ability to teleport is their most dangerous. The Uhn Miners essentially negate your long-range attackers by teleporting to close quarters. Boost melee resistances to counter the Miners' attacks. When the Uhn teleport, retarget your attacks to eliminate the threat quickly.

ern wall (**18**) to recharge a power. After the main path bends east (**19**), find another War Pedestal.

The path splits north and east. Follow the eastern route to a door (**20**) that leads into additional mine caves that are part of the Vix's Vengeance secondary quest. Resume course north along the primary quest path. Battle large groups of Uhn and Lithid (**21**); the path bends west and curves around to the northern edge of the lower mines. Squads of Morden and Uhn defend a teleporter in the north-western corner.

Tip

*Discover a ridge stretching south from the lower mine teleporter. The heavily defended corner contains additional treasure, as well as the fourth Ancient Dwarven Chest (**22**) that's part of the Dwarven Song of Ore secondary quest.*

You're nearing the battle against the Dark Wizards; take the opportunity to return to town to restock potions and adjust equipment. Follow the tracks east toward a mammoth lift station. Ride the lift to the summit.

The Summit of the Dark Wizards

Proceed east to a second lift station (**23**) and ascend to the upper platform. The battle against the Dark Wizards (**24**) begins.

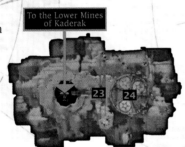

The Summit of the Dark Wizards

The battle rages on a circular platform. There are three War Pedestals along the rear edge of the platform. Recharge your most potent powers during the battle. The three Dark Wizards combine their magic to summon the formidable Xzeihoranth, a beast created from electricity. All its attacks are melee-based. Bombard the Xzeihoranth and the Dark Wizards with melee and ranged attacks, spells, and powers.

The Dark Wizards summon a Xzeihoranth during the battle.

You must defeat all three Dark Wizards to complete the task and recover the Aegis of Life. The wizards invoke the crystal shield; attack the crystals to disable the shield that protects the wizards from sustaining damage. The Dark Wizards also employ a series of elemental attacks, which they can combine for bigger damage. Focus your attacks on a single wizard and eliminate them one at a time.

Return to Kalrathia. Cast a Summon Town Portal spell or retrace your steps to the teleporter in the Lower Mines of Kaderak. Once in Kalrathia, enter Kalrathia Hall and locate Lord Kalrathia in his bedroom. Speak with him to conclude this quest and automatically initiate your next task.

Chapter 6—The Agallan Trial

This quest consists primarily of puzzles. An ancient chamber beneath Kalrathia holds a mighty cistern. Restoring water to four waterways opens access to the Agallan Peaks. Rustguards patrol the caverns around the waterway and you must defeat Advisor Kynos in battle to recover the key that unlocks the ancient chamber. This quest's intended level is 37. Quest tasks are the following:

◆ Speak to and defeat Advisor Kynos.

◆ Unlock and enter the ancient chamber below Kalrathia.

- ◆ Restore water to the northern, southern, western, and eastern waterways.

- ◆ Go through the portal to the Agallan Peaks.

Find Advisor Kynos in Kalrathia Hall and speak with him. Kynos doesn't trust you; he holds the key that unlocks the way to the Agallan chambers beneath Kalrathia, but he's unwilling to give it up. When Kynos becomes aggressive, defeat the advisor and recover the Kalrathia Crystal. Talk with Tehruth before leaving.

Exit Kalrathia Hall and approach the fountain at the center of town. Three statues flank the fountain and one pedestal remains empty. Place the Kalrathia Crystal on the empty pedestal to activate the lift into the Agallan chambers. Step onto the lift and descend beneath Kalrathia. Follow the ancient stairway west.

> ### Tip
>
> When you eliminate Advisor Kynos, you receive the Kalrathian House Key. Find a door on the northern wall east of Berseba's start location. Open the door to use the key automatically. Search the home for any treasures left behind.

Speak with the Azunite Ancestor. A cistern lies at the center of the Agallan chamber. You must restore the flow of water to four channels to restore a missing walkway that leads to a portal to the Agallan Peaks. Exit through the western door and descend the stairwell toward the ancient waterworks.

The Agallan Chambers beneath Kalrathia

The magnificent cistern is east of your start position. Proceed down the steps into the western waterway. Restore water to the western waterway with the following steps:

- ◆ Pull the lever on the left wall (**1**) to open the western waterway gate.

- ◆ Use the exposed valve (**2**) to the west; you've now restored water to the western walkway.

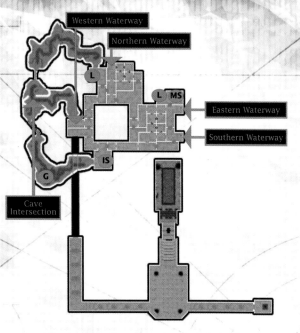

The Agallan Chambers beneath Kalrathia

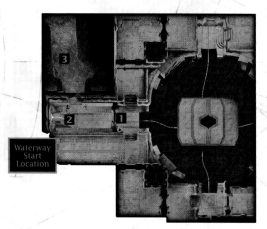

Western Waterway

Proceed through the open cavern (**3**) to the north. Rustguards patrol the cavern; defeat them as you maneuver through. You reach the cavern intersection where the path splits north and south; proceed north and continue to eliminate the Rustguards. You're now in the northern section of the Agallan chamber. Find a lectern on the western wall; it contains a mysterious chant, the Greater Chant of Summon Friends.

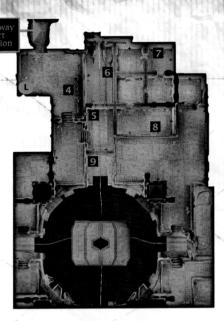

Northern Waterway

From the northern waterway, follow the path southwest. Press the button on the wall to open passage back to the chamber's position. Reenter the Rustguard-filled cavern. At the cavern intersection, go south. Defeat groups of Rustguards. Spot the ghostly spirit where the path bends east. Move east toward the southern waterway. Find the Incantation Shrine. Restore the water using the following moves:

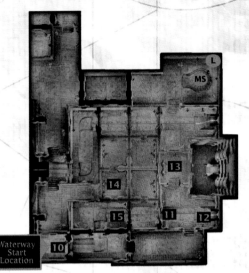

Southern Waterway

Approach the three buttons (**4**) overlooking the waterway and a series of rooms, doors, and more buttons. You must use the three buttons to adjust doors and clear a route through the rooms. The directions indicated assume you're facing the three buttons. Restore water to the northern walkway by completing the following moves:

- Use the middle button.

- Use the right button.

- Lower the first (left) waterway gate (**5**).

- Pull the lever that starts the water flow (**6**).

- Use the button in the back-corner (northeast) room (**7**).

- Use the button in the long (eastern) room on the opposite side (**8**).

- Go north through the open passage. Continue along the open path. It bends south then west to the end of the northern waterway. You now have access to the last waterway gate.

- Use the lever (**9**) to lower the final waterway gate, allowing the water flow to reach the center cistern. You've restored the northern waterway.

- From the entrance, follow the waterway east and use the levers to open two walls blocking passage (**10**).

- Go east and follow the waterway to its start and open the first door on the left (**11**).

- Use the valve (**12**) on the right to start water flowing.

- Go north to the two buttons (**13**) and face them (you'll face west).

- Use the left button.

- Use the right button.

- Use the button in southwestern room (**14**).

- Exit south into the waterway and use the levers to open two adjacent gates (**15**). You've restored water to the southern waterway.

From the southern waterway, return west toward the area's start position. A button on the wall opens passage to the western waterway. Go east to spot another button (**16**). Press it to reveal a passage, though it's still blocked. Instead, turn south and descend into the end of the eastern waterway. Clear the way using the following steps.

Eastern Waterway

◆ From the end of the eastern waterway, use the levers to open the first gate (**17**).

◆ Return to the chamber's start position and traverse the cavern. Go south at the cavern intersection to return toward the southern waterway.

◆ Move through the southern waterway to the two buttons used previously (**18**).

◆ Use the buttons to align the walls from the southern waterway walkthrough.

◆ Move into the southwestern room (**19**) and use the button.

◆ Move north to the adjacent room and use the button (**20**). The door on the northern wall should be open.

◆ Use the lever to lower the gate (**21**).

◆ Use the button in the southwestern room again (**19**).

◆ Go east and use the button (**22**).

◆ Return to the southwestern room and use the button again (**19**).

◆ The passage is now open toward the northeastern room (**23**).

◆ Return to the two buttons and use the one on the right.

◆ Use the southwestern button again (**19**). The passage to the eastern waterway is now open.

◆ Open the two gates using the lever (**24**).

◆ Go to the valve (**25**) and use it to restore water to the eastern waterway.

Ascend the steps north to the Mana Shrine. Use the button on the west wall (**26**) to open the passage. The opposite wall is open if you used the corresponding button (**16**) earlier in this walkthrough. If not, you'll have to take the long way back to the start position.

Go west toward the cavern entrance. Ascend the southern steps and traverse the large stairwell. Move north past the Azunite Scholar. You can now cross the connected walkway. Collect treasure from the big chests then enter the portal to the Agallan Peaks.

Chapter 7—The Agallan Giants

Completing this quest is straightforward—locate the Agallan Giants and speak with them about the Aegis. The intended level for this quest is 37. Quest tasks are as follows:

◆ Investigate the Agallan Peaks.

◆ Use the portal to travel to Zaramoth's Horns.

The Agallan Peaks

Arrive from the portal beneath Kalrathia. Go east through the great halls. Grab the Meaning of the Obelisks Lore Book (**1**). Locate the three Agallan Giants on their thrones (**2**). Speak with Elandir, the Agallan Giant Leader. Complete the conversation. The Agallan Giants reforge the Aegis using the lost fragment: Drevin's Medallion! You receive the Shield of Azunai.

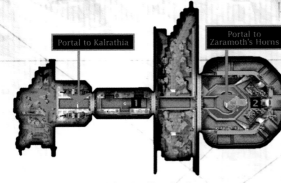

Portal to Kalrathia

Portal to Zaramoth's Horns

The Agallan Peaks

Speak with Elandir, the Agallan Giant Leader, and learn the mystery of the Shield of Azunai's lost fragment.

A portal materializes behind you. Enter the portal to Zaramoth's Horns, which triggers the next primary quest.

Chapter 8—Zaramoth's Horns

You're nearing the final confrontation with Valdis. Enemies defending Valdis's fortress, Zaramoth's Horns, are stronger than any faced before. Increase resistances to lightning and fire magic to counter the Qatall and Kluun spellcasters that crowd the fortress's halls. This quest is intended for level-37 characters. The quest's tasks:

◆ Ascend to the top of the mountain.

◆ Defeat the Archmage.

Zaramoth's Horns, Part 1

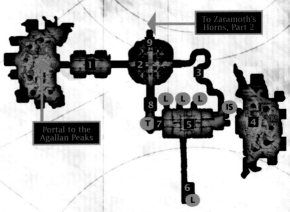

To Zaramoth's Horns, Part 2

Portal to the Agallan Peaks

Zaramoth's Horns, Part 1

You arrive via portal from Agallan Peaks. You're instantly under assault from Harpies. Defeat the winged menaces then move east and down the steps into the fortress interior.

Expect to face mixed groups of Kluun and Qatall defending the first chamber. The room contains an Eye of Zaramoth statue (**1**). Break the Eye of Zaramoth to fire a beam of energy that damages any enemy in front of the statue. Cross the room and traverse the narrow bridge (**2**). Move quickly past the fireball trap at the bridge's center. Enter the spiral staircase. Ascend the staircase (**3**) and battle fierce defenders through the halls. At the southern edge, the path forks east and west.

East leads to an optional exterior cliff (**4**) populated with minions. Turn west into the large prison chamber.

Kluun and Qatall

The Kluun are Valdis's close council. Completely loyal to their leader, the Kluun patrol Zaramoth's Horns and defend it against any who are opposed to Valdis and his cause. The Kluun Legionnaire is a powerful melee foe and wields a mighty sword. The Kluun magic users, the Conjuring Kluun Legionnaires, cast fire-magic spells along with Aquatic Embrace and Drown.

The Qatall were servants of Zaramoth and now mutely serve Valdis, the one who wields Zaramoth's sword. Created from bodies of Valdis's fallen followers, the Qatall, like the Kluun, feature melee and spellcaster variations. Qatall Minions attack with swords and wear massive armor (and can cast Wind Embrace and Decay Armor), and Qatall Runecasters utilize lightning magic and cast Wind Embrace and Wrath of Magic. Expect to also encounter Qatall Attendants (which are stronger versions of Minions) and Qatall Runeshapers (which are stronger Runecasters). Qatall float through Zaramoth's Horns, which enables these enemies to attack your party from above. Move cautiously through Zaramoth's Horns and focus your attacks on Qatall that drop in front of your party.

A series of lifts connects the prison cages. The cages block passage through most of the bottom floor. You must descend and ascend lifts to cross through the prison. Descend the first lift and defeat the Kluun and Qatall guards. Enter the western cage and ascend the lift to the prison's center platform. Find an Agallan Obelisk on the platform. Use the obelisk to grant your party temporary invulnerability. The prison's center platform (**5**) contains four lifts. You arrive from the lift on the southeastern side of the platform.

The northeast lift leads to a ranged Sanctuary Door (level 35) that conceals a lectern with the Greater Chant of Ranged Skill. A door to the east takes you to an Incantation Shrine and a melee Sanctuary Door (level 35) that holds a lectern with the Greater Chant of Melee Skill. The platform's southwest lift leads into a southern treasure room (**6**) that holds a lectern with the Chant of Power. Take the platform's northwest lift and find nature magic and combat magic Sanctuary Doors (both level 35). Both magic Sanctuary Doors conceal a lectern with the Greater Chant of Magic Skill. Use the lift in this cage to reach the upper western platform. Find the three exit doors (**7**). Proceed through them and battle the beasts guarding the area's teleporter.

Return to Kalrathia if needed before resuming course north. Recharge a power using the War Pedestal (**8**). Cross the narrow bridge (**9**)—it's simply a higher level of the same room you explored before.

Zaramoth's Horns, Part 2

Zaramoth's Horns, Part 2

Enter the northern room and combat the monsters inside. Three doors exit the room. The northern and western doors lead to treasure chambers; take the eastern passage and ascend the spiral staircase. Maneuver through several small rooms before exiting north to a cliff (**10**). Expect to face a menacing Ganth supported by Harpies. Move northwest and cross a narrow rock bridge (**11**) toward the western ruins. Search a ridge south of the ruins to find a ghostly spirit. Some of Valdis's fiercest defenders populate the ruins (**12**), including Stygian Hulking Beasts, Ganth, and minibosses.

Invoke a chant at the Incantation Shrine up the western stairs to aid your party during the tough battle. South of the shrine find a button that opens a secret passage. The area contains a lectern with the Chant of Chaotic Skill. Find a War Pedestal in the southwest corner. Search the southeastern corner to discover a lever that opens a treasure room. Exit through the door along the south wall.

Cross the narrow walkway (**13**). The path bends west. Defeat groups of Kluun, Qatall, and assorted beasts. Proceed through the double doors to the north (**14**). Monsters crowd the room. There's a Life Shrine down the next hall; ascend the western staircase and find the shrine at the top near an Agallan Obelisk (**15**). Use the obelisk for temporary invulnerability. Exit through a western passage and return to an exterior cliff.

Traverse the cliff south (**16**) and battle through hordes of Harpies, Qatall, and assorted Zaramoth monsters. Find an entrance to the fortress in the southeastern corner of the cliff. Combat Valdis's forces among the statues through the fortress chamber (**17**). Break the Eye of Zaramoth statue in the room's center and use the beam to damage nearby creatures. Follow the room northeast and exit onto the narrow bridge.

The Archmage's Chamber

Continue east and locate the lift at the far end. Pull the lever (**18**) and ride the lift to the upper walkway. Maneuver south to another exterior cliff. Crush Valdis's forces along the cliff (**19**) and move north to another fortress entrance on the west wall. Use the teleporter inside to return to Kalrathia. A difficult battle awaits you; take the opportunity to restock your potions or acquire better equipment.

Follow the hall to the north into the circular chamber (**20**). The Archmage is Valdis's most

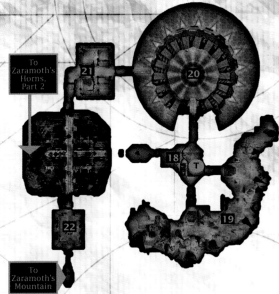

The Archmage's Chamber

powerful minion—and he's responsible for the destruction of Aman'lu.

Agallan Obelisks surround the exterior of the Archmage's circular chamber. Use the Obelisks to invoke temporary invulnerability on your party members (some of the Archmage's attacks remove the invulnerability, which forces you to return to an obelisk to regain it). But the Archmage can twist the obelisks for his own purpose. Your enemy casts Aegis Terminus around the obelisk, making it unusable. And if left unchecked, the obelisk launches projectiles at your party. The longer you leave the obelisks affected, the more projectiles appear. Attack the affected obelisk to end Aegis Terminus.

The Archmage also invokes Aegis Apocryphal to shield himself from your damaging attacks. Focus your assault on the Apocryphal shield to eliminate the magic protecting the Archmage. Once eliminated, resume your assault against the Archmage by using your most damaging spells and powers. Locate two War Pedestals on the chamber's northern end to recharge your two most potent powers.

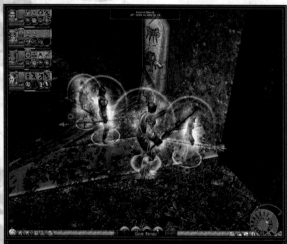

The Archmage's chamber contains Agallan Obelisks, which the Archmage can twist for his own purpose.

Beware of the Archmage's shockwave attack. The ground shakes around the Archmage, inflicting significant damage to any party members within the blast radius. Move away from the Archmage, drink a health potion, then resume the assault against Valdis's lackey. Destroy the Archmage to complete the task.

Follow the circular stairwell on the northern side. Collect treasures from the chests at the top. Exit through the western hallway. Eliminate the Kluun and Shail guards within the prison chamber (**21**). Lure enemies into the doorway and bombard them with powers. Cross the narrow bridge south and repel a Qatall ambush. Enter the southern door. Defeat the Kluun, Qatall, and other beasts guarding the chamber (**22**). Collect the treasure that surrounds the center statue. Exit to the south.

Chapter 9—The Final Ascent

This is the final ascent up Zaramoth's Mountain and to the Temple of Valdis...and it won't be easy. Hordes of Harpies, Qatall, Kluun, Shail, and Ganth guard the steps up the mountain. Before you reach the temple, increase resistance to fire damage to better counter Valdis's devastating attacks. This quest is intended for level-38 characters. There are two final quest tasks:

◆ Locate the Temple of Valdis.

◆ Destroy Valdis.

Zaramoth's Mountain

Exit onto the cliff. Expect to combat Harpies, Ganth, and Qatall near the entrance (**1**). You must proceed south initially; the ridges along the mountain cliff loop around to the east and west and connect to staircases. You can take either staircase; both connect to the same location (**2**)—the foot of a third staircase that ascends the mountain and leads north toward the Temple of Valdis.

The staircase defenders have a significant height advantage over your party. Manage your most potent area-effect powers carefully. Maximize the powers' damage potential against the highest number of enemies possible. The stairs connect at a narrow ridge guarded by swarming Harpies and other beasts. Clear the ridge and begin the ascent north up the center staircase.

Zaramoth's Mountain

The stairs eventually level into a bridge (**3**) crowded with Harpies, Qatall, Kluun, and Shail. Move slowly across the bridge and focus your attacks on small groups to avoid triggering the aggressions of the entire enemy force. Cross the bridge and reach a wide courtyard (**4**). Eliminate the enemies protecting the courtyard and continue north toward the Temple of Valdis.

The Temple of Valdis

The Temple of Valdis

Maneuver north into the temple. Find four War Pedestals (**5**) within the temple to recharge party powers. Confront Valdis in the northern chamber.

Valdis's chamber contains Agallan Obelisks, used to provide your party with temporary invulnerability. The chamber (**6**) also contains four Eye of Zaramoth statues in a square formation near the chamber's entrance. Valdis is completely invulnerable during this first encounter. None of your attacks, spells, or powers will damage him. You must use the statues to inflict damage.

Don't get close to Valdis; his most powerful attacks at this stage are close-range. You must lure him in front of one of the Eye of Zaramoth statues. If you have summoned creatures, allow Valdis to defeat them so he focuses his attacks on your party. Move to the opposite side of a statue so it lies between you and the approaching Valdis. As Valdis nears, attack the statue until it fires its damaging beam and forces Valdis backward. You must lure Valdis into a statue's beam three times to complete the first stage of this battle.

> ### Tip
>
> The Eye of Zaramoth statue beams will inflict massive damage to anything in their path, including any of your party members or pets! In Mercenary mode, a beam inflicts 1,000 points of damage to any party member or pet unfortunate enough to walk into it.

The Azunite Scholar enters the chamber...and he's not looking friendly. After he takes the Shield of Azunai from you, the second stage of the battle against Valdis begins. The Eye of Zaramoth statues are gone and pools of lava stretch along the sides of the room. Stay out of the magma!

Valdis now sustains damage from your attacks. Unleash your powers and your most powerful spells and abilities against him. Valdis has several new attacks, including two separate fireball assaults. When Valdis begins to glow in yellow flame, he's charging a fireball attack. This is a relatively slow, but high-damage attack. Back away quickly or maneuver your party in a circular motion around Valdis to stay ahead of the attack. The fiery projectile inflicts massive damage if it connects.

Use the Eye of Zaramoth to wound Valdis in the first confrontation.

A second fireball attack is much quicker and harder to avoid (though not as damaging). Valdis summons two balls of molten lava from the pools surrounding the chamber, and hurls them in a fantastic flash. This attack inflicts devastating damage if it connects, and it's so fast it's difficult to avoid. Move to one side to avoid the strike. At close range, Valdis can also punch the ground and create a shockwave that knocks your party back and possibly into the lava

During the battle, Valdis morphs into three versions and heals himself. Immediately attack the real Valdis to end the healing process. Valdis invokes this spell the first time his health drops below 80%, the first time his health drops below 60%, and the first time his health drops below 40%.

Valdis is knocked back after you've reduced his health by a third. At this point, Qatall enter the chamber from every corner. Focus your attacks on the Qatall intruders. If Valdis begins to heal himself, immediately return your attacks to your nemesis and end his healing attempt.

A large object at the far end of the chamber begins to break. Eventually the object breaks apart, which reveals a massive Eye of Zaramoth statue. With the statue fully exposed, lure Valdis in front of the eye. Attack the Eye of Zaramoth to "break" the statue. Hit Valdis with the crushing beam of light to conclude the battle.

:PART 7:
SECONDARY QUESTS WALKTHROUGH

Dungeon Siege II *offers dozens of secondary quests for adventurers willing to explore off the primary story path. These tasks are completely optional but their valuable rewards—which range from random magic equipment to one-of-a-kind unique or set items—makes completion more than worth your effort. This section provides complete walkthroughs and maps for all of* Dungeon Siege II's *secondary quests.*

Act I Secondary Quests

The Armorer's Apprentice

Visit the merchant shop in Eirulan and speak with Apprentice Telinu. She's been ordered to create Dryad armor but can't remember the exact formula. This quest is intended for level-3 characters. The task for this secondary quest:

◆ Read the Tome of Smithing and tell Telinu the correct material list for Dryad armor.

Leave the merchant shop and proceed to the Terrace of Wisdom. Find the Tome of Smithing on a table inside the Great Hall. Add the book to your journal and read its contents. Learn the correct recipe for Dryad armor:

> **Developer Tip**
>
> *It's possible to answer Apprentice Telinu's dilemma without even picking up the Tome of Smithing. If you guess, you have a 20% chance of being correct. Or you can simply select the third dialog option and be correct 100% of the time! However, merely guessing the correct recipe without recovering the Tome of Smithing provides less reward. —Ryan Gibson*

five squares of leather, three pots of boiling wax, twelve stoneshroom discs, and two baskets of leaves. Coat the leather with wax, apply the discs, then fasten the leaves to the resulting armor.

Return to Apprentice Telinu and speak with her again. When you select the correct recipe from the choices, Apprentice Telinu crafts armor with good modifiers for you; answer incorrectly, and receive armor with mediocre modifiers.

Lumilla's Salve

Speak with Enchantress Lumilla in the Eirulan merchant shop. Ask Lumilla about her special reagent to initiate the quest. This quest is intended for level-3 characters. The quest task:

◆ Collect four Nettle Clusters and give them to Enchantress Lumilla.

The four Nettle Clusters are scattered throughout Act I. Find enough at the following locations:

◆ Go southwest from the Dryad Exile Colony in the Eastern Greilyn Jungle. Find the Nettle Cluster near mana bushes just outside a small cave (the cave that contains Hrawn the Hak'u).

◆ Exit Eirulan through the southern gate into the Southern Greilyn Jungle. Take the first fork east. Find the Nettle Cluster just outside a dark, bone-filled cave (the cave in Taar's Investigation).

- In the Kithraya Valley just before the Lower Kithraya Caverns, find a Nettle Cluster near an abandoned tower on the path opposite the Kithraya Valley teleporter.

- On Eastern Greilyn Beach after destroying the Shard, find a Nettle Cluster before the Incantation Shrine.

- You can also find Nettle Clusters available at an Arcanist as well as randomly dropped from monsters or quest rewards.

Return to the Eirulan merchant shop with all four Nettle Clusters and give them to Lumilla. In return she creates a special reagent, Lumilla's Salve, which bestows +10 health and +5% health regeneration.

Lelani's Sorrow

Initiate this secondary quest by speaking with Lelani in Eirulan. Find her in her home south of the pet shop. Lelani's late daughter's favorite place was Aman'lu, and Lelani hopes to find a keepsake that would remind her of the town. This quest—which spans all three acts—is a unique scavenger hunt in which you seek out characters looking for specific objects and those willing to give up their own wares. Complete the quest and receive the Hunter's Mark unique amulet. The tasks follow:

- Talk to Lelani about the strange doll on the table next to her. Bring Lelani a keepsake from Aman'lu.

- Bring Fenella a toy to cheer up her child.

- Bring Soldier Balamar something special to quench his thirst.

- Bring Soldier Jordhan some fresh meat.

- Bring Soldier Kiernan something to change his luck.

- Bring Alar'ithil a trophy of the enemy that he can display.

- Bring Prospector Gareth some supplies.

- Bring Nalus something ancient and interesting that he can study.

- Bring Ithir'renne the Fletcher a new material to use for crafting arrows.

- Bring Lelani a keepsake from Aman'lu.

The following table reveals all characters in the Lelani's Sorrow quest, their locations, what items they possess, and what items they want.

Character	Location	Has	Wants
Lelani	Eirulan (south of the pet shop)	Child's Doll	Aman'lu Orchid
Fenella	Eirulan (first house in the Terrace of the Falls)	Flask of Elven Ale	Child's Doll
Soldier Balamar	Azunite Desert (in the fort near the portal from Greilyn)	Skath Cat Ribs	Flask of Elven Ale
Soldier Jordhan	Eirulan Tavern (second floor of the inn room)	Lucky Statuette of Xeria	Skath Cat Ribs
Soldier Kiernan	Snowbrook Haven Courtyard (in the dining hall below the commander rendezvous point)	Morden Head on a Pike	Lucky Statuette of Xeria
Alar'ithil	South Aman'lu	Bottle of Elven Water	Morden Head on a Pike
Prospector Gareth	Some Crumbling Ruins (in the abandoned tower in the Northern Plain of Tears)	Battered Agallan Relic	Bottle of Elven Water
Nalus	Kalrathia (a rampart in the middle of the north wall)	Bundle of Harpy Feathers	Battered Agallan Relic
Ithir'renne the Fletcher	Aman'lu (east of the north gate)	Aman'lu Orchid	Bundle of Harpy Feathers

Secrets of the Elven Shrine

Speak with Laenne in her Eirulan hut above the pet shop to trigger this secondary quest. Using the secret button within the Elven Shrine before speaking to Laenne also initiates the quest. This quest is intended for level-8 characters. The quest task list:

Map Legend
- **IS** Incantation Shrine
- **MS** Mana Shrine
- **LS** Life Shrine
- **G** Ghostly Spirit
- **L** Chant lectern
- **T** Teleporter

- Find the secret rooms rumored to be within the Elven Shrine.

- Find the Lost Sapphire of the Elves. Take it to Laenne in Eirulan.

Green Socket Room in the Elven Shrine

Locate the Elven Shrine in the Western Greilyn Jungle; it's the same shrine you explored in the Act I primary quest The Plague. After descending on the first lift, find a hidden switch on the western wall (**1**) to open a secret chamber. Enter the secret room, pick a Green Life Cube from the pile (**2**), and place it in the socket. Descend the elevator by using the lever.

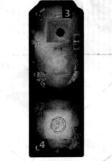

Yellow Socket Room in the Elven Shrine

Hit a button on the northern wall (**3**) to open another hidden room to the south. Pick a Yellow Sight Cube from the pile in the first room and place it in the socket. Pick two Red Blindness Cubes from the pile (**4**) and another Yellow Sight Cube.

Red and Purple Socket Rooms in the Elven Shrine

Descend the lift and press the button on the eastern wall. This opens a southern room. Place the Red Blindness Cube in the socket (**5**). Pick two Purple Death Cubes from the pile (**6**). Place one Purple Death Cube in the socket near the lift to open a new passage to the north. The new area (**7**) contains two closed sockets and an open Yellow Sight Cube socket. Place the Yellow Sight Cube from your inventory in the socket (if you forgot to get a second, return up the lift). This opens the Red Blindness socket; place the Red Blindness Cube inside. Now the Purple Death socket is open. Place the Purple Death Cube to activate the nearby lift.

Use the lift to ascend into a hidden room containing the Lost Sapphire of the Elves (**8**). Grab it. The room also contains three lecterns. Pick up the Chant of Lesser Fighter Power, Chant of Lesser Mage Power, and Chant of Lesser Ranger Power. Return to Laenne in Eirulan and speak with her for your reward, which includes the Outrider's Signet unique ring.

The Kithraya Hive

Initiate this secondary quest by speaking with Tamari in Eirulan. Visit the Terrace of the Falls; go past the gorgeous waterfalls and return to another section of Eirulan. Find Tamari in her hut. You can also trigger the quest by locating the Kithraya Hive Queen. The Queen is weak to death magic, so prepare your equipment and spells before venturing out. She can also cast Impale, so increase death resistance to counter. This quest is intended for level-13 characters. The quest features the following tasks:

◆ Destroy the Kithraya Hive Queen.

◆ Show the Severed Head of the Kithraya Hive Queen to Tamari in Eirulan.

Kithraya Queen in the Lower Kithraya Caverns

As part of the Act I primary quest Leaving Greilyn Isle, you pass through the Lower Kithraya Caverns. Before the caverns' east exit, the path splits north and south. Take the southern route toward the Kithraya Queen.

This section of the Lower Kithraya Caverns is extremely challenging; ensure your party is prepared with potions, recharged powers, and the best equipment available. Follow the path south and expect to encounter plagued groups (**1**) of Larvax, Carver Bats, Boggrots, Veesh, Kurtle, and Shard Souls. Follow the cave west and back north. Defeat Maltratar (**2**) on sight—the creatures can heal other monsters. You certainly wouldn't want a Maltratar near the Kithraya Queen!

Defeat the mighty Queen in the Lower Kithraya Caverns to complete the quest.

The Hak'u Caves

Continue through the cavern west and back south (**3**) toward the queen's lair. The Kithraya Hive Queen occupies the chamber's center (**4**). She's weak against death magic. Clear out any other creatures before entering the chamber, and focus all attacks on the queen. Autocast curse spells to weaken the queen against your most deadly attacks and powers, and use summon spells to provide the queen other targets. The queen can cast Cripple (slowing your attack rate) and Impale, a death-magic spell.

Eliminate the queen to receive the Severed Head of the Kithraya Hive Insect Queen quest item. You also have a chance to recover the Queen's Husk unique ring after the queen's death; if not, receive the Queen's Husk from Tamari in Eirulan when you show her the severed head.

The Hak'u, Part I

Initiate this secondary quest by speaking with Hesla in the Eirulan infirmary. You can also trigger the quest during the Act I primary quest The Morden Towers when you spot Morain chasing a Hak'u in the Northern Greilyn Jungle. This quest is intended for level-7 characters. Quest tasks:

◆ Find the hidden rear entrance to the Hak'u caves.

◆ Rescue Hesla's daughter, Tanzi.

◆ Speak with Hesla in the Eirulan infirmary.

The hidden rear entrance to the Hak'u caves is in the Western Greilyn Jungle. Find it down a western path just before the fourth Morden Tower and north of the Western Greilyn Jungle teleporter. The gate into the caves remains locked until you initiate the quest. If the quest is triggered, you'll spot a Hak'u running through an opened gate when you approach.

Defeat the mixed Hak'u groups around the entrance. Move south then west to find caged Tanzi (**1**). A brief cut scene shows a Hak'u helping Tanzi escape! Tanzi flees back to Eirulan. You can return to Eirulan immediately to complete the quest. Speak with Hesla in the Eirulan infirmary (on the Terrace of Wisdom) to finish the last task.

You can also take time to explore the rest of the Hak'u caves. Connect the bridge (**2**) to the south using the lever. Grab the Lore Book (**3**) near the ghostly spirit. The path splits. The southern path (**4**) offers one exit into the Northern Greilyn Jungle. You can also continue east past an Incantation Shrine to battle a large group of mixed Hak'u (**5**). Locate a second exit (**6**) into the Northern Greilyn Jungle.

The Hak'u, Part II

Complete the secondary quest The Hak'u and speak with Hesla in the Eirulan infirmary to initiate the second part. After Tanzi reveals a Hak'u named Hrawn helped her escape, Hesla wants to take the opportunity to strike while the Hak'u may be in civil war. This quest is intended for level-10 characters. Tasks for the quest are as follows:

- Find Hrawn the Hak'u.

- Kill the Hak'u leader who stands against your allies.

- Return to Hesla in the Eirulan infirmary.

Locate Hrawn the Hak'u inside a small cave in the Eastern Greilyn Jungle. Move through the Dryad Exile Colony and take the southwest path. Locate the cave entrance near the Incantation Shrine. Enter the cave and speak with Hrawn the Hak'u (**1**). You have three choices of how to complete the quest.

Hrawn's Cave in the Eastern Greilyn Jungle

- Select the dialogue option regarding killing the Usurper instead of Hrawn. Locate the Usurper's hideout west of the Western Greilyn Jungle teleporter near an Incantation Shrine. There's also a ghostly spirit on the far western side. Use the door (**2**) in the ruins and tell the Usurper you have a message from the High Priest. Enter and battle the Usurper and his minions. Recover the Hak'u Headdress.

Usurper's Hideout in the Western Greilyn Jungle

- Select the dialogue option regarding killing Hrawn and not the Usurper. Hrawn will beg you to reconsider, and offer a bribe. Don't accept the bribe; kill Hrawn, the High Priest, and other Hak'u to obtain the Hak'u Headdress.

- Select the dialogue option regarding killing Hrawn instead of the Usurper. When Hrawn begs you to reconsider and offers the bribe, take it. You receive the Hak'u Headdress.

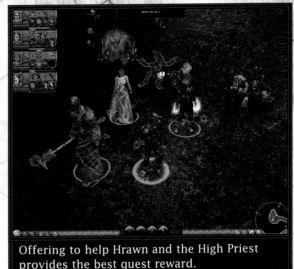

Offering to help Hrawn and the High Priest provides the best quest reward.

After obtaining the Hak'u Headdress through one of the three options, return to Hesla in the Eirulan infirmary and speak with her. The quality of reward depends on your choice. You receive the best equipment reward for killing the Usurper and the worse rewards for killing or bribing Hrawn and the High Priest.

Dire Wolf

Initiate this quest by speaking with Pet Seller Neda inside the Eirulan Pet Shop. Ask her about special pets and discuss the Dire Wolf. This quest is intended for level-10 characters. The quest's tasks follow:

- Speak with Rokhar the Nature Mage in the town of Eirulan.

- Go to Rokhar's Rift Site. Kill all the Nawl Beasts that come through the rift.

- Remind Rokhar to send the Dire Wolf back to Pet Seller Neda. Return to Pet Seller Neda in the Eirulan Pet Shop.

Go to the Great Hall in Eirulan and speak with Rokhar the Mage about the Dire Wolf. He requests a meeting at a special rift site in the Eastern Greilyn Jungle. After moving past the amphitheater (Razka's Ruins), search the cave north of the main road. Proceed through the small cave and exit into Rokhar's Rift Site. Find Rokhar (**1**) there waiting for you. Speak with him to trigger the next objective.

Rokhar's Rift Site in the Eastern Greilyn Jungle

While Rokhar holds the rift (**2**) open, protect him from Nawl Beasts emerging from the rift. Utilize your area-effect powers against the Nawl Beasts and a Morden mage. After the battle, speak with Rokhar again to remind him to send the Dire Wolf back to Eirulan. Return to Eirulan and speak with Pet Seller Neda; now the Dire Wolf pet is available for purchase.

Taar's Investigation

You must have Taar in your party to initiate this secondary quest. You can recruit her after completing the Act I primary quest The Plague. With Taar in your party, speak with Arianne in her hut on the Terrace of Wisdom. This quest is intended for level-10 characters. The quest's tasks:

- ◆ Confirm or deny the existence of the Hak'u Ceremonial Blade.

- ◆ Investigate the rumors of the Hak'u beast. Slay the Garganturax.

- ◆ Take proof of the beast's death to Arianne in Eirulan.

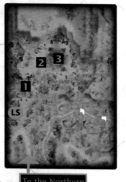

Hak'u Ceremonial Grounds (Northern Greilyn Jungle)

Exit Eirulan through the north gate. Go past the Dryad Outpost, following the main path north then the bend east. At the broken bridge, turn north and proceed past the Life Shrine and across the bridge (**1**). The Hak'u Ceremonial Grounds is just to the northeast; a tribe (**2**) of Hak'u protects the altar. Defeat the defenders. Pick up the Hak'u Ceremonial Blade off of the altar (**3**).

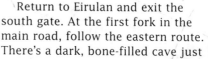

A Dark, Bone-Filled Cave (Southern Greilyn Jungle)

Return to Eirulan and exit the south gate. At the first fork in the main road, follow the eastern route. There's a dark, bone-filled cave just ahead. Find the menacing but just two-foot-tall Garganturax in the cave's rear (**4**). You must have the Hak'u Ceremonial Blade equipped to inflict any damage on the Garganturax. All other attacks have no effect. Defeat the beast by using the Hak'u blade and receive the Garganturax Head quest item.

Return to Eirulan and speak with Arianne. The Garganturax Head is proof enough that the beast has been slain. Collect your rewards from Arianne.

> **Tip**
>
> The Hak'u Ceremonial Blade is the only weapon that can slay the Garganturax...but it's useless after that battle. The unique dagger's base damage is a meager 2 to 5.

> **Tip**
>
> If you enter the dark, bone-filled cave before activating the quest, the Garganturax won't be inside. If you trigger the quest but fail to recover the Hak'u Ceremonial Blade, the Garganturax will be present in the cave but you will be unable to slay it.

Feldwyr the Blacksmith

Locate the entrance to an underground shelter within the Eastern Greilyn Jungle. Inside, speak with Feldwyr the Blacksmith to initiate the quest. This quest is intended for level-12 characters. The tasks are as follows:

- Find Feldwyr's anvil, Mythril Ore, and hammer, and return the items to him.

- Speak to Blacksmith Apprentice Fyrndolf in the town of Aman'lu.

An Underground Shelter in the Eastern Greilyn Jungle

Battle Hak'u near the underground shelter's entrance. Search a southern room (**1**) for treasure. Continue east to battle assorted Hak'u and locate Blacksmith Feldwyr in the southern portion of the room (**2**). Speak with him; this opens a new route to the east. Check the room south of the blacksmith to find a lift (**3**) to the Eastern Greilyn Jungle.

> ### Tip
> *The northern side of the underground shelter (containing the Mythril Ore) contains level-12 monsters; the southern side is populated by level-24 monsters. After securing the Mythril Ore, it's best to leave the shelter and return later after your party has gained levels. The more difficult southern section contains the Blacksmith's anvil.*

Proceed into the opened eastern route. Pull a lever on a column in the adjacent room (**4**) to open a northern chamber containing treasure. A button on a western wall opens access to another treasure room. Continue down a staircase east and battle Hak'u and Taclak at the three-way intersection. There's also a War Pedestal here (**5**). Move north. Battle a large Hak'u group (**6**); eliminate the Witch Doctors quickly to avoid summon and resurrect spells. Open the eastern door.

Invaders have stolen Feldwyr the Blacksmith's valuable equipment.

You can search the northern and center sections for additional combat and possible treasure. Find levers to open all routes. In the furthest northwest room in the water-logged area, pull a lever on the southern wall to access an armor stand. Search the southern side (**7**) to locate a Taclak miniboss holding the blacksmith's Mythril Ore. Kill the beast to recover the quest item.

The southern section is much tougher with high-level monsters. It's wise to leave the shelter and return later after your party has gained levels. Once back inside the shelter, return to the intersection and proceed south. Battle Taclak in the large chamber (**8**). Search the side rooms for treasure; two rooms contain switches (**9**) that open more treasure areas. In the southeastern chamber, battle another miniboss (**10**) to recover the blacksmith's anvil.

Return to Feldwyr with both quest items. Now his hammer has been stolen. Proceed north from Feldwyr. There's a melee Sanctuary Door (level

9) on the western side of the hall (**11**). Continue north into the cavern. Defeat Taclak minibosses and supporting minions to recover the hammer. Use a nearby War Pedestal to recharge a power. Return to Feldwyr. He says to speak with his brother, Blacksmith Apprentice Fyrndolf, in Aman'lu for your reward.

After proceeding into the portal upon completion of Act I, find Fyrndolf in the Aman'lu Armory and speak with him.

A Family Heirloom

Trigger this secondary quest by finding and speaking with Master Thestrin in a tower in the Azunite Desert. The tower is northeast of the Azunite portal. This quest is intended for level-14 characters. The quest's tasks follow:

◆ Enter the crypt described by Master Thestrin. Solve the Guardian of the Crypt's riddle.

◆ Enter the ruined crypt vault and find the heirloom. Return to Master Thestrin with the heirloom sword.

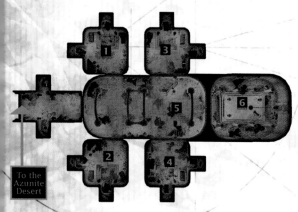

A Ruined Crypt in the Azunite Desert

Move to the southeast corner of the Azunite Desert and enter a ruined crypt. Undead Azunites occupy the crypt's side rooms. Search the first northern room (**1**) to find a squad of undead guarding a War Pedestal. The first southern room (**2**) holds another War Pedestal and a few containers. The second northern room (**3**) bears treasure, and the second southern room (**4**) contains additional undead, containers, and a third War Pedestal.

Speak with the Statue Guardian (**5**) on the eastern side of the main hall. Answer his riddle in the following order:

1. Azunai, for he was a man and quickest to move.

2. Xeria, for war followed closely in the footsteps of men.

3. Elandir, for the Agallans never believed in war.

4. Zaramoth, for his sword struck Azunai's shield and brought about the second age of man.

The correct answer opens another room to the east (**6**). Defeat the miniboss and supporting undead. Grab the unique sword, Thestrin's family heirloom, and loot the big chest. Return to Thestrin's tower and speak with the old man. He immediately provides a reward, a mysterious chant, "Magnum Erupto." Then he asks for the sword.

You can choose to ignore Thestrin's demands and keep the sword for yourself, or you can hand it over. If you give him the sword, Thestrin reveals the secret chant was actually a curse. For handing over the sword, he teaches you a rewarding chant, "Requo Amicum Es," which is the Lesser Chant of Summon Friends.

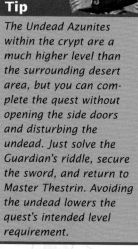

Tip

The Undead Azunites within the crypt are a much higher level than the surrounding desert area, but you can complete the quest without opening the side doors and disturbing the undead. Just solve the Guardian's riddle, secure the sword, and return to Master Thestrin. Avoiding the undead lowers the quest's intended level requirement.

Tip

The Heirloom Sword is a unique weapon that adds +15 to its maximum damage. You've certainly found better melee weapons by this point in the game, so the Heirloom Sword isn't likely worth equipping. The sword is involved in the Act II secondary quest A Family Heirloom, Part II so keep it in a town storage vault. You can still initiate the Act II quest if you return the sword to Thestrin.

The Imprisoned Half-Giant

A Half-Giant named Sartan has been imprisoned by Captain Dathry on suspicion of being quite mad. Initiate this quest by speaking with Sartan in his "prison" in Windstone Fortress. He's in a hole near Captain Darthry. This quest is intended for level-19 characters. The quest's tasks:

- ◆ Talk to the soldiers about releasing Sartan once Windstone Fortress is safe.

- ◆ Talk to the newly freed Sartan.

After activating the Azunite Artifact within the Windstone Fortress Inner Vault (part of the Act I primary quest Windstone Fortress), bring the activated artifact back to Captain Dathry. Speak with the captain. Explosives clear the northern path and the captain leads the Windstone troops toward the Temple of Xeria.

Before following them north, speak with Soldier Orayne about releasing Sartan. Once Sartan is free, speak with the Half-Giant. Your reward for completing the quest is the ability to add Sartan, a level-19 warrior, to your party.

The Missing Squadron

Initiate this secondary quest by talking to Squadron Leader Taarth at the northern end of Windstone Fortress. He reveals that three privates are missing. Alternatively, you can trigger the quest if you find any of the three privates, speak to them, and accept the quest. This quest is intended for level-18 characters. The quest task:

- ◆ Find Private Nolan, Private Banos, and Private Caiden and escort them back to Squadron Leader Taarth.

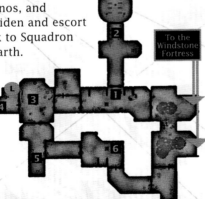

Windstone Fortress Barracks

After speaking with Taarth, find Private Nolan is in the Windstone Fortress Barracks. Locate the entrance across from the Windstone teleporter on the western side of the road. Proceed into the northern entrance. Mixed groups of Plagued Windstone troops have overrun the barracks. Advance north and locate a hidden switch (**1**) along the northern wall. Explore the northern room to find a second switch, (**2**) in the northern alcove. Use this switch to open a northern treasure room.

Search farther west and enter a populated room containing a War Pedestal (**3**). Locate Private Nolan in a small room (**4**) on the far western side of this hallway. The room also contains a lectern with the Lesser Chant of Magic Skill. You can escort him to Squadron Leader Taarth immediately, or explore the rest of the barracks. You'll find a combat magic (level 17) Sanctuary Door to the south (**5**) and a War Pedestal to the east (**6**).

Tip

Have no fear when escorting the privates back to Squadron Leader Taarth. Enemy attacks can't hurt or kill these characters. Of course, the privates won't assist your party in a tough fight, either!

Find Private Caiden in the Eastern Windstone Fortress Gatehouse. Enter using the west entrance north of the Windstone Fortress entrance. Plagued Windstone troops crowd the gatehouse hall. Use the War Pedestal south (**7**) of the entrance to recharge a power. Find Private Caiden (**8**) in the southwestern corner. Grab the Lore Book nearby. Break the urns to reach and speak with him. Search the opposite corner for a lectern containing the Chant of Lesser Melee Skill.

Eastern Windstone Fortress Gatehouse

Explore the Western Windstone Fortress Gatehouse and find Private Banos in a southern room in a hall east of the entrance (**9**). You had to move through this area during the Act I primary quests. Speak with Private Banos and offer to escort him out of danger. Escort the privates to Taarth.

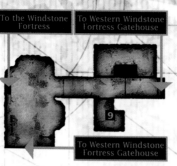

Western Windstone Fortress Gatehouse

Speak with Squadron Leader Taarth after rescuing all three privates. He offers a Dusty Vault Key as your reward. The key unlocks a secret chamber inside the Windstone Fortress Inner Vault. The room contains four Purple Death Hexahedron Sockets. Pick up four Hexahedrons from the pile in the previous chamber north of the Font of Azunite Fire. Place all four Hexahedrons in their sockets to open a hidden treasure room.

Secrets of Xeria's Temple

Talk with the Grizzled Bar Patron in the Eirulan Tavern to initiate this secondary quest. You can also trigger the quest by beginning the puzzle inside the Temple of Xeria. This quest is intended for level-19 characters. Quest tasks:

◆ Enter the Temple of Xeria and place the Stone of Life within its socket. Finish exploring the Temple of Xeria.

◆ Return to the Grizzled Bar Patron in the Eirulan Tavern.

Temple of Xeria Puzzle

You'll enter the Temple of Xeria as part of the final primary quest in Act I. Proceed through the temple and enter the large chamber (**1**) containing the Yellow Sight Stone and Green Life Stone sockets. Pick up a Green Life Stone from the pile (**2**) in the southeastern corner and place it in the Green Life Socket in the chamber's center. A western passage opens.

The new room (**3**) contains a pile of Yellow Sight Stones and four closed sockets (one for each stone type). Grab a Yellow Sight Stone and return to the previous chamber. Place the stone in the socket to open a new room to the south (**4**). It contains yellow and green sockets. Pick up another Yellow Sight Stone and Green Life Stone from the piles and place them in the two sockets. Filling the yellow socket opens a room (**5**) to the south; filling the green socket opens a room (**6**) to the east.

You'll automatically initiate this secondary quest upon placing the Green Life Stone in its socket.

Move to the eastern room and pick up a Red Blindness Stone. Return to the southern room opened by the yellow socket and place the Red Blindness Stone in the open socket. A new room to the north opens (**7**) and a second Red Blindness socket opens. Grab another Red Blindness Stone and place it in the socket. An adjacent room opens to the south, which contains a pile of Purple Death Stones (**8**).

Grab three Purple Death Stones to fill all open sockets (**9**). You'll eventually connect to the room containing four sockets, one for each type of stone. The sockets are open. Pick up one of each remaining stone type and place it in an open socket. A final room that opens to the west (**10**) contains a big chest and a lectern holding the Chant of Scholars.

Complete the quest by returning to Eirulan and speaking with the Grizzled Bar Patron inside the tavern. He gives you a unique ring, Xeria's Seal, as part of your reward.

Act II Secondary Quests

Tywlis' Broken Staff

Speak to Tywlis the Mage in her home near Aman'lu's north gate. She's looking for a colorful reagent used as a headpiece on her grandfather's staff. The quest's tasks are as follows:

◆ Find the reagent Tywlis needs to repair her grandfather's staff.

◆ Return to Tywlis the Mage.

The reagent Tywlis is searching for is the Rainbow Trinket (+5% chance to find magic items). Locate the reagent while treasure-hunting on any other quest; you'll also find one in a frigid cave in Snowbrook Valley (see Part 5 for the location). Return to Tywlis and talk to her with the Rainbow Trinket in your inventory to collect your reward. Tell Tywlis you don't need a gold reward and your kindness is rewarded with a unique ring, Gleamstone.

A Dark Ohm

Initiate this quest by speaking with Mage Lyssanore in the Aman'lu Magic Shop. Ask her about spirits. You're asked to find and eavesdrop on a Vai'kesh ritual to memorize their chants. This quest is intended for level-26 characters. The quest's tasks follow:

◆ Observe the Vai'kesh during one of their rituals.

◆ Return to Mage Lyssanore in Aman'lu.

A Small Vai'kesh Cave in the Vai'kesh Forest

Investigate a small Vai'kesh cave in the Vai'kesh Forest. Find the cave north of the main path between the large Vai'kesh cavern and Arinth's Ravine. Defeat the Vai'kesh within the cave and approach a door (**1**) on the cave's north side. Observe the Vai'kesh ritual (**2**) in the next chamber. After witnessing the chant, you can slaughter the Vai'kesh. Loot the room for treasure, including a lectern with the Chant of Fortification.

Return to the Aman'lu Magic Shop and speak with Mage Lyssanore. She translates the chants and rewards your effort with the Chant of the Dead (the power to speak with the ghostly spirits scattered throughout the game). Invoke "Vox Mortem" at any Incantation Shrine to temporarily receive the power.

> **Tip**
>
> *Completing A Dark Ohm is necessary for completing several other secondary quests: A Servant's Haunt; A Servant's Haunt, Part II; Spirits of Aranna; Arinth's Legendary Staff; and Arinth the Mad.*

Spirits of Aranna

To initiate Spirits of Aranna, you must first complete the A Dark Ohm secondary quest and receive the Chant of the Dead. Invoke the chant at any Incantation Shrine then speak with one of the 18 ghostly spirits scattered throughout the game to initiate this quest. The quest's task:

◆ Find the 18 restless spirits.

With the Chant of the Dead active, speak with one of the 18 ghostly spirits and complete the conversation. The ghostly spirit disappears and leaves a pile of treasure behind. A counter on the bottom of the screen reveals how many spirits are left. The following table reveals all 18 spirit locations, instructions for how to find the ghostly spirit, and the direction of the closest Incantation Shrine. The quest's reward includes the rings from the Ghostly Visions set: Spirit of Unrest, Spirit of Rest, and Spirit of Repose.

Location	Directions
Lost Valley of the Azunites	South from the Ancient Azunite Shrine exit. Incantation Shrine to the east.
Northern Greilyn Jungle	Southeastern side of the Hak'u Caves. Incantation Shrine to the northwest.
Western Greilyn Jungle	West of the main road in the ruins (Usurper's location from The Hak'u Part II secondary quest). Incantation Shrine to the east.
Eastern Greilyn Beach	North along the main road. Incantation Shrine to the south.
Eirulan	Terrace of the Falls on the wooden bridge. Incantation Shrine at the terrace entrance.
Temple of Xeria	On a balcony on the west side of the room south of the Incantation Shrine.
A Tranquil Cave	Behind a waterfall on the western side of the road in the Northern Greilyn Jungle. Incantation Shrine to the north.
Snowbrook Haven Living Quarters	Eastern side of the living quarters just south of the Cavern of Frost. Incantation Shrine to the west (lower floor).
Arinth's Ravine	In the caves just before the Knotted Shambler; in the northeast alcove. Incantation Shrine in an adjacent cave.
Aman'lu Tavern and Inn	On a second-floor balcony. Incantation Shrine at the northwest of town.
A Cellar Beneath Aman'lu	Access the cellar from Tywlis the Mage's home. Incantation Shrine also in the cellar.
Garden of the Ancients (secret area)	In the southern section of the Garden of the Ancients, Part 2. The area is accessible only from the Azunite Burial Grounds. Find the spirit on the east side and an Incantation Shrine to the west.
Eastern Plain of Tears	North of the main road east of the area's teleporter. Incantation Shrine to the east.
Kalrathia	On the ramparts on the southwest side of Kalrathia, south of the teleporter. Incantation Shrine just outside the north gate.
Mines of Kaderak	Upper Mines of Kaderak, Part 2. Find the spirit north of the area's teleporter. Incantation Shrine on the highest floor to the east.
Darthrul	Southeast section of the center courtyard. Incantation Shrine in the District of the Crossbow to the southwest.
Agallan Chamber Beneath Kalrathia	In the southern cavern that leads to the southern waterway. Incantation Shrine to the east.
Zaramoth's Horns	On the south end of a ridge before the ruins. Incantation Shrine upstairs in the ruins.

Viperclaw

Speak with Eumenidie in Aman'lu to trigger this secondary quest. She's attempting to re-create the legendary reagent known as Viperclaw, and she needs your help. The tasks:

◆ Find these reagents: Jagged Arrowheads, Griffon Feather, and Onyx Fragment.

◆ Return to Eumenidie.

You'll find these reagents through normal play of primary and secondary quests, as well as available from Arcanists. Search chests and other containers diligently and remember which reagents you're searching for. There are also specific places to find these three reagents.

◆ Jagged Arrowheads: Leave Aman'lu via the north gate exit. While crossing the eastbound bridge right outside the town, double back towards the town to the south. The arrowheads are submerged in a corner of the creek.

◆ Griffon Feather: On the western side of the Elen'lu Isles, there is a lift that leads down into a flooded chamber. Once inside the chamber, fight your way west past the Taclak to another lift leading up. The Griffon Feather is on the eastern side of the island.

◆ Onyx Fragment: Take the Western End of Arinth's Ravine teleporter and follow the path south and west. The Onyx Fragment is hidden in a crevice in a small Vai'kesh cave.

Return all three to Eumenidie to complete the quest. Eumenidie crafts the Viperclaw from the three ingredients, and it's added to your inventory. The Viperclaw is a ranged-weapon-specific reagent and adds +15 to minimum and maximum damage, and +8 to +12 to death damage.

Arinth's Legendary Staff

Speak to Eolanda in Aman'lu to initiate this secondary quest. To complete the quest, you must have the Chant of the Dead. Complete the A Dark Ohm secondary quest to receive the chant. This quest is intended for level-26 characters. The tasks are listed below:

◆ Find the Carved Rod, Jeweled Staff, and Focusing Stone.

◆ Return to Eolanda in the town of Aman'lu with the pieces of Arinth's Legendary Staff.

You'll find the parts of Arinth's Legendary Staff in three separate dungeons spread across the game. The dungeons can be explored in any order. Before descending into the dungeons, find an Incantation Shrine and invoke the Chant of the Dead while standing on the shrine. The following list reveals all three locations and their contents.

Eolanda, Aman'lu's combat mage, initiates the quest to find the pieces to Arinth's staff.

1. Descend into one of the three legendary staff dungeons in the northern corner of the Northern Vai'lutra Forest, originally explored during Act II. Proceed north along the main path after the entrance from the Elven Hills, Part 2. There's an Incantation Shrine south of the entrance to invoke the Chant of the Dead. Descend the lift into the dungeon and walk to the northern end. With the incantation active, speak with the ghostly spirit (**1**). Open the big chest and receive the Carved Rod. A button on the east wall opens a treasure room near the lift.

An Ancient Elven Reliquary in Northern Vai'lutra Forest

Tip

All three dungeons in Arinth's Legendary Staff are labeled on the corresponding maps in the primary walkthrough sections. Check the maps in Parts 4 through 6 for precise locations of the dungeons that hold the three pieces of Arinth's staff.

2. Locate an entrance into one of the three legendary staff dungeons on the western side of Snowbrook Valley, explored during Act II. Find it along a river just northwest of a bridge and east of an Incantation Shrine (use it to invoke the Chant of the Dead). Speak with the ghostly spirit at the northern end of the dungeon. Open the chest to recover the Jeweled Staff. A button on the west side of the staircase opens a treasure room near the lift.

An Ancient Elven Reliquary in Snowbrook Valley

3. Find an entrance into one of the three legendary staff dungeons in the southwestern corner of Isteru's Caverns, originally explored during Act I. Find an Incantation Shrine (to invoke the Chant of the Dead) to the east. Find the ghostly spirit on the dungeon's southern side. Talk with the ghost then open the chest to recover the Stone of Focus.

An Ancient Elven Reliquary in Isteru's Caverns

After recovering all three pieces to Arinth's Legendary Staff, return to Aman'lu and speak with Eolanda. She reassembles the legendary staff, which you can add to your inventory and even equip. She also warns you not to take the staff to Arinth.

Arinth the Mad

You don't have to listen to Eolanda! Taking the staff to Arinth and freeing him offers the chance for some valuable rewards. Trigger this secondary quest by taking Arinth's Legendary Staff (reassembled during the secondary quest of the same name) to Arinth the Mad. Destroy the enchanted pillar using the staff to free Arinth. Prepare for the quest by increasing fire resistance—Arinth attacks with Fireball and Plasma Globes. This quest is intended for level-26 characters. You have one quest task:

◆ Track down and defeat Arinth.

An Elven Prison in the Lost Valley of the Azunites

The entrance into Arinth the Mad's Elven prison is on the eastern side of the Lost Valley of the Azunites, originally explored during Act I. It's directly east of the area's teleporter within some ruins. Descend the lift into the underground prison.

The initial chamber (**1**) contains a War Pedestal. A button in the northern room (**2**) opens the southern passage. Search for another button (**3**) in the south room to open a new passage to the southeast. Another button (**4**) opens the eastern passage. And finally, yet another button (**5**) exposes a spiral staircase to the east. Follow the staircase to find Arinth the Mad (**6**) incarcerated at the bottom. Equip Arinth's Legendary Staff and use it to break the enchanted pillar. Arinth escapes!

Before tracking down Arinth, increase your fire resistance to counter his fire spells, Fireball and Plasma Globes. Arinth can also cast Dehydrate (which lowers your fire resistance) and Wrath of Magic (which alters magic damage). Locate Arinth the Mad in the Temple of Istaura and Isteru in the Northern Vai'lutra Forest. Find the temple east of the area's teleporter. Arinth demands his staff and starts a battle! Defeat Arinth to recover his unique armor Arinth's Robe. After completing the quest, return to Eolanda in Aman'lu for an additional reward.

Mythrilhorn

Trigger this secondary quest by speaking with Pet Seller Galeron in Aman'lu. Ask him about special animals, and he tells of the Mythrilhorn, a powerful creature with a distinctive silver horn. If one can be caught, he could offer the mighty beast for sale. This quest is intended for level-33 characters. The quest tasks:

◆ Find Khartos the Wise and defeat him in a duel.

◆ Go to the Rift Site.

◆ Cover Khartos while he captures the Mythrilhorn. Speak to Khartos.

◆ Speak to Pet Seller Galeron in Aman'lu.

Find and speak with Khartos in the Kalrathia Tavern. Khartos is clearly drunk and more interested in a fight than conversation. Attack Khartos and defeat him in combat to complete the next task. Upon his defeat, he agrees to help with the Mythrilhorn search.

Locate Khartos' rift site in the northeast section of The Northern Plain of Tears (also northeast of the area's teleporter). Find Khartos (**1**) at the rift site already engaged in combat with hostile Morden. He approaches the rift (**2**) and Durvla flood the area. Attack the Durvla and any other creatures around Khartos.

Khartos' Rift Site in The Northern Plain of Tears

After the battle, speak with Khartos near the rift. The Mythrilhorn and Khartos leave the area. Return to Aman'lu and speak with Pet Seller Galeron in the pet shop. This completes the task and the Mythrilhorn becomes available for purchase at the Aman'lu Pet Shop.

A Family Heirloom, Part II

To initiate this secondary quest, you must first complete the A Family Heirloom secondary quest from Act I. After completing the quest, speak with Athelas in the Aman'lu Tavern. He claims that Master Thestrin, the old man you helped in the other secondary quest, is actually an agent of the Vai'kesh. The demon attacks with Multispark (lightning magic) and Leech Life (death magic), so prepare resistances. This quest is intended for level-26 characters. The quest tasks follow:

- ◆ Locate and destroy the demon.

- ◆ Speak with Athelas.

Locate the demon in a small Vai'kesh prison at the southern corner of the Vai'kesh Forest. The entrance is south of the area's teleporter near a Life Shrine. Walk into the dungeon and find the Demon of the Vai'kesh (**1**) at the southern end— released by Thestrin and the heirloom sword! Eliminate the demon. Along with his lightning and death-magic attacks, the demon can also cast Blind (which alters your chance to hit melee and ranged) and Infect (which alters cast rate and weakens death resistance). Recover the treasure, which includes the unique ring Soulreaver. Speak with Athelas (**2**) up the steps toward the dungeon's exit to complete the quest and receive your reward.

A Small Vai'kesh Prison in the Vai'kesh Forest

Defeat Thestrin's demon to complete the task.

The quest plays out differently if you didn't return the Heirloom Sword to Thestrin and decided to keep it for yourself. In this scenario, you must equip the Heirloom Sword to destroy the demon's prison and the demon.

Lothar's Innocence

With Lothar in your party, speak with Roland in the Aman'lu Tavern and Inn. Lothar plans to prove his innocence after Roland accuses the Half-Giant of thievery. This quest is intended for level-24 characters. The quest tasks are as follows:

- ◆ Find Roland's golden cloak.

- ◆ Find and defeat Magrus.

- ◆ Return to Roland.

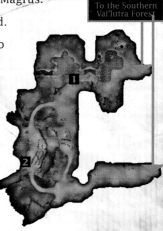

A Watery Cavern

Your first goal is to find the cave Roland spoke of and see if the cloak happens to be inside. Find the cave in the Southern Vai'lutra Forest. The cave contains primarily Forest Va'arths (**1**). Cross a rock bridge and find Magrus (**2**) on an elevated cliff on the cave's southwestern side. Speak with Magrus (with Lothar in your party) to discover he's the thief that stole Roland's cloak. Magrus disappears, leaving behind the Elven House Key quest item.

Locate Magrus's house north of the watery cavern within the Southern Vai'lutra Forest. It's on a side path east of the main road, in a small clearing (**3**). Open the door using the Elven House Key, and speak with Magrus. A battle ensues. Fight Magrus until he yields (when he has approximately 20% health remaining). Recover Roland's Golden Cloak quest item.

Magrus' House in Southern Vai'lutra Forest

Return to the Aman'lu Tavern and Inn and speak with Roland now that you have proof of Lothar's innocence. Collect your reward.

Deru's Treasure Hunt

With Deru in your party, locate Prospector Albain by the river in the southeast corner of Aman'lu (southeast of the pet shop). Speak with him and hear his story. You receive the Prospector's Key and the Prospector's Map. It reveals possible treasure in a ruined amphitheater. This quest is intended for level-19 characters. The quest tasks are listed below:

◆ Find and explore the location identified on the map the Elven prospector gave Deru.

◆ Find and explore the location identified by Razka's Riddle.

◆ Find and explore the location identified by Razka's Second Riddle.

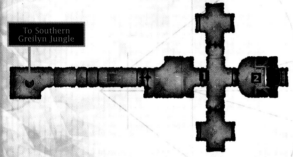

Razka's Ruins in the Southern Greilyn Jungle

You passed the ruined amphitheater during your exploration of the Southern Greilyn Jungle in Act I—it's Razka's Ruins (just west of the entrance into the Eastern Greilyn Jungle and east of the Southern Greilyn Jungle teleporter). Descend the lift at the bottom of the amphitheater. Combat mixed groups of Morden enemies (including a possible miniboss) then open the eastern locked door (**1**) using the Prospector's Key. Open the big chest (**2**) in the eastern room to receive Razka's Riddle and the Silver-Riddle Inscribed Key. Both point the way to the next treasure on this elaborate scavenger hunt.

Razka's Riddle reads "Use the key in the Frozen Heart of the Corrupted Forest." This describes a location in Arinth's Ravine, explored during Act II. Locate a frozen Vai'kesh cavern on the southern side of Arinth's Ravine (the first southern cave after the ravine's entrance from the Vai'kesh Forest). Defeat the Vai'kesh guarding their domain.

A Frozen Vai'kesh Cavern in Arinth's Ravine

Locate the locked door (**3**) south of the cavern entrance. Open the door using the Silver-Riddle Inscribed Key. Open the big chest (**4**) in the room beyond. Recover Razka's Second Riddle and the Golden-Riddle Inscribed Key.

A Magical Oasis in the Northern Plain of Tears

Razka's Second Riddle reads "Seek water in the heart of the desert." This describes a location in The Northern Plain of Tears, explored during Act III. Find a magical oasis in the northeast section of the Northern Plain of Tears.

Move east through the oasis to the locked door (**5**). Grab the Chant of Health from the lectern beside the door. Open the door using the Golden-Riddle Inscribed Key. Open the big chest (**6**) in the next room to receive the quest's rewards.

Mark of the Assassin

Initiate this secondary quest by picking up the intriguing stone inside an abandoned home near Aman'lu's south gate. The home is east of the main road. This quest is intended for level-35 characters. The quest's tasks:

- Pick up the intriguing stone.

- Encounter the assassin. Speak to Danadel.

- Investigate the Liantir Stone in the town of Kalrathia.

- Bring a Dwarven Mythril Ring to Enchantress Valeria in Kalrathia.

- Find Merchant Kendril.

- Find and defeat the assassin.

An assassin attacks after you pick up the stone. Danadel arrives and explains the situation. The stone was the Liantir Stone, the assassin's gift to the one he intends to kill. The intended target was Merchant Kendril. Danadel suggests traveling to Kalrathia and speaking with Enchantress Valeria about the stone.

Find Enchantress Valeria in the Kalrathia Magic Shop. Tell her Danadel of Aman'lu sent you. To escape the Liantir Stone's effects, you must kill the assassin who created it. However, that assassin is invisible to common men. Valeria promises to enchant a special ring that will allow you to see through the assassin's mirage. You must find a Dwarven Mythril Ring.

The Dwarven Mythril Ring is in the first part of the Upper Mines of Kaderak south of the entrance from The Desert of Kaderak. Pull a lever (1) in the southern room to open an adjacent hidden chamber. Open a Mystical Dwarven Chest (2) to locate the Dwarven Mythril Ring.

Return to the Kalrathia Magic Shop and speak with Enchantress Valeria with the Dwarven Mythril Ring in your inventory. She enchants the ring and it becomes the Dwarven Mythril Ring of Sight. Equip the ring.

To find the assassin, you must seek out his intended target, Merchant Kendril. Locate the

Dwarven Mythril Ring in Upper Mines of Kaderak, Part 1

merchant in the Kalrathia Inn (upstairs from the tavern) and speak with him. Luun the Assassin appears near the merchant. Battle and defeat Luun. Recover Geithaa and Citaa, two swords from Luun's Deathblades set. Speak with Merchant Kendril after defeating Luun for a gold reward.

The Aman'lu Arena

In the Aman'lu Tavern and Inn, speak with Barkeeper Drudwyn. Don't acknowledge any of his "adventurous" stories, and you'll learn of the Aman'lu Arena, a sort of underground fight club. This quest is intended for level-19 characters. The quest's tasks:

- Defeat nine waves of combatants in the Aman'lu Arena.

- Defeat the arena masters.

Proceed behind the bar in Aman'lu Tavern and find the lift station. Ride the lift into the wine cellar. Pull the west lever to open a passage. Speak with Tristeth (1) and say the password, "Cuivador," to gain entry. Descend the spiral staircase (2) to the arena.

A Cellar Beneath Aman'lu

Talk to Daesthai (3) inside the arena. To engage in a round of combat, you must purchase a token from Daesthai. Place the Arena Token on the pedestal (4) to begin combat. Defeat the wave of adversaries to receive a special key that unlocks a corresponding treasure room. Succeed against all nine waves, and you'll face the arena masters in the championship wave.

The Aman'lu Arena

Defeat the masters and receive a bonus key, the ability to purchase a special pet, and the title of Champion of the Aman'lu Arena.

The following table reveals all 10 rounds of the Aman'lu Arena and possible adversaries. Each wave includes at least one miniboss. After receiving the key rewards, search the corresponding treasure room in the arena. If you defeat the masters, take Daesthai's Gold Key to the door on the western side, behind the iron door. Speak with the Elf Summoner to purchase a special pet, the Light Naiad.

> **Tip**
>
> *If you need additional gold to purchase an Arena Token, sell any unneeded items to Daesthai!*

Wave	Token Cost	Enemies	Key
1	1,000	Taclak	Black Key of the First
2	1,500	Forest Va'arth	Blue Key of the Second
3	2,000	Vai'kesh	Turquoise Key of the Third
4	3,000	Undead Azunites	Green Key of the Fourth
5	4,000	Plagued Snowbrook Soldiers	Yellow Key of the Fifth
6	6,000	Korven	Orange Key of the Sixth
7	8,000	Morden-Durvla and Ganth	Red Key of the Seventh
8	12,000	Uhn	Purple Key of the Eighth
9	16,000	Qatall	Iron Key of the Ninth
Championship	25,000	Qatall Runeshapers and Rustguards	Daesthai's Gold Key

A Servant's Haunt, Part I

Talk to Eldoriath Wilwarin in South Aman'lu; he asks you to contact the ghost of his father, Threnith Wilwarin, former servant at the Levreth Estate. Threnith was accused of murdering his master and now haunts his former domain. This quest is intended for level-26 characters. The quest's tasks are as follows:

- Enter the Levreth Estate.
- Speak with the ghost of Threnith Wilwarin.
- Follow the ghost of Threnith Wilwarin and look for clues.

- Find the jewels of the Levreth Estate.
- Bring proof of Threnith's innocence back to Eldoriath Wilwarin in the town of Aman'lu.

To complete this secondary quest, you must have already earned the Chant of the Dead from the A Dark Ohm secondary quest. Invoke "Vox Mortem" at any Incantation Shrine before entering the Levreth Estate so you can speak with the ghost of Threnith Wilwarin.

The Levreth Estate

Find the entrance to the Levreth Estate in the Southern Vai'lutra Forest (east of the area's teleporter); the lift into the estate lies within a soaring atrium along the forest's main path. Descend a duo of lifts into the estate.

The lift into the Levreth Estate lies within this magnificent atrium.

Speak with the ghost (**1**) of Threnith Wilwarin and learn about his troubled past. Follow the ghost south and pick up a Portrait of the Lady of the Estate (**2**). Speak with the ghost again then follow Threnith west to find a Lock of Golden Hair (**3**). Speak to Threnith then follow him south to find the Burned Letter (**4**). Talk to the ghost then follow him into the western room again; a secret passage opens to the north. Open the big chest in the northern chamber (**5**) to recover the Jewels of the Levreth Estate. Before leaving, search the northern area of the estate for various forest beasts. Grab the Chant of Fighter Health from the lectern (**6**) in the northern room. Go into the northwest room and find a War Pedestal, a couple lecterns with the Chant of Mage Health and Chant of Ranger Health, and a hidden button (**7**) that opens a small treasure room.

Return to South Aman'lu and speak with Eldoriath Wilwarin in his home to complete the quest and receive your rewards.

A Servant's Haunt, Part II

Once you complete the secondary quest A Servant's Haunt, the ghost of Threnith Wilwarin appears and remains in Eldoriath Wilwarin's house in South Aman'lu. Speak with the ghost to initiate this follow-up secondary quest. This quest is intended for level-26 characters. The tasks:

- ◆ Confront Lady Levreth in the town of Eirulan.

- ◆ Confront and defeat Wethril the Guardian Commander in the town of Aman'lu.

- ◆ Speak with Celeb'hel the Elder in Aman'lu's Alt'orn Hall about the Guardian Commander's deception.

Lady Levreth was responsible for her husband's death and currently hangs out in the Eirulan Tavern. Travel there and confront her. She confesses to being involved in her husband's death, but it was her brother, the Guardian Commander of Aman'lu, who committed the act. Find Wethril, Celeb'hel the Elder's most trusted advisor, inside Alt'orn Hall in Aman'lu.

Speak with Wethril; he doesn't appreciate the accusation, and he attacks! Kill Wethril (resistant to ice magic). Complete the quest by speaking with Celeb'hel the Elder about Wethril's crime and deception.

You must have Amren as a current party member to initiate his unique character quest. Begin the quest by finding one of the four circular mushroom formations scattered throughout the game. Approach a mushroom circle to trigger Amren's vision. The circle hides a lift; use one of the mushrooms as a lever to lower the lift. Your goal is to locate and explore all four locations revealed in the vision. This quest is intended for level-19 characters. Quest tasks:

- ◆ Find and explore the first, second, third, and fourth locations in Amren's visions.

- ◆ Investigate the portal in Amren's vision.

Tip

All four of Amren's mushroom circles are labeled on the corresponding map in the primary walkthrough sections. Check the maps in Parts 4 through 6 for precise locations of the mushroom circles in Amren's vision.

You can visit Amren's vision locations in any order. The list below reveals all four locations and their contents.

1. Find a mushroom circle from Amren's vision in the Eastern Greilyn Jungle, originally visited during Act I. After descending into the small shrine, go south and find The Path of Life Lore Book (**1**) near a doorway (**2**) that only Amren can open. Use the statue (**3**) in the southern room. This shrine contains the Tree of Life Azunite symbol.

Amren's Vision Location 1—A Mysterious Shrine in the Eastern Greilyn Jungle

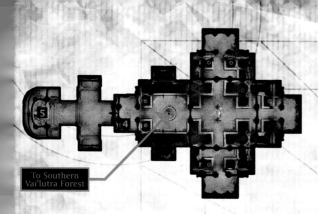

3. Discover a mushroom circle in the Garden of the Ancients, originally explored during Act II. Enter the mysterious shrine and proceed south. Pick up The Path of Death Lore Book (**6**) before using the statue (**7**)

Amren's Vision Location 2—A Mysterious Shrine in the Southern Vai'lutra Forest

Amren's Vision Location 3—A Mysterious Shrine in the Garden of the Ancients

2. Locate a mushroom circle in the Southern Vai'lutra Forest, originally visited during Act II. Descend into the mysterious shrine and go west. Grab The Path of the Sight Lore Book (**4**) and use the statue (**5**). This shrine features the Eye of Sight Azunite symbol.

in the southern corner. This shrine features the Tree of Death Azunite symbol.

Guide Amren to the four locations revealed in his vision.

Amren's Vision Location 4—A Mysterious Shrine in The Ruins of Okaym

4. Find a mushroom circle in The Ruins of Okaym, originally visited during Act III. Descend into the mysterious shrine and go west. Grab The Path of Blindness Lore Book (**8**) and use the statue (**9**) in the corner. This shrine contains the Eye of Darkness Azunite symbol.

Amren's Vision Reward Dungeon

After exploring all four mushroom circle shrines and activating all four statues, a portal in each shrine's center activates. Enter any one of the four mysterious portals to journey to Amren's reward. Open the big chest (**10**) to the west and recover the Virtuous Rebellion unique bow among other valuable treasures.

Finala's Contempt

Finala's unique secondary quest begins when you locate a broken lift—Finala must be in your party at the time. She's Aman'lu's engineer and quite handy at fixing things. This quest is intended for level-22 characters. Quest tasks:

- Explore the hidden Morden intelligence camp.
- Burn down the Morden towers in the Southern Greilyn Jungle and the Northern Greilyn Jungle.
- Destroy the hatchery.
- Find and explore the second Morden intelligence camp.

Find a broken lift in the Upper Kithraya Caverns near the exit into the Kithraya Valley. With Finala selected in your party, attempt to use the lift; Finala repairs

A Hidden Morden Stronghold in the Upper Kithraya Caverns

the lever and you can descend into the Morden camp. Loot various containers and search the western corner (**1**) for a big chest that contains Morden battle plans (describing the attack at the game's beginning) and a map revealing the location of hidden Morden towers. You receive the Morden Map of the Greilyn Jungle.

Explore the Southern Greilyn Jungle originally visited during Act I. Find some abandoned ruins south of the primary road. Finala discovers a secret door on the eastern wall (**2**), which automatically lowers when Finala moves near. Traverse the eastern cavern, a hidden Morden passage, to a lift (**3**) that returns to the jungle. There's a hidden Morden tower near the lift (**4**). Defeat any Morden guards then burn down the tower using the same method as you did during the Act I primary quest. Break the wooden cage; pick up and equip the cage fragment; use the cage fragment on the campfire;

Some Abandoned Ruins in the Southern Greilyn Jungle

Hidden Morden Tower in the Southern Greilyn Jungle

then use the flaming cage fragment on the tower. When finished, search the path north for more Morden and potential treasure.

There are ruins just north of the Northern Greilyn Jungle teleporter. Approach the ruins with Finala in your party to open the secret door (**5**). Explore the new path southeast to discover the second hidden Morden tower (**6**). Crush any defenders and burn the tower. Follow the path north and burn a third (**7**) and fourth (**8**) tower to complete the task.

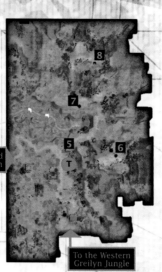

Hidden Morden Towers in the Northern Greilyn Jungle

Upon burning down the last tower, Finala recovers a map and the Morden Elevator Gear quest item. The map (the City of Darthrul) reveals the location of a secret Durvla hatchery and another Morden intelligence camp.

Hidden Hatchery Entrance in Darthrul

You'll explore the Morden city of Darthrul during Act III. With Finala in the party, search the walls at the end of the eastern alcove (**9**). A secret passage opens into the Durvla hatchery.

Defeat mixed groups of Morden-Durvla and Morden-Viir throughout (**10**) the hidden hatchery. Eliminate enemies around the southern corner and locate the bomb near the gate (**11**). Attack the bomb to destroy the hatchery. Open the gate and search the big chest. You receive the Morden Wrench quest item. You now have two quest items to repair the next broken elevator.

A Durvla Hatchery

Locate the broken lift over the second Morden intelligence camp in the Desert of Kaderak; find it on a hill (**12**) just north of the teleporter. Approach the lever with Finala and use the broken lever to administer repairs. Descend into the large Morden intelligence camp.

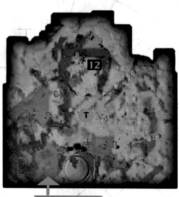

Second Morden Intelligence Camp Entrance in the Desert of Kaderak

Combat mixed squads of Morden-Durvla, Morden-Viir, and Morden-Urg protecting their underground camp. Expect to encounter a Morden miniboss near the northern side. You must defeat all enemies before you can open the north-eastern gate (**13**). Open the big chest in the alcove (**14**) to recover more battle plans and your quest rewards.

A Large Morden Intelligence Camp

Rahvan's Curse

Initiate this secondary quest by returning all four Champion's Death Masks to Rahvan during the Act II primary quest Princess Evangeline. See Part 5 for the complete solution and maps for recovering all four masks. Speak with Rahvan after returning all four masks to trigger this quest. Prepare for Letiso by equipping spells or weapons that inflict fire damage. Letiso uses Leech Life, a death-magic spell, and can summon bone minions. This quest is intended for level-28 characters. The quest's tasks are as follows:

◆ Find and defeat Letiso the Lich.

◆ Return Captain Rahvan's Soulstone.

Letiso the Lich in the Azunite Catacombs

Rahvan says to find Letiso in the Azunite Catacombs. You must stand on the Azunite Symbol of Death outside in a southern alcove within the Azunite Catacombs, and speak the name "Letiso" to enter. It's just west of the lift used after using the symbol-combination mechanism.

The southern alcove (**1**) contains a War Pedestal before the floor symbol. Stand on the Azunite Symbol of Death (**2**), the dying tree, and open the chat window. Speak the word "Letiso" to open the tomb. Defeat Letiso the Lich (resistant to ice and death magic and weak to fire) and recover the Rahvan's Soulstone. Letiso can resurrect fallen undead, so it's wise to eliminate Letiso quickly. Letiso's chamber (**3**) also includes a lectern with the Chant of Purity. Return to Rahvan and speak with him to return the Soulstone and receive your reward, which includes the unique ring Rahvan's Fist.

Evangeline's Folly

Add Evangeline to your party and return to the caravan in the Southern Vai'lutra Forest (near the area's south teleporter). Speak with the wounded caravan driver Mylindril. He reveals that the Vai'kesh kidnapped Jessic and other soldiers; the Vai'kesh took the prisoners deep inside the dark Elves' territory. This quest is intended for level-28 characters. Your task:

◆ Seek Jessic and the soldiers in the first, second, and third Vai'kesh stronghold.

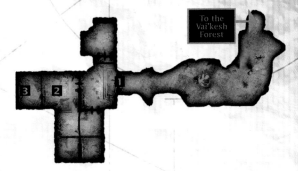

A Small Vai'kesh Cave in the Vai'kesh Forest

The caravan prisoners have been taken into three separate locations: two Vai'kesh caves and the Vai'kesh stronghold. The two caves contain captured royal guards and the stronghold holds the captive Jessic.

Return to the caravan with Eva in your party and speak with the wounded driver.

Find the first small Vai'kesh cave in the Vai'kesh Forest. It's in a southern alcove east of the area's teleporter (follow the main road). Defeat Vai'kesh defenders and approach the closed door (**1**) to the west. Speak with the Vai'kesh Zealot on the other side of the door. Eva gets the party inside. Eliminate the Vai'kesh Jailor (**2**) inside to recover the Bronze Vai'kesh Jail Key (the jailors are weak to lightning and resistant to death magic). Free the Royal Guard of the Northern Reaches (**3**) using the Bronze Key and speak with him.

Find the second Vai'kesh stronghold in a large cavern in Arinth's Ravine. It's the first northern cave east of the area's western teleporter. Defeat the Vai'kesh defending the cavern. Approach the closed door on the western side (**4**). Eva again talks her way inside the Vai'kesh cave. Battle the Vai'kesh defenders and the Jailor (**5**) to recover the Silver Vai'kesh Jail Key. Use the key to free another Royal Guard of the Northern Reaches (**6**). Talk with the guard.

A Large Vai'kesh Cavern in Arinth's Ravine

Locate the third Vai'kesh stronghold in Arinth's Ravine. It's on the northern side east of the second Vai'kesh cavern containing one of the guard prisoners. Eva breaks down the strong-

A Large Vai'kesh Cavern in Arinth's Ravine

hold door. Battle the Vai'kesh defenders. Use a War Pedestal to recharge a power (**7**). Defeat the Vai'kesh Jailor (**8**) to the west and recover the Gold Vai'kesh Jail Key. Move to the eastern side of the stronghold. Open a melee Sanctuary Door (level 24) to find treasure (**9**). Find another War Pedestal (**10**) near the jail cells. Use the Gold Key to free Jessic from his cell (**11**). Open the big chest inside the cell to receive your quest rewards.

Act III Secondary Quests

Dwarven Song of Ore

Find Historian Leontia in Kalrathia Hall and speak with her. Select the dialogue option "How might I assist you?" to initiate the quest. She's searching for stanzas from the Dwarven Song of Ore. All stanzas can be found in the Mines of Kaderak. This quest is intended for level-35 characters. The quest tasks:

- Find the Silver, Iron, and Gold Stanzas.

- Return all stanzas, including the bonus fourth Mythril Stanza, to Historian Leontia.

Silver Stanza Location in the Upper Mines of Kaderak, Part 1

Travel through The Desert of Kaderak and descend into the Upper Mines of Kaderak. Locate the Silver Stanza in an Ancient Dwarven Chest (**1**) east of the teleporter and the Life Shrine. Open the chest to recover the quest item automatically.

The Iron Stanza is in the Upper Mines of Kaderak, Part 2. From the area's teleporter, walk north up the eastern steps and move through rooms toward the western side. Find the Ancient Dwarven Chest (**2**) in a room on the western edge. Open the chest to recover the Iron Stanza quest item.

Iron Stanza Location in the Upper Mines of Kaderak, Part 2

Find the Gold Stanza in the southeastern area of the Upper Mines of Kaderak, Part 2. Move south from the Shard destroyed in the primary quest. Go into the western barracks and pull a hidden lever to expose the room that contains the Ancient Dwarven Chest (**3**). Open the chest to receive the Gold Stanza quest item.

Gold Stanza Location in the Upper Mines of Kaderak, Part 2

Before returning to Kalrathia, locate a bonus stanza in the Lower Mines of Kaderak. Explore the dead-end path south of the area's teleporter (west of the entrance into the Summit of the Dark Wizards). Find the Ancient Dwarven Chest (**4**) in the back corner. Open the chest to receive the Mythril Stanza quest item.

Return to Kalrathia Hall and speak with Historian Leontia after you've collected all the stanzas. She rewards your effort with two incantations: the Chant of Prosperity for finding three stanzas and the Greater Chant of Prosperity for finding all four. Find all four to also receive the unique ring, Stoutgrip.

Mythril Stanza in the Lower Mines of Kaderak

The Lore of Aranna

Talk to Telgrey the Scholar in a home in the northeast corner of the top level of Kalrathia to initiate this secondary quest. Telgrey hopes to collect all 20 volumes of the Lore of Aranna Lore Book collection. These Lore Books are scattered throughout the game. This quest is intended for level-33 characters. The quest's task:

◆ Find the Lore of Aranna collection and return to Telgrey the Scholar.

The table on the next page reveals all 20 volumes and their locations. Return to Telgrey with all 20 volumes to receive the quest rewards.

Volume	Title	Location
1	Kings and Queens of the Northern Reaches	Snowbrook Haven Living Quarters, upper level near the bridge
2	The Dark Wizards	Vai'kesh Sanctuary
3	Downfall of the Manu Ostar	Alar'ithil in South Aman'lu
4	Valdis and his Armies	Tywlis's house in Aman'lu
5	Turmanar and its Aftermath	Alt'orn Hall in Aman'lu
6	The Skath	Near Vix in the Eastern Greilyn Jungle
7	The Deeds of Xeria	Windstone Fortress Gatehouse
8	The Death of Xeria	Temple of Xeria
9	The War of Legions	Temple of Xeria
10	The Legend of Arinth the Mad	Eolanda in Aman'lu
11	The Dryads and their Customs	Near Eolanda in Aman'lu
12	Zaramoth's Ascendance and Downfall	Aman'lu Magic Shop
13	Elandir's Life and Teachings	Aman'lu Tavern and Inn
14	Fables and Ancient Artifacts	Near Eolanda in Aman'lu
15	Symbology of the Azunites	Aman'lu Magic Shop
16	The Legacy of Azunai	Kalrathia, in a room on the northeastern side
17	The Path of the Life	A mysterious shrine in the Eastern Greilyn Jungle (part of the Amren's Vision quest)
18	The Path of the Sighted Eye	A mysterious shrine in the Southern Vai'lutra Forest (part of the Amren's Vision quest)
19	The Path of Death	A mysterious shrine in The Garden of the Ancients (part of the Amren's Vision quest)
20	The Path of Blindness	A mysterious shrine in The Ruins of Okaym (part of the Amren's Vision quest)

The Lost Jewels of Soranith

Begin this secondary quest by speaking to Kevarre the Explorer in the Kalrathia Tavern. The ancient vault is in The Northern Plain of Tears. Follow the aqueduct to a tall, stone tower then head east and down the hill. A tower on the right side leads into the vault. This quest is intended for level-33 characters. Tasks are:

◆ Enter the ancient vault.

◆ Solve the second puzzle within the vault and see if there are any jewels locked within.

◆ Solve the third puzzle within the vault and investigate the area for more jewels.

◆ Return to Kevarre the Explorer in the Kalrathia Tavern.

To the Northern Plain of Tears

Proceed south into the vault. Encounter Korven lurking through the halls. Kevarre has already solved the first puzzle room (**1**). Move south into the next puzzle room (**2**) and defeat the occupying Korven.

There are five buttons in the room. Pressing a button creates a glowing blue line to another button. You must activate the buttons in a specific order—including pressing some more than once—to fill the grooves with the glowing blue light. The goal is to "draw" an unbroken line without doubling the line on any path. These puzzles have multiple solutions.

A Mysterious Vault in the Northern Plain of Tears

Activate the buttons in the order shown on the map. If needed, use the statue on the room's southern end to reset the puzzle.

After solving the second puzzle, go south and enter the western room to find a big chest (**3**). Open it and recover Soranith's Silver Ring from the Secrets of the Forgotten set. Continue south down the spiral staircase and enter the third puzzle room: now with nine statues (**4**).

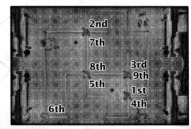

Puzzle Solution: Five-Button Room

The puzzle is similar to the second. Activate the buttons in the order shown on the map below. Once you've completed the puzzle, continue south to the big chest (**5**). Grab the mysterious chant, the Greater Chant of Random Item, from the lectern then open the chest and recover Soranith's Gold Ring.

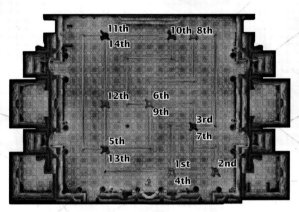

Puzzle Solution: Nine-Button Room

Return to Kalrathia with both rings and speak to Kevarre the Explorer in the Kalrathia Tavern. He rewards your effort with the third piece of the Secrets of the Forgotten set: Soranith's Amulet.

The Legendary Mace of Agarrus

Initiate this secondary quest by speaking with Berseba in Kalrathia's lower courtyard. She points the way to an explorer in Aman'lu that has information on the mythical mace. This quest is intended for level-33 characters. The quest's tasks:

- ◆ Talk to Explorer Tai'esse in Aman'lu.
- ◆ Find the stone tablet fragment.
- ◆ Return the stone tablet fragment to Explorer Tai'esse in Aman'lu.
- ◆ Enter the Tomb of Agarrus and locate the mace.

Proceed to the Aman'lu Tavern and find Explorer Tai'esse inside. Speak with her and ask her about the history of the Mace of Agarrus. She has recovered many fragments of a stone tablet that's rumored to identify the final resting place of the mace—but she's missing one

small fragment. Tai'esse hands you the Stone Key quest item and tells you the fragment's in the Snowbrook Grotto, an underground side area in the Snowbrook Foothills.

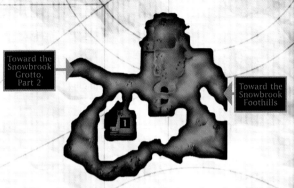

The Missing Fragment in the Snowbrook Grotto

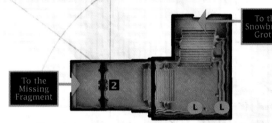

The Missing Fragment in the Snowbrook Grotto

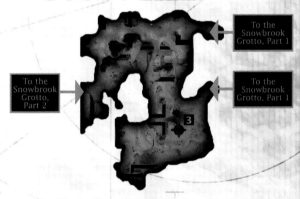

The Missing Fragment in The Snowbrook Grotto

Explore the Snowbrook Grotto. Descend a staircase (**1**) in the southern section of the grotto. If you didn't find them previously, grab the Chant of Magic Skill and Chant of Melee Skill from the lecterns. Follow the staircase to a locked door (**2**). The Stone Key Tai'esse provided opens the door. Continue through the passage and find the stone tablet fragment (**3**) on the dungeon floor.

Return to the Aman'lu Tavern and speak with Explorer Tai'esse after recovering the tablet fragment. Tai'esse reassembles the tablet and discovers the mace's location in the Lost Valley of the Azunites. The stone tablet is the key to unlocking the Tomb of Agarrus. You receive the Repaired Stone Tablet quest item.

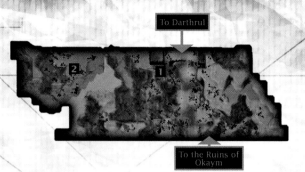

Finding the Apprentice in the Ruins of Okaym

The Tomb of Agarrus is in an Azunite cavern first explored during Act I. The entrance into the tomb is west of the mirror puzzle you solved to reach the Lost Vault of the Azunites. The button that controls the lift is under a breakable rock. Destroy the rock then use the button to lower the lift into the tomb. The Repaired Stone Tablet opens the door to the north (**4**). Speak with Guardian Magentus inside the next chamber (**5**).

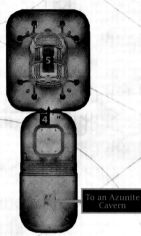

The Tomb of Agarrus in an Azunite Cavern

After a brief conversation, he rewards you with a unique weapon: the Mace of Agarrus.

The Mage's Apprentice

Talk to Mage Boden in the Kalrathia Magic Shop to begin this secondary quest. He asks you to search for his missing apprentice as well as his research journal. This quest is intended for level-34 characters. Quest tasks are as follows:

◆ Find Apprentice Darek and Mage Boden's research journal.

◆ Return to Mage Boden with his journal. Defeat Mage Boden.

◆ Speak with Apprentice Darek.

After speaking with Mage Boden, you receive the Golden Mirror quest item. Find the entrance into the dungeon containing the apprentice in the Ruins of Okaym. Go north toward the city of Darthrul. Right before the bridge into Darthrul, look west toward the tower. Find a narrow path (**1**) around the tower. Go through the trench and locate the dungeon entrance (**2**) on the opposite side.

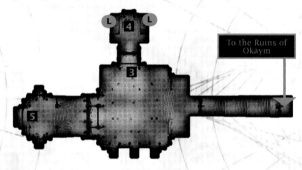

Some Ancient Ruins in the Ruins of Okaym

Move west through the corridor and into a room with many statues and mirrors. The northernmost statue lacks a mirror (**3**). Click on the statue to automatically attach the Golden Mirror quest item. There are two locked doors in the chamber, one to the west and one to the north. The goal is to adjust the statues to bounce a beam of light off the mirrors and toward one of the locked doors. (See the accompanying graphics for each puzzle solution.)

Apprentice Darek (**4**) is behind the northern locked door. Treasure is behind the western locked door. Opening the north door is part of the quest; opening the western door nets additional treasure. The room holding Apprentice Darek also contains a couple lecterns with the Greater Chant of Casting and Greater Chant of Fighter Power.

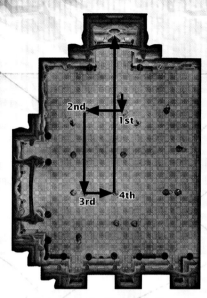

Unlocking the Northern Door

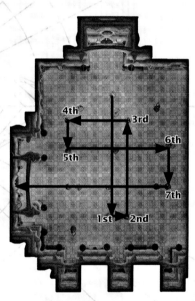

Unlocking the Western Door

Mage Boden had his apprentice locked away, and the research journal is proof of Boden's involvement with the Morden. You receive the Journal of the Mage's Apprentice quest item. Gather a couple of chants from their lecterns before leaving the room.

Return to the Kalrathia Magic Shop. Before you speak with Boden, boost fire resistances to prepare for his fire damage attacks. Speak with Boden after recovering his journal. After you expose his collaboration with the Morden, Boden attacks. Fire resistance will help protect you from his Firespray spell and the Thrusk he may summon. Mage Boden is also 100% resistant to freeze, stun, silence, slow, ignite, immobilize, knockback, slide, and fear attacks. Eliminate him then speak with Apprentice Darek; he shows up after the battle. Now you'll speak with Apprentice Darek to shop for spells, potions, and magic jewelry! Your reward also includes the Spellbinder unique ring.

The Kalrathian Nexus

Talk to Nora the Nature Mage in Kalrathia to initiate this secondary quest. She asks you to imbue a Soulstaff at three separate locations and use the imbued staff to destroy a seal placed over the Kalrathian Nexus. This quest is intended for level-33 characters. Quest tasks:

◆ Imbue the Soulstaff at the Node of Earth, Node of Frost, and Node of the Phoenix.

◆ Use the Soulstaff of the Elements to destroy the seal on the Kalrathian Nexus.

◆ Return to Nora.

1. Locate the Cavern of the Phoenix in the southern edge of the Lost Valley of the Azunites, originally explored during Act I. Go south from the area's teleporter until you reach

The Cavern of the Phoenix in the Lost Valley of the Azunites

the very bottom of the map. As instructed by Nora, move to the symbol on the floor (**1**) in the cavern's center. Equip the Soulstaff and invoke the chant "Arcesso Arcanum" to imbue the staff at this node.

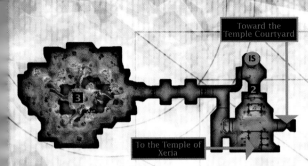

The Cavern of Earth in the Temple of Xeria

2. The Cavern of Earth is in the Temple of Xeria (originally explored during Act I), west of the area's teleporter. Go to the temple's northern end near the Incantation Shrine. Activate the statue (**2**) to open a western passage. Proceed west into the cavern. Stand on the symbol in the cavern's center (**3**). Equip the Soulstaff and invoke the chant "Arcesso Arcanum" to imbue the staff at this node.

3. Find the Cavern of Frost in the northeastern section of the Snowbrook Haven Servants' Quarters, originally explored during Act II. Instead of exiting the area on the western side, explore the north-

The Cavern of Frost in the Snowbrook Haven Living Quarters

eastern route to find the cavern. Stand on the symbol in the cavern's center (**4**). Equip the Soulstaff and invoke the chant "Arcesso Arcanum" to imbue the staff at this node.

4. After imbuing the staff at the three cavern nodes, travel to the Eastern Plain of Tears. Find a cave on the northern edge of the area just east of Kalrathia. The cave is the Kalrathian Nexus. Walk to the seal of dark magic (**5**) in the cave's center. Equip the Soulstaff and attack the seal. Pick up the Sigil of the Kalrathian Nexus.

The Kalrathian Nexus in the Eastern Plain of Tears

Return to Kalrathia and speak with Nora. She combines the Soulstaff and the Sigil you recovered to create a unique weapon, the Soulstaff of the Nexus, as your reward for completing the quest.

Sartan's Suspicion

With Sartan in your party, travel to the Kalrathia Tavern and speak with Feltan the Drunkard. He mentions Osric, a possible spy for the Morden that's traveled here from Windstone Fortress. Feltan thinks Osric is hiding in a cave in the Eastern Plain of Tears. This quest is intended for level-33 characters. The tasks:

◆ Find Osric, a suspected spy working for the Morden.

◆ Find the Morden arsenal. Free the prisoners.

◆ Return to Soldier Orayne.

Locate Osric's hideout in the south-eastern corner of the Eastern Plain of Tears. Proceed east through the mysterious cavern. Search northern alcoves for treasure (a button opens a hidden room) and the southern alcove for a melee Sanctuary Door (level 31).

A Mysterious Cavern in the Eastern Plain of Tears

Act III Secondary Quests

Go to the cavern's eastern side and click on the door (**1**). After a brief discussion, Sartan gets inside the room and eliminates Osric, the spy...or was he? It turns out Osric was working undercover trying to locate a secret Morden arsenal. He wasn't a traitor. Sartan attempts to redeem his mistake by taking over Osric's mission.

Help Sartan find redemption by locating the Morden arsenal and freeing its prisoners.

The Morden arsenal is in the Ruins of Okaym. Find the entrance west of the area's teleporter. Knock on the entrance door (**2**), which Sartan breaks down. Defeat

A Morden Arsenal in the Ruins of Okaym

the Morden guarding the initial room; there's a War Pedestal in the corner in case you need to recharge a power.

Explore a northern room for a button (**3**) that opens a side treasure chamber. The western and southern paths connect (**4**). Continue west toward the prison cells (**5**). Detonate the four bombs in front of the cell doors to free the prisoners. Check the southwestern cell for a big chest containing the quest's rewards. Return to Soldier Orayne in the mysterious cavern in the Eastern Plain of Tears and speak with him to conclude the quest.

The Morden Riders

Initiate this secondary quest by talking to Nordax or Neilliok, disgruntled Morden Riders in a hidden camp east of the city of Darthrul. This quest is intended for level-35 characters. The quest tasks are as follows:

◆ Find a Morden Tent, a Sack of Morden Rations, and a Pack of Klask Rations.

◆ Bring the supplies to Nordax and Neilliok.

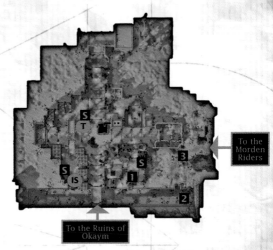

The City of Darthrul

The Morden Riders in a Desert Canyon

Explore the southeastern district of Darthrul (you'll need a key to the District of the Lance which is found during the Act III primary quest The Morden Chief) and find a lift station (**1**) in the southeastern corner. Descend on the lift and walk out to the trench. Follow the trench east; harvest potions from a group of health bushes (**2**) before climbing the steps north. Follow the path east of Darthrul (**3**). Battle assorted groups of Blastwings, Shaggrots, Korven, Morden, Mercrus, and Mucrim.

Find Nordax and Neilliok (**4**) with their pet Klask northeast near the wall. Speak with either rider. The riders were exiled from the Morden and need supplies to continue their journey. You receive the Darthrul Supply Key. There are three locked supply vaults in Darthrul; each one contains supplies (see the following list). Return to the riders with all three supplies to complete the quest.

◆ A supply room is in the southeast district just northeast of the lift you used to reach the trench. Open the Morden Supply Chest and receive the Pack of Klask Rations.

◆ Explore the southwest district (District of the Crossbow) and find the supply room near the Incantation Shrine along the southern wall. Open the chest to recover the Morden Tent.

◆ Find the third supply room in the northwest district (District of the Lance) north of the area's teleporter. The chest contains the Sack of Morden Rations.

Return to Nordax and Neilliok with all three supplies. Your reward: the riders' pet Klask Bruno knocks down the wall, permitting access to the treasure vault (**5**) in the adjacent canyon.

Vix's Vengeance

With Vix in your party, go to the Lower Mines of Kaderak. There's a door on the eastern side (near the entrance from the Upper Mines of Kaderak, Part 2). Click on the door; Vix suggests exploring the additional mine caverns to ensure all Shards are destroyed. This quest is intended for level-37 characters. Quest tasks are as follows:

◆ Investigate the additional mine caverns Vix discovered.

◆ Destroy the first, second, and third cluster of Shards.

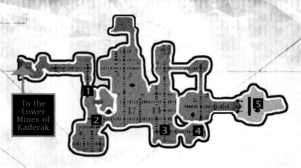

Additional Mine Caverns in the Lower Mines of Kaderak

There are three Shard clusters in the additional cavern. Move down the ramp and then east from the start position to locate the first Shard. Use the lever on the floor to adjust the track, then activate the second lever to send the mine cart into the first Shard (**1**). Proceed through the tunnel left empty by the demolished Shard.

Locate the second Shard, south of the first. Perform the same actions: use the lever to adjust the track then a second lever to move the mine cart into the Shard. Destroy the second Shard (**2**) like the first, then move through the vacant tunnel.

Move east, and when you reach the larger chamber, find the third Shard to the southeast (**3**). Use the levers to adjust the track and send the mine cart into the Shard. Explore the tunnel behind the former Shard cluster to discover a big chest (**4**) holding your quest rewards.

Tip

*From the third Shard, find a bridge to the north. Go east across this bridge and then south across a second bridge. Continue east into a magnificent side cavern (**5**). Enjoy the view!*

PART 8
STATISTICS

This section compiles *Dungeon Siege II* *statistics, including class skills and powers, weapons, armor, monsters, unique items, set items, and spells.*

Explanations for certain table entries follow (spell entries are explained in their sections):

- **1H/2H**: The number of hands required to wield the weapon.

- **Bonuses**: The unique item's benefits.

- **Defense**: The armor's Defense rating. The higher the rating, the better the defense.

- **Effects**: The prefix or suffix's effect or modification to a particular item.

- **Object Types**: The types of objects the enchantment can affect. For example, "Melee" means the enchantment can be applied to a melee weapon, "Ranged" means it affects a ranged weapon, and "Mage" means the enchantment can be applied to a mage weapon.

- **Range**: The bow, crossbow, or thrown weapons' range in meters. The greater the number, the longer the weapon's attack range.

- **Requirements**: The class-level requirements to equip the armor.

- **Resists**: The percentage of the different resistances the monster possesses.

- **Spell**: Any spells used by the monster.

- **Value**: The formula governing the incantation's benefits.

- **XP**: The number of experience points received from slaying the monster.

Class Skills

This section provides statistics for every class skill at every possible level. You receive one skill point for each character level gained. It's important to spend your skill points wisely! See Part 2, "Character Development," for strategies on maximizing your skill choices.

Melee Skills

FORTITUDE

Adding points to Fortitude increases your character's maximum health and meets a prerequisite for unlocking the Whirling Strike power. Health is certainly vital to the Melee class, which is always in the thick of battle. Unless you're specifically trying to unlock Whirling Strike, focus most of your skill points elsewhere, though. You can use equipment modifiers to boost maximum health and health regeneration and save your points for specialized skills. Half-Giants possess two points in Fortitude.

Prerequisite: Melee Level 1

Level	Maximum Health +%	Cumulative Total
1	+6%	6%
2	+4%	10%
3	+4%	14%
4	+4%	18%
5	+3%	21%
6	+3%	24%
7	+2%	26%
8	+2%	28%
9	+2%	30%
10	+2%	32%
11	+2%	34%
12	+2%	36%
13	+2%	38%
14	+1%	39%
15	+1%	40%
16	+1%	41%

(continued)

Level	Maximum Health +%	Cumulative Total
17	+1%	42%
18	+1%	43%
19	+1%	44%
20	+1%	45%

Critical Strike

The Critical Strike skill increases your character's chance of inflicting 200% damage in a single attack. Add points to Critical Strike if you want to unlock the Brutal Attack, Whirling Strike, War Cry, or Elemental Rage powers. Ten to eleven points in Critical Strike provide a strong chance, as approximately every two out of five hits will inflict 200% damage. The Elf race features one point in Critical Strike.

Prerequisite: Melee Level 1

Level	Chance to Inflict Critical Hit +%	Cumulative Total
1	+8%	8%
2	+6%	14%
3	+4%	18%
4	+4%	22%
5	+3.5%	25.5%
6	+3%	28.5%
7	+2.5%	31%
8	+2.5%	33.5%
9	+2.5%	36%
10	+2%	38%
11	+2%	40%
12	+1.5%	41.5%
13	+1.5%	43%
14	+1.5%	44.5%
15	+1.5%	46%
16	+1%	47%
17	+1%	48%
18	+1%	49%
19	+0.5%	49.5%
20	+0.5%	50%

Barricade

Barricade is the prerequisite for equipping shields and can increase your character's Defense dramatically. You should add points to Barricade only if you plan to equip a shield. Changing to a two-handed weapon or dual-wielding later in the game will weaken your character; points in Barricade will be essentially wasted. Adding points to Barricade meets the prerequisite for the Provoke power.

Prerequisites: Melee Level 5, Fortitude Level 1

Level	Shield Armor +%	Cumulative Total	Chance to Block Melee and Ranged Attack +%	Cumulative Total
1	+20%	20%	+2%	2%
2	+15%	35%	+2%	4%
3	+10%	45%	+2%	6%
4	+10%	55%	+2%	8%
5	+8%	63%	+1%	9%
6	+7%	70%	+1%	10%
7	+6%	76%	+1%	11%
8	+6%	82%	+1%	12%
9	+6%	88%	+1%	13%
10	+5%	93%	+1%	14%
11	+5%	98%	+1%	15%
12	+4%	102%	+1%	16%
13	+4%	106%	+0.5%	16.5%
14	+3%	109%	+0.5%	17%
15	+3%	112%	+0.5%	17.5%
16	+2%	114%	+0.5%	18%
17	+2%	116%	+0.5%	18.5%
18	+2%	118%	+0.5%	19%
19	+1%	119%	+0.5%	19.5%
20	+1%	120%	+0.5%	20%

Overbear

Overbear is the prerequisite for equipping a two-handed weapon and increases your two-handed weapon's damage. You should add points to Overbear only if you plan to equip a two-handed weapon; otherwise you're wasting points that would be better spent on your primary weapon or defensive choice. Overbear is the primary prerequisite for the Staggering Blow power.

Prerequisites: Melee Level 5, Critical Strike Level 1

Level	Two-handed Weapon Damage +%	Cumulative Total
1	+8%	8%
2	+6%	14%
3	+4%	18%
4	+4%	22%
5	+3.5%	25.5%
6	+3%	28.5%
7	+2.5%	31%
8	+2.5%	33.5%
9	+2.5%	36%
10	+2%	38%
11	+2%	40%
12	+1.5%	41.5%
13	+1.5%	43%
14	+1.5%	44.5%
15	+1.5%	46%
16	+1%	47%
17	+1%	48%
18	+1%	49%
19	+0.5%	49.5%
20	+0.5%	50%

Dual Wield

Dual Wield is the prerequisite for equipping a one-handed weapon in both hands. This skill adds to your character's dual-wielding damage. Add points to Dual Wield only if you plan to equip two one-handed weapons; otherwise these points are better spent on Barricade or Overbear for shield or two-handed weapon use. Dual Wield is the primary prerequisite for the Waves of Force power.

(continued)

Level	Dual-Wield Damage +%	Cumulative Total
1	+8%	8%
2	+7%	15%
3	+6%	21%
4	+5%	26%
5	+5%	31%
6	+5%	36%
7	+4%	40%
8	+4%	44%
9	+4%	48%
10	+4%	52%
11	+3%	55%
12	+3%	58%
13	+2%	60%
14	+2%	62%
15	+2%	64%
16	+2%	66%
17	+1%	67%
18	+1%	68%
19	+1%	69%
20	+1%	70%

Toughness

The Toughness skill increases the character's resistance to melee and ranged attacks and is also a prerequisite for the Provoke and Staggering Blow powers. Add points to Toughness, which is handy if you're stressing defense over damage—specifically if you're focusing on the use of a shield with Barricade and Provoke.

Prerequisites: Melee Level 12, Fortitude Level 1

Level	Physical Damage Resistance +%	Cumulative Total
1	+3%	3%
2	+2%	5%
3	+2%	7%
4	+2%	9%
5	+2%	11%
6	+1.5%	12.5%
7	+1.5%	14%
8	+1.5%	15.5%
9	+1.5%	17%
10	+1%	18%
11	+1%	19%
12	+1%	20%
13	+1%	21%
14	+1%	22%
15	+1%	23%
16	+1%	24%
17	+0.5%	24.5%
18	+0.5%	25%
19	+0.5%	25.5%
20	+0.5%	26%

Alacrity

Alacrity is the perfect complement to Dual Wield; this skill increases the character's melee attack speed. Add points to Alacrity to unlock the upper levels of the Waves of Force power, which is specifically for Dual Wield melee characters.

Level	Melee Attack Speed +%	Cumulative Total
1	+3%	3%
2	+2%	5%
3	+2%	7%
4	+2%	9%
5	+1%	10%
6	+1%	11%
7	+1%	12%
8	+1%	13%
9	+1%	14%
10	+1%	15%
11	+1%	16%
12	+1%	17%
13	+1%	18%
14	+1%	19%
15	+1%	20%
16	+1%	21%
17	+1%	22%
18	+1%	23%
19	+1%	24%
20	+1%	25%

Reinforced Armor

The Reinforced Armor skill provides a percentage boost to your character's Armor rating and is a prerequisite for the upper levels of the Provoke power. Reinforced Armor is in the "sword and shield" Melee class path and should be used by characters focusing on Barricade over Dual Wield and Overbear.

Prerequisites: Melee Level 24, Barricade Level 1

Level	Armor +%	Cumulative Total
1	+4%	4%
2	+3%	7%
3	+3%	10%
4	+3%	13%
5	+2%	15%
6	+2%	17%
7	+2%	19%
8	+2%	21%
9	+2%	23%
10	+1.5%	24.5%
11	+1.5%	26%
12	+1.5%	27.5%
13	+1.5%	29%
14	+1%	30%
15	+1%	31%
16	+1%	32%
17	+1%	33%
18	+1%	34%
19	+0.5%	34.5%
20	+0.5%	35%

Smite

The Smite skill adds a chance to stun during a two-handed weapon attack. Characters focused on Overbear and two-handed weapons should boost Smite, which is also a prerequisite for the highest level of Staggering Blow, a power that inflicts damage and stuns multiple enemies.

Prerequisites: Melee Level 24, Overbear Level 1, Toughness Level 1

Level	Two-Handed Weapon Stun Chance +%	Cumulative Total	Stun Duration	Cumulative Total
1	+5%	5%	+1 s	1 s
2	+5%	10%	+0 s	1 s
3	+4%	14%	+0 s	1 s
4	+4%	18%	+0 s	1 s
5	+4%	22%	+0 s	1 s
6	+3%	25%	+0.25 s	1.25 s
7	+3%	28%	+0 s	1.25 s
8	+3%	31%	+0 s	1.25 s
9	+3%	34%	+0 s	1.25 s
10	+2%	36%	+0 s	1.25 s
11	+2%	38%	+0.25 s	1.5 s
12	+2%	40%	+0 s	1.5 s
13	+2%	42%	+0 s	1.5 s
14	+2%	44%	+0 s	1.5 s
15	+1%	45%	+0 s	1.5 s
16	+1%	46%	+0.5 s	2 s
17	+1%	47%	+0 s	2 s
18	+1%	48%	+0 s	2 s
19	+1%	49%	+0 s	2 s
20	+1%	50%	+0 s	2 s

Fierce Renewal

Fierce Renewal increases the character's melee power recovery rate. The skill is in the Dual Wield path but is valuable for any melee character hoping to unleash powers at a higher rate. To unlock Fierce Renewal you must spend a point in Dual Wield and Alacrity, which may mean at least one wasted point for characters focusing on two-handed weapons or shields. Fierce Renewal is also a prerequisite for the Elemental Rage power.

Prerequisites: Melee Level 24, Alacrity Level 1

Level	Melee Power Recovery Rate +%	Cumulative Total
1	+3%	3%
2	+3%	6%
3	+2%	8%
4	+2%	10%
5	+2%	12%
6	+2%	14%
7	+2%	16%
8	+1.5%	17.5%
9	+1.5%	19%
10	+1.5%	20.5%
11	+1.5%	22%
12	+1%	23%
13	+1%	24%
14	+1%	25%
15	+1%	26%
16	+0%	26%
17	+1%	27%
18	+1%	28%
19	+1 %	29%
20	+1%	30%

Rebuke

The Rebuke skill is for characters focused on Barricade and the use of a shield. Dual Wield and Overbear characters have no reason to place any skill points in Rebuke. This skill adds damage when your character blocks a monster's melee attack, which will happen only with a shield equipped. The potency of Rebuke ties in with Barricade, which increases your character's chance to block melee attacks. Rebuke is the prerequisite for the highest level of the Provoke power.

Prerequisites: Melee Level 36, Reinforced Armor Level 1

Level	Rebuke Damage (x Melee Level)	Cumulative Total (x Melee Level)	Rebuke Stun Time	Cumulative Total
1	+0.4	0.4	+1 s	1 s
2	+0.3	0.7	+0 s	1 s
3	+0.2	0.9	+0 s	1 s
4	+0.2	1.1	+0 s	1 s
5	+0.2	1.3	+0 s	1 s
6	+0.15	1.45	+0.25 s	1.25 s
7	+0.15	1.6	+0 s	1.25 s
8	+0.1	1.7	+0 s	1.25 s
9	+0.1	1.8	+0 s	1.25 s
10	+0.1	1.9	+0 s	1.25 s
11	+0.08	1.98	+0.25 s	1.5 s
12	+0.08	2.06	+0 s	1.5 s
13	+0.08	2.14	+0 s	1.5 s
14	+0.08	2.22	+0 s	1.5 s
15	+0.08	2.3	+0 s	1.5 s
16	+0.04	2.34	+0.5 s	2 s
17	+0.04	2.38	+0 s	2 s
18	+0.04	2.42	+0 s	2 s
19	+0.04	2.46	+0 s	2 s
20	+0.04	2.5	+0 s	2 s

Deadly Strike

Deadly Strike increases the damage inflicted by a critical hit and ties in well with the Critical Strike skill, which increases the chance of inflicting a critical hit. Deadly Strike is part of the prerequisites for the higher levels of the Waves of Force, War Cry, and Elemental Rage powers.

Prerequisites: Melee Level 36, Critical Strike Level 1

Level	Increased Critical Hit Damage %	Cumulative Total
1	+224%	224%
2	+18%	242%
3	+14%	256%
4	+12%	268%
5	+11%	279%
6	+9%	288%
7	+8%	296%
8	+7%	303%
9	+7%	310%
10	+6%	316%
11	+6%	322%
12	+5%	327%
13	+5%	332%
14	+4%	336%
15	+4%	340%

(continued)

Level	Increased Critical Hit Damage %	Cumulative Total
16	+3%	343%
17	+3%	346%
18	+2%	348%
19	+1%	349%
20	+1%	350%

Ranged Skills

Critical Shot

The Critical Shot skill increases the character's chance of inflicting a critical hit with a ranged weapon (critical hits deal 200% damage). This is certainly a valuable skill for a character focusing on bow, crossbow, or thrown weapons. Critical Shot is a prerequisite for the Take Aim, Flurry (thrown weapons), and Charged Shots (bow or crossbow) powers.

Prerequisite: Ranged Level 1

1	+8%	8%
2	+6%	14%
3	+4%	18%
4	+4%	22%
5	+3.5%	25.5%
6	+3%	28.5%
7	+2.5%	31%
8	+2.5%	33.5%
9	+2.5%	36%
10	+2%	38%
11	+2%	40%
12	+1.5%	41.5%
13	+1.5%	43%
14	+1.5%	44.5%
15	+1.5%	46%
16	+1%	47%
17	+1%	48%
18	+1%	49%
19	+0.5%	49.5%
20	+0.5%	50%

Dodge

Dodge increases the character's chance to dodge melee or ranged attacks; 10 skill points in Dodge mean approximately a quarter of all melee and ranged attacks will be dodged. Select the Dryad race to automatically receive one point in Dodge. It's a defensive skill and best used if you want to unlock the Silence or Repulse power. Otherwise you're better focusing points in a bow, crossbow, or thrown-weapon discipline.

Prerequisite: Ranged Level 1

Level	Chance to Dodge Melee or Ranged Attacks +%	Cumulative Total
1	+4%	4%
2	+3%	7%
3	+3%	10%
4	+3%	13%
5	+3%	16%
6	+2%	18%
7	+2%	20%
8	+2%	22%
9	+2%	24%
10	+2%	26%
11	+2%	28%
12	+2%	30%
13	+2%	32%
14	+2%	34%
15	+1%	35%
16	+1%	36%
17	+1%	37%
18	+1%	38%
19	+1%	39%
20	+1%	40%

Biting Arrow

Biting Arrow enhances bow or crossbow damage and is the prerequisite for equipping a crossbow as well as the Thunderous Shot power. Ranged characters using bow or crossbow should certainly focus points in Biting Arrow, eventually up to 12 to reach a prerequisite for the highest level of Thunderous Shot. Thrown-weapon users have no use for this skill.

Prerequisites: Ranged Level 5, Critical Shot Level 1

Level	Bow and Crossbow Damage +%	Cumulative Total
1	+8%	8%
2	+6%	14%
3	+4%	18%
4	+4%	22%
5	+3.5%	25.5%
6	+3%	28.5%
7	+2.5%	31%
8	+2.5%	33.5%
9	+2.5%	36%
10	+2%	38%
11	+2%	40%
12	+1.5%	41.5%
13	+1.5%	43%
14	+1.5%	44.5%
15	+1.5%	46%
16	+1%	47%
17	+1%	48%
18	+1%	49%
19	+0.5%	49.5%
20	+0.5%	50%

Quick Draw

Quick Draw enhances thrown weapon firing rate and is the prerequisite for equipping a thrown weapon as well as the Shrapnel Blast power. Ranged characters equipped with a thrown weapon should focus points into this skill, eventually at least 10 to reach a prerequisite for the highest level of Shrapnel Blast. Bow and crossbow characters have no use for this skill.

Prerequisites: Ranged Level 5, Critical Shot Level 1

Level	Throw Weapon Firing Rate +%	Cumulative Total
1	+3%	3%
2	+2%	5%
3	+2%	7%

(continued)

(continued)

4	+2%	9%
5	+1%	10%
6	+1%	11%
7	+1%	12%
8	+1%	13%
9	+1%	14%
10	+1%	15%
11	+1%	16%
12	+1%	17%
13	+1%	18%
14	+1%	19%
15	+1%	20%
16	+1%	21%
17	+1%	22%
18	+1%	23%
19	+1%	24%
20	+1%	25%

Level	Bow and Crossbow Range +%	Cumulative Total
3	+4%	14%
4	+4%	18%
5	+4%	22%
6	+3%	25%
7	+3%	28%
8	+3%	31%
9	+3%	34%
10	+3%	37%
11	+3%	40%
12	+3%	43%
13	+3%	46%
14	+2%	48%
15	+2%	50%
16	+2%	52%
17	+2%	54%
18	+2%	56%
19	+2%	58%
20	+2%	60%

Far Shot

Far Shot increases bow and crossbow range, allowing the user to remain even farther away from threatening monsters. Far Shot has no effect on thrown weapon range and only users equipped with bows or crossbows should spend points in this skill. Far Shot is a prerequisite for the Thunderous Shot power.

Prerequisites: Ranged Level 12, Biting Arrow Level 1

Level	Bow and Crossbow Range +%	Cumulative Total
1	+6%	6%
2	+4%	10%

(continued)

Bleed

Bleed is a skill that benefits thrown weapon users only. Each strike from a thrown weapon has a chance to bleed, which inflicts additional damage over the next four seconds (same for all skill levels). The chance to cause bleed caps at skill level five, though bleed damage continues to increase. Bleed is also a prerequisite for the Shrapnel Blast power. Bleed damage is shown in actual values; the values shown in-game are rounded up.

(continued)

Survival

Survival is a unique skill that offers no damage, critical hit, or armor bonuses—it's the only skill that specifically increases character resistances to fire, ice, and lightning damage. Astute equipment selection can accomplish these same benefits, though Survival is also the prerequisite for harvesting health potions from health bushes, and is part of the prerequisite for the Silence and Repulse powers.

Prerequisite: Ranged Level 5

Level	Fire Damage Resistance +%	Cumulative Total	Ice Damage Resistance +%	Cumulative Total	Lightning Damage Resistance +%	Cumulative Total	Health Potions
1	+10%	10%	+10%	10%	+10%	10%	Small
2	+7%	17%	+7%	17%	+7%	17%	Small
3	+5%	22%	+5%	22%	+5%	22%	Small
4	+5%	27%	+5%	27%	+5%	27%	Normal
5	+4%	31%	+4%	31%	+4%	31%	Normal
6	+4%	35%	+4%	35%	+4%	35%	Normal
7	+3%	38%	+3%	38%	+3%	38%	Normal
8	+3%	41%	+3%	41%	+3%	41%	Large
9	+3%	44%	+3%	44%	+3%	44%	Large
10	+2.5%	46.5%	+2.5%	46.5%	+2.5%	46.5%	Large
11	+2.5%	49%	+2.5%	49%	+2.5%	49%	Large
12	+2%	51%	+2%	51%	+2%	51%	Super
13	+2%	53%	+2%	53%	+2%	53%	Super
14	+2%	55%	+2%	55%	+2%	55%	Super
15	+1%	56%	+1%	56%	+1%	56%	Super
16	+1%	57%	+1%	57%	+1%	57%	Colossal
17	+1%	58%	+1%	58%	+1%	58%	Colossal
18	+1%	59%	+1%	59%	+1%	59%	Colossal
19	+0.5%	59.5%	+0.5%	59.5%	+0.5%	59.5%	Colossal

Level	Chance to Cause Bleed %	Cumulative Total	Bleed Damage (x Dexterity)	Cumulative Total
1	+10%	10%	+.06	.06
2	+5%	15%	+.05	.11
3	+3%	18%	+.04	.15
4	+4%	22%	+.04	.19
5	+3%	25%	+.04	.23
6	+0%	25%	+.03	.26
7	+0%	25%	+.03	.29
8	+0%	25%	+.025	.315
9	+0%	25%	+.025	.34
10	+0%	25%	+.02	.36
11	+0%	25%	+.02	.38
12	+0%	25%	+.02	.40
13	+0%	25%	+.02	.42
14	+0%	25%	+.015	.435
15	+0%	25%	+.015	.45
16	+0%	25%	+.01	.46
17	+0%	25%	+.01	.47
18	+0%	25%	+.01	.48
19	+0%	25%	+.01	.49
20	+0%	25%	+.01	.50

Shockwave

The Shockwave skill adds additional damage when a bow, arrow, or crossbow bolt travels a certain distance. To maximize this skill's benefit, keep your Ranged-class character as far from the action as possible. Increasing Shockwave lowers the required distance; also, increasing Far Shot increases bow and crossbow range, which certainly aids Shockwave, as well, since you can fire from a greater distance, ensuring shockwave damage. This skill is a prerequisite for the Charged Shots power. The radius for shockwave damage is always two meters.

Prerequisites: Ranged Level 24, Far Shot Level 1

Level	Shockwave Damage (+% of Projectile Damage)	Cumulative Total	Shockwave when arrow or bolt travels farther than x meters	Cumulative Total
1	+8%	8%	+9	9
2	+4%	12%	0	9
3	+4%	16%	0	9
4	+4%	20%	-0.5	8.5
5	+3%	23%	0	8.5
6	+3%	26%	-0.5	8
7	+2%	28%	0	8
8	+2%	30%	0	8
9	+2%	32%	-0.5	7.5
10	+2%	34%	0	7.5
11	+2%	36%	0	7.5
12	+2%	38%	-0.5	7
13	+2%	40%	0	7
14	+2%	42%	0	7
15	+2%	44%	0	7
16	+2%	46%	0	7
17	+1%	47%	0	7
18	+1%	48%	0	7
19	+1%	49%	0	7
20	+1%	50%	0	7

Penetrate

Penetrate adds a chance that projectiles (from bow, crossbow, or thrown weapon) will penetrate through an enemy and inflict damage on other foes. Penetrate is primarily a prerequisite for the thrown-weapon power Shrapnel Blast but is certainly a valuable counterpart to any bow or crossbow user.

Prerequisite: Ranged Level 24

Level	Chance Projectile will Penetrate Enemies +%	Cumulative Total
1	+12%	12%
2	+10%	22%
3	+8%	30%
4	+6%	36%
5	+5%	41%
6	+5%	46%
7	+4%	50%
8	+4%	54%
9	+3%	57%
10	+3%	60%
11	+3%	63%
12	+2%	65%
13	+2%	67%
14	+2%	69%
15	+1.5%	70.5%
16	+1.5%	72%
17	+1%	73%
18	+1%	74%
19	+0.5%	74.5%
20	+0.5%	75%

Cunning Renewal

The Cunning Renewal skill increases ranged power recovery. It's primarily a thrown-weapon skill; its perquisites include Bleed, which requires Quick Draw. Also, Cunning Renewal is a prerequisite for the thrown-weapon power Flurry. This skill certainly benefits any Ranged-class character, though bow and crossbow users will have to spend two points in thrown weapon skills to start increasing Cunning Renewal.

Prerequisites: Ranged Level 24, Bleed Level 1

Level	Ranged Power Recovery +%	Cumulative Total
1	+3%	3%
2	+3%	6%
3	+2%	8%
4	+2%	10%
5	+2%	12%
6	+2%	14%
7	+2%	16%
8	+1.5%	17.5%
9	+1.5%	19%

(continued)

(continued)

Level	Ranged Power Recovery +%	Cumulative Total
10	+1.5%	20.5%
11	+1.5%	22%
12	+1%	23%
13	+1%	24%
14	+1%	25%
15	+1%	26%
16	+0%	26%
17	+1%	27%
18	+1%	28%
19	+1%	29%
20	+1%	30%

Mortal Wound

Add points to Mortal Wound to increase damage inflicted by a critical hit from a bow or crossbow. Mortal Wound is tied to Critical Shot, which increases the chance of inflicting a critical hit, and is a prerequisite for the bow and crossbow power Charged Shots, as well as Silence.

Prerequisites: Ranged Level 36, Far Shot Level 1, Penetrate Level 1

Level	Bow and Crossbow Critical Hit Damage +%	Cumulative Total
1	+224%	224%
2	+18%	242%
3	+14%	256%
4	+12%	268%
5	+11%	279%
6	+9%	288%
7	+8%	296%
8	+7%	303%
9	+7%	310%
10	+6%	316%
11	+6%	322%
12	+5%	327%
13	+5%	332%
14	+4%	336%
15	+4%	340%
16	+3%	343%
17	+3%	346%
18	+2%	348%
19	+1%	349%
20	+1%	350%

Ricochet

Ricochet causes thrown-weapon critical hits to ricochet to a nearby enemy, inflicting a percentage of the original projectile damage. Gain additional benefit for this skill by improving Critical Shot, which increases the chance of inflicting a critical hit. Bow and crossbow users have no use for this skill, which is also a prerequisite for the higher levels of the thrown-weapon power Flurry, as well as Repulse.

Prerequisites: Ranged Level 36, Penetrate Level 1, Bleed 1

Level	Ricochet Damage (+% of Projectile Damage)	Cumulative Total
1	+66%	66%
2	+12%	78%
3	+8%	86%
4	+8%	94%
5	+7%	101%
6	+6%	107%
7	+5%	112%
8	+5%	117%
9	+5%	122%
10	+4%	126%
11	+4%	130%
12	+3%	133%
13	+3%	136%
14	+3%	139%
15	+3%	142%
16	+2%	144%
17	+2%	146%
18	+2%	148%
19	+1%	149%
20	+1%	150%

Combat Magic Skills

Brilliance

Brilliance increases maximum mana, which helps a mage afford repeated casts of expensive high-damage spells. Mana is the lifeblood of a mage, but you can gain a similar benefit from proper equipment selection and crafted-item creation. Select an elemental-damage path instead and add points to Brilliance after unlocking the path's upgraded powers. Brilliance is a prerequisite for the Energy Orb power. The Elf race includes one point in Brilliance.

Prerequisite: Combat Magic Level 1

Level	Maximum Mana +%	Cumulative Total
1	+7%	7%
2	+7%	14%
3	+7%	21%
4	+7%	28%
5	+8%	36%
6	+8%	44%
7	+8%	52%
8	+8%	60%
9	+8%	68%
10	+8%	76%
11	+7%	83%
12	+7%	90%
13	+7%	97%
14	+8%	105%
15	+8%	113%
16	+8%	121%
17	+8%	129%
18	+7%	136%
19	+7%	143%
20	+7%	150%

Devastation

Devastation is an all-encompassing skill that increases all combat magic damage. It's also the prerequisite for a power from each of the three elemental paths. Spend 10 to 12 points in Devastation to unlock the highest levels of Harvest Soul, Flame Nexus, or Chain

(continued)

Class Skills

Lightning. Alternate spending points into Devastation and the elemental-damage skills to maximize increases and power unlocks.

Prerequisite: Combat Magic Level 1

Level	Combat Magic Damage +%	Cumulative Total
1	+10%	10%
2	+7%	17%
3	+5%	22%
4	+5%	27%
5	+4%	31%
6	+4%	35%
7	+3%	38%
8	+3%	41%
9	+3%	44%
10	+2.5%	46.5%
11	+2.5%	49%
12	+2%	51%
13	+2%	53%
14	+2%	55%
15	+1%	56%
16	+1%	57%
17	+1%	58%
18	+1%	59%
19	+0.5%	59.5%
20	+0.5%	60%

Debilitation

Debilitation increases the power and duration of the combat mage's curses, spells that inflict a harmful enchantment on monsters. Debilitation would be considered the tool of a death mage; it's the prerequisite for the Corrosive Eruption power. Mages focusing on fire or lightning would be better off spending on those skills to unlock their powers sooner.

Prerequisite: Combat Magic Level 5

Level	Curse Spell Power +%	Cumulative Total	Curse Spell Duration +%	Cumulative Total
1	+24%	24%	+32%	32%
2	+18%	42%	+24%	56%
3	+12%	54%	+16%	72%
4	+12%	66%	+16%	88%
5	+11%	77%	+14%	102%
6	+9%	86%	+12%	114%
7	+8%	94%	+10%	124%
8	+8%	102%	+10%	134%
9	+7%	109%	+10%	144%
10	+6%	115%	+8%	152%
11	+6%	121%	+8%	160%
12	+5%	126%	+6%	166%
13	+5%	131%	+6%	172%
14	+4%	135%	+6%	178%
15	+4%	139%	+6%	184%
16	+3%	142%	+4%	188%
17	+3%	145%	+4%	192%
18	+2%	147%	+4%	196%
19	+2%	149%	+2%	198%
20	+1%	150%	+2%	200%

Searing Flames

Searing Flames is the skill of the fire mage and a prerequisite for the Flame Nexus and Detonation powers. Searing Flames increases fire-spell damage and power damage in equal measure.

Prerequisites: Combat Magic Level 5, Devastation Level 1

Level	Fire Magic Damage +%	Cumulative Total
1	+8%	8%
2	+6%	14%
3	+6%	20%
4	+4%	24%
5	+4%	28%
6	+4%	32%
7	+4%	36%
8	+3%	39%
9	+3%	42%
10	+2%	44%
11	+2%	46%
12	+2%	48%
13	+2%	50%
14	+2%	52%
15	+2%	54%
16	+2%	56%
17	+1%	57%
18	+1%	58%
19	+1%	59%
20	+1%	60%

Amplified Lightning

Amplified Lightning is the skill of the lightning mage and a prerequisite for the Chain Lightning and Gathered Bolt powers. Amplified Lightning increases lightning-spell damage and power damage in equal measure.

Prerequisites: Combat Magic Level 5, Devastation Level 1

Level	Lightning Magic Damage +%	Cumulative Total
1	+8%	8%
2	+6%	14%
3	+6%	20%
4	+4%	24%
5	+4%	28%
6	+4%	32%
7	+4%	36%
8	+3%	39%
9	+3%	42%
10	+2%	44%
11	+2%	46%
12	+2%	48%
13	+2%	50%
14	+2%	52%
15	+2%	54%
16	+2%	56%
17	+1%	57%
18	+1%	58%
19	+1%	59%
20	+1%	60%

Summon Alacrity

A combat mage can improve the damage potential of his summoned creatures with this skill; Summon Alacrity increases summoned-creature attack speed. There are no combat-magic powers associated with this skill. Nature magic includes several summoned-creature skills; a nature mage could dabble in combat magic and spend points in Summon Alacrity to boost his own enhanced summons.

Prerequisite: Combat Magic Level 12

Level	Summon Creature Attack Speed +%	Cumulative Total
1	+7%	7%
2	+5%	12%
3	+4%	16%
4	+3%	19%
5	+3%	22%
6	+2%	24%
7	+2%	26%
8	+2%	28%
9	+1.5%	29.5%
10	+1.5%	31%
11	+1.5%	32.5%
12	+1.5%	34%
13	+1%	35%
14	+1%	36%
15	+1%	37%
16	+1%	38%
17	+0.5%	38.5%
18	+0.5%	39%
19	+0.5%	39.5%
20	+0.5%	40%

Grim Necromancy

Grim Necromancy is the skill of the death mage and a prerequisite for the Corrosive Eruption and Harvest Soul powers. Grim Necromancy increases death-spell damage and power damage in equal measure.

Prerequisites: Combat Magic Level 12, Devastation Level 1

Level	Death Magic Damage +%	Cumulative Total
1	+8%	8%
2	+6%	14%
3	+6%	20%
4	+4%	24%
5	+4%	28%
6	+4%	32%
7	+4%	36%
8	+3%	39%
9	+3%	42%
10	+2%	44%
11	+2%	46%
12	+2%	48%
13	+2%	50%
14	+2%	52%
15	+2%	54%
16	+2%	56%
17	+1%	57%
18	+1%	58%
19	+1%	59%
20	+1%	60%

Quickened Casting

Faster casting can mean higher damage potential. It also means more mana consumption. Maintain a robust stock of mana potions or apply big boosts to your mana reserve and regeneration with the appropriate equipment. Adding points to Brilliance complements a faster firing rate, but skill points for unlocking powers are better spent elsewhere. Elevate mana through equipment first. Quickened Casting is a prerequisite for the Gathered Bolt power.

Prerequisites: Combat Magic Level 24, Brilliance Level 1

Level	Cast Speed +%	Cumulative Total
1	+4%	4%
2	+3%	7%
3	+3%	10%
4	+2%	12%
5	+2%	14%
6	+1.5%	15.5%
7	+1.5%	17%
8	+1%	18%
9	+1%	19%
10	+1%	20%
11	+1%	21%
12	+0.75%	21.75%
13	+0.75%	22.5%
14	+0.5%	23%
15	+0.5%	23.5%
16	+0.5%	24%
17	+0.25%	24.25%
18	+0.25%	24.5%
19	+0.25%	24.75%
20	+0.25%	25%

Vampirism

Vampirism essentially adds life-leeching power to all death-magic damage spells. Vampirism is a prerequisite for the Harvest Soul power.

Prerequisites: Combat Magic Level 24, Grim Necromancy Level 1

Level	Amount of Death Magic Damage Added to Health +%	Cumulative Total
1	+3%	3%
2	+3%	6%
3	+2%	8%
4	+2%	10%
5	+2%	12%
6	+2%	14%
7	+1%	15%
8	+1%	16%
9	+1%	17%
10	+1%	18%
11	+1%	19%
12	+1%	20%
13	+1%	21%
14	+1%	22%
15	+0.5%	22.5%
16	+0.5%	23%
17	+0.5%	23.5%
18	+0.5%	24%
19	+0.5%	24.5%

(continued)

Level	Amount of Death Magic Damage Added to Health +%	Cumulative Total
20	+0.5%	25%

Ignite

Ignite provides a chance that fire-damage spells will ignite a monster and inflict burn damage over three seconds. Ignite is the prerequisite for the highest level of the Flame Nexus power. Note that the Ignite Damage values are accurate and the values shown in the game are rounded to the nearest whole number.

Prerequisites: Combat Magic Level 24, Searing Flames Level 1

Level	Chance to Ignite +%	Cumulative Total	Ignite Damage Per Second (× Intelligence)	Cumulative Total
1	+5%	5%	+0.08	0.08
2	+3%	8%	+0.06	0.14
3	+3%	11%	+0.04	0.18
4	+2%	13%	+0.04	0.22
5	+2%	15%	+0.03	0.25
6	+2%	17%	+0.03	0.28
7	+1.5%	18.5%	+0.2	0.31
8	+1.5%	20%	+0.2	0.33
9	+1.5%	21.5%	+0.2	0.35
10	+1%	22.5%	+0.2	0.37
11	+1%	23.5%	+0.2	0.39
12	+1%	24.5%	+0.2	0.41
13	+1%	25.5%	+0.2	0.43
14	+1%	26.5%	+0.1	0.44
15	+0.75%	27.25%	+0.1	0.45
16	+0.75%	28%	+0.1	0.46
17	+0.5%	28.5%	+0.1	0.47
18	+0.5%	29%	+0.1	0.48
19	+0.5%	29.5%	+0.1	0.49
20	+0.5%	30%	+0.1	0.50

Arcane Fury

Arcane Fury increases combat-magic and nature-magic power damage, which is likely already boosted by the specific elemental damage skills. Arcane Fury is a prerequisite for the upper levels of the Detonation, Gathered Bolt, and Corrosive Eruption powers.

Prerequisites: Combat Magic Level 36, Quickened Casting Level 1

Level	Combat- and Nature-Magic Power Damage +%	Cumulative Total
1	+3%	3%
2	+3%	6%
3	+2%	8%
4	+2%	10%
5	+2%	12%
6	+2%	14%
7	+2%	16%
8	+1.5%	17.5%
9	+1.5%	19%
10	+1.5%	20.5%
11	+1.5%	22%
12	+1%	23%
13	+1%	24%
14	+1%	25%

Level	Combat- and Nature-Magic Power Damage +%	Cumulative Total
15	+1%	26%
16	+0%	26%
17	+1%	27%
18	+1%	28%
19	+1%	29%
20	+1%	30%

Arcing

Arcing adds a possibility of "chain lightning" to every lightning-damage spell. Arcing is the prerequisite for the highest levels of the Chain Lightning power. Note that the Arc Damage values here are accurate; the values shown in the game are rounded to the nearest whole number.

Prerequisites: Combat Magic Level 36, Amplified Lightning Level 1

Level	Chance to Arc +%	Cumulative Total	Arc Damage (× Intelligence)	Cumulative Total
1	+5%	5%	+0.18	0.18
2	+3%	8%	+0.12	0.30
3	+3%	11%	+0.08	0.38
4	+2%	13%	+0.07	0.45
5	+2%	15%	+0.07	0.52
6	+2%	17%	+0.06	0.58
7	+1.5%	18.5%	+0.05	0.63
8	+1.5%	20%	+0.05	0.68
9	+1.5%	21.5%	+0.05	0.73
10	+1%	22.5%	+0.04	0.77
11	+1%	23.5%	+0.04	0.81
12	+1%	24.5%	+0.03	0.84
13	+1%	25.5%	+0.03	0.87
14	+1%	26.5%	+0.03	0.9
15	+0.75%	27.25%	+0.02	0.92
16	+0.75%	28%	+0.02	0.94
17	+0.5%	28.5%	+0.02	0.96
18	+0.5%	29%	+0.02	0.98
19	+0.5%	29.5%	+0.01	0.99
20	+0.5%	30%	+0.01	1.00

Nature Magic Skills

Natural Bond

Natural Bond decreases the mana cost of spells. This would aid an ice nature mage primarily because of the frequency of casting expensive high-damage ice spells. Summon spells are extremely expensive but infrequently cast. Natural Bond would also be valuable to a combat mage multiclassing; spend skill points in Natural Bond instead of Brilliance, then increase mana using equipment to compound both benefits. Natural Bond is a prerequisite for the Gravity Stone and Circle of Frost powers, as well as for harvesting mana potions from mana bushes. The Dryad race includes one point in Natural Bond.

Prerequisite: Nature Magic Level 1

Level	Mana Cost of Spells: -%	Cumulative Total	Mana Potions
1	-6%	-6%	Small
2	-6%	-12%	Small

(continued)

(continued)

Level	Mana Cost of Spells: -%	Cumulative Total	Mana Potions
3	-5%	-17%	Small
4	-5%	-22%	Small
5	-4%	-26%	Normal
6	-4%	-30%	Normal
7	-4%	-34%	Normal
8	-3%	-37%	Normal
9	-3%	-40%	Large
10	-3%	-43%	Large
11	-2%	-45%	Large
12	-2%	-47%	Super
13	-2%	-49%	Super
14	-2%	-51%	Super
15	-2%	-53%	Super
16	-2%	-55%	Colossal
17	-2%	-57%	Colossal
18	-1%	-58%	Colossal
19	-1%	-59%	Colossal
20	-1%	-60%	Colossal (2)

Aquatic Affinity

Aquatic Affinity increases the effectiveness of healing magic and the damage of ice spells. This is an essential skill for a nature mage focusing on ice damage; it's a prerequisite for the Icicle Blast power. A mage balancing heal support with ice damage would also benefit from spending points in this skill.

Prerequisite: Nature Magic Level 1

Level	Healing Magic +%	Cumulative Total	Ice Magic Damage +%	Cumulative Total
1	+5%	5%	+5%	7%
2	+4%	9%	+5%	10%
3	+3%	12%	+4%	14%
4	+3%	15%	+3%	17%
5	+3%	18%	+3%	20%
6	+3%	21%	+2%	22%
7	+3%	24%	+2%	24%
8	+2%	26%	+2%	26%
9	+2%	28%	+1.5%	27.5%
10	+2%	30%	+1.5%	29%
11	+2%	32%	+1.5%	30.5%
12	+2%	34%	+1.5%	32%
13	+2%	36%	+1%	33%
14	+2%	38%	+1%	34%
15	+2%	40%	+1%	35%
16	+2%	42%	+1%	36%
17	+2%	44%	+1%	37%
18	+2%	46%	+1%	38%
19	+2%	48%	+1%	39%
20	+2%	50%	+1%	40%

Summon Fortitude

Increase summoned-creature health with this skill. Nature magic offers two skills and powers focused on summoned creatures. Summon Fortitude is a prerequisite for the Summon Provoke power.

Prerequisite: Nature Magic Level 5

Level	Summoned-creature Health +%	Cumulative Total
1	+16%	16%
2	+12%	28%
3	+8%	36%
4	+8%	44%
5	+7%	51%
6	+6%	57%
7	+5%	62%
8	+5%	67%
9	+5%	72%
10	+4%	76%
11	+4%	80%
12	+3%	83%
13	+3%	86%
14	+3%	89%
15	+3%	92%
16	+2%	94%
17	+2%	96%
18	+2%	98%
19	+1%	99%
20	+1%	100%

Enveloping Embrace

Enveloping Embrace increases the power and duration of the "embrace" spells, which add enchantments to party members. A nature mage focused on party support should add points in this skill and Feral Wrath. Enveloping Embrace is the prerequisite for the Invulnerability power.

Prerequisite: Nature Magic Level 5

Level	Embrace Spell Power +%	Cumulative Total	Embrace Spell Duration +%	Cumulative Total
1	+20%	20%	+32%	32%
2	+16%	36%	+24%	56%
3	+12%	48%	+16%	72%
4	+10%	58%	+16%	88%
5	+10%	68%	+14%	102%
6	+10%	78%	+12%	114%
7	+10%	88%	+10%	124%
8	+8%	96%	+10%	134%
9	+8%	104%	+10%	144%
10	+8%	112%	+8%	152%
11	+6%	118%	+8%	160%
12	+6%	124%	+6%	166%
13	+6%	130%	+6%	172%
14	+4%	134%	+6%	178%
15	+4%	138%	+6%	184%
16	+4%	142%	+4%	188%
17	+2%	144%	+4%	192%
18	+2%	146%	+4%	196%
19	+2%	148%	+2%	198%
20	+2%	150%	+2%	200%

Arctic Mastery

Arctic Mastery is a focused ice-mage skill; it increases ice magic and power damage in equal measure. Arctic Mastery is the prerequisite for the upper levels of the Icicle Blast and Circle of Frost powers.

Class Skills

Prerequisites: Nature Magic Level 5, Aquatic Affinity Level 1

Level	Ice Magic Damage +%	Cumulative Total
1	+8%	8%
2	+6%	14%
3	+6%	20%
4	+4%	24%
5	+4%	28%
6	+4%	32%
7	+4%	36%
8	+3%	39%
9	+3%	42%
10	+2%	44%
11	+2%	46%
12	+2%	48%
13	+2%	50%
14	+2%	52%
15	+2%	54%
16	+2%	56%
17	+1%	57%
18	+1%	58%
19	+1%	59%
20	+1%	60%

Summon Might

A nature mage aiding the party with summoned creatures should add points into this skill, which increases summoned-creature damage, and Summon Fortitude. Summon Might is a prerequisite for the Summon Provoke and Aether Blast powers.

Prerequisites: Nature Magic Level 12, Summon Fortitude Level 1

Level	Summoned-creature Damage +%	Cumulative Total
1	+24%	24%
2	+18%	42%
3	+12%	54%
4	+12%	66%
5	+11%	77%
6	+9%	86%
7	+8%	94%
8	+8%	102%
9	+7%	109%
10	+6%	115%
11	+6%	121%
12	+5%	126%
13	+5%	131%
14	+4%	135%
15	+4%	139%
16	+3%	142%
17	+3%	145%
18	+2%	147%
19	+2%	149%
20	+1%	150%

Feral Wrath

Feral Wrath increases the power and duration of the "wrath" spells, which add enchantments to party members. A nature mage focused on party support should add points in this skill and Enveloping Embrace. Feral Wrath is the prerequisite for the Glacial Aura power.

Prerequisites: Nature Magic Level 12, Enveloping Embrace Level 1

Level	Wrath Spell Power +%	Cumulative Total	Wrath Spell Duration +%	Cumulative Total
1	+20%	20%	+32%	32%
2	+16%	36%	+24%	56%
3	+12%	48%	+16%	72%
4	+10%	58%	+16%	88%
5	+10%	68%	+14%	102%
6	+10%	78%	+12%	114%
7	+10%	88%	+10%	124%
8	+8%	96%	+10%	134%
9	+8%	104%	+10%	144%
10	+8%	112%	+8%	152%
11	+6%	118%	+8%	160%
12	+6%	124%	+6%	166%
13	+6%	130%	+6%	172%
14	+4%	134%	+6%	178%
15	+4%	138%	+6%	184%
16	+4%	142%	+4%	188%
17	+2%	144%	+4%	192%
18	+2%	146%	+4%	196%
19	+2%	148%	+2%	198%
20	+2%	150%	+2%	200%

Nurturing Gift

Nurturing Gift increases the restorative power of healing spells, an important skill for a nature mage focused on party support. Nurturing Gift is a prerequisite for the higher levels of the Invulnerability power.

Prerequisites: Nature Magic Level 12, Aquatic Affinity Level 1

Level	Healing Magic +%	Cumulative Total
1	+8%	8%
2	+8%	16%
3	+8%	24%
4	+6%	30%
5	+6%	36%
6	+6%	42%
7	+6%	48%
8	+6%	54%
9	+6%	60%
10	+5%	65%
11	+5%	70%
12	+5%	75%
13	+4%	79%
14	+4%	83%
15	+4%	87%
16	+3%	90%
17	+3%	93%
18	+3%	96%
19	+2%	98%
20	+2%	100%

Arcane Renewal

Arcane Renewal increases combat- and nature-magic power recovery rate and is a prerequisite for the higher levels of Aether Blast, Invulnerability, and Gravity Stone. After unlocking upper-level powers, any nature mage should focus points here to increase damage potential: more-frequent powers equal higher damage.

Level	Combat- and Nature-Magic Power Recovery Rate +%	Cumulative Total
1	+3%	3%
2	+3%	6%
3	+2%	8%
4	+2%	10%
5	+2%	12%
6	+2%	14%
7	+2%	16%
8	+1.5%	17.5%
9	+1.5%	19%
10	+1.5%	20.5%
11	+1.5%	22%
12	+1%	23%
13	+1%	24%
14	+1%	25%
15	+1%	26%
16	+0%	26%
17	+1%	27%
18	+1%	28%
19	+1%	29%
20	+1%	30%

Freezing

Freezing adds a chance to freeze for all ice-damage spells. A frozen monster can't attack and is left vulnerable to all of your party (and summoned creature) damage. Freezing is a prerequisite for the higher levels of the Icicle Blast, Circle of Frost, and Glacial Aura powers.

Level	Chance to Freeze +%	Cumulative Total	Freeze Duration	Cumulative Total
1	+5%	5%	+1 s	1 s
2	+3%	8%	+0 s	1 s
3	+3%	11%	+0 s	1 s
4	+2%	13%	+0 s	1 s
5	+2%	15%	+0 s	1 s
6	+2%	17%	+0.25 s	1.25 s
7	+1.5%	18.5%	+0 s	1.25 s
8	+1.5%	20%	+0 s	1.25 s
9	+1.5%	21.5%	+0 s	1.25 s
10	+1%	22.5%	+0 s	1.25 s
11	+1%	23.5%	+0.25 s	1.5 s
12	+1%	24.5%	+0 s	1.5 s
13	+1%	25.5%	+0 s	1.5 s
14	+1%	26.5%	+0 s	1.5 s
15	+0.75%	27.25%	+0 s	1.5 s
16	+0.75%	28%	+0.5 s	2 s
17	+0.5%	28.5%	+0 s	2 s
18	+0.5%	29%	+0 s	2 s
19	+0.5%	29.5%	+0 s	2 s
20	+0.5%	30%	+0 s	2 s

Summon Bond

Summon Bond essentially turns a summoned creature into an active health potion. When a mage suffers damage, a percentage of that damage is transferred as health from the summoned creature. Summon Bond is a prerequisite for the higher levels of the Summon Provoke and Aether Blast powers.

Level	Percentage of Damage Transferred +%	Cumulative Total
1	+12%	12%
2	+8%	20%
3	+6%	26%
4	+5%	31%
5	+4%	35%
6	+4%	39%
7	+3%	42%
8	+3%	45%
9	+2.5%	47.5%
10	+2.5%	50%
11	+2.5%	52.5%
12	+2%	54.5%
13	+2%	56.5%
14	+2%	58.5%
15	+1.5%	60%
16	+1.5%	61.5%
17	+1.5%	63%
18	+1%	64%
19	+1%	65%
20	+1%	66%

Absorption

Absorption allows a nature mage to absorb a percentage of monster magic damage and transfer a percentage of that damage into mana. Absorption is a prerequisite for the higher levels of the Glacial Aura power.

Level	Magic Damage Absorbed +%	Cumulative Total	Percentage of Absorbed Damage Added to Mana +%	Cumulative Total
1	+14%	14%	+8%	8%
2	+10%	24%	+6%	14%
3	+7%	31%	+4%	18%
4	+7%	38%	+4%	22%
5	+6%	44%	+3.5%	25.5%
6	+5%	49%	+3%	28.5%
7	+4%	53%	+2.5%	31%
8	+4%	57%	+2.5%	33.5%
9	+4%	61%	+2.5%	36%
10	+3%	64%	+2%	38%
11	+3%	67%	+2%	40%
12	+2.5%	69.5%	+1.5%	41.5%
13	+2.5%	72%	+1.5%	43%
14	+2.5%	74.5%	+1.5%	44.5%
15	+2.5%	77%	+1.5%	46%
16	+2%	79%	+1%	47%
17	+2%	81%	+1%	48%
18	+2%	83%	+1%	49%
19	+1%	84%	+0.5%	49.5%
20	+1%	85%	+0.5%	50%

Class Powers

This section provides statistics for every power at every level. Unlock powers through careful skill selection. See Part 2, "Character Development," for strategies on spending skill points to maximize power availability.

Melee Powers

Brutal Attack

Brutal Attack enhances the next melee attack with added damage. Ensure the Brutal Attack is focused on the toughest present monster. This power can be used only with a melee weapon and is a fast recharge.

Prerequisites: ◆ Level 1: Critical Strike Level 1 ◆ Level 2: Critical Strike Level 5 ◆ Level 3: Critical Strike Level 8

Level	+% Damage with Next Strike
1	1500 +25 × melee level
2	1750 + 48 × melee level
3	2000 + 60 × melee level

Whirling Strike

Use Whirling Strike when surrounded by monsters. The character whirls in a circle and damages and stuns surrounding enemies. This power can be used only with a melee weapon and automatically targets surrounding monsters within range. It is a normal recharge. This is a skill for any melee discipline, but spending heavy points in Critical Strike and Fortitude would limit other power options.

Prerequisites: ◆ Level 1: Critical Strike Level 6, Fortitude Level 8 ◆ Level 2: Critical Strike Level 8, Fortitude Level 10, Reinforced Armor Level 6 ◆ Level 3: Critical Strike Level 12, Fortitude Level 12, Reinforced Armor Level 12

Level	+% Normal Damage to Enemies	Radius	Stun Duration
1	920 + 9 × melee level	3 (5 enemies)	1.5 s
2	1070 + 15.4 × melee level	3.5 (5 enemies)	1.5 s
3	1400 + 19 × melee level	4 (5 enemies)	1.5 s

Provoke

When you activate Provoke, surrounding monsters become angry and attack your character. Provoke also increases the user's armor to help protect against the onslaught. With monsters distracted, other party members concentrate attacks or powers to eliminate the threat. Provoke can be used only when equipped with a shield, so it's best suited for a melee character focusing on the Barricade skill. It's a fast-recharge power.

Prerequisites: ◆ Level 1: Barricade Level 1 ◆ Level 2: Barricade Level 6, Toughness Level 4 ◆ Level 3: Barricade Level 10, Toughness Level 10, Rebuke Level 5

Level	Armor Bonus %	Radius	Duration
1	+25%	6 m	5 s
2	+30%	7 m	8 s
3	+50%	8 m	10 s

Staggering Blow

Staggering Blow enhances the next two-handed-weapon melee attack with added damage and stun (which can afflict multiple enemies within the shockwave's radius). Staggering Blow can only be used with a two-handed weapon, so it's suited for melee characters focusing on Overbear. It's a normal recharge.

Prerequisites: ◆ Level 1: Overbear Level 1 ◆ Level 2: Overbear Level 5, Toughness Level 4 ◆ Level 3: Overbear Level 12, Toughness Level 10, Smite Level 8

Level	% Normal Damage to Enemies	Stun Radius	Stun Duration
1	400 + 7 × melee level	2.8 m (3 enemies)	6 s
2	425 + 10 × melee level	3.3 m (4 enemies)	8 s
3	800 + 12 × melee level	4 m (4 enemies)	10 s

War Cry

Invoke War Cry to cause nearby enemies to flee in fear, reduce enemy damage, and cause the next series of attacks to inflict 200% damage. War Cry can be used with any melee weapon. Use when there are several monsters positioned in front of the melee caster. This is a normal-recharge power.

Prerequisites: ◆ Level 1: Critical Strike Level 8, Smite Level 1 ◆ Level 2: Critical Strike Level 12, Smite Level 8, Deadly Strike Level 2 ◆ Level 3: Critical Strike Level 12, Smite Level 12, Deadly Strike Level 8

Level	Next Attacks are Critical Hits	Enemy Armor Reduced by %	Reduced Armor Duration
1	8	35%	20 s
2	12	50%	20 s
3	15	60%	20 s

Waves of Force

Waves of Force can be used only when dual wielding two weapons, so it's suited for melee characters focusing on the Dual Wield skill. The power sends a series of five damaging waves from the melee character; use when many monsters are positioned in front of the melee character. It's a normal-recharge power.

Prerequisites: ◆ Level 1: Dual Wield Level 1 ◆ Level 2: Dual Wield Level 5, Alacrity Level 4 ◆ Level 3: Dual Wield Level 10, Alacrity Level 10, Deadly Strike Level 8

Level	% Main Hand Damage per Wave	Waves	Distance	Speed
1	200 + 3.6 × melee level	5	12	10
2	280 + 7 × melee level	5	12	10
3	490 + 9 × melee level	5	12	10

Elemental Rage

Elemental Rage adds elemental damage to all dual-wielding attacks. It also increases attack rate but at the expense of lowering resistance to physical damage. It's a relatively short-lived power; maximize its potential by strengthening the dual-wielder with enchantments then invoking Elemental Rage against a large group of monsters—attack as many monsters as quickly as possible. This is a slow-recharge power.

Prerequisites: ◆ Level 1: Critical Strike Level 8, Fierce Renewal Level 2 ◆ Level 2: Critical Strike Level 10, Fierce Renewal Level 6, Deadly Strike Level 1 ◆ Level 3: Critical evel 14, Fierce Renewal Level 12, Deadly Strike Level 12

Level	Elemental Damage	Attack Rate Bonus %	Vulnerability to Melee and Ranged Damage	Duration
1	**Minimum**: (3.7 + 0.9 × melee level) × (2.0 + 0.015 × melee level) **Maximum**: (6.2 + 1.54 × melee level) × (2.0 + 0.015 × melee level)	+10%	-12%	15 s
2	**Minimum**: (3.6 + 0.87 × melee level) × (2.0 + 0.029 × melee level) **Maximum**: (5.9 + 1.48 × melee level) × (2.0 + 0.029 × melee level)	+15%	-15%	15 s
3	**Minimum**: (3.4 + 0.83 × melee level) × (2.5 + 0.036 × melee level) **Maximum**: (5.7 + 1.42 × melee level) × (2.5 + 0.036 × melee level)	+20%	-20%	15 s

Ranged Powers

Take Aim

Take Aim enhances the next bow, crossbow, or thrown-weapon attack with increased damage. Use the high-damage ranged attack against the toughest present monster. It's a fast-recharge power.

Prerequisites: ◆ **Level 1: Critical Shot Level 1** ◆ **Level 2: Critical Shot Level 5** ◆ **Level 3: Critical Shot Level 8, Penetrate Level 1**

Level	+% Damage with Next Attack
1	1500 + 25 × ranged level
2	1700 + 48 × ranged level
3	2500 + 60 × ranged level

Shrapnel Blast

Shrapnel Blast adds explosive area-of-effect damage to a thrown weapon. Use Shrapnel Blast against a packed group of monsters for maximum damage. At impact, the thrown weapon explodes and the shrapnel spread inflicts additional damage. It's a normal-recharge power.

Prerequisites: ◆ **Level 1: Quick Draw Level 1** ◆ **Level 2: Quick Draw Level 5, Bleed Level 5** ◆ **Level 3: Quick Draw Level 10, Bleed Level 8, Penetrate Level 6**

Level	% Normal Damage to Enemies	Explosive Damage	Number of Missiles
1	950 + 17 × ranged level	80 + 1.5 × ranged level	5
2	1450 + 24 × ranged level	130 + 3.0 × ranged level	7
3	1700 + 30 × ranged level	200 + 6.0 × ranged level	9

Thunderous Shot

Thunderous Shot fires an arrow or bolt projectile that passes through enemies and leaves them stunned for a short duration. Use this power against a line of approaching enemies or to temporarily stun a tough monster. Thunderous Shot can be used only with a bow or crossbow and is normal-recharge.

Prerequisites: ◆ **Level 1: Biting Arrow Level 1** ◆ **Level 2: Biting Arrow Level 8, Far Shot Level 1** ◆ **Level 3: Biting Arrow Level 12, Far Shot Level 8, Mortal Wound Level 5**

Level	Damage Bonus	Stun Duration
1	530 + 9 × ranged level	6 s
2	1025 + 16 × ranged level	8 s
3	1225 + 21 × ranged level	10 s

Flurry

Flurry temporarily increases the firing rate and damage of thrown weapons, but at the expense of accuracy. It's optimal to fight for the power's entire duration, so use Flurry when facing several tough monsters. Flurry can be used only with a thrown weapon and is slow-recharge.

Prerequisites: ◆ **Level 1: Critical Shot Level 8, Cunning Renewal Level 4** ◆ **Level 2: Critical Shot Level 10, Cunning Renewal Level 8, Ricochet Level 8** ◆ **Level 3: Critical Shot Level 14, Cunning Renewal Level 12, Ricochet Level 12**

Level	Attack Rate Multiplier	% Normal Damage to Enemies	Duration
1	1.2	180 + 1.4 × ranged level	15 s
2	1.4	205 + 2.2 × ranged level	15 s
3	1.5	210 + 2.6 × ranged level	15 s

Silence

Silence is an area-of-effect spell that prevents affected monsters from casting damage, heal, summon, enhancement, curse, or resurrect spells. You should generally save this spell for use against groups of monster mages or a strong enemy mage, though other monster types can cast spells. Silence is a fast-recharge power.

Prerequisites: ◆ **Level 1: Dodge Level 5, Survival Level 3** ◆ **Level 2: Dodge Level 10, Survival Level 6, Mortal Wound Level 1** ◆ **Level 3: Dodge Level 14, Survival Level 10, Mortal Wound Level 12**

Level	Silence Radius	Duration
1	4 m	15 s
2	5 m	20 s
3	6 m	25 s

Repulse

Repulse knocks back monsters surrounding the user. Monster stun duration is short, so Repulse can be difficult to use as a setup for another power. Ideally, use it when surrounded by several monsters; target stunned monsters with other attacks or powers. Repulse remains around the user for a short duration, preventing monsters from approaching or attacking. It's a slow-recharge power.

Prerequisites: ◆ **Level 1: Dodge Level 4, Survival Level 3** ◆ **Level 2: Dodge Level 10, Survival Level 6, Ricochet Level 1** ◆ **Level 3: Dodge Level 14, Survival Level 10, Ricochet Level 12**

Class Powers

Level	Repulse Radius	Knockback Distance	Stun Duration	Power duration
1	3 m	3 m	1.5 s	12 s
2	3.5 m	5 m	1.5 s	16 s
3	4 m	7 m	1.5 s	20 s

Charged Shots

Charged Shots adds lightning damage to every bow or crossbow projectile. This power is even more devastating against monsters that are weak to lightning damage, and less so against monsters that are resistant to lightning. Charged Shots can be used only with a bow or crossbow and is slow-recharge.

Prerequisites: ◆ Level 1: Critical Shot Level 8, Shockwave Level 4 ◆ Level 2: Critical Shot Level 10, Shockwave Level 8, Mortal Wound Level 8 ◆ Level 3: Critical Shot Level 14, Shockwave Level 12, Mortal Wound Level 12

Level	Lightning Damage	Duration
1	**Minimum:** (18 + 4.5 × ranged level) × (2.0 + 0.015 × ranged level) **Maximum:** (30 + 7.5 × ranged level) × (2.0 + 0.015 × ranged level)	12 s
2	**Minimum:** (15 + 3.6 × ranged level) × (2.6 + 0.029 × ranged level) **Maximum:** (25 + 6.25 × ranged level) × (2.6 + 0.029 × ranged level)	14 s
3	**Minimum:** (13.8 + 3.5 × ranged level) × (2.9 + 0.036 × ranged level) **Maximum:** (23 + 5.8 × ranged level) × (2.9 + 0.036 × ranged level)	15 s

Combat-Magic Powers

Flame Nexus

Flame Nexus allows the user to launch a devastating fireball that continues through monsters and inflicts high fire damage. It attacks monsters in front of the user; activate Flame Nexus when facing a large pack of monsters. The power is even stronger against monsters weak to fire; it's weaker against monsters resistant to fire. Flame Nexus is a normal-recharge power.

Prerequisites: ◆ Level 1: Devastation Level 2, Searing Flames Level 1 ◆ Level 2: Devastation Level 5, Searing Flames Level 4 ◆ Level 3: Devastation Level 12, Searing Flames Level 8, Ignite Level 5

Level	Fire Damage
1	(40 + 10 × combat magic level) × (0.82 + 0.015 × combat magic level) × (1 + (increased power damage percentage × .01)) × ((1+ increased fire damage × .01))
2	(40 + 10 × combat magic level) × (1.15 + 0.029 × combat magic level) × (1 + (increased power damage percentage × .01)) × ((1+ increased fire damage × .01))
3	(40 + 10 × combat magic level) × (2.00 + 0.036 × combat magic level) × (1 + (increased power damage percentage × .01)) × ((1+ increased fire damage × .01))

Detonation

Detonation is an area-of-effect power that inflicts high fire damage against monsters caught in the blast radius. Save this slow-recharge power to use against huge groups of monsters. Lure monsters into position if needed. Detonation is even better against monsters weak to fire.

Prerequisites: ◆ Level 1: Ignite Level 1, Searing Flames Level 8 ◆ Level 2: Ignite Level 6, Searing Flames Level 12 ◆ Level 3: Ignite Level 10, Searing Flames Level 16, Arcane Fury Level 8

Level	Fire Damage	Radius
1	(67.5 + 16.9 × combat magic level) × (2.0 + 0.015 × combat magic level) × (1+ (increased power damage percentage × .01)) + 1 + (increased fire damage × .01)	3 m (4 targets)
2	(67.5 + 16.9 × combat magic level) × (2.0 + 0.029 × combat magic level) × (1+ (increased power damage percentage × .01)) + 1 + (increased fire damage × .01)	3.5 m (4 targets)
3	(67.5 + 16.9 × combat magic level) × (2.7 + 0.036 × combat magic level) × (1+ (increased power damage percentage × .01)) + 1 + (increased fire damage × .01)	4 m (4 targets)

Harvest Soul

Harvest Soul is an area-of-effect death-damage power. Like Detonation, activate Harvest Soul against a group of tightly packed monsters (lure them into position if necessary). A percentage of death damage inflicted is returned to the party as health. This is a normal-recharge power.

Prerequisites: ◆ Level 1: Devastation Level 6, Grim Necromancy Level 5 ◆ Level 2: Devastation Level 8, Grim Necromancy Level 8, Vampirism Level 4 ◆ Level 3: Devastation Level 10, Grim Necromancy Level 12, Vampirism Level 10

Level	Death Damage	Radius	Percentage of Damage Healed
1	(40 + 10 × combat magic level) × (1.5 + 0.015 × combat magic level) × (1 + (increased power damage percentage × .01)) × (1 + (increased death damage × .01))	3 m	6%
2	(40 + 10 × combat magic level) × (2.0 + 0.029 × combat magic level) × (1 + (increased power damage percentage × .01)) × (1 + (increased death damage × .01))	3 m	6%
3	(40 + 10 × combat magic level) × (2.5 + 0.036 × combat magic level) × (1 + (increased power damage percentage × .01)) × (1 + (increased death damage × .01))	3 m	6%

Energy Orb

This power summons an Energy Orb above the user; the orb also fires projectile attacks against monsters. Prerequisites for this power are inexpensive, but spending points in Brilliance early delays availability of other powers. This is a fast-recharge power.

Prerequisites: ◆ Level 1: Brilliance Level 1 ◆ Level 2: Brilliance Level 4, Devastation Level 2 ◆ Level 3: Brilliance Level 8, Devastation Level 4

Level	Damage	Duration
1	**Minimum**: (20 + 5 × combat magic level) × (0.82 + 0.015 × combat magic level) × (1+ (increased power damage percentage × .01)) **Maximum**: (30 + 7.5 × combat magic level) × (0.82 + 0.015 × combat magic level) × (+1 (increased power damage percentage × .01))	20 s
2	**Minimum**: (20 + 5 × combat magic level) × (1.00 + 0.029 × combat magic level) × (1+ (increased power damage percentage × .01) **Maximum**: (30 + 7.5 × combat magic level) × (1.00 + 0.029 × combat magic level) × (+1 (increased power damage percentage × .01))	20 s
3	**Minimum**: (20 + 5 × combat magic level) × (1.20 + 0.036 × combat magic level) × (1+ (increased power damage percentage × .01) **Maximum**: (30 + 7.5 × combat magic level) × (1.20 + 0.036 × combat magic level) × (+1 (increased power damage percentage × .01))	20 s

Chain Lightning

Chain Lightning hurls a bolt of lightning that shocks the nearest enemy then jumps to nearby monsters. The lightning bolt inflicts reduced damage with each jump. Activate it when the closest monster is one of the strongest. Chain Lightning is even stronger against enemies weak to lightning damage. This is a fast-recharge power.

Prerequisites: ◆ Level 1: Amplified Lightning Level 1, Devastation Level 2 ◆ Level 2: Amplified Lightning Level 4, Devastation Level 5 ◆ Level 3: Amplified Lightning Level 8, Devastation Level 12, Arcing Level 5

Level	Lightning Damage	Number of Jumps	Damage on Next Hit
1	(66.4 + 16.6 × combat magic level) × (0.82 + 0.015 × combat magic level) × (1 + (increased power damage percentage × .01)) + (1 + increased lightning damage × .01))	2	38%
2	(66.4 + 16.6 × combat magic level) × (1.20 + 0.029 × combat magic level) × (1 + (increased power damage percentage × .01)) + ((1 + increased lightning damage × .01))	4	22%
3	(66.4 + 16.6 × combat magic level) × (2.00 + 0.036 × combat magic level) × (1 + (increased power damage percentage × .01)) + (1 + increased lightning damage × .01))	6	15%

Gathered Bolt

Gathered Bolt is an area-of-effect lightning-damage power. Target an enemy or terrain; within the next couple of seconds, the massive lightning bolt crashes down. Because there is a small delay, target the ter-

rain where you expect monsters to be within a couple of seconds, not where the monsters currently stand. Gathered belt has a slow recharge.

Prerequisites: ◆ Level 1: Amplified Lightning Level 8, Quickened Casting Level 1 ◆ Level 2: Amplified Lightning Level 10, Quickened Casting Level 6, Arcane Fury Level 1 ◆ Level 3: Amplified Lightning Level 14, Quickened Casting Level 12, Arcane Fury Level 6

Level	Lightning Damage	Radius
1	(70 + 17.5 × combat magic level) × (1.85 + 0.015 × combat magic level) × (1 + (increased power damage percentage × .01)) + ((1 + increased lightning damage × .01))	3.5 m
2	(70 + 17.5 × combat magic level) × (2.00 + 0.029 × combat magic level) × (1 + (increased power damage percentage × .01)) + ((1 + increased lightning damage × .01))	4 m
3	(70 + 17.5 × combat magic level) × (2.5 + 0.036 × combat magic level) × (1 + (increased power damage percentage × .01)) + ((1 + increased lightning damage × .01))	5 m

Corrosive Eruption

Corrosive Eruption is an area-of-effect power. Activate the power against a packed group of monsters; the monsters will be caught within a poisonous gas cloud. When a monster dies from the effect, it inflicts additional damage against nearby monsters. This is a normal-recharge power.

Prerequisites: ◆ Level 1: Debilitation Level 1 ◆ Level 2: Debilitation Level 5, Grim Necromancy Level 4 ◆ Level 3: Debilitation Level 12, Grim Necromancy Level 10, Arcane Fury Level 4

Level	Cloud Radius	Curse Duration	Eruption Damage (% of Max. Monster Health)	Eruption Radius
1	4 m	30 s	45 × (1 + (increase power damage percentage × .01)) × (1 + (increased death damage × .01))	2.5 m
2	5 m	60 s	60 × (1 + (increase power damage percentage × .01)) × (1 + (increased death damage × .01))	2.5 m
3	6 m	300 s	70 × (1 + (increase power damage percentage × .01)) × (1 + (increased death damage × .01))	2.5 m

Nature-Magic Powers

Gravity Stone

Activate Gravity Stone to summon a massive stone that pulls monsters close and holds them in place. This is an excellent way of setting up a follow-up area-of-effect power; the Gravity Stone packs monsters together, leaving them vulnerable to another power's blast radius. This is a fast-recharge power.

Prerequisites: ◆ Level 1: Natural Bond Level 1 ◆ Level 2: Natural Bond Level 5 ◆ Level 3: Natural Bond Level 8, Arcane Renewal Level 6

Level	Radius	Duration
1	4 m	4 s
2	5 m	5 s
3	6 m	6 s

Icicle Blast

Icicle Blast launches shards of ice in front of the user. Activate when facing several monsters in close proximity. Icicle Blast inflicts ice damage (even more powerful against monsters weak to ice) and knocks monsters back. It's normal-recharge.

Prerequisites:
◆ **Level 1: Aquatic Affinity Level 2** ◆ **Level 2: Aquatic Affinity Level 5, Arctic Mastery Level 5** ◆ **Level 3: Aquatic Affinity Level 10, Arctic Mastery Level 10, Freezing Level 8**

Level	Ice Damage
1	(56 + 14 × nature magic level) × (0.82 + 0.015 × nature magic level) × (1 + (increased power damage percentage × .01)) × (1+ (increased ice damage × .01))
2	(56 + 14 × nature magic level) × (1.3 + 0.029 × nature magic level) × (1 + (increased power damage percentage × .01)) × (1+ (increased ice damage × .01))
3	(56 + 14 × nature magic level) × (2.0 + 0.036 × nature magic level) × (1 + (increased power damage percentage × .01)) × (1+ (increased ice damage × .01))

Circle of Frost

Circle of Frost is an area-of-effect power that inflicts ice damage and freezes damaged monsters for a long duration. Focus subsequent attacks on frozen monsters or activate a second power to take advantage of the immobilized creatures. This is a slow-recharge power.

Prerequisites: ◆ **Level 1: Natural Bond Level 5, Arctic Mastery Level 8, Freezing Level 1** ◆ **Level 2: Natural Bond Level 6, Arctic Mastery Level 10, Freezing Level 6** ◆ **Level 3: Natural Bond Level 8, Arctic Mastery Level 12, Freezing Level 12**

Level	Ice Damage	Freeze Duration	Radius
1	(13.3 + 3.3 × nature magic level) × (2.0 + 0.015 × nature magic level) × (1 + (increased power damage percentage × .01)) × (1 + (increased ice damage × .01))	12 s	3.5 m
2	(13.3 + 3.3 × nature magic level) × (2.0 + 0.029 × nature magic level) × (1 + (increased power damage percentage × .01)) × (1 + (increased ice damage × .01))	15 s	4 m
3	(13.3 + 3.3 × nature magic level) × (2.5 + 0.036 × nature magic level) × (1 + (increased power damage percentage × .01)) × (1 + (increased ice damage × .01))	18 s	4.5 m

Summon Provoke

Summon Provoke causes monsters to focus their wrath on a mage's summoned creature. Take advantage of the monsters' distraction and eliminate them. This power can only be used when the mage has summoned a creature, and it's fast-recharge. The power targets monsters around the caster, so move the mage into position for optimum results.

Prerequisites: ◆ **Level 1: Summon Fortitude Level 3, Summon Might Level 1** ◆ **Level 2: Summon Fortitude Level 7, Summon Might Level 4** ◆ **Level 3: Summon Fortitude Level 12, Summon Might Level 6, Summon Bond Level 6**

Level	Radius
1	6 m
2	7 m
3	8 m

Aether Blast

Aether Blast essentially creates a summoned-creature bomb. Aether Blast causes a mage's summoned creature to explode; the more powerful the summoned creature, the more deadly the blast. A duo of nature mages could use Summon Provoke then Aether Blast as a one-two explosive punch. This is a normal-recharge power.

Prerequisites: ◆ **Level 1: Summon Might Level 8, Arcane Renewal Level 1** ◆ **Level 2: Summon Might Level 10, Arcane Renewal Level 6, Summon Bond Level 2** ◆ **Level 3: Summon Might Level 14, Arcane Renewal Level 8, Summon Bond Level 12**

Level	Blast Radius	Stun Duration	Blast Damage
1	3.5 m	5 s	(240 + 1.8 × nature magic level) × (1 + (increased power damage percentage × .01))
2	4 m	5 s	(240 + 3.5 × nature magic level) × (1 + (increased power damage percentage × .01))
3	5 m	5 s	(350 + 4.3 × nature magic level) × (1 + (increased power damage percentage × .01))

Glacial Aura

Glacial Aura creates a frozen mist around the user. These waves of frost damage briefly freeze any monsters they touch. Move the user near monsters to freeze and inflict ice damage. This is a slow-recharge power.

Prerequisites: ◆ **Level 1: Feral Wrath Level 8, Freezing Level 1** ◆ **Level 2: Feral Wrath Level 12, Freezing Level 12, Absorption Level 6** ◆ **Level 3: Feral Wrath Level 14, Freezing Level 15, Absorption Level 12**

Level	Ice Damage Per Wave	Aura Duration	Freeze Duration	Radius
1	(2.6 + 0.65 × nature magic level) × (2.0 + 0.015 × nature magic level) × (1 + (increase power damage percentage × .01)) × (1 + (increased ice damage × .01))	10 s	4 s	2 m
2	(2.2 + 0.54 × nature magic level) × (2.6 + 0.029 × nature magic level) × (1 + (increase power damage percentage × .01)) × (1 + (increased ice damage × .01))	12 s	5 s	2 m

(continued)

Level	Ice Damage Per Wave	Aura Duration	Freeze Duration	Radius
3	(1.7 + 0.44 × nature magic level) × (2.9 + 0.036 × nature magic level) × (1 + (increase power damage percentage × .01)) × (1 + (increased ice damage × .01))	15 s	6 s	2 m

Invulnerability

This power makes all party members invulnerable for a short period of time. Activate this valuable power when facing a large group of tough monsters or a boss. Maximize its use by aggressively attacking while the party remains invulnerable. It's a normal-recharge power.

Prerequisites: ◆ Level 1: Enveloping Embrace Level 1 ◆ Level 2: Enveloping Embrace Level 6, Nurturing Gift Level 4 ◆ Level 3: Enveloping Embrace Level 12, Nurturing Gift Level 8, Arcane Renewal Level 6

Level	Duration
1	6 s
2	8 s
3	12 s

Weapons

These charts include detailed statistics for all base weaponry. Most base weapons include more than one variant. Although the weapon's name is the same, its statistics are different. In general, the earlier in the game you are, the lower the requirement to wield a weapon and the lower damage it dishes out. Enchantment prefixes and suffixes are added to these base items to create a near-infinite combination of magic items.

Axes

Name	Requirements	Damage	1H/2H	Gold Value	Inventory Height, Width
Feeble Battle Axe	Melee 1	4–7	1H	34	3,1
Battle Axe	Melee 1	4–7	1H	34	3,1
	Melee 10	9–15	1H	124	3,1
	Melee 28	19–32	1H	304	3,1
	Melee 40	25–43	1H	424	3,1
	Melee 52	32–54	1H	544	3,1
Forest Pick	Melee 5	6–10	1H	74	3,2
	Melee 19	14–23	1H	214	3,2
	Melee 32	21–35	1H	344	3,2
	Melee 48	30–50	1H	504	3,2
	Melee 61	37–62	1H	634	3,2
Elven Axe	Melee 18	13–22	1H	204	3,1
	Melee 35	23–38	1H	374	3,1
	Melee 63	38–64	1H	654	3,1
	Melee 68	41–69	1H	704	3,1
	Melee 78	46–78	1H	804	3,1
Vai'Kesh Cleaver	Melee 24	16–28	1H	264	3,1
	Melee 54	33–56	1H	564	3,1
	Melee 77	46–77	1H	794	3,1
	Melee 82	49–81	1H	844	3,1
	Melee 87	51–86	1H	894	3,1
Rift Axe	Melee 31	20–34	1H	334	3,1
	Melee 71	43–71	1H	734	3,1
	Melee 80	48–80	1H	824	3,1
	Melee 90	53–89	1H	924	3,1
	Melee 92	54–91	1H	944	3,1
War Axe	Melee 7, Overbear 1	12–20	2H	94	3,2
	Melee 15, Overbear 1	19–32	2H	174	3,2
	Melee 33, Overbear 1	35–59	2H	354	3,2
	Melee 44, Overbear 1	45–75	2H	464	3,2
	Melee 60, Overbear 1	59–99	2H	624	3,2
Viper Axe	Melee 25, Overbear 1	28–47	2H	274	3,1
	Melee 49, Overbear 1	49–83	2H	514	3,1
	Melee 75, Overbear 1	73–122	2H	774	3,1

(continued)

Name	Requirements	Damage	1H/2H	Gold Value	Inventory Height, Width
	Melee 83, Overbear 1	80–134	2H	854	3,1
	Melee 88, Overbear 1	84–141	2H	904	3,1

Bows

Name	Requirements	Damage	Range	Gold Value	Inventory Height, Width
Short Bow	N/A	2–3	9	4	3,1
	Ranged 6, Character 7	6–11	9	94	3,1
	Ranged 15, Character 19	12–20	9	214	3,1
	Ranged 27, Character 32	18–31	9	344	3,1
	Ranged 35, Character 41	23–38	9	434	3,1
Scout Bow	Ranged 1	3–6	9	34	4,1
	Ranged 12	9–15	9	144	4,1
	Ranged 26	15–26	9	284	4,1
	Ranged 38	21–36	9	404	4,1
	Ranged 47	26–43	9	494	4,1
Dryad Bow	Ranged 5	5–9	9	74	4,1
	Ranged 14	10–16	9	164	4,1
	Ranged 34	19–33	9	364	4,1
	Ranged 43	24–40	9	454	4,1
	Ranged 54	29–49	9	564	4,1
Composite Bow	Ranged 10	8–13	9	124	4,1
	Ranged 21	13–22	9	234	4,1
	Ranged 40	22–37	9	424	4,1
	Ranged 48	26–44	9	504	4,1
	Ranged 60	32–54	9	624	4,1
Curve Bow	Ranged 13, Character 17	11–19	9	194	3,1
	Ranged 24, Character 29	17–28	9	314	3,1
	Ranged 35, Character 45	25–41	9	474	3,1
	Ranged 46, Character 52	28–47	9	544	3,1
	Ranged 55, Character 65	34–58	9	674	3,1
Stalker Bow	Ranged 23	14–24	9	254	3,1
	Ranged 37	21–35	9	394	3,1
	Ranged 51	28–46	9	534	3,1
	Ranged 58	31–52	9	604	3,1
	Ranged 71	37–63	9	734	3,1
Elven Longbow	Ranged 27	16–27	9	294	4,1
	Ranged 42	23–39	9	444	4,1
	Ranged 55	30–50	9	574	4,1
	Ranged 63	33–56	9	654	4,1
	Ranged 78	41–69	9	814	4,1
Ironwood Bow	Ranged 31	18–30	9	334	4,1
	Ranged 49	27–45	9	514	4,1
	Ranged 68	36–60	9	704	4,1
	Ranged 76	40–67	9	784	4,1
	Ranged 84	44–73	9	864	4,1
Swift Bow	Ranged 35	20–33	9	374	4,1
	Ranged 73	38–64	9	754	4,1
	Ranged 82	43–72	9	844	4,1
	Ranged 87	45–76	9	894	4,1
	Ranged 91	47–79	9	934	4,1

Cestus

Name	Requirements	Damage	1H/2H	Gold Value	Inventory Height, Width
Weak Arcane Cestus	Mage 1	1–3	2H	34	2,2
Arcane Cestus	Mage 10	4–6	2H	124	2,2
	Mage 20	6–10	2H	224	2,2
	Mage 41	11–18	2H	434	2,2

(continued)

Name	Requirements	Damage	1H/2H	Gold Value	Inventory Height, Width
	Mage 49	13–21	2H	514	2,2
	Mage 58	15–25	2H	604	2,2
Cryptic Cestus	Mage 25	7–12	2H	274	2,2
	Mage 44	11–19	2H	464	2,2
	Mage 54	14–23	2H	564	2,2
	Mage 61	15–26	2H	634	2,2
	Mage 71	18–30	2H	734	2,2
Spirit Cestus	Mage 34	9–16	2H	364	2,2
	Mage 66	17–28	2H	684	2,2
	Mage 79	20–33	2H	814	2,2
	Mage 85	21–35	2H	874	2,2
	Mage 90	22–37	2H	924	2,2

Clubs

Name	Requirements	Damage	1H/2H	Gold Value	Inventory Height, Width
Club	N/A	2–4	1H	4	2,1
	Melee 5, Character 6	6–11	1H	84	2,1
	Melee 13, Character 16	12–20	1H	184	2,1
	Melee 22, Character 27	18–31	1H	294	2,1
	Melee 30, Character 36	23–39	1H	384	2,1
Spiked Club	Melee 2, Character 2	4–7	1H	44	2,1
	Melee 18, Character 23	16–27	1H	254	2,1
	Melee 44, Character 50	31–52	1H	524	2,1
	Melee 50, Character 56	34–57	1H	584	2,1
	Melee 58, Character 64	39–65	1H	664	2,1

Crossbows

Name	Requirements	Damage	Range	Gold Value	Inventory Height, Width
Mercenary Crossbow	Ranged 4, Biting Arrow 1	9–15	9	64	3,2
	Ranged 8, Biting Arrow 1	12–21	9	104	3,2
	Ranged 20, Biting Arrow 1	23–39	9	224	3,2
	Ranged 28, Biting Arrow 1	30–51	9	304	3,2
	Ranged 38, Biting Arrow 1	39–66	9	404	3,2
Light Crossbow	Ranged 11, Biting Arrow 1	15–26	9	134	3,2
	Ranged 11, Biting Arrow 1	21–35	9	194	3,2
	Ranged 30, Biting Arrow 1	33–56	9	334	3,2
	Ranged 44, Biting Arrow 1	46–77	9	474	3,2
	Ranged 57, Biting Arrow 1	57–95	9	594	3,2
Heavy Crossbow	Ranged 14, Biting Arrow 1	18–30	9	164	3,2
	Ranged 41, Biting Arrow 1	42–71	9	434	3,2
	Ranged 53, Biting Arrow 1	53–89	9	554	3,2
	Ranged 61, Biting Arrow 1	60–101	9	634	3,2
	Ranged 70, Biting Arrow 1	68–114	9	724	3,2
Arbalest	Ranged 24, Biting Arrow 1	27–45	9	264	3,2
	Ranged 49, Biting Arrow 1	49–83	9	514	3,2
	Ranged 64, Biting Arrow 1	63–105	9	664	3,2
	Ranged 74, Biting Arrow 1	72–120	9	764	3,2
	Ranged 80, Biting Arrow 1	77–129	9	824	3,2
Ballista	Ranged 34, Biting Arrow 1	36–60	9	364	3,2
	Ranged 67, Biting Arrow 1	66–110	9	694	3,2
	Ranged 77, Biting Arrow 1	75–125	9	794	3,2
	Ranged 85, Biting Arrow 1	82–137	9	874	3,2
	Ranged 89, Biting Arrow 1	85–143	9	914	3,2

Daggers

Name	Requirements	Damage	1H/2H	Gold Value	Inventory Height, Width
Dagger	N/A	2–4	1H	4	2,1
	Melee 7, Character 9	8–14	1H	94	2,1
	Melee 24, Character 29	19–32	1H	264	2,1
	Melee 31, Character 37	24–40	1H	334	2,1
	Melee 39, Character 45	28–47	1H	414	2,1
Royal Dagger	Melee 28, Character 34	22–37	1H	304	2,1
	Melee 54, Character 60	36–61	1H	564	2,1
	Melee 71, Character 77	46–77	1H	734	2,1
	Melee 79, Character 85	50–84	1H	814	2,1
	Melee 82, Character 88	52–87	1H	834	2,1

Hammers

Name	Requirements	Damage	1H/2H	Gold Value	Inventory Height, Width
Hammer	N/A	3–5	1H	14	3,1
	Melee 8	8–13	1H	104	3,1
	Melee 21	15–25	1H	234	3,1
	Melee 33	21–36	1H	354	3,1
	Melee 42	26–44	1H	444	3,1
Dryad Hammer	Melee 3	5–8	1H	54	3,1
	Melee 14	11–19	1H	164	3,1
	Melee 39	25–42	1H	414	3,1
	Melee 46	29–48	1H	484	3,1
	Melee 58	35–59	1H	604	3,1
Spiked Hammer	Melee 17	13–21	1H	194	3,2
	Melee 43	27–45	1H	454	3,2
	Melee 51	31–53	1H	534	3,2
	Melee 59	36–60	1H	614	3,2
	Melee 69	41–69	1H	714	3,2
Sledge	Melee 4, Overbear 1	9–15	2H	64	3,2
	Melee 11, Overbear 1	15–26	2H	134	3,2
	Melee 21, Overbear 1	24–41	2H	234	3,2
	Melee 27, Overbear 1	30–50	2H	294	3,2
	Melee 37, Overbear 1	39–65	2H	394	3,2
Soldier Hammer	Melee 17, Overbear 1	21–35	2H	174	4,2
	Melee 31, Overbear 1	33–56	2H	334	4,2
	Melee 42, Overbear 1	43–72	2H	444	4,2
	Melee 55, Overbear 1	55–92	2H	574	4,2
	Melee 67, Overbear 1	66–110	2H	694	4,2

Maces

Name	Requirements	Damage	1H/2H	Gold Value	Inventory Height, Width
Mace	N/A	3–6	1H	24	3,1
	Melee 12	10–17	1H	144	3,1
	Melee 28	19–32	1H	304	3,1
	Melee 38	24–41	1H	404	3,1
	Melee 47	29–49	1H	494	3,1
Flanged Mace	Melee 20	14–24	1H	224	3,1
	Melee 53	33–55	1H	554	3,1
	Melee 66	40–67	1H	684	3,1
	Melee 72	43–72	1H	744	3,1
	Melee 81	48–81	1H	834	3,1

Staffs

Name	Requirements	Damage	1H/2H	Gold Value	Inventory Height, Width
Fighter Staff	Melee 4, Overbear 1	9–15	2H	64	4,1

(continued)

Name	Requirements	Damage	1H/2H	Gold Value	Inventory Height, Width
	Melee 12, Overbear 1	16–27	2H	144	4,1
	Melee 28, Overbear 1	30–51	2H	304	4,1
	Melee 44, Overbear 1	45–75	2H	464	4,1
	Melee 60, Overbear 1	59–99	2H	624	4,1
Bladed Staff	Melee 20, Overbear 1	23–39	2H	224	4,1
	Melee 36, Overbear 1	38–63	2H	384	4,1
	Melee 52, Overbear 1	52–87	2H	544	4,1
	Melee 68, Overbear 1	66–111	2H	704	4,1
	Melee 77, Overbear 1	75–125	2H	794	4,1
Bent Druid Staff	Mage 1	4–7	2H	34	4,1
Ritual Staff	N/A	3–5	2H	14	4,1
	Mage 7	8–14	2H	94	4,1
	Mage 17	14–24	2H	194	4,1
	Mage 36	27–45	2H	384	4,1
	Mage 46	33–55	2H	484	4,1
Druid Staff	Mage 3	6–10	2H	54	4,1
	Mage 14	13–21	2H	164	4,1
	Mage 27	21–35	2H	294	4,1
	Mage 51	36–61	2H	534	4,1
	Mage 64	44–74	2H	664	4,1
Elven Staff	Mage 22	18–30	2H	244	4,1
	Mage 29	22–37	2H	314	4,1
	Mage 56	39–66	2H	584	4,1
	Mage 69	48–80	2H	714	4,1
	Mage 77	53–88	2H	794	4,1
Yearling Staff	Mage 31	23–39	2H	334	4,1
	Mage 39	28–48	2H	414	4,1
	Mage 74	51–85	2H	764	4,1
	Mage 82	56–93	2H	844	4,1
	Mage 87	59–99	2H	894	4,1

Swords

Name	Requirements	Damage	1H/2H	Gold Value	Inventory Height, Width
Rusty Short Sword	N/A	3–6	1H	24	3,1
Short Sword	N/A	3–6	1H	24	3,1
	Melee 11	9–16	1H	134	3,1
	Melee 30	20–33	1H	324	3,1
	Melee 40	25–43	1H	424	3,1
	Melee 49	30–51	1H	514	3,1
Dryad Sword	Melee 3, Character 4	5–9	1H	64	3,1
	Melee 10, Character 13	10–18	1H	154	3,1
	Melee 28, Character 34	22–37	1H	364	3,1
	Melee 38, Character 44	28–46	1H	464	3,1
	Melee 45, Character 55	34–56	1H	574	3,1
Gladius	Melee 7	7–12	1H	94	3,1
	Melee 25	17–29	1H	274	3,1
	Melee 47	29–49	1H	494	3,1
	Melee 57	35–58	1H	594	3,1
	Melee 67	40–68	1H	694	3,1
Long Sword	Melee 15	11–19	1H	174	3,1
	Melee 31	20–34	1H	334	3,1
	Melee 53	33–55	1H	554	3,1
	Melee 62	38–63	1H	644	3,1
	Melee 73	44–73	1H	754	3,1
Elven Sword	Melee 22	15–26	1H	244	3,1
	Melee 41	26–44	1H	434	3,1
	Melee 70	42–70	1H	724	3,1

(continued)

Weapons

Name	Requirements	Damage	1H/2H	Gold Value	Inventory Height, Width
	Melee 75	45–75	1H	774	3,1
	Melee 84	50–83	1H	864	3,1
Broad Sword	Melee 26	18–30	1H	284	3,1
	Melee 65	39–66	1H	674	3,1
	Melee 79	47–79	1H	814	3,1
	Melee 86	51–85	1H	884	3,1
	Melee 89	53–88	1H	914	3,1
Katana	Melee 37	24–40	1H	394	4,1
	Melee 74	44–74	1H	764	4,1
	Melee 83	49–82	1H	854	4,1
	Melee 91	54–90	1H	934	4,1
	Melee 93	55–92	1H	954	4,1
Bastard Sword	Melee 5, Overbear 1	10–17	2H	74	4,1
	Melee 13, Overbear 1	17–29	2H	154	4,1
	Melee 28, Overbear 1	31–53	2H	314	4,1
	Melee 39, Overbear 1	40–68	2H	414	4,1
	Melee 51, Overbear 1	51–86	2H	534	4,1
Totem Sword	Melee 7, Character 9, Overbear 1	13–23	2H	114	4,1
	Melee 15, Character 19, Overbear 1	22–38	2H	214	4,1
	Melee 40, Character 46, Overbear 1	47–78	2H	484	4,1
	Melee 52, Character 58, Overbear 1	57–96	2H	604	4,1
	Melee 58, Character 64, Overbear 1	63–105	2H	664	4,1
Hunter Sword	Melee 23, Overbear 1	26–44	2H	234	4,1
	Melee 53, Overbear 1	53–89	2H	554	4,1
	Melee 62, Overbear 1	61–102	2H	644	4,1
	Melee 73, Overbear 1	71–119	2H	754	4,1
	Melee 77, Overbear 1	75–125	2H	794	4,1
Hero's Sword	Melee 35, Overbear 1	37–62	2H	374	4,1
	Melee 70, Overbear 1	68–114	2H	724	4,1
	Melee 77, Overbear 1	77–129	2H	794	4,1
	Melee 86, Overbear 1	83–138	2H	884	4,1
	Melee 91, Overbear 1	87–146	2H	934	4,1

Thrown Weapons

Name	Requirements	Damage	Range	Gold Value	Inventory Height, Width
Throwing Knife	Ranged 4, Quick Draw 1	6–11	7.5	64	2,1
	Ranged 11, Quick Draw 1	11–18	7.5	134	2,1
	Ranged 21, Quick Draw 1	17–29	7.5	234	2,1
	Ranged 35, Quick Draw 1	26–44	7.5	374	2,1
	Ranged 45, Quick Draw 1	33–55	7.5	474	2,1
Throwing Axe	Ranged 6, Quick Draw 1	8–13	7.5	84	2,1
	Ranged 13, Quick Draw 1	12–20	7.5	154	2,1
	Ranged 26, Quick Draw 1	20–34	7.5	284	2,1
	Ranged 42, Quick Draw 1	31–52	7.5	444	2,1
	Ranged 52, Quick Draw 1	37–62	7.5	544	2,1
Throwing Crescent	Ranged 7, Character 9, Quick Draw 1	9–16	7.5	114	2,1
	Ranged 14, Character 18, Quick Draw 1	15–26	7.5	204	2,1
	Ranged 27, Character 32, Quick Draw 1	24–41	7.5	344	2,1
	Ranged 48, Character 54, Quick Draw 1	39–65	7.5	564	2,1
	Ranged 55, Character 61, Quick Draw 1	43–72	7.5	634	2,1
Throwing Star	Ranged 16, Quick Draw 1	14–24	7.5	184	2,1
	Ranged 28, Quick Draw 1	22–37	7.5	304	2,1
	Ranged 47, Quick Draw 1	34–57	7.5	494	2,1
	Ranged 63, Quick Draw 1	44–74	7.5	654	2,1
	Ranged 71, Quick Draw 1	49–83	7.5	734	2,1
Glaive	Ranged 23, Quick Draw 1	19–31	7.5	254	2,2
	Ranged 40, Quick Draw 1	29–49	7.5	424	2,2

(continued)

Name	Requirements	Damage	Range	Gold Value	Inventory Height, Width
	Ranged 56, Quick Draw 1	40–67	7.5	584	2,2
	Ranged 68, Quick Draw 1	48–80	7.5	704	2,2
	Ranged 76, Quick Draw 1	53–88	7.5	784	2,2
Chakram	Ranged 30, Quick Draw 1	23–39	7.5	324	2,2
	Ranged 50, Quick Draw 1	36–60	7.5	524	2,2
	Ranged 65, Quick Draw 1	46–76	7.5	674	2,2
	Ranged 79, Quick Draw 1	55–91	7.5	814	2,2
	Ranged 84, Quick Draw 1	58–97	7.5	864	2,2
Throwing Shiv	Ranged 37, Quick Draw 1	28–46	7.5	394	3,1
	Ranged 59, Quick Draw 1	42–70	7.5	614	3,1
	Ranged 73, Quick Draw 1	51–85	7.5	754	3,1
	Ranged 82, Quick Draw 1	57–95	7.5	844	3,1
	Ranged 87, Quick Draw 1	60–100	7.5	894	3,1

Armor

The following charts include detailed statistics for base armor. Pieces of armor feature more than one variant. Although the armor's base name remains the same, its statistics will be different. In general, you'll find armor with lower requirements and poorer defense earlier in the game. Enchantment prefixes and suffixes are added to these base items to create a near-infinite combination of magic items.

Body Armor

Name	Requirements	Defense	Gold Value	Inventory Height, Width
Tattered Apprentice Robe	N/A	7	4	2,2
Apprentice Robe	Combat Magic 1	8	6	2,2
	Combat Magic 7	15	18	2,2
	Combat Magic 16	26	36	2,2
	Combat Magic 31	44	66	2,2
	Combat Magic 43	58	90	2,2
Elementalist Robe	Combat Magic 4	12	12	2,2
	Combat Magic 13	22	30	2,2
	Combat Magic 25	37	54	2,2
	Combat Magic 46	62	96	2,2
	Combat Magic 52	69	108	2,2
Adept Robe	Combat Magic 8, Character 10	19	24	2,2
	Combat Magic 17, Character 22	33	48	2,2
	Combat Magic 34, Character 40	55	84	2,2
	Combat Magic 52, Character 58	76	120	2,2
	Combat Magic 58, Character 64	84	132	2,2
Sorcerer Robe	Combat Magic 19	30	42	3,2
	Combat Magic 34	48	72	3,2
	Combat Magic 55	73	114	3,2
	Combat Magic 70	91	144	3,2
	Combat Magic 76	98	156	3,2
Warlock Robe	Combat Magic 28	40	60	3,2
	Combat Magic 49	66	102	3,2
	Combat Magic 67	87	138	3,2
	Combat Magic 79	102	162	3,2
	Combat Magic 85	109	174	3,2
Archmage Robe	Combat Magic 37	51	78	3,2
	Combat Magic 61	80	126	3,2
	Combat Magic 73	94	150	3,2
	Combat Magic 82	105	168	3,2
	Combat Magic 88	112	180	3,2
Leather Jerkin	Melee 1	14	6	2,2
	Melee 7	26	18	2,2
	Melee 16	44	36	2,2
	Melee 25	62	54	2,2

(continued)

Name	Requirements	Defense	Gold Value	Inventory Height, Width
	Melee 34	80	72	2,2
Studded Tunic	Melee 3, Character 4	20	12	2,2
	Melee 8, Character 10	32	24	2,2
	Melee 15, Character 19	50	42	2,2
	Melee 34, Character 40	92	84	2,2
	Melee 43, Character 49	110	102	2,2
Chain Mail	Melee 13	38	30	3,2
	Melee 28	68	60	3,2
	Melee 46	104	96	3,2
	Melee 55	122	114	3,2
	Melee 61	134	126	3,2
Full Plate	Melee 22	56	48	3,2
	Melee 43	98	90	3,2
	Melee 58	128	120	3,2
	Melee 67	146	138	3,2
	Melee 73	158	150	3,2
Obsidian Armor	Melee 31	74	66	3,2
	Melee 52	116	108	3,2
	Melee 70	152	144	3,2
	Melee 79	170	162	3,2
	Melee 85	182	174	3,2
Mythril Armor	Melee 37	86	78	3,2
	Melee 64	140	132	3,2
	Melee 76	164	156	3,2
	Melee 82	176	168	3,2
	Melee 88	188	180	3,2
Dirty Woven Tunic	N/A	7	4	2,2
Woven Tunic	Nature Magic 2	9	8	2,2
	Nature Magic 8	16	20	2,2
	Nature Magic 17	27	38	2,2
	Nature Magic 26	38	56	2,2
	Nature Magic 35	49	74	2,2
Tribal Armor	Nature Magic 4, Character 5	13	14	2,2
	Nature Magic 9, Character 11	20	26	2,2
	Nature Magic 16, Character 20	31	44	2,2
	Nature Magic 35, Character 41	56	86	2,2
	Nature Magic 44, Character 50	67	104	2,2
Raven Armor	Nature Magic 14	24	32	2,2
	Nature Magic 29	42	62	2,2
	Nature Magic 47	63	98	2,2
	Nature Magic 56	74	116	2,2
	Nature Magic 62	81	128	2,2
Ancestral Armor	Nature Magic 23	34	50	3,2
	Nature Magic 44	60	92	3,2
	Nature Magic 59	78	122	3,2
	Nature Magic 68	88	140	3,2
	Nature Magic 74	96	152	3,2
Dragon Armor	Nature Magic 32	45	68	3,2
	Nature Magic 53	70	110	3,2
	Nature Magic 71	92	146	3,2
	Nature Magic 80	103	164	3,2
	Nature Magic 86	110	176	3,2
Mystic Armor	Nature Magic 38	52	80	3,2
	Nature Magic 65	85	134	3,2
	Nature Magic 77	99	158	3,2
	Nature Magic 83	106	170	3,2
	Nature Magic 89	114	182	3,2

(continued)

Name	Requirements	Defense	Gold Value	Inventory Height, Width
Broken Leaf Jerkin	N/A	9	4	3,2
Leaf Jerkin	Ranged 2	12	8	2,2
	Ranged 8	22	20	2,2
	Ranged 17	36	38	2,2
	Ranged 32	60	68	2,2
	Ranged 44	80	92	2,2
Carved Tunic	Ranged 5	17	14	2,2
	Ranged 14	32	32	2,2
	Ranged 26	51	56	2,2
	Ranged 47	84	98	2,2
	Ranged 53	94	110	2,2
Explorer Armor	Ranged 9, Character 11	27	26	3,2
	Ranged 18, Character 23	46	50	3,2
	Ranged 35, Character 41	75	86	3,2
	Ranged 53, Character 59	104	122	3,2
	Ranged 59, Character 65	113	134	3,2
Elven Armor	Ranged 20	41	44	3,2
	Ranged 35	65	74	3,2
	Ranged 56	99	116	3,2
	Ranged 71	123	146	3,2
	Ranged 77	132	158	3,2
Arboreal Armor	Ranged 29	56	62	3,2
	Ranged 50	89	104	3,2
	Ranged 68	118	140	3,2
	Ranged 80	137	164	3,2
	Ranged 86	147	176	3,2
Twilight Armor	Ranged 38	70	80	3,2
	Ranged 62	108	128	3,2
	Ranged 74	128	152	3,2
	Ranged 83	142	170	3,2
	Ranged 89	152	182	3,2
Windstone Armor	Character 9	30	22	2,2

Boots

Name	Requirements	Defense	Gold Value	Inventory Height, Width
Apprentice Boots	Combat Magic 1	2	6	2,1
	Combat Magic 6	4	16	2,1
	Combat Magic 15	7	34	2,1
	Combat Magic 30	12	64	2,1
	Combat Magic 42	17	88	2,1
Elementalist Boots	Combat Magic 3	3	10	2,1
	Combat Magic 12	6	28	2,1
	Combat Magic 24	10	52	2,1
	Combat Magic 45	18	94	2,1
	Combat Magic 51	20	106	2,1
Adept Boots	Combat Magic 7, Character 9	5	22	2,1
	Combat Magic 17, Character 21	9	46	2,1
	Combat Magic 33, Character 39	16	82	2,1
	Combat Magic 51, Character 57	22	118	2,1
	Combat Magic 57, Character 63	24	130	2,1
Sorcerer Boots	Combat Magic 18	8	40	2,1
	Combat Magic 33	14	70	2,1
	Combat Magic 54	21	112	2,1
	Combat Magic 69	27	142	2,1
	Combat Magic 75	29	154	2,1
Warlock Boots	Combat Magic 27	11	58	2,1
	Combat Magic 48	19	100	2,1

(continued)

ARMOR

Name	Requirements	Defense	Gold Value	Inventory Height, Width
	Combat Magic 66	25	136	2,1
	Combat Magic 78	30	160	2,1
	Combat Magic 84	32	172	2,1
Archmage Boots	Combat Magic 36	15	76	2,1
	Combat Magic 60	23	124	2,1
	Combat Magic 72	28	148	2,1
	Combat Magic 81	31	166	2,1
	Combat Magic 87	33	178	2,1
Leather Boots	Melee 1	4	6	2,1
	Melee 6	7	16	2,1
	Melee 15	12	34	2,1
	Melee 24	18	52	2,1
	Melee 33	23	70	2,1
Studded Boots	Melee 3, Character 3	5	10	2,1
	Melee 7, Character 9	9	22	2,1
	Melee 14, Character 18	14	40	2,1
	Melee 33, Character 39	27	82	2,1
	Melee 42, Character 48	32	100	2,1
Chain Boots	Melee 12	10	28	2,1
	Melee 27	19	58	2,1
	Melee 45	30	94	2,1
	Melee 54	36	112	2,1
	Melee 60	39	124	2,1
Plate Greaves	Melee 21	16	46	2,1
	Melee 42	28	88	2,1
	Melee 57	37	118	2,1
	Melee 66	43	136	2,1
	Melee 72	46	148	2,1
Obsidian Greaves	Melee 30	21	64	2,1
	Melee 51	34	106	2,1
	Melee 69	45	142	2,1
	Melee 78	50	160	2,1
	Melee 84	54	172	2,1
Mythril Greaves	Melee 36	25	76	2,1
	Melee 63	41	130	2,1
	Melee 75	48	154	2,1
	Melee 81	52	166	2,1
	Melee 87	55	178	2,1
Woven Boots	Nature Magic 1	2	6	2,1
	Nature Magic 7	4	18	2,1
	Nature Magic 16	7	36	2,1
	Nature Magic 25	11	54	2,1
	Nature Magic 34	14	72	2,1
Tribal Boots	Nature Magic 3, Character 4	3	12	2,1
	Nature Magic 8, Character 10	5	24	2,1
	Nature Magic 15, Character 19	9	42	2,1
	Nature Magic 34, Character 40	16	84	2,1
	Nature Magic 43, Character 49	19	102	2,1
Raven Boots	Nature Magic 13	6	30	2,1
	Nature Magic 28	12	60	2,1
	Nature Magic 46	18	96	2,1
	Nature Magic 55	21	114	2,1
	Nature Magic 61	24	126	2,1
Ancestral Boots	Nature Magic 22	10	48	2,1
	Nature Magic 43	17	90	2,1
	Nature Magic 58	23	120	2,1
	Nature Magic 67	26	138	2,1

(continued)

Name	Requirements	Defense	Gold Value	Inventory Height, Width
	Nature Magic 73	28	150	2,1
Dragon Boots	Nature Magic 31	13	66	2,1
	Nature Magic 52	20	108	2,1
	Nature Magic 70	27	144	2,1
	Nature Magic 79	30	162	2,1
	Nature Magic 85	32	174	2,1
Mystic Boots	Nature Magic 37	15	78	2,1
	Nature Magic 64	25	132	2,1
	Nature Magic 76	29	156	2,1
	Nature Magic 82	31	168	2,1
	Nature Magic 88	33	180	2,1
Leaf Boots	Ranged 1	3	6	2,1
	Ranged 7	6	18	2,1
	Ranged 16	10	36	2,1
	Ranged 31	17	66	2,1
	Ranged 43	23	90	2,1
Carved Boots	Ranged 4	5	12	2,1
	Ranged 13	9	30	2,1
	Ranged 25	14	54	2,1
	Ranged 46	24	96	2,1
	Ranged 52	27	108	2,1
Explorer Boots	Ranged 8, Character 10	7	24	2,1
	Ranged 17, Character 22	13	48	2,1
	Ranged 34, Character 40	22	84	2,1
	Ranged 52, Character 58	30	120	2,1
	Ranged 58, Character 64	33	132	2,1
Elven Boots	Ranged 19	12	42	2,1
	Ranged 34	19	72	2,1
	Ranged 55	29	114	2,1
	Ranged 70	36	144	2,1
	Ranged 76	39	156	2,1
Arboreal Boots	Ranged 28	16	60	2,1
	Ranged 49	26	102	2,1
	Ranged 67	35	138	2,1
	Ranged 79	40	162	2,1
	Ranged 85	43	174	2,1
Twilight Boots	Ranged 37	20	78	2,1
	Ranged 61	32	126	2,1
	Ranged 73	37	150	2,1
	Ranged 82	42	168	2,1
	Ranged 88	45	180	2,1
Windstone Boots	Character 8	8	20	2,1

Gloves

Name	Requirements	Defense	Gold Value	Inventory Height, Width
Apprentice Gloves	Combat Magic 1	2	6	2,1
	Combat Magic 6	4	16	2,1
	Combat Magic 15	7	34	2,1
	Combat Magic 30	12	64	2,1
	Combat Magic 42	17	88	2,1
Elementalist Gloves	Combat Magic 3	3	10	2,1
	Combat Magic 12	6	28	2,1
	Combat Magic 24	10	52	2,1
	Combat Magic 45	18	94	2,1
	Combat Magic 51	20	106	2,1
Adept Gloves	Combat Magic 7, Character 9	5	22	2,1
	Combat Magic 17, Character 21	9	46	2,1

(continued)

ARMOR

Name	Requirements	Defense	Gold Value	Inventory Height, Width
	Combat Magic 33, Character 39	16	82	2,1
	Combat Magic 51, Character 57	22	118	2,1
	Combat Magic 63	24	130	2,1
Sorcerer Gloves	Combat Magic 18	8	40	2,1
	Combat Magic 33	14	70	2,1
	Combat Magic 54	21	112	2,1
	Combat Magic 69	27	142	2,1
	Combat Magic 75	29	154	2,1
Warlock Gloves	Combat Magic 27	11	58	2,1
	Combat Magic 48	19	100	2,1
	Combat Magic 66	25	136	2,1
	Combat Magic 78	30	160	2,1
	Combat Magic 84	32	172	2,1
Archmage Gloves	Combat Magic 36	15	76	2,1
	Combat Magic 60	23	124	2,1
	Combat Magic 72	28	148	2,1
	Combat Magic 81	31	166	2,1
	Combat Magic 87	33	178	2,1
Leather Gloves	Melee 1	4	6	2,1
	Melee 6	7	16	2,1
	Melee 15	12	34	2,1
	Melee 24	18	52	2,1
	Melee 33	23	70	2,1
Studded Gloves	Melee 3, Character 3	5	10	2,1
	Melee 7, Character 9	9	22	2,1
	Melee 14, Character 18	14	40	2,1
	Melee 33, Character 39	27	82	2,1
	Melee 42, Character 48	32	100	2,1
Chain Gloves	Melee 12	10	28	2,1
	Melee 27	19	58	2,1
	Melee 45	30	94	2,1
	Melee 54	36	112	2,1
	Melee 60	39	124	2,1
Plate Gauntlets	Melee 21	16	46	2,1
	Melee 42	28	88	2,1
	Melee 57	37	118	2,1
	Melee 66	43	136	2,1
	Melee 72	46	148	2,1
Obsidian Gauntlets	Melee 30	21	64	2,1
	Melee 51	34	106	2,1
	Melee 69	45	142	2,1
	Melee 78	50	160	2,1
	Melee 84	54	172	2,1
Mythril Gauntlets	Melee 36	25	76	2,1
	Melee 63	41	130	2,1
	Melee 75	48	154	2,1
	Melee 81	52	166	2,1
	Melee 87	55	178	2,1
Woven Gloves	Nature Magic 1	2	6	2,1
	Nature Magic 7	4	18	2,1
	Nature Magic 16	7	36	2,1
	Nature Magic 25	11	54	2,1
	Nature Magic 34	14	72	2,1
Tribal Gloves	Nature Magic 3, Character 4	3	12	2,1
	Nature Magic 8, Character 10	5	24	2,1
	Nature Magic 15, Character 19	9	42	2,1
	Nature Magic 34, Character 40	16	84	2,1

(continued)

Name	Requirements	Defense	Gold Value	Inventory Height, Width
	Nature Magic 43, Character 49	19	102	2,1
Raven Gloves	Nature Magic 13	6	30	2,1
	Nature Magic 28	12	60	2,1
	Nature Magic 46	18	96	2,1
	Nature Magic 55	21	114	2,1
	Nature Magic 61	24	126	2,1
Ancestral Gloves	Nature Magic 22	10	48	2,1
	Nature Magic 43	17	90	2,1
	Nature Magic 58	23	120	2,1
	Nature Magic 67	26	138	2,1
	Nature Magic 73	28	150	2,1
Dragon Gloves	Nature Magic 31	13	66	2,1
	Nature Magic 52	20	108	2,1
	Nature Magic 70	27	144	2,1
	Nature Magic 79	31	162	2,1
	Nature Magic 85	32	174	2,1
Mystic Gloves	Nature Magic 37	15	78	2,1
	Nature Magic 64	25	132	2,1
	Nature Magic 76	29	156	2,1
	Nature Magic 82	31	168	2,1
	Nature Magic 88	33	180	2,1
Leaf Gloves	Ranged 1	3	6	2,1
	Ranged 7	6	18	2,1
	Ranged 16	10	36	2,1
	Ranged 31	17	66	2,1
	Ranged 43	23	90	2,1
Carved Gloves	Ranged 4	4	12	2,1
	Ranged 13	9	30	2,1
	Ranged 25	14	54	2,1
	Ranged 46	24	96	2,1
	Ranged 52	27	108	2,1
Explorer Gloves	Ranged 8, Character 10	7	24	2,1
	Ranged 17, Character 22	13	48	2,1
	Ranged 34, Character 40	22	84	2,1
	Ranged 52, Character 58	30	120	2,1
	Ranged 58, Character 64	33	132	2,1
Elven Gloves	Ranged 19	12	42	2,1
	Ranged 34	19	72	2,1
	Ranged 55	29	114	2,1
	Ranged 70	36	144	2,1
	Ranged 76	39	156	2,1
Arboreal Gloves	Ranged 28	16	60	2,1
	Ranged 49	26	102	2,1
	Ranged 67	35	138	2,1
	Ranged 79	40	162	2,1
	Ranged 85	43	174	2,1
Twilight Gloves	Ranged 37	20	78	2,1
	Ranged 61	32	126	2,1
	Ranged 73	37	150	2,1
	Ranged 82	42	168	2,1
	Ranged 88	45	180	2,1
Windstone Gloves	Character 8	8	20	2,1

Helmets

Name	Requirements	Defense	Gold Value	Inventory Height, Width
Apprentice Hood	Combat Magic 2	3	8	2,2
	Combat Magic 8	6	20	2,2

(continued)

Name	Requirements	Defense	Gold Value	Inventory Height, Width
	Combat Magic 17	11	38	2,2
	Combat Magic 32	18	68	2,2
	Combat Magic 44	24	92	2,2
Elementalist Cap	Combat Magic 5	5	14	2,2
	Combat Magic 14	9	32	2,2
	Combat Magic 26	15	56	2,2
	Combat Magic 47	25	98	2,2
	Combat Magic 53	28	110	2,2
Adept Helm	Combat Magic 9, Character 11	8	26	2,2
	Combat Magic 18, Character 23	13	50	2,2
	Combat Magic 35, Character 41	22	86	2,2
	Combat Magic 53, Character 59	31	122	2,2
	Combat Magic 59, Character 65	34	134	2,2
Sorcerer Cowl	Combat Magic 20	12	44	2,2
	Combat Magic 35	19	74	2,2
	Combat Magic 56	29	116	2,2
	Combat Magic 71	36	146	2,2
	Combat Magic 77	39	158	2,2
Warlock Mask	Combat Magic 29	16	62	2,2
	Combat Magic 50	26	104	2,2
	Combat Magic 68	35	140	2,2
	Combat Magic 80	41	164	2,2
	Combat Magic 86	44	176	2,2
Archmage Hood	Combat Magic 38	21	80	2,2
	Combat Magic 62	32	128	2,2
	Combat Magic 74	38	152	2,2
	Combat Magic 83	42	170	2,2
	Combat Magic 89	45	182	2,2
Leather Helm	Melee 2	6	8	2,2
	Melee 8	11	20	2,2
	Melee 17	18	38	2,2
	Melee 26	25	56	2,2
	Melee 35	32	74	2,2
Studded Helm	Melee 4, Character 5	8	14	2,2
	Melee 9, Character 11	13	26	2,2
	Melee 16, Character 20	20	44	2,2
	Melee 35, Character 41	37	86	2,2
	Melee 44, Character 50	44	104	2,2
Chain Helm	Melee 14	16	32	2,2
	Melee 29	28	62	2,2
	Melee 47	42	98	2,2
	Melee 56	49	116	2,2
	Melee 62	54	128	2,2
Plate Helm	Melee 23	23	50	2,2
	Melee 44	40	92	2,2
	Melee 59	52	122	2,2
	Melee 68	59	140	2,2
	Melee 74	64	152	2,2
Obsidian Helmet	Melee 32	30	68	2,2
	Melee 53	47	110	2,2
	Melee 71	61	146	2,2
	Melee 80	68	164	2,2
	Melee 86	73	176	2,2
Mythril Helmet	Melee 38	35	80	2,2
	Melee 65	56	134	2,2
	Melee 77	66	158	2,2
	Melee 83	71	170	2,2

(continued)

Name	Requirements	Defense	Gold Value	Inventory Height, Width
	Melee 89	76	182	2,2
Woven Hood	Nature Magic 3	4	10	2,2
	Nature Magic 9	7	22	2,2
	Nature Magic 18	11	40	2,2
	Nature Magic 27	15	58	2,2
	Nature Magic 36	20	76	2,2
Tribal Headdress	Nature Magic 5, Character 6	5	16	2,2
	Nature Magic 10, Character 12	8	28	2,2
	Nature Magic 17, Character 21	12	46	2,2
	Nature Magic 36, Character 42	23	88	2,2
	Nature Magic 45, Character 51	27	106	2,2
Raven Cap	Nature Magic 15	10	34	2,2
	Nature Magic 30	17	64	2,2
	Nature Magic 48	25	100	2,2
	Nature Magic 57	30	118	2,2
	Nature Magic 63	33	130	2,2
Ancestral Helm	Nature Magic 24	14	52	2,2
	Nature Magic 45	24	94	2,2
	Nature Magic 60	31	124	2,2
	Nature Magic 69	36	142	2,2
	Nature Magic 75	38	154	2,2
Dragon Helm	Nature Magic 33	18	70	2,2
	Nature Magic 54	28	112	2,2
	Nature Magic 72	37	148	2,2
	Nature Magic 81	41	166	2,2
	Nature Magic 87	44	178	2,2
Mystic Helm	Nature Magic 39	21	82	2,2
	Nature Magic 66	34	136	2,2
	Nature Magic 78	40	160	2,2
	Nature Magic 84	43	172	2,2
	Nature Magic 90	46	184	2,2
Leaf Hood	Ranged 3	5	10	2,2
	Ranged 9	9	22	2,2
	Ranged 18	15	40	2,2
	Ranged 33	24	70	2,2
	Ranged 45	32	94	2,2
Carved Cap	Ranged 6	7	16	2,2
	Ranged 15	13	34	2,2
	Ranged 27	21	58	2,2
	Ranged 48	34	100	2,2
	Ranged 54	38	112	2,2
Explorer Helm	Ranged 10, Character 12	11	28	2,2
	Ranged 19, Character 24	19	52	2,2
	Ranged 36, Character 42	30	88	2,2
	Ranged 54, Character 60	42	124	2,2
	Ranged 60, Character 66	46	136	2,2
Elven Helm	Ranged 21	17	46	2,2
	Ranged 36	26	76	2,2
	Ranged 57	40	118	2,2
	Ranged 72	49	148	2,2
	Ranged 78	53	160	2,2
Arboreal Horns	Ranged 30	23	64	2,2
	Ranged 51	36	106	2,2
	Ranged 69	48	142	2,2
	Ranged 81	55	166	2,2
	Ranged 87	59	178	2,2
Twilight Hood	Ranged 39	28	82	2,2

(continued)

Name	Requirements	Defense	Gold Value	Inventory Height, Width
	Ranged 63	44	130	2,2
	Ranged 75	51	154	2,2
	Ranged 84	57	172	2,2
	Ranged 90	61	184	2,2
Windstone Helmet	Character 10	12	24	2,2

Shields

Name	Requirements	Defense	Gold Value	Inventory Height, Width
Buckler	Melee 4, Barricade 1	8	12	2,2
	Melee 9, Barricade 1	12	22	2,2
	Melee 15, Barricade 1	16	34	2,2
	Melee 26, Barricade 1	25	56	2,2
	Melee 37, Barricade 1	34	78	2,2
Small Shield	Melee 7, Barricade 1	10	18	2,2
	Melee 13, Barricade 1	15	30	2,2
	Melee 21, Barricade 1	21	46	2,2
	Melee 40, Barricade 1	36	84	2,2
	Melee 45, Barricade 1	40	94	2,2
Heater Shield	Melee 9, Character 11, Barricade 1	13	26	2,2
	Melee 15, Character 19, Barricade 1	20	42	2,2
	Melee 27, Character 33, Barricade 1	31	70	2,2
	Melee 42, Character 48, Barricade 1	43	100	2,2
	Melee 50, Character 56, Barricade 1	49	116	2,2
Large Shield	Melee 17, Barricade 1	18	38	3,2
	Melee 28, Barricade 1	27	60	3,2
	Melee 42, Barricade 1	38	88	3,2
	Melee 54, Barricade 1	48	112	3,2
	Melee 64, Barricade 1	56	132	3,2
Tower Shield	Melee 24, Barricade 1	24	52	3,2
	Melee 51, Barricade 1	45	106	3,2
	Melee 61, Barricade 1	53	126	3,2
	Melee 69, Barricade 1	60	142	3,2
	Melee 74, Barricade 1	64	152	3,2
Kite Shield	Melee 30, Barricade 1	28	64	3,2
	Melee 59, Barricade 1	52	122	3,2
	Melee 72, Barricade 1	62	148	3,2
	Melee 79, Barricade 1	68	162	3,2
	Melee 85, Barricade 1	72	174	3,2
Ceremonial Shield	Melee 35, Barricade 1	32	74	2,2
	Melee 66, Barricade 1	57	136	2,2
	Melee 76, Barricade 1	65	156	2,2
	Melee 82, Barricade 1	70	168	2,2
	Melee 88, Barricade 1	75	180	2,2

Unique Items

These charts reveal detailed statistics for unique weapons, armor, and quest items. Unique items carry specific—and quite robust—bonuses, and are extremely rare. Gold values are for the base item.

Unique Hand-to-Hand Weapons

Unique Item	Base Item	Bonuses	Requirements	Base Damage	1H/2H	Gold Value	Inventory Height, Width
Heartwood Cudgel	Club	+30 health, +15% health regeneration, +50% damage	Melee 4	5–9	1H	64	2,1
Thorn	Spiked Club	+22 max. damage, 25% of physical damage reflected to enemy, +20% fire resistance, +18% ranged resistance	Melee 33	21–36	1H	354	3,1
Assassin's Kiss	Dagger	+4 strength, +4 dexterity, +4 max. damage, +2 health per hit, +18% gold dropped	Melee 6	6–11	1H	84	2,1
Heartseeker	Royal Dagger	+55% weapon damage, +12 health per hit, +6% chance to dodge melee attacks, +3 to Critical Strike, Dual Wield, Alacrity	Melee 80	48–80	1H	824	2,1
Purgestone	Mace	+3–4 fire damage, +8% health regeneration, +8 armor, +15% death resistance	Melee 13	10–18	1H	154	3,1
Gravecage	Flanged Mace	+124 health, +20–33 ice damage, +44 armor, +25% ice resistance	Melee 57	35–58	1H	594	3,1
Claw of Kajj	Short Sword	+7 min. damage, +20% damage, 5% health stolen, +10% chance to find magic items	Melee 10	9–15	1H	124	3,1
Frost Talon	Dryad Sword	+11 strength, +26% damage, +5–8 ice damage, +17% fire resistance, +2 to Critical Strike, Dual Wield, Alacrity	Melee 21	15–25	1H	234	3,1
Gemcrust	Gladius	+20 strength, +12% magic resistance, +14% power recharge rate, +35% chance to find magic items, +80% to gold dropped	Melee 37	24–40	1H	394	3,1
Mourneblade	Long Sword	+32 min. damage, +12–20 death damage, +34 armor, +22% fire resistance	Melee 42	26–44	1H	444	3,1
Feanden's Lash	Elven Sword	+60 max. damage, +15–45 lightning damage, +15% chance to dodge ranged attacks, +3 to Critical Strike, Dual Wield, Alacrity	Melee 62	38–63	1H	644	3,1
Bloodletter	Broad Sword	+80 max. damage, +64% damage, +29–48 death damage, +10% melee resistance	Melee 72	43–72	1H	744	4,1
Xeria's Fury	Katana	+11 strength, +25–74 lightning damage, +30% lightning resistance, +4 to Critical Strike, Dual Wield, Alacrity	Melee 83	49–81	1H	854	4,1
Champion's Edge	Battle Axe	+8 strength, +16 health, +10 armor, +4% melee and ranged resistance, +2 to Barricade, Toughness, Reinforced Armor	Melee 17	13–21	1H	194	3,1
Grimsteel Reaver	Forest Pick	+18 strength, +30% weapon damage, +7–21 death damage, 10% health stolen, -75% heath regeneration, +20% death resistance	Melee 29	19–32	1H	314	3,2
Silver Dawn	Elven Axe	+42 strength, +11–34 lightning damage, +24% death resistance, +3 to Barricade, Toughness, Reinforced Armor	Melee 52	32–54	1H	544	3,2
Addiction	Vai'Kesh Cleaver	+200 health, +26 min. damage, 16% health stolen, -25% death resistance, +20% power recharge rate	Melee 67	40–68	1H	694	3,2
Desert Fire	Rift Axe	+68% damage, +38–47 fire damage, 12% health stolen, +18% magic damage resistance	Melee 76	45–76	1H	784	3,2
Fortune's Favor	Hammer	+20% damage, +6% chance to dodge melee attacks, +10% chance to find magic items, +25% to gold dropped	Melee 8	8–13	1H	104	3,1
Earthcrafter	Dryad Hammer	+65 health, +15 max. damage, +30% damage, +12% health regeneration, +20% lightning resistance	Melee 25	17–29	1H	274	3,2
Gregor's Diligence	Spiked Hammer	+72 strength, +250 health, +78 armor, +4 to Barricade, Toughness, Reinforced Armor	Melee 80	48–80	1H	824	3,2

(continued)

Unique Items

Unique Item	Base Item	Bonuses	Requirements	Base Damage	1H/2H	Gold Value	Inventory Height, Width
Galeblade	Bastard Sword	+9 min. damage, +3–8 lightning damage, +7% health stolen, +8% lightning resistance, +2 to Fortitude, Overbear, Smite	Melee 18, Overbear 1	21–36	2H	204	4,1
Blackened Tooth of Karsha	Totem Sword	+15 min. damage, +9–15 death damage, +8 health per hit, +22 armor	Melee 34, Overbear 1	36–60	2H	364	4,1
Frenzy	Hunter Sword	+55 strength, +85% damage, +18 health per hit, -40 armor, +3 to Fortitude, Overbear, Smite	Melee 63, Overbear 1	62–104	2H	654	4,1
Rahvan's Sunsword	Hero's Sword	+260 health, +43–52 fire damage, +25% health regeneration, +14% melee resistance, +4 to Fortitude, Overbear, Smite	Melee 81, Overbear 1	78–131	2H	834	4,1
Soulburn	War Axe	+66 health, +30% damage, +7–9 fire damage, 25% of physical damage reflected to enemy, +20% ice resistance	Melee 26, Overbear 1	29–48	2H	284	3,2
Istaura's Justice	Viper Axe	+65 strength, +29–48 ice damage, +64 armor, +3 to melee skills	Melee 72, Overbear 1	70–117	2H	744	4,2
Bloodpounder	Sledge	+4 strength, +6 max. damage, +3 health per hit, +3% melee and ranged resistance	Melee 7, Overbear 1	12–20	2H	94	4,2
Dragonheart	Soldier Hammer	+100 health, +16–19 fire damage, +18% health regeneration, +1 to melee skills	Melee 44, Overbear 1	45–75	2H	464	4,2
Fury of the Elements	Fighter Staff	+2–4 ice damage, +3–4 fire damage, +2–5 lightning damage, +7% magic resistance	Melee 12, Overbear 1	16–27	2H	144	4,1
Crimson Hunter	Bladed Staff	+65 max. damage, 12% health stolen, +12% chance to dodge melee attacks, +12% chance to dodge ranged attacks	Melee 54, Overbear 1	54–90	2H	564	4,1
Gnarlcharm	Ritual Staff	+2 intelligence, +17 mana, +5% mana regeneration, +5% chance to find magic items	Mage 4	6–11	2H	64	4,1
The Soul Vortex	Druid Staff	+4 intelligence, 5% mana stolen, +6 armor, +8% magic damage resistance	Mage 10	10–17	2H	124	4,1
Rubicon's Bracers	Arcane Cestus	+37 health, +10% health regeneration, +9 armor, +4% melee and ranged resistance	Mage 16	5–9	2H	184	2,2
Manastorm Spire	Elven Staff	+13 intelligence, +105 mana, +15% nature magic damage, +15% combat magic damage, +20% lightning resistance	Mage 29	22–37	2H	314	4,1
Ancestor's Hands	Cryptic Cestus	10% health stolen, +24% mana regeneration, +22% fire resistance, +16% power recharge rate, +40% chance to find magic items	Mage 49	13–21	2H	514	2,2
Isteru's Wisdom	Yearling Staff	+52 intelligence, +360 mana, 12% mana stolen, +12% melee resistance	Nature Magic 73	50–84	2H	754	4,1
Endless Memory	Spirit Cestus	+65 to intelligence, +40% nature magic damage, +40% combat magic damage, +3 to nature magic skills, +3 to combat magic skills	Combat Magic 83	21–35	2H	854	2,2
The Curving Stream	Ritual Staff	+10 intelligence, +15% nature magic damage, +18% ice resistance, +2 to Aquatic Affinity, Arctic Mastery, Freezing	Nature Magic 24	19–32	2H	264	4,1
Druid's Companions	Arcane Cestus	+100 mana, +18% mana regeneration, +20% death resistance, +2 to Summon Fortitude, Summon Might, Summon Bond, +1 to Fortitude and Toughness	Nature Magic 33	9–15	2H	354	2,2
Oakheart Gift	Druid Staff	+100 health, 10% health stolen, +32 armor, +22% ranged resistance	Nature Magic 40	29–49	2H	424	4,1
Genesis	Cryptic Cestus	+200 mana, +20% mana regeneration, +14% magic resistance, +3 to Summon Fortitude, Summon Might, Summon Bond, +3 to Nurturing Gift, Enveloping Embrace, Feral Wrath	Nature Magic 52	13–22	2H	544	2,2
Rimen's Dragoneye Staff	Yearling Staff	+45 intelligence, +35% nature magic damage, +50% ice resistance, +2 to nature magic skills, +4 to Aquatic Affinity, Arctic Mastery, Freezing	Mage 65	45–75	2H	674	4,1

(continued)

Unique Item	Base Item	Bonuses	Requirements	Base Damage	1H/2H	Gold Value	Inventory Height, Width
Ruin's Herald	Ritual Staff	+8 intelligence, +15% combat magic damage, +18% fire resistance, +2 to Devastation, Searing Flames, Ignite	Combat Magic 20	16–28	2H	224	4,1
Reckless	Arcane Cestus	+112 mana, +18% mana regeneration, +20% lightning resistance, +14% power recharge rate, +3 to Summoned Alacrity and Quickened Casting	Combat Magic 35	9–16	2H	374	2,2
Nightmarrow	Elven Staff	+25 intelligence, 10% health stolen, 10% mana stolen, +24% death resistance, +3 to Debilitation, Grim Necromancy, Vampirism	Combat Magic 46	33–55	2H	224	4,1
Archon's Grip	Cryptic Cestus	+175 health, +250 mana, 40% of physical damage reflected to enemy, +15% magic resistance, +3 to Brilliance, Amplified Lightning, Arcing	Combat Magic 58	15–25	2H	604	2,2
Apocalypse	Spirit Cestus	+42 intelligence, +35% to combat magic damage, +2 to combat magic skills, +3 to Debilitation, Grim Necromancy, Vampirism, +3 to Brilliance, Amplified Lightning, Arcing, +3 to Devastation, Searing Flames, Ignite	Mage 64	16–27	2H	664	2,2

Unique Ranged Weapons

Unique Item	Base Item	Bonuses	Requirements	Base Damage	Range	Gold Value	Inventory Height, Width
Lyssa's Bow	Short Bow	+4 dexterity, +1–2 fire damage, +5% chance to find magic items, +15% gold dropped	Ranged 4	5–8	9	64	3,1
Demonstring	Scout Bow	+6 max. damage, +2–3 death damage, 15% of physical damage reflected to enemy, 6% health stolen, -75% health regeneration	Ranged 10	8–13	9	124	4,1
Lunar Grace	Dryad Bow	+11 dexterity, +24% weapon damage, +3 health per hit, +2 to Critical Shot, Dodge, Survival	Ranged 16	11–18	9	184	4,1
Purestrike	Composite Bow	+35% damage, +5–14 lightning damage, +20% death resistance, +2 to Biting Arrow, Far Shot, Shockwave	Ranged 29	17–28	9	314	4,1
The Blood Rose Thorn	Curve Bow	+40 dexterity, +13–21 ice damage, 10% health stolen, +18% health regeneration	Ranged 43	24–40	9	454	3,1
Despair of the Void	Stalker Bow	+54% damage, +20–33 death damage, +24% ice resistance, +3 to Critical Shot, Dodge, Survival	Ranged 57	31–51	9	594	3,1
Venerable Hunter	Elven Longbow	+300 health, +20 health per hit, +25% health regeneration, +65 armor	Ranged 64	34–57	9	664	3,1
Dalziel's Forsaker	Ironwood Bow	+88 dexterity, +33–41 fire damage, +18% magic damage resistance, +4 to Biting Arrow, Far Shot, Shockwave	Ranged 70	37–62	9	724	4,1
Starfall	Swift Bow	+30 min. damage, +36–60 ice damage, +20% magic resistance, +4 to Critical Shot, Dodge, Survival	Ranged 82	43–72	9	844	4,1
Spikeshell	Mercenary Crossbow	+16 health, +1–2 ice damage, +5% health regeneration, +5 armor	Ranged 6, Biting Arrow 1	11–18	9	84	3,2
Siegebolt	Light Crossbow	+42 health, +15 max. damage, +18% fire resistance, +2 to Biting Arrow, Far Shot, Shockwave	Ranged 22, Biting Arrow	25–42	9	244	3,2
Undermountain Catapult	Heavy Crossbow	+20 strength, +25 max. damage, +42% damage, +15% power recharge rate, +100% to gold dropped	Ranged 36, Biting Arrow 1	38–63	9	384	3,2
Crystal Cloudstrike	Arbalest	+11–32 lightning damage, +45 armor, +20% lightning resistance, +3 to Biting Arrow, Far Shot, Shockwave	Ranged 50, Biting Arrow 1	50–84	9	524	3,2

(continued)

Unique Items

Unique Item	Base Item	Bonuses	Requirements	Base Damage	Range	Gold Value	Inventory Height, Width
Warmaker	Ballista	+68% damage, +90 armor, +25% fire resistance, +2 to ranged skills	Ranged 76, Biting Arrow 1	74–123	9	784	4,2
Spellbreaker	Throwing Knife	+6 min. damage, +8% magic resistance, +6% power recharge rate, +10% chance to find magic items	Ranged 8, Quick Draw 1	9–15	7.5	104	2,1
Rogue's Spirit	Throwing Axe	+13 dexterity, +3–8 lightning damage, +4% melee and ranged resistance, +2 to Quick Draw, Bleed, Penetrate	Ranged 18, Quick Draw 1	15–26	7.5	204	2,1
Blastspine	Throwing Crescent	+35% damage, +9–11 fire damage, 30% of physical damage reflected to enemy, +7 health per hit, +12% power recharge rate	Ranged 30, Quick Draw 1	23–39	7.5	324	2,1
Abyssal Avatar	Throwing Star	+112 health, +16–19 fire damage, +13–22 death damage, +24% death resistance	Ranged 44, Quick Draw 1	32–54	7.5	464	2,2
Balance	Glaive	+65 dexterity, +22 min. damage, +25% ranged resistance, +3 to Quick Draw, Bleed, Penetrate	Ranged 58, Quick Draw 1	41–69	7.5	604	2,2
Circle of the Night	Chakram	+75 max. damage, +28–46 ice damage, 12% health stolen, +25% ice resistance	Ranged 70, Quick Draw 1	49–82	7.5	724	2,2
Flawless	Throwing Shiv	+112 dexterity, +100 max. damage, +72% damage, +14% melee resistance, +4 to Quick Draw, Bleed, Penetrate	Ranged 82, Quick Draw 1	57–95	7.5	844	3,1

Unique Armor

Unique Item	Base Item	Bonuses	Requirement	Base Defense	Gold Value	Inventory Height, Width
Dusk	Leather Jerkin	+8 armor, +13% lightning resistance, +13% death resistance, +6% chance to dodge melee attacks, +18% chance to find magic items	Melee 14	40	32	2,2
Ravager's Skin	Studded Tunic	+10 strength, +50 health, 20% of physical damage reflected to enemy, +80% armor	Melee 23	58	50	2,2
Lescanza Skin	Chain Mail	+22 armor, +22% lightning resistance, +12% chance to dodge ranged attacks, +1 to melee skills	Melee 38	88	80	3,2
Resplendent Mail	Full Plate	+42 strength, +20% health regeneration, +120% armor, +25% fire resistance	Melee 58	128	120	3,2
Forgotten Armor	Obsidian Armor	+200 health, +58 armor, +20% magic damage resistance, +2 to Barricade, Toughness, Reinforced Armor, +40% chance to find magic items	Melee 68	148	140	3,2
The Radiant Sun	Mythril Armor	+78 strength, +300 health, +140% armor, +10% melee and ranged resistance, +2 to melee skills	Melee 83	178	170	3,2
Lunar Petals	Leaf Jerkin	+10 dexterity, +8% health regeneration, +15% ice resistance, +15% fire resistance	Ranged 18	38	40	2,2
Oakcase	Carved Tunic	+50 health, +13 armor, +16% death resistance, +6% melee resistance	Ranged 24	48	52	2,2
Artech's Raiment	Explorer Armor	+30 dexterity, +105% armor, +14% magic resistance, +1 to ranged skills	Ranged 35	65	74	3,2
Etched Spirit	Elven Armor	+160 health, +145% armor, +22% fire resistance, +3 to Critical Shot, Dodge, Survival	Ranged 55	97	114	3,2
Woodland Finery	Arboreal Armor	+5% health regeneration, +60 armor, +25% ice resistance, +25% chance to dodge ranged attacks	Ranged 69	120	142	3,2
The Ageless Hunter	Twilight Armor	+110 dexterity, +300 health, +200% armor, +2 to ranged skills	Ranged 83	142	170	3,2
Sylvan Garb	Woven Tunic	+5 intelligence, +30 health, +10% mana regeneration, +14% death resistance	Nature Magic 16	26	36	2,2
Prongtotem	Tribal Armor	+85 mana, 25% of physical damage reflected to enemy, +12 armor, +18% ice resistance, +30% chance to find magic items	Nature Magic 27	39	58	2,2
Trickster Feathers	Raven Armor	+18 intelligence, +115% armor, +22% fire resistance, +1 to nature magic skills	Nature Magic 39	54	82	2,2

(continued)

Unique Item	Base Item	Bonuses	Requirement	Base Defense	Gold Value	Inventory Height, Width
Wildclaw	Ancestral Armor	+205 health, +22% health regeneration, +58 armor, +10% melee and ranged resistance	Nature Magic 59	78	122	3,2
Ancient's Majesty	Dragon Armor	+240 health, +20% to nature magic damage, +25% mana regeneration, +180% armor	Nature Magic 73	94	150	3,2
Nature's Avatar	Mystic Armor	+60 intelligence, +525 mana, +200% armor, +2 to nature magic skills	Nature Magic 83	106	170	3,2
Traveler's Robe	Apprentice Robe	+25 health, +35 mana, +14% ice resistance, +3% melee and ranged resistance	Combat Magic 14	24	32	2,2
Inferno Mantle	Elementalist Robe	+10 intelligence, +56 health, +18 armor, +18% fire resistance, +18% lightning resistance	Combat Magic 26	38	56	2,2
Serpent Vestment	Adept Robe	+165 mana, +16% health regeneration, +120% armor, +1 to combat magic skills	Combat Magic 42	57	88	2,2
The Encrusted Masterpiece	Sorcerer Robe	+42 intelligence, +65 armor, +18% magic resistance, +3 to Brilliance, Amplified Lightning, Arcing	Combat Magic 63	82	130	3,2
Bloodspeaker Robe	Warlock Robe	+20% combat magic damage, 6% health stolen, +25% mana regeneration, +180% armor, +25% death resistance	Combat Magic 72	93	148	3,2
Entropy	Archmage Robe	+60 intelligence, +525 mana, +200% armor, +2 to combat magic skills	Combat Magic 83	106	170	3,2
Gloamhand	Leather Gloves	+3–5 damage, +3 armor, +10% death resistance, +20% to gold dropped	Melee 4	6	12	2,1
Ragetalon	Studded Gloves	+3 strength, +15 health, +2 health per hit, +1 to Fortitude, Overbear, Smite	Melee 8	8	20	2,1
Stormhold	Chain Gloves	+12 strength, +4–12 damage, +12 armor, +18% lightning resistance, +5% power recharge rate	Melee 26	19	56	2,1
Noblegrip	Plate Gauntlets	+8 health per hit, +80% armor, +20% fire resistance, +1 to melee skills, +80% gold dropped	Melee 34	24	72	2,1
Shattering Gauntlets	Obsidian Gauntlets	+30 strength, +14–23 damage, +30 armor, +25% ice resistance, +3 to Fortitude, Overbear, Smite	Melee 46	31	96	2,1
Gauntlets of Cleansing Fire	Mythril Gauntlets	+36–44 damage, 10% health stolen, +50 armor, +14% power recharge rate, +4 to Critical Strike, Dual Wield, Alacrity	Melee 73	47	150	2,1
Moon Needle	Leaf Gloves	+6 max. damage, +10% to nature magic damage, +3 health per hit, +8% health regeneration, +12% ice resistance	Ranged 11	8	26	2,1
Thief's Finesse	Carved Gloves	+8 dexterity, +2–6 damage, +8 armor, +15% chance to find magic items, +50% gold dropped	Ranged 15	10	34	2,1
Horizon's Reach	Explorer Gloves	+65 health, +22 armor, +7% power recharge rate, +2 to Quick Draw, Bleed, Penetrate	Ranged 31	17	66	2,1
Archer's Tradition	Elven Gloves	+55 dexterity, +15 health per hit, +140% armor, +10% power recharge rate, +3 to Biting Arrow, Far Shot, Shockwave	Ranged 51	27	106	2,1
Ethaniel's Gloves	Arboreal Gloves	+200 health, +24–40 damage, +25% health regeneration, +52 armor, +12% power recharge rate	Ranged 64	33	132	2,1
Exalted Mastery	Twilight Gloves	+110 dexterity, +95 max. damage, +12% health stolen, +15 health per hit, +70 armor, +14% power recharge rate	Ranged 80	41	164	2,1
Verdant Touch	Woven Gloves	+18 mana, +4% mana stolen, +5 armor, +12% ice resistance	Nature Magic 7	4	18	2,1
Wolfspirit	Tribal Gloves	+5 intelligence, +10% nature magic damage, +10% mana regeneration, +12% ranged resistance	Nature Magic 14	7	32	2,1
Bloodtalons	Raven Gloves	+70 mana, +6% health stolen, +15 armor, +18% fire resistance, +5% power recharge rate	Nature Magic 24	10	52	2,1
Beastguards	Ancestral Gloves	+110 health, +8% mana stolen, +18% health regeneration, +120% armor, +8% power recharge rate	Nature Magic 43	17	90	2,1
Scaled Blessing	Dragon Gloves	+40 armor, +24% death resistance, +10% power recharge rate, +3 to Nurturing Gift, Enveloping Embrace, Feral Wrath	Nature Magic 55	21	114	2,1
Protector's Oath	Mystic Gloves	+58 intelligence, +25% nature magic damage, +70 armor, +14% power recharge rate, +4 to Summon Fortitude, Summon Might, Summon Bond	Nature Magic 77	29	158	2,1

(continued)

Unique Items

Unique Item	Base Item	Bonuses	Requirement	Base Defense	Gold Value	Inventory Height, Width
Prestidigitators	Apprentice Gloves	+25 mana, 4% mana stolen, +12% death resistance, +10% chance to dodge ranged attacks, +10% chance to find magic items	Combat Magic 10	5	24	2,1
Phosphorsilk	Elementalist Gloves	+6 intelligence, +18% of physical damage reflected to enemy, +15% fire resistance, +2 to Devastation, Searing Flames, Ignite	Combat Magic 17	8	38	2,1
Wyrmscale Gloves	Adept Gloves	+12% combat magic damage, +7% mana stolen, +20 armor, +8% power recharge rate	Combat Magic 30	12	64	2,1
Ruby Gauntlets	Sorcerer Gloves	+200 mana, +135% armor, +22% fire resistance, +10% power recharge rate, +3 to Devastation, Searing Flames, Ignite	Combat Magic 50	20	104	2,1
Culling Touch	Warlock Gloves	+12% mana stolen, +40 armor, +24% death resistance, +12% power recharge rate, +3 to Debilitation, Grim Necromancy, Vampirism	Combat Magic 58	23	120	2,1
Runes of Command	Archmage Gloves	+60 to intelligence, +25% to combat magic damage, +70 armor, +20% magic resistance, +14% power recharge rate	Combat Magic 79	30	162	2,1
Grace of Night	Leather Boots	+12 health, +4 armor, +12% ice resistance, +8% chance to dodge ranged attacks	Melee 6	7	16	2,1
Grimstomp	Studded Boots	+5 strength, +6% health regeneration, +8 armor, +13% fire resistance	Melee 12	10	28	2,1
Infused Boots	Chain Boots	+8 strength, +12 armor, +16% lightning resistance, +6% chance to dodge melee attacks, +70% gold dropped	Melee 20	15	44	2,1
Norick's Preservation	Plate Greaves	+90 health, +16% health regeneration, +90% armor, +3 to Barricade, Toughness, Reinforced Armor, +30% chance to find magic items	Melee 42	28	88	2,1
Kale's Resolve	Obsidian Greaves	+38 strength, +130 health, +40% of physical damage reflected to enemy, +40 armor, +25% death resistance	Melee 54	36	112	2,1
Dawntread	Mythril Greaves	+240 health, +60 armor, +30% fire resistance, +10% melee resistance, +4 to Fortitude, Overbear, Smite	Melee 76	49	156	2,1
Grovestep	Leaf Boots	+3 dexterity, +5% health regeneration, +5% chance to dodge melee attacks, +20% gold dropped	Ranged 5	5	14	2,1
Nimblefoot	Carved Boots	+5 to dexterity, +5 armor, +12% lightning resistance, +10% chance to dodge ranged attacks	Ranged 9	7	22	2,1
Farwalkers	Explorer Boots	+40 health, +10% health regeneration, +12 armor, +2 to Quick Draw, Bleed, Penetrate	Ranged 21	12	46	2,1
Tracker's Boots	Elven Boots	+115% armor, +22% ice resistance, +22% fire resistance, +3 to Critical Shot, Dodge, Survival, +35% to chance to find magic items	Ranged 39	21	82	2,1
Forest Dancers	Arboreal Boots	+48 dexterity, +125 health, +40 armor, +12% chance to dodge melee attacks	Ranged 47	25	98	2,1
Gilded Striders	Twilight Boots	+96 dexterity, +25% health regeneration, +70 armor, +20% magic damage resistance	Ranged 74	38	152	2,1
Lifewalk	Woven Boots	+10 health, 4% health stolen, +5% health regeneration, +10% fire resistance	Nature Magic 5	3	14	2,1
Panther's Paw	Tribal Boots	+16 health, +6% mana regeneration, +12% death resistance, +3% chance to dodge ranged and melee attacks	Nature Magic 9	5	22	2,1
Companion's Wisdom	Raven Boots	+8 intelligence, +12 armor, +8% magic damage resistance, +2 to Summon Fortitude, Summon Might, Summon Bond	Nature Magic 21	9	46	2,1
Feral Stalkers	Ancestral Boots	+16 intelligence, +18% mana regeneration, +105% armor, +3 to Nurturing Gift, Enveloping Embrace, Feral Wrath, +35% chance to find magic items	Nature Magic 35	14	74	2,1
Wyrmriders	Dragon Boots	+125 health, +20% health regeneration, +40 armor, +24% lightning resistance, +3 to Summon Fortitude, Summon Might, and Summon Bond	Nature Magic 47	19	98	2,1
Growth of Ages	Mystic Boots	+50 intelligence, +340 mana, +25% mana regeneration, +70 armor, +4 to Aquatic Affinity, Arctic Mastery, Freezing	Nature Magic 70	27	144	2,1

(continued)

Unique Item	Base Item	Bonuses	Requirement	Base Defense	Gold Value	Inventory Height, Width
Wanderer's Boots	Apprentice Boots	+2 intelligence, +5% mana regeneration, +10% ice resistance, +25% gold dropped	Combat Magic 6	4	16	2,1
Stormdancers	Elementalist Boots	+22 health, +12% lightning resistance, +12% chance to dodge ranged attacks, +2 to Brilliance, Amplified Lightning, Arcing	Combat Magic 12	6	28	2,1
Chimaera Tracks	Adept Boots	+8 intelligence, +45 health, +15 armor, +16% fire resistance	Combat Magic 23	10	50	2,1
Sapphire Boots	Sorcerer Boots	+125 mana, +20% mana regeneration, +110% armor, +22% ice resistance, +35% to chance to find magic items	Combat Magic 38	15	80	2,1
Corrupting Wake	Warlock Boots	+155 health, 40% of physical damage reflected to enemy, +50 armor, +24% death resistance	Combat Magic 54	21	112	2,1
Planar Travelers	Archmage Boots	+56 intelligence, +390 mana, +70 armor, +2 to combat magic skills	Combat Magic 76	29	156	2,1
Nightwolf Crest	Leather Helm	+6% health regeneration, +12% fire resistance, +5% chance to dodge melee attacks, +1 to Fortitude, Overbear, Smite	Melee 10	12	24	2,2
Chaos Glare	Studded Helm	+8 strength, +30 health, 18% of physical damage reflected to enemy, +3 health per hit	Melee 17	18	38	2,2
Elfhame	Chain Helm	+15 strength, +22 armor, +20% lightning resistance, +30% chance to find magic items	Melee 30	28	64	2,2
Pulsing Horns	Plate Helm	+120 health, 8% health stolen, +35 armor, +1 to melee skills	Melee 50	44	104	2,2
Glacial Crown	Obsidian Helmet	+180 health, +20% health regeneration, +120% armor, +28% ranged resistance, +2 to melee skills	Melee 63	55	130	2,2
Helm of Glory	Mythril Helmet	+72 strength, +90 max. damage, +70 armor, +20% magic resistance, +2 to Barricade, Toughness, Reinforced Armor	Melee 79	68	162	2,2
Rogue's Hood	Leaf Hood	+15 health, 10% of physical damage reflected to enemy, +11% lightning resistance, +10% chance to find magic items	Ranged 7	8	18	2,2
Arborwood	Carved Cap	+24 health, +2 health per hit, +14% ice resistance, +6% melee resistance, +1 to Critical Shot, Dodge, Survival	Ranged 13	12	30	2,2
Restless Gaze	Explorer Helm	+18 dexterity, +18 armor, +6% chance to dodge, +2 to Critical Shot, Dodge, Survival	Ranged 27	21	58	2,2
Wyrmskin Cowl	Elven Helm	+110 health, 10% health stolen, +35 armor, +1 to ranged skills	Ranged 43	31	90	2,2
Thicket Horns	Arboreal Helm	+66 dexterity, +24% health regeneration, +150% armor, +2 to ranged skills	Ranged 59	41	122	2,2
Polaris	Twilight Helm	+105 dexterity, +25 health per hit, +70 armor, +15% melee and ranged resistance	Ranged 77	53	158	2,2
Forest Shroud	Woven Hood	+3 intelligence, +12% lightning resistance, +10% ranged resistance, +12% chance to dodge ranged attacks	Nature Magic 11	8	26	2,2
Sight of the Eagle	Tribal Headdress	+6 intelligence, +50 mana, +5% mana stolen, +12 armor	Nature Magic 18	11	40	2,2
Gram's Relic	Raven Cap	+70 health, +100% armor, +18% death resistance, +2 to Aquatic Affinity, Arctic Mastery, Freezing, +30% chance to find magic items	Nature Magic 31	17	66	2,2
Untamed Eyes	Ancestral Helm	+30 intelligence, +10% nature magic damage, +20% mana regeneration, +46 armor, +24% ice resistance	Nature Magic 51	27	106	2,2
Tyrant's Horns	Dragon Helm	12% health stolen, 12% mana stolen, +160% armor, +30% fire resistance, +35% chance to find magic items	Nature Magic 64	33	132	2,2
Harmony of All	Mystic Helm	+60 intelligence, +15% nature magic damage, +75 armor, +20% magic resistance, +2 to nature magic skills	Nature Magic 80	41	164	2,2
Vagabond's Hood	Apprentice Hood	+2 intelligence, +4% health regeneration, +10% fire resistance, +5% melee resistance	Combat Magic 4	4	12	2,2
Soulchannel	Elementalist Cap	+54 mana, 4% health stolen, +5% mana regeneration, +12% death resistance	Combat Magic 8	6	20	2,2

(continued)

Unique Items

Unique Item	Base Item	Bonuses	Require-ment	Base Defense	Gold Value	Inventory Height, Width
Devilhorn	Adept Helm	+6 intelligence, +40 health, +75% armor, +15% fire resistance, +2 to Debilitation, Grim Necromancy, Vampirism	Combat Magic 20	12	44	2,2
Diamond Mask	Sorcerer Cowl	+105 mana, +10% combat magic damage, +25 armor, +22% lightning resistance, +2 to Brilliance, Amplified Lightning, Arcing	Combat Magic 34	19	72	2,2
Calix's Mask	Warlock Mask	+25 intelligence, 35% of physical damage reflected to enemy, +125% armor, +22% ice resistance, +3 to Devastation, Searing Flames, Ignite	Combat Magic 46	24	96	2,2
The Omniscient Oracle	Archmage Hood	+45 intelligence, +15% combat magic damage, +25% mana regeneration, +65 armor, +2 to combat magic skills	Combat Magic 68	35	140	2,2
Glimmerhold	Buckler	+15 health, +12% lightning resistance, +8% chance to block melee attacks, +10% chance to find magic items	Melee 8, Barricade 1	11	20	2,2
Utraean Bulwark	Small Shield	+8 strength, +35 health, +8% health regeneration, +10% chance to block ranged attacks	Melee 18, Barricade 1	19	40	2,2
Flame of Ibsen Yamas	Heater Shield	+9–11 damage, +15 armor, +20% fire resistance, +10% chance to block melee attacks	Melee 30, Barricade 1	28	64	2,2
Flechette Ward	Large Shield	+25 strength, +90% armor, +22% ranged resistance, +15% chance to block ranged attacks	Melee 42, Barricade 1	38	88	3,2
Razor Mane of Culahn	Tower Shield	40% of physical damage reflected to enemy, +40 armor, +20% death resistance, +12% chance to block melee attacks, +20% chance to block ranged attacks	Melee 54, Barricade 1	48	112	4,2
Will of the Last Justiciar	Kite Shield	+200 health, +120% armor, +16% magic resistance, +15% chance to block melee attacks	Melee 66, Barricade 1	57	136	4,2
Rowain's Indomitability	Ceremonial Shield	+70 strength, +70 armor, +8% melee and ranged resistance, +10% chance to block melee attacks, +25% chance to block ranged attacks	Melee 78, Barricade 1	67	160	2,2

Unique Rings and Amulets

Unique Item	Base Item	Bonuses	Requirement
Hunter's Mark	Talisman	+25 dexterity, +12 max. damage, +20 armor, +1 to ranged skills	Character Level 34
Xeria's Seal	Silver Ring	+5 strength, +6 max. damage, +3 health per hit, +10 armor	Character Level 20
Rahvan's Fist	Gold Ring	+10 strength, +10 max. damage, +12 armor, +8% magic damage resistance	Character Level 30
Stoutgrip	Gold Ring	+15 strength, +65 health, +5% power recharge rate, +40% gold dropped	Character Level 36
Gleamstone	Jeweled Ring	+40 health, +40 mana, +25% gold dropped, +15% chance to find magic items	Character Level 28
Queen's Husk	Elaborate Ring	+6 armor, +2% health stolen, +10 health, +10% death resistance	Character Level 13
Soulreaver	Adorned Ring	+30 health, +3–5 damage, +15% fire resistance, +4% melee and ranged resistance	Character Level 26
Outrider's Signet	Gilded Ring	+4 dexterity, +3 intelligence, +5% mana regeneration, +8% ice resistance	Character Level 10
Spellbinder	Ornate Ring	+12 intelligence, +75 mana, +5% combat magic damage, +5% nature magic damage	Character Level 34

Unique Quest-Specific Items

Unique Item	Type	Bonuses
Hero's Amulet	Amulet	+4% magic damage resistance
Hero's Ring	Ring	+10 health, +5 armor
Heirloom Sword	Sword	+15 max. damage
Arinth's Staff	Staff	+62 mana, 20% of physical damage reflected to enemy, +7% health stolen, +8% melee resistance
Arinth's Robe	Archmage Robe	+77 mana, +18 armor, +19% fire resistance, +25% chance to find magic items
Virtuous Rebellion	Bow	+24 dexterity, +35% damage, +6-7 lightning damage, +2 to Biting Arrow, Far Shot, Shockwave
Mace of Agarrus	Mace	+30 strength, +22 max. damage, +40% damage
Hak'u Ceremonial Blade	Hak'u Ceremonial Blade	Imbued with Hak'u Magic

(continued)

Unique Item	Type	Bonuses
Soulstaff of the Nexus	Staff	+15 intelligence, +32 mana, +10–20 fire damage, +24 armor, +20% ice resistance

Set Items

The following tables reveal *Dungeon Siege II*'s set items. These are very rare, unique items that are part of larger sets. If you equip more than one item from a set, you receive additional bonuses. Each set table is followed by a table that reveals these bonuses.

Dual Wield Set 1—Night's Shadow

Name	Base Name	Requirement	Effects
Nightspirit	Gloves	Melee 22	+9 strength, +12 armor, +16% fire resistance, +75% to gold dropped
Shadowstep	Boots	Melee 16	+7 armor, +8% melee resistance, +12% chance to dodge ranged attacks, +15% chance to find magic items
Smoke's Cowl	Hood	Melee 13	+16 health, +5% health regeneration, +12% death resistance, +4% power recharge rate
Phantom Razor	Falchion	Melee 29	+14 strength, +7–12 ice damage, 8% health stolen, +2 to Critical Strike, Dual Wield, Alacrity
Whisper	Dirk	Melee 19	+12 max. damage, +25% damage, +4–7 death damage, +5% chance to dodge melee attacks

Night's Shadow Set Bonuses

Number of Items Equipped	+% Health Steal	% Chance to Dodge Melee Attack	+ to Critical Strike, Dual Wield, Alacrity	+% Chance to find Magic Items	+ Melee Damage	+Armor
2	3%	4%	0	20%	3	0
3	4%	6%	1	25%	5	2
4	5%	10%	1	30%	8	4
5	7%	12%	2	40%	14	6

Dual Wield Set 2—The Furious Tempest

Name	Base Name	Requirements	Effects
Windstep	Boots	Melee 48	+36 armor, +25% lightning resistance, +25% chance to dodge ranged attacks, +2 to Critical Shot, Dodge, Survival
Torrent	Sword	Melee 51	+125 health, +12 health per hit, +20% health regeneration, +3 to Critical Strike, Dual Wield, Alacrity
Thunderstroke	Heavy Edged Axe	Melee 44	+28 strength, +9–26 lightning damage, +20% lightning resistance, +2 to Barricade, Toughness, Reinforced Armor
Eye of the Tempest	Amulet	Melee 56	+43 strength, +150 health, +15% magic resistance, +8% melee resistance

The Furious Tempest Set Bonuses

Number of Items Equipped	+ STR	+% Health Regeneration	+% Melee Resistance	+ to Melee Skills	+ Melee Damage
2	20	+5%	4%	1	3
3	35	+10%	6%	2	6
4	50	+15%	10%	2	10

Dual Wield Set 3—Luun's Deathblades

Name	Base Name	Requirements	Effects
Citaa	Long Sword	Melee 34	+28 dexterity, +42% damage, +9–15 death damage, +2 to Critical Strike, Dual Wield, Alacrity
Giethaa	Short Sword	Melee 34	+18 strength, +67 health, +9–15 death damage

Luun's Deathblades Set Bonuses

Number of Items Equipped	+ Death Damage	% Health Stolen	+% Power Recharge Rate	+ to Critical Strike, Dual Wield, Alacrity
2	10–16	+8%	6%	2

1H Weapon / Shield Set 1—Lorethal's Legacy

Name	Base Name	Requirements	Effects
Lorethal's Courage	Full Plate	Melee 28	+14 strength, +100% armor, +6% melee resistance, +1 to melee skills

(continued)

Name	Base Name	Requirements	Effects
Lorethal's Grace	Gauntlets	Melee 6	+3 strength, +5 armor, +10% lightning resistance, +3% power recharge rate
Lorethal's Determination	Greaves	Melee 12	+22 health, +7 armor, +12% ice resistance, +12% fire resistance
Lorethal's Nobility	Bascinet	Melee 9	5% health stolen, +33% armor, +12% death resistance, +1 to Barricade, Toughness, Reinforced Armor
Lorethal's Command	Shield	Melee 24, Barricade 1	+10% health regeneration, +80% armor, +12% ranged resistance, +26% chance to block melee attacks
Lorethal's Sacrifice	Flanged Mace	Melee 15	+6 strength, +8 max. damage, +25% damage, +4–5 fire damage
Lorethal's Honor	Amulet	Melee 3	+7 health, +1–2 damage, +3 armor, +8% chance to find magic items
Lorethal's Eminence	Ring	Melee 18	+6% health stolen, +12% health regeneration, +8% magic resistance, +1 to Barricade, Toughness, Reinforced Armor

Lorethal's Legacy Set Bonuses

Number of Items Equipped	+ STR	+ Armor	+% Magic Damage Resistance	+ Melee Skills	+ to Barricade, Toughness, Reinforced Armor	+Min. & Max. Damage
2	3	5	2%	0	0	0
3	5	12	4%	0	0	0
4	6	18	6%	0	1	0
5	8	25	8%	0	1	5
6	10	35	10%	1	1	10
7	14	50	12%	1	2	20
8	18	65	15%	2	3	27

1H Weapon / Shield Set 2—Vistira's Undoing

Name	Base Name	Requirements	Effects
Fangs of Vistira	Gauntlets	Melee 43	+28 strength, +33 max. damage, +11% health stolen, +6% power recharge rate
Skin of Vistira	Greaves	Melee 36	+16% health regeneration, +20 armor, +15% magic resistance, +1 to melee skills
Serpent of Vistira	Helm	Melee 48	+120 health, 40% of physical damage reflected to enemy, +30 armor, +3 to Barricade, Toughness, Reinforced Armor
Mirror of Vistira	Shield	Melee 40, Barricade 1	30% of physical damage reflected to enemy, +90% armor, +24% death resistance, +15% chance to block melee attacks

Vistira's Undoing Set Bonuses

Number of Items Equipped	+ Health	% Physical Damage Reflected to Enemy	+% Magic Damage Resistance	+ to Barricade, Toughness, Reinforced Armor	+ Armor
2	50	20%	4%	1	4
3	100	30%	8%	2	8
4	150	45%	12%	3	18

2H Weapon Set 1—Frostheim's Trappings

Name	Type	Requirements	Effects
Frostheim's Grip	Gauntlets	Melee 30	+55 health, +15 armor, +20% ice resistance, +2 to Fortitude, Overbear, Smite
Frostheim	Flamberge	Melee 27, Overbear 1	+16 strength, +35% damage, +6–11 ice damage, +18% fire resistance
Frostheim's Claw	Ring	Melee 21	+8 strength, +5–8 weapon damage, 20% of physical damage reflected to enemy, +7% health stolen
Frostheim's Binding	Ring	Melee 33	+36 max. damage, +12% health regeneration, +20% ice resistance, +6% power recharge rate

Frostheim's Trappings Set Bonuses

Number of Items Equipped	+ STR	+ Ice Damage	+% Ice Resistance	+ Melee Skills	+ Melee Damage	+ Armor
2	12	5–9	15	0	0	4
3	18	7–12	20	1	8	5
4	25	9–15	25	2	15	8

2H Weapon Set 2—Legend of the Fire King

Name	Type	Requirements	Effects
Fire King's Trappings	Body Armor	Melee 54	+40 strength, +140 health, +100% armor, +14% ranged resistance
Fire King's Crown	Helm	Melee 51	40% of physical damage reflected to enemy, +32 armor, +25% fire resistance, +10% melee resistance
Fire King's Foecrusher	Maul	Melee 60, Overbear 1	+45 strength, +65% damage, +24–29 fire damage, +3 to Fortitude, Overbear, Smite
Fire King's Will	Ring	Melee 43	+20% health regeneration, +25% fire resistance, +6% power recharge rate, +1 to melee skills

Legend of the Fire King Set Bonuses

Number of Items Equipped	+ STR	+ Melee Damage	+ Fire Damage	+% Fire Resistance	+ Fortitude, Overbear, Smite
2	20	10–35	10–15	20%	1
3	40	15–50	20–25	25%	3
4	56	25–65	29–36	30%	4

Bow Set 1—Olimarch's Bane

Name	Type	Requirements	Effects
Savior's Signal	Gloves	Ranged 10	+6 dexterity, +12% ice resistance, +3% power recharge rate, +1 to Critical Shot, Dodge, Survival
Savior's Trail	Boots	Ranged 4	+8 health, +10% fire resistance, +5% chance to dodge melee attacks, +8% to chance to find magic items
Skewer of Olimarch	Bow	Ranged 16	+9 dexterity, +22% damage, +2–7 lightning damage, +1 to Biting Arrow, Far Shot, Shockwave
Savior's Halo	Ring	Ranged 7	+25 health, +5% health stolen, +5% health regeneration, +12% lightning resistance

Olimarch's Bane Set Bonuses

Number of Items Equipped	+ DEX	+ Ranged Max. Damage	+% Magic Damage Resistance	+ Critical Shot, Dodge, Survival	+Biting Arrow, Far Shot, Shockwave	+ Armor
2	5	4	3%	0	0	0
3	8	6	6%	1	1	2
4	12	9	10%	1	2	6

Bow Set 2—Bloody Vengeance

Name	Base Name	Requirement	Effects
Envy	Gloves	Ranged 55	+57 dexterity, +14 health per hit, +3 to Barricade, Toughness, Reinforced Armor, +3 to Critical Shot, Dodge, Survival
Spite	Helm	Ranged 55	+100 health, +36 max. damage, 35% of physical damage reflected to enemy, +35 armor
Vengeance	Composite Bow	Ranged 48	+52% damage, +15–25 death damage, +2 to ranged skills, +3 to Biting Arrow, Far Shot, Shockwave
Ire	Amulet	Ranged 42	+35 dexterity, 35% of physical damage reflected to enemy, +20% health regeneration, +7% power recharge rate

Bloody Vengeance Set Bonuses

Number of Items Equipped	+ Death Damage	% Health Stolen	+ Ranged Skills	+Biting Arrow, Far Shot, Shockwave	+ Ranged Damage	+ Armor
2	10–20	5%	1	2	0	2
3	15–25	8%	1	3	0	4
4	21–36	12%	2	4	14	12

Crossbow Set—The Fallen Soldier's Gift

Name	Base Name	Requirements	Effects
Soldier's Reborn Shroud	Body Armor	Ranged 32	+100% armor, +22% death resistance, +8% melee and ranged resistance, +3 to Critical Shot, Dodge, Survival
Soldier's Vigilance	Gloves	Ranged 28	+18 dexterity, +15 armor, +12% magic resistance, +6% power recharge rate
Soldier's Justice	Arbalest	Ranged 37, Biting Arrow 1	+30 dexterity, +26 max. damage, +45% damage, +12–15 fire damage, +2 to ranged skills

The Fallen Soldier's Gift Set Bonuses

Number of Items Equipped	+ Health	+ Fire Damage	+ Armor	+ Critical Shot, Dodge, Survival
2	75	11–23	25	2
3	100	13–16	40	3

Thrown Weapon Set—Winds of Kel'drassil

Name	Base Name	Requirements	Effects
Gale Raiment	Hauberk	Ranged 34	+10 dexterity, +65% armor, +5% power recharge rate, +15% health regeneration, +1 to ranged skills
The Fourth Wind	Glaive	Ranged 26, Quick Draw 1	+16 dexterity, +16 max. damage, +33% damage, +2 to Quick Draw, Bleed, Penetrate
Wind of Calamity	Ring	Ranged 22	+13 max. damage, +10 min. damage, 20% of physical damage reflected to enemy, +1 to Quick Draw, Bleed, Penetrate
Wind of Recovery	Ring	Ranged 29	+55 health, +6 health per hit, +15% health recovery, +6% power recharge rate
Wind of Omens	Ring	Ranged 46	+18 armor, +8% chance to dodge melee attacks, +2 to Critical Shot, Dodge, Survival, +40% chance to find magic items

Winds of Kel'drassil Set Bonuses

Number of Items Equipped	+ DEX	+ Health Per Hit	+ Ranged Skills	+ Quick Draw, Bleed, Penetrate	+ Armor
2	12	4	1	1	0
3	18	6	1	1	0
4	24	8	2	2	4
5	32	10	2	3	14

Staff Set 1—Thena's Serenity

Name	Base Name	Requirement	Effects
Thena's Soothing Touch	Gloves	Nature Magic 12	+22 mana, +2 mana per hit, +12% death resistance, +1 to Nurturing Gift, Enveloping Embrace, Feral Wrath
Thena's Tranquil Path	Boots	Nature Magic 4	+5% mana regeneration, +5 armor, +10% ice resistance, +10% fire resistance
Thena's Calming Gaze	Hood	Nature Magic 16	+6 intelligence, 6% mana stolen, +80% armor, +1 to Summon Fortitude, Summon Might, Summon Bond
Thena's Companion	Shillelah	Nature Magic 8	+3 intelligence, +12 health, +10% nature magic damage, +10% chance to find magic items

Thena's Serenity Set Bonuses

Number of Items Equipped	+ INT	+ Mana	+% Magic Damage Resistance	+ Summon Fortitude, Summon Might, Summon Bond	+ Nurturing Gift, Enveloping Embrace, Feral Wrath	+ Armor
2	3	20	3%	0	0	0
3	5	30	6%	1	1	2
4	8	40	10%	2	2	5

Staff Set 2—North Keeper's Vestments

Name	Base Name	Requirement	Effects
Mantle of the North	Body	Nature Magic 49	+25 intelligence, +125% armor, +25% ice resistance, +3 to Aquatic Affinity, Arctic Mastery, Freezing
Guardian of the North	Staff	Nature Magic 56	+150 health, +30% nature magic damage, +48 armor, +3 to Nurturing Gift, Enveloping Embrace, Feral Wrath
Soul of the North	Amulet	Nature Magic 45	10% mana stolen, +15% magic damage resistance, +8% power recharge rate, +1 to nature magic skills

North Keeper's Vestments Set Bonuses

Number of Items Equipped	+% Nature Magic Damage	+% Ice Resistance	+% Ranged Resistance	+ Aquatic Affinity, Arctic Mastery, Freezing	+ Nurturing Gift, Enveloping Embrace, Feral Wrath
2	20%	18%	20%	2	2
3	30%	25%	25%	3	3

Cestus Set 1—Chaos' Avatar

Name	Type	Requirement	Effects
Endbringer's Vestment	Vestment	Combat Magic 22	+48 mana, 20% of physical damage reflected to enemy, +60% armor, +2 to Brilliance, Amplified Lightning, Arcing
Unraveler's Boots	Boots	Combat Magic 26	+12 intelligence, +12% mana regeneration, +22 armor, +2 to Debilitation, Grim Necromancy, Vampirism
Chaos Grips	Cestus	Combat Magic 32	+14 intelligence, +20% combat magic damage, +6% power recharge rate, +2 to Devastation, Searing Flames, Ignite

Chaos' Avatar Set Bonuses

Number of Items Equipped	+ Mana	+% Combat Magic Damage	+% Power Recharge Rate	+ Combat Magic Skills	+ Armor
2	80	12%	3%	1	4
3	110	20%	6%	2	13

Cestus Set 2—The Lich's Carcass

Name	Base Name	Requirement	Effects
The Lich's Eye	Ornate Crown	Combat Magic 54	+30 intelligence, +48 armor, +15% magic damage resistance, +3 to Brilliance, Amplified Lightning, Arcing
The Lich's Hands	Cestus	Combat Magic 62	+35% combat magic damage, 12% health stolen, 12% mana stolen, +3 to Debilitation, Grim Necromancy, Vampirism
The Lich's Heart	Amulet	Combat Magic 58	+160 health, +25% death resistance, +12% melee and ranged resistance, +3 to combat magic skills
The Lich's Tooth	Ring	Combat Magic 50	+30% combat magic damage, +14 mana per hit, +8% power recharge rate, +3 to Devastation, Searing Flames, Ignite

The Lich's Carcass Set Bonuses

Number of Items Equipped	+ INT	% Mana Stolen	+% Death Resistance	+ Debilitation, Grim Necromancy, Vampirism	+ Brilliance, Amplified Lightning, Arcing	+ Devastation, Searing Flames, Ignite
2	20	10%	20%	2	0	1
3	35	13%	25%	3	1	2
4	50	16%	30%	4	2	3

Armor Set 1: Ranger—Eternal Grace

Name	Type	Requirement	Effects
Eternal Dignity	Jerkin	Ranged 12	+15 health, +50% armor, +1 to Biting Arrow, Far Shot, Shockwave, +1 to Quick Draw, Bleed, Penetrate
Eternal Elegance	Boots	Ranged 25	+9 dexterity, +9 armor, +15% fire resistance, +12% chance to dodge melee attacks
Eternal Beauty	Hood	Ranged 20	+5% health stolen, +12% health regeneration, +70% armor, +1 to Critical Shot, Dodge, Survival
Eternal Finesse	Gloves	Ranged 14	+13 dexterity, +8 max. damage, +7% health stolen, +8 armor, +8% power recharge rate

Eternal Grace Set Bonuses

Number of Items Equipped	+ DEX	+ Armor	+% Melee Resistance	+ Ranged Skills
2	8	12	6%	0
3	14	20	8%	1
4	22	35	10%	1

Armor Set 2: Magic—The Circle of Four

Name	Type	Requirement	Effects
Azuka of Four's Robe	Robe	Mage 46	+150 mana, +120% armor, +3 to Summon Fortitude, Summon Might, Summon Bond, +3 to Nurturing Gift, Enveloping Embrace, Feral Wrath
Treil of Four's Boots	Boots	Mage 37	10% mana stolen, +25 armor, +1 to combat magic skills, +2 to Devastation, Searing Flames, Ignite
Corum of Four's Helm	Helm	Mage 33	+14 intelligence, +22% combat magic damage, +20 armor, +2 to Brilliance, Amplified Lightning, Arcing
Kreya of Four's Pendant	Amulet	Melee 35	+18 intelligence, +25% nature magic damage, +1 to nature magic skills, +2 to Aquatic Affinity, Arctic Mastery, Freezing

The Circle of Four Set Bonuses

Number of Items Equipped	+ Mana	% Health Stolen	+% Ranged Resistance	+ Summon Fortitude, Summon Might, Summon Bond	+ Armor
2	100	8	15%	2	2
3	150	10	20%	3	4
4	200	12	25%	4	15

Armor Set 3: Magic—Silks of the Master

Name	Type	Requirement	Effects
Magesilk Gloves	Gloves	Mage 9	+15 mana, +5% mana regeneration, +6 armor, +12% fire resistance
Magesilk Boots	Boots	Mage 6	+3 intelligence, +5% health regeneration, +5 armor, +10% lightning resistance
Master's Focusing Charm	Amulet	Mage 20	+10% nature magic damage, +10% combat magic damage, +6% mana stolen, +1 to Aquatic Affinity, Arctic Mastery, Freezing
Master's Insight	Ring	Mage 13	+5 intelligence, +6% magic damage resistance, +4% power recharge rate, +1 to Devastation, Grim Necromancy, Vampirism

Silks of the Master Set Bonuses

Number of Items Equipped	+ INT	+% Nature Magic Damage	+% Combat Magic Damage	% Mana Stolen	+ Armor
2	3	10%	10%	4	2
3	5	15%	15%	6	4
4	8	20%	20%	8	8

Armor Set 4: Melee—Treasures of the Dwarven Lords

Name	Base Name	Requirement	Effects
Stonecase	Layered Plate	Melee 42	+95 health, +20 armor, +75% armor, +3 to Barricade, Toughness, Reinforced Armor
Forge Gauntlets	Gauntlets	Melee 47	+32 strength, +30 armor, +15% ranged resistance, +2 to melee skills
The Iron Crown	Helm	Melee 36	+20 strength, +25 max. damage, +20 armor, +8% melee resistance

Treasures of the Dwarven Lords Set Bonuses

Number of Items Equipped	+ STR	+ Health	+% Melee Resistance	+% Chance to find Magic Items	+ Armor
2	20	50	6%	8%	4
3	40	100	10%	15%	12

Armor Set 5: Magic—Keh's Regalia

Name	Base Name	Requirement	Effects
Keh's Majesty	Robe	Mage 60	+35 intelligence, +160 health, +150% armor, +25% fire resistance
Keh's Liberators	Gloves	Mage 52	+46 armor, +25% death resistance, +8% power recharge rate
Keh's Rulership	Ring	Mage 66	+45 intelligence, +275 mana, +16% magic resistance, +2 to nature magic skills, +2 to combat magic skills
Keh's Might	Ring	Mage 55	+35% nature magic damage, +35% combat magic damage, 12% mana stolen, +20% health regeneration, +15% melee resistance

Keh's Regalia Set Bonuses

Number of Items Equipped	+ INT	+% Mana Regeneration	+% Power Recharge Rate	+ Nature Magic Skills	+ Combat Magic Skills
2	20	10%	8%	1	1
3	40	15%	12%	2	2
4	52	20%	15%	3	3

Armor Set 6: Melee—The Undying Warlord

Name	Base Name	Requirement	Effects
The Warlord's Cage	Scaled Plate	Melee 72	+62 strength, +29–48 damage, +120% armor, +4 to Barricade, Toughness, Reinforced Armor
The Warlord's Tread	Greaves	Melee 58	+160 health, 45% of physical damage reflected to enemy, +40 armor, +3 to Critical Strike, Dual Wield, Alacrity
The Warlord's Horns	Helm	Melee 61	+15–44 damage, 12% health stolen, +45 armor, +3 to Fortitude, Overbear, Smite

(continued)

Name	Base Name	Requirement	Effects
The Warlord's Crest	Amulet	Melee 66	+54 strength, +67 max. damage, +10% melee resistance, +2 to melee skills
The Warlord's Sign	Ring	Melee 52	+125 health, +20–25 damage, +15% magic resistance, +10% power recharge rate

The Undying Warlord Set Bonuses

Number of Items Equipped	+ STR	+ Weapon Max. Damage	+ Armor	+% Melee and Ranged Resistance	+ Melee Skills
2	20	30	30	4%	1
3	40	50	50	7%	2
4	60	70	70	10%	3
5	76	90	100	12%	4

Armor Set 7: Ranged—Plainswalker's Journey

Name	Base Name	Requirement	Effects
Plainswalker's Passing	Suit	Ranged 70	+150% armor, +16% magic resistance, +12% melee and ranged resistance, +4 to Critical Shot, Dodge, Survival
Plainswalker's Travelers	Boots	Ranged 42	+38 dexterity, +25% ice resistance, +12% chance to dodge melee attacks, +3 to Quick Draw, Bleed, Penetrate
Plainswalker's Heroism	Spiked Helmet	Ranged 58	+54 max. damage, +52 armor, +25% magic resistance, +4 to Biting Arrow, Far Shot, Shockwave
Plainswalker's Legend	Amulet	Ranged 51	+45 dexterity, +130 health, +25% lightning resistance, +2 to ranged skills
Plainswalker's Relic	Ring	Ranged 46	+9–28 damage, 11% health stolen, +25% death resistance, +10% power recharge rate

Plainswalker's Journey Set Bonuses

Number of Items Equipped	+ DEX	+ Ranged Max. Damage	+% Magic Damage Resistance	+% Chance to Dodge attack	+ Ranged Skills	+ Armor
2	30	30	5%	8%	1	0
3	52	50	8%	10%	2	8
4	76	70	10%	12%	3	20
5	100	90	12%	16%	4	45

Armor Set 8—Jewels of the Nexus

Name	Base Name	Requirement	Effects
Nexus Prism	Amulet	Character Level 34	+68 health, +12% magic resistance, +1 to Barricade, Toughness, Reinforced Armor, +1 to Critical Shot, Dodge, Survival, +1 to Aquatic Affinity, Arctic Mastery, Freezing, +1 to Devastation, Searing Flames, Ignite
Jewel of Fire	Ring	Character Level 4	+4 strength, +1–2 damage, +10% fire resistance, +8% chance to find magic items
Jewel of Lightning	Ring	Character Level 12	+6 dexterity, +2–5 damage, +12% lightning resistance, +60% to gold dropped
Jewel of Ice	Ring	Character Level 19	+4–7 damage, +8 armor, +16% ice resistance, +14% ranged resistance
Jewel of Death	Ring	Character Level 27	+10 intelligence, +6–11 damage, +5 health per hit, +18% death resistance

Jewels of the Nexus Set Bonuses

Number of Items Equipped	+ Ice Damage	+ Fire Damage	+ Lightning Damage	+ Death Damage	+ Melee Skills	+ Ranged Skills	+ Nature Magic Skills	+ Combat Magic Skills
2	2–4	2–4	2–5	2–4	0	0	0	0
3	4–7	5–6	3–8	4–7	0	0	0	0
4	7–12	8–10	5–14	7–12	1	1	1	1
5	10–16	12–14	6–19	10–16	2	2	2	2

Armor Set 9—Secrets of the Forgotten

Name	Base Name	Requirement	Effects
Soranith's Amulet	Amulet	Character Level 32	+15 intelligence, +15% mana regeneration, +20% death resistance
Soranith's Gold Ring	Ring	Character Level 32	+20 strength, +4–6 damage, +20% fire resistance
Soranith's Silver Ring	Ring	Character Level 32	+27 dexterity, +4–6 damage, +20% lightning resistance

Secrets of the Forgotten Set Bonuses

Number of Items Equipped	+ Health Stolen	+% Magic Damage Resistance	+% Chance to Magic Items
2	3	4%	20%
3	5	6%	40%

Armor Set 10—Nature's Vigilance

Name	Base Name	Requirement	Effects
Vigilant Hauberk	Dryad Armor	Character Level 4	+4 strength, +12 health
Vigilant Crest	Dryad Helm	Character Level 8	+4 intelligence, +20 mana, +5% death resistance
Vigilant Boots	Dryad Boots	Character Level 6	+4 dexterity, +5% health regeneration, +4 armor
Vigilant Gloves	Dryad Gloves	Character Level 2	+4% nature magic damage, +5% mana regeneration, +4% lightning resistance

Nature's Vigilance Set Bonuses

Number of Items Equipped	+% Lightning Resistance	+ Armor	+ Health
2	5%	0	0
3	8%	6	0
4	10%	15	20

Armor Set 11—Ghostly Visions

Name	Type	Requirement	Effects
Spirit of Rest	Ring	Character Level 26	+35 health, +35 mana, +12% mana regeneration, +12 health regeneration
Spirit of Unrest	Ring	Character Level 26	+4–6 damage, +5% health stolen, 20% of physical damage reflected to enemy, +15% death resistance
Spirit of Repose	Amulet	Character Level 38	+80 health, +80 mana, +3% power damage, +6% power recharge rate

Ghostly Vision Set Bonuses

Number of Items Equipped	+ Health Regeneration	+ Mana Regeneration	+% Magic Damage Resistance	+ Armor
2	8%	8%	4%	8
3	15%	15%	8%	20

Enchantments

These prefixes and suffixes enhance the various base items found within the game. Adventurers should seek out the many combinations of items and enchantments to obtain the best equipment possible for the party.

Enchantment Prefixes

Modifier	Effects	Object Types
Cruel	+10% to melee damage	Melee
Wicked	+15% to melee damage	Melee
Callous	+20% to melee damage	Melee
Heartless	+25% to melee damage	Melee
Vicious	+32% to melee damage	Melee
Ruthless	+40% to melee damage	Melee
Rancorous	+48% to melee damage	Melee
Excruciating	+56% to melee damage	Melee
Sharp	+10% to ranged damage	Ranged
Honed	+15% to ranged damage	Ranged
Stinging	+20% to ranged damage	Ranged
Jagged	+26% to ranged damage	Ranged
Fine	+33% to ranged damage	Ranged
Serrated	+40% to ranged damage	Ranged
Keen	+48% to ranged damage	Ranged
Razor	+56% to ranged damage	Ranged
Feral	+4% to nature magic damage	Mage
Savage	+8% to nature magic damage	Mage

Modifier	Effects	Object Types
Wild	+10% to nature magic damage	Mage
Ferocious	+12% to nature magic damage	Mage
Bestial	+15% to nature magic damage	Mage
Rabid	+18% to nature magic damage	Mage
Overgrown	+22% to nature magic damage	Mage
Arboreal	+25% to nature magic damage	Mage
Destructive	+4% to combat magic damage	Mage
Eradicating	+8% to combat magic damage	Mage
Ruinous	+12% to combat magic damage	Mage
Devastating	+15% to combat magic damage	Mage
Annihilating	+20% to combat magic damage	Mage

(continued)

(continued)

Modifier	Effects	Object Types
Demolishing	+24% to combat magic damage	Mage
Obliterating	+28% to combat magic damage	Mage
Tragic	+32% to combat magic damage	Mage
Chilling	+3–4 ice damage	Melee
Shivering	+5–8 ice damage	Melee
Frigid	+8–14 ice damage	Melee
Arctic	+13–22 ice damage	Melee
Glacial	+19–32 ice damage	Melee
Boreal	+27–45 ice damage	Melee
Frosted	+3–4 ice damage	Ranged
Snowy	+5–8 ice damage	Ranged
Icy	+8–14 ice damage	Ranged
Frozen	+13–22 ice damage	Ranged
Wintery	+19–32 ice damage	Ranged
Polar	+27–45 ice damage	Ranged
Scorching	+2–4 fire damage	Melee
Burning	+4–6 fire damage	Melee
Searing	+10–12 fire damage	Melee
Flaming	+16–20 fire damage	Melee
Blistering	+25–30 fire damage	Melee
Cremating	+36–46 fire damage	Melee
Heated	+3–3 fire damage	Ranged
Smoking	+4–6 fire damage	Ranged
Cauterizing	+10–12 fire damage	Ranged
Igneous	+16–20 fire damage	Ranged
Carbonizing	+25–30 fire damage	Ranged
Incinerating	+36–46 fire damage	Ranged
Jolting	+2–5 lightning damage	Melee
Electrified	+4–12 lightning damage	Melee
Charged	+6–20 lightning damage	Melee
Shocking	+12–32 lightning damage	Melee
Thundering	+16–50 lightning damage	Melee
Storming	+24–70 lightning damage	Melee
Glimmering	+2–5 lightning damage	Ranged
Glowing	+4–12 lightning damage	Ranged
Radiating	+6–20 lightning damage	Ranged
Dazzling	+12–32 lightning damage	Ranged
Suffused	+16–50 lightning damage	Ranged
Incandescent	+24–70 lightning damage	Ranged
Grim	+4–6 death damage	Melee
Corrupt	+6–12 death damage	Melee
Vile	+10–18 death damage	Melee
Gruesome	+16–28 death damage	Melee
Depraved	+24–40 death damage	Melee
Necromantic	+35–58 death damage	Melee
Somber	+4–6 death damage	Ranged
Dispiriting	+6–12 death damage	Ranged
Mournful	+10–18 death damage	Ranged
Desolate	+16–28 death damage	Ranged
Caliginous	+24–40 death damage	Ranged
Stygian	+35–58 death damage	Ranged
Stout	+2 to armor	Armor, Shield, Ring, Amulet
Repellant	+4 to armor	Armor, Shield, Ring, Amulet

Modifier	Effects	Object Types
Stable	+6 to armor	Armor, Shield, Ring, Amulet
Enforced	+8 to armor	Armor, Shield, Ring, Amulet
Tough	+10 to armor	Armor, Shield, Ring, Amulet
Hardened	+15 to armor	Armor, Shield, Ring, Amulet
Durable	+22 to armor	Armor, Shield, Ring, Amulet
Rugged	+30 to armor	Armor, Shield, Ring, Amulet
Fortified	+40 to armor	Armor, Shield, Ring, Amulet
Impenetrable	+53 to armor	Armor, Shield, Ring, Amulet
Masterwork	+68 to armor	Armor, Shield, Ring, Amulet
Adamantine	+85 to armor	Armor, Shield, Ring, Amulet
Steadfast	+26% to armor	Armor, Shield
Vigilant	+39% to armor	Armor, Shield
Resolute	+52% to armor	Armor, Shield
Persistent	+65% to armor	Armor, Shield
Unremitting	+78% to armor	Armor, Shield
Relentless	+90% to armor	Armor, Shield
Abiding	+103% to armor	Armor, Shield
Eternal	+116% to armor	Armor, Shield
Twilight	Magic damage reduced by 5%	Amulet, Spellbook
Dusk	Magic damage reduced by 8%	Amulet, Spellbook
Midnight	Magic damage reduced by 12%	Amulet, Spellbook
Dawn	Magic damage reduced by 15%	Amulet, Spellbook
Azure	Ice magic damage reduced by 10%	Armor, Shield, Ring, Amulet, Spellbook
Beryl	Ice magic damage reduced by 14%	Armor, Shield, Ring, Amulet, Spellbook
Blue	Ice magic damage reduced by 18%	Armor, Shield, Ring, Amulet, Spellbook
Cerulean	Ice magic damage reduced by 22%	Armor, Shield, Ring, Amulet, Spellbook
Sapphire	Ice magic damage reduced by 25%	Armor, Shield, Ring, Amulet, Spellbook
Crimson	Fire magic damage reduced by 10%	Armor, Shield, Ring, Amulet, Spellbook
Scarlet	Fire magic damage reduced by 14%	Armor, Shield, Ring, Amulet, Spellbook
Red	Fire magic damage reduced by 18%	Armor, Shield, Ring, Amulet, Spellbook
Bloodshot	Fire magic damage reduced by 22%	Armor, Shield, Ring, Amulet, Spellbook

(continued)

(continued)

Enchantments

Modifier	Effects	Object Types
Ruby	Fire magic damage reduced by 25%	Armor, Shield, Ring, Amulet, Spellbook
Pale	Lightning magic damage reduced by 10%	Armor, Shield, Ring, Amulet, Spellbook
Ivory	Lightning magic damage reduced by 14%	Armor, Shield, Ring, Amulet, Spellbook
White	Lightning magic damage reduced by 18%	Armor, Shield, Ring, Amulet, Spellbook
Crystalline	Lightning magic damage reduced by 22%	Armor, Shield, Ring, Amulet, Spellbook
Pearl	Lightning magic damage reduced by 25%	Armor, Shield, Ring, Amulet, Spellbook
Indigo	Death magic damage reduced by 10%	Armor, Shield, Ring, Amulet, Spellbook
Lavender	Death magic damage reduced by 14%	Armor, Shield, Ring, Amulet, Spellbook
Purple	Death magic damage reduced by 18%	Armor, Shield, Ring, Amulet, Spellbook
Violet	Death magic damage reduced by 22%	Armor, Shield, Ring, Amulet, Spellbook
Amethyst	Death magic damage reduced by 25%	Armor, Shield, Ring, Amulet, Spellbook
Noble	Physical damage reduced by 3%	Shield, Amulet
Regal	Physical damage reduced by 5%	Shield, Amulet
Imperial	Physical damage reduced by 7%	Shield, Amulet
Sovereign	Physical damage reduced by 10%	Shield, Amulet
Formidable	Melee damage reduced by 5%	Armor, Shield
Imposing	Melee damage reduced by 7%	Armor, Shield
Daunting	Melee damage reduced by 9%	Armor, Shield
Intimidating	Melee damage reduced by 11%	Armor, Shield
Fearsome	Melee damage reduced by 14%	Armor, Shield
Disorienting	Ranged damage reduced by 8%	Armor, Shield
Obscuring	Ranged damage reduced by 12%	Armor, Shield
Blurring	Ranged damage reduced by 15%	Armor, Shield
Confounding	Ranged damage reduced by 18%	Armor, Shield
Displacing	Ranged damage reduced by 20%	Armor, Shield
Rousing	Increase power recharge rate by 5%	Weapon, Amulet

Modifier	Effects	Object Types
Energizing	Increase power recharge rate by 7%	Weapon, Amulet
Invigorating	Increase power recharge rate by 10%	Weapon, Amulet
Warrior's	+1 to melee skills	Melee, Amulet
Champion's	+2 to melee skills	Melee, Amulet
Adventurer's	+1 to ranged skills	Ranged, Amulet
Ranger's	+2 to ranged skills	Ranged, Amulet
Watcher's	+1 to nature magic skills	Mage, Amulet, Spellbook
Druid's	+2 to nature magic skills	Mage, Amulet, Spellbook
Ravager's	+1 to combat magic skills	Mage, Amulet, Spellbook
Apocalyptic	+2 to combat magic skills	Mage, Amulet, Spellbook
Knight's	+2 to Barricade, Toughness, Reinforced Armor	Melee, Amulet
Templar's	+3 to Barricade, Toughness, Reinforced Armor	Melee, Amulet
Paladin's	+4 to Barricade, Toughness, Reinforced Armor	Melee, Amulet
Brawler's	+2 to Fortitude, Overbear, Smite	Melee, Amulet
Barbarian's	+3 to Fortitude, Overbear, Smite	Melee, Amulet
Berserker's	+4 to Fortitude, Overbear, Smite	Melee, Amulet
Duelist's	+2 to Critical Strike, Dual Wield, Alacrity	Melee, Amulet
Slayer's	+3 to Critical Strike, Dual Wield, Alacrity	Melee, Amulet
Hurricane's	+4 to Critical Strike, Dual Wield, Alacrity	Melee, Amulet
Wanderer's	+2 to Critical Shot, Dodge, Survival	Ranged, Amulet
Nomad's	+3 to Critical Shot, Dodge, Survival	Ranged, Amulet
Vagabond's	+4 to Critical Shot, Dodge, Survival	Ranged, Amulet
Archer's	+2 to Biting Arrow, Far Shot, Shockwave	Ranged, Amulet
Marksman's	+3 to Biting Arrow, Far Shot, Shockwave	Ranged, Amulet
Sniper's	+4 to Biting Arrow, Far Shot, Shockwave	Ranged, Amulet
Assassin's	+2 Quick Draw, Point Blank Throw, Penetrate	Ranged, Amulet
Tempest's	+3 to Quick Draw, Point Blank Throw, Penetrate	Ranged, Amulet
Fusilier's	+4 to Quick Draw, Point Blank Throw, Penetrate	Ranged, Amulet
Caller's	+2 to Summon Fortitude, Summon Might, Summon Bond	Mage, Amulet, Spellbook
Summoner's	+3 to Summon Fortitude, Summon Might, Summon Bond	Mage, Amulet, Spellbook
Beastwalker's	+4 to Summon Fortitude, Summon Might, Summon Bond	Mage, Amulet, Spellbook

(continued)

(continued)

Modifier	Effects	Object Types
Rime	+2 to Aquatic Affinity, Arctic Mastery, Freezing	Mage, Amulet, Spellbook
Winter	+3 to Aquatic Affinity, Arctic Mastery, Freezing	Mage, Amulet, Spellbook
Aquamancer's	+4 to Aquatic Affinity, Arctic Mastery, Freezing	Mage, Amulet, Spellbook
Advocate's	+2 to Nurturing Gift, Enveloping Embrace, Feral Wrath	Mage, Amulet, Spellbook
Protector's	+3 to Nurturing Gift, Enveloping Embrace, Feral Wrath	Mage, Amulet, Spellbook
Warden's	+4 to Nurturing Gift, Enveloping Embrace, Feral Wrath	Mage, Amulet, Spellbook
Vanquisher's	+2 to Debilitation, Grim Necromancy, Vampirism	Mage, Amulet, Spellbook
Necromancer's	+3 to Debilitation, Grim Necromancy, Vampirism	Mage, Amulet, Spellbook
Blightwalker's	+4 to Debilitation, Grim Necromancy, Vampirism	Mage, Amulet, Spellbook
Luminous	+2 to Brilliance, Amplified Lightning, Arcing	Mage, Amulet, Spellbook
Blinding	+3 to Brilliance, Amplified Lightning, Arcing	Mage, Amulet, Spellbook
Shining	+4 to Brilliance, Amplified Lightning, Arcing	Mage, Amulet, Spellbook
Blazing	+2 to Devastation, Searing Flames, Ignite	Mage, Amulet, Spellbook
Incendiary	+3 to Devastation, Searing Flames, Ignite	Mage, Amulet, Spellbook
Pyromancer's	+4 to Devastation, Searing Flames, Ignite	Mage, Amulet, Spellbook
Fortunate	+4–6% to magic find	Ring, Amulet, Spellbook
Charmed	+8–12% to magic find	Ring, Amulet, Spellbook
Lucky	+16–24% to magic find	Ring, Amulet, Spellbook
Fated	+25–34% to magic find	Ring, Amulet, Spellbook
Serendipitous	+35–45% to magic find	Ring, Amulet, Spellbook
Glittering	+5% to gold dropped	Melee, Ranged, Mage, Ring, Amulet, Spellbook
Wealthy	+15% to gold dropped	Ring, Amulet, Spellbook
Opulent	+40% to gold dropped	Ring, Amulet, Spellbook
Affluent	+70% to gold dropped	Ring, Amulet, Spellbook

Enchantment Suffixes

Modifier	Effects	Object Types
Of Hardiness	+1 to Strength	Weapon, Armor, Shield, Ring, Amulet
Of Sturdiness	+3 to Strength	Weapon, Armor, Shield, Ring, Amulet
Of Vigor	+7 to Strength	Weapon, Armor, Shield, Ring, Amulet
Of Tenacity	+12 to Strength	Weapon, Armor, Shield, Ring, Amulet
Of Force	+20 to Strength	Weapon, Armor, Shield, Ring, Amulet
Of Virulence	+30 to Strength	Weapon, Armor, Shield, Ring, Amulet
Of Might	+42 to Strength	Weapon, Armor, Shield, Ring, Amulet
Of Prominence	+56 to Strength	Weapon, Armor, Shield, Ring, Amulet
Of Colossus	+72 to Strength	Weapon, Armor, Shield, Ring, Amulet
Of the Swift	+1 to Dexterity	Weapon, Armor, Ring, Amulet
Of the Spry	+4 to Dexterity	Weapon, Armor, Ring, Amulet
Of the Nimble	+9 to Dexterity	Weapon, Armor, Ring, Amulet
Of Proficiency	+16 to Dexterity	Weapon, Armor, Ring, Amulet
Of Expertise	+27 to Dexterity	Weapon, Armor, Ring, Amulet
Of Finesse	+40 to Dexterity	Weapon, Armor, Ring, Amulet
Of Deftness	+57 to Dexterity	Weapon, Armor, Ring, Amulet
Of Adroitness	+76 to Dexterity	Weapon, Armor, Ring, Amulet
Of Effortlessness	+100 to Dexterity	Weapon, Armor, Ring, Amulet
Of Awareness	+1 to Intelligence	Weapon, Armor, Ring, Amulet, Spellbook
Of Insight	+3 to Intelligence	Weapon, Armor, Ring, Amulet, Spellbook
Of Judgment	+6 to Intelligence	Weapon, Armor, Ring, Amulet, Spellbook
Of Foresight	+10 to Intelligence	Weapon, Armor, Ring, Amulet, Spellbook
Of Acumen	+16 to Intelligence	Weapon, Armor, Ring, Amulet, Spellbook
Of Knowledge	+24 to Intelligence	Weapon, Armor, Ring, Amulet, Spellbook
Of Brilliance	+33 to Intelligence	Weapon, Armor, Ring, Amulet, Spellbook
Of Enlightenment	+45 to Intelligence	Weapon, Armor, Ring, Amulet, Spellbook
Of Omniscience	+60 to Intelligence	Weapon, Armor, Ring, Amulet, Spellbook
Of the Rat	+4 to Health	Armor, Shield, Ring, Amulet, Spellbook
Of the Weasel	+9 to Health	Armor, Shield, Ring, Amulet, Spellbook
Of the Fox	+15 to Health	Armor, Shield, Ring, Amulet, Spellbook
Of the Badger	+24 to Health	Armor, Shield, Ring, Amulet, Spellbook
Of the Panther	+36 to Health	Armor, Shield, Ring, Amulet, Spellbook
Of the Ram	+50 to Health	Armor, Shield, Ring, Amulet, Spellbook
Of the Boar	+67 to Health	Armor, Shield, Ring, Amulet, Spellbook
Of the Wolf	+90 to Health	Armor, Shield, Ring, Amulet, Spellbook

(continued)

(continued)

Enchantments

Modifier	Effects	Object Types
Of the Tiger	+116 to Health	Armor, Shield, Ring, Amulet, Spellbook
Of the Horse	+150 to Health	Armor, Shield, Ring, Amulet, Spellbook
Of the Bear	+188 to Health	Armor, Ring, Amulet, Spellbook
Of the Lion	+237 to Health	Armor, Ring, Amulet, Spellbook
Of the Toad	+4 to Mana	Mage Weapons, Mage Armor, Ring, Amulet, Spellbook
Of the Hawk	+13 to Mana	Mage Weapons, Mage Armor, Ring, Amulet, Spellbook
Of the Lizard	+21 to Mana	Mage Weapons, Mage Armor, Ring, Amulet, Spellbook
Of the Eagle	+30 to Mana	Mage Weapons, Mage Armor, Ring, Amulet, Spellbook
Of the Serpent	+43 to Mana	Mage Weapons, Mage Armor, Ring, Amulet, Spellbook
Of the Falcon	+59 to Mana	Mage Weapons, Mage Armor, Ring, Amulet, Spellbook
Of the Raven	+81 to Mana	Mage Weapons, Mage Armor, Ring, Amulet, Spellbook
Of the Owl	+107 to Mana	Mage Weapons, Mage Armor, Ring, Amulet, Spellbook
Of the Griffon	+136 to Mana	Mage Weapons, Mage Armor, Ring, Amulet, Spellbook
Of the Hydra	+175 to Mana	Mage Weapons, Mage Armor, Ring, Amulet, Spellbook
Of the Phoenix	+218 to Mana	Mage Weapons, Mage Armor, Ring, Amulet, Spellbook
Of the Dragon	+274 to Mana	Mage Weapons, Mage Armor, Ring, Amulet, Spellbook
Of Wounding	+1 to melee max. damage	Melee
Of Pain	+4 to melee max. damage	Melee
Of Torment	+12 to melee max. damage	Melee
Of Injury	+25 to melee max. damage	Melee
Of Mutilation	+45 to melee max. damage	Melee
Of Torture	+72 to melee max. damage	Melee
Of Accuracy	+1 to ranged max. damage	Ranged
Of Focus	+4 to ranged max. damage	Ranged
Of Sighting	+11 to ranged max. damage	Ranged
Of Precision	+25 to ranged max. damage	Ranged

(continued)

Modifier	Effects	Object Types
Of Seeking	+44 to ranged max. damage	Ranged
Of Mastery	+72 to ranged max. damage	Ranged
Of Affliction	+3 to melee min. damage	Melee
Of Disaster	+4 to melee min. damage	Melee
Of Grief	+6 to melee min. damage	Melee
Of Misery	+9 to melee min. damage	Melee
Of Calamity	+13 to melee min. damage	Melee
Of Desolation	+18 to melee min. damage	Melee
Of Piercing	+3 to ranged min. damage	Ranged
Of Driving	+4 to ranged min. damage	Ranged
Of Puncturing	+6 to ranged min. damage	Ranged
Of Boring	+9 to ranged min. damage	Ranged
Of Perforating	+13 to ranged min. damage	Ranged
Of Penetrating	+18 to ranged min. damage	Ranged
Of Reversal	10% of damage received reflected back to attacker	Armor, Shield
Of Punishment	20% of damage received reflected back to attacker	Armor, Shield
Of Vengeance	30% of damage received reflected back to attacker	Armor, Shield
Of Retribution	40% of damage received reflected back to attacker	Armor, Shield
Of the Parasite	3% health stolen	Weapon
Of the Predator	5% health stolen	Weapon
Of the Vampire	7% health stolen	Weapon
Of Blood	8% health stolen	Weapon
Of Consumption	+2 health stolen per hit	Weapon
Of Gorging	+6 health stolen per hit	Weapon
Of Feasting	+14 health stolen per hit	Weapon
Of Devouring	+23 health stolen per hit	Weapon
Of the Phantom	3% mana stolen	Weapon
Of the Ghost	5% mana stolen	Weapon
Of the Specter	7% mana stolen	Weapon
Of the Wraith	8% mana stolen	Weapon
Of Candlelight	+2 mana stolen per hit	Weapon
Of Moonlight	+6 mana stolen per hit	Weapon
Of Daylight	+14 mana stolen per hit	Weapon
Of Starlight	+23 mana stolen per hit	Weapon

(continued)

Modifier	Effects	Object Types
Of Mending	+4% to health recovery	Melee/Ranged Armor, Shield, Ring, Amulet
Of Reconstruction	+6% to health recovery	Melee/Ranged Armor, Shield, Ring, Amulet
Of Suturing	+10% to health recovery	Melee/Ranged Armor, Shield, Ring, Amulet
Of Regeneration	+12% to health recovery	Melee/Ranged Armor, Shield, Ring, Amulet
Of Brightening	+4% to mana recovery	Mage Armor, Ring, Amulet, Spellbook
Of Illumination	+6% to mana recovery	Mage Armor, Ring, Amulet, Spellbook
Of Awakening	+10% to mana recovery	Mage Armor, Ring, Amulet, Spellbook
Of Visions	+12% to mana recovery	Mage Armor, Ring, Amulet, Spellbook
Of Repulsion	5% chance to block melee attack	Shield

Modifier	Effects	Object Types
Of Prevention	10% chance to block melee attack	Shield
Of Obstruction	15% chance to block melee attack	Shield
Of Deflection	5% chance to block ranged attack	Shield
Of Interception	12% chance to block ranged attack	Shield
Of Defense	20% chance to block ranged attack	Shield

(continued)

Reagents

This chart reveals all reagents and their effects. Reagents can be applied to enchantable weapons, armor, and jewelry. The quality of an enchantable weapon, armor, or jewelry piece determines how many separate reagents can be applied. There are no other limits to reagent application.

Reagent	Effects	Object Types	Inventory Height, Width
Pine Splinter	+3 to Strength	Weapon, Armor, Shield, Ring, Amulet	1,1
Oak Branch	+7 to Strength	Weapon, Armor, Shield, Ring, Amulet	1,4
Ironwood Timber	+18 to Strength	Weapon, Armor, Shield, Ring, Amulet	2,4
Dryad Bead	+3 to Dexterity	Weapon, Armor, Ring, Amulet	1,1
Elven Oil	+7 to Dexterity	Weapon, Armor, Ring, Amulet	1,4
Quicksilver Oil	+18 to Dexterity	Weapon, Armor, Ring, Amulet	2,4
Gral Eye	+2 to Intelligence	Weapon, Armor, Ring, Amulet, Spellbook	1,1
Malachite Powder	+5 to Intelligence	Weapon, Armor, Ring, Amulet, Spellbook	4,1
Spectral Dust	+12 to Intelligence	Weapon, Armor, Ring, Amulet, Spellbook	4,2
Nettle Cluster	+6 to Health	Armor, Shield, Ring, Amulet, Spellbook	1,1
Mandrake Root	+14 to Health	Armor, Shield, Ring, Amulet, Spellbook	2,1
Ash Leaves	+34 to Health	Armor, Shield, Ring, Amulet, Spellbook	3,1
Rowan Leaves	+70 to Health	Armor, Shield, Ring, Amulet, Spellbook	4,1
Angelica Root	+130 to Health	Armor, Shield, Ring, Amulet, Spellbook	3,2
Henbane Leaves	+8 to Mana	Mage Weapons, Mage Armor, Ring, Amulet, Spellbook	1,1
Gardenia Leaves	+22 to Mana	Mage Weapons, Mage Armor, Ring, Amulet, Spellbook	1,2
Valerian Root	+50 to Mana	Mage Weapons, Mage Armor, Ring, Amulet, Spellbook	1,3
Wormwood Essence	+85 to Mana	Mage Weapons, Mage Armor, Ring, Amulet, Spellbook	1,4
Verbena Flowers	+150 to Mana	Mage Weapons, Mage Armor, Ring, Amulet, Spellbook	2,3
Raptor Tooth	+2 to melee max. damage	Melee	1,1
Rhinock Horn	+8 to melee max. damage	Melee	1,4
Trilisk Fang	+50 to melee max. damage	Melee	2,4
Jagged Arrowheads	+2 to ranged max. damage	Ranged	1,2
Serrated Arrowheads	+7 to ranged max. damage	Ranged	1,4
Keen Arrowheads	+50 to ranged max. damage	Ranged	2,4
Whetstone	+2 to melee min. damage	Melee	1,1

(continued)

Reagent	Effects	Object Types	Inventory Height, Width
Mythril Alloy	+5 to melee min. damage	Melee	1,3
Meteoric Alloy	+25 to melee min. damage	Melee	1,4
Hawk Feather	+1 to ranged min. damage	Ranged	1,1
Griffon Feather	+3 to ranged min. damage	Ranged	1,2
Phoenix Feather	+22 to ranged min. damage	Ranged	1,4
Sapphire Splinter	+2–3 ice damage	Melee	2,1
Sapphire Pommelstone	+4–6 ice damage	Melee	4,2
Sapphire Ornament	+19–31 ice damage	Melee	4,3
Coral Fragment	+2–3 ice damage	Ranged	3,1
Coral Spangle	+5–8 ice damage	Ranged	4,1
Coral Filament	+15–25 ice damage	Ranged	3,2
Ruby Splinter	+2–3 fire damage	Melee	2,2
Ruby Pommelstone	+3–5 fire damage	Melee	3,3
Ruby Ornament	+18–22 fire damage	Melee	4,4
Amber Fragment	+4–6 fire damage	Ranged	2,1
Amber Spangle	+2–6 fire damage	Ranged	4,1
Amber Filament	+16–20 fire damage	Ranged	4,2
Crystal Splinter	+1–3 lightning damage	Melee	1,2
Crystal Pommelstone	+3–8 lightning damage	Melee	1,4
Crystal Ornament	+11–33 lightning damage	Melee	2,4
Diamond Fragment	+1–2 lightning damage	Ranged	2,3
Diamond Spangle	+2–6 lightning damage	Ranged	3,3
Diamond Filament	+8–23 lightning damage	Ranged	4,4
Jet Splinter	+3–5 death damage	Melee	1,3
Jet Pommelstone	+5–8 death damage	Melee	2,3
Jet Ornament	+23–38 death damage	Melee	3,3
Onyx Fragment	+3–5 death damage	Ranged	1,2
Onyx Spangle	+5–8 death damage	Ranged	1,4
Onyx Filament	+18–30 death damage	Ranged	2,4
Ivory Thorns	8% of damage received reflected back to attacker	Armor, Shield	2,2
Diamond Thorns	15% of damage received reflected back to attacker	Armor, Shield	2,3
Ensorcelled Thorns	35% of damage received reflected back to attacker	Armor, Shield	3,4
Wolf Jaw	3% health steal	Weapon	2,3
Vampire Jaw	4% health steal	Weapon	2,4
Demon Jaw	6% health steal	Weapon	3,4
Eagle Talon	3% mana steal	Weapon	3,2
Raven Talon	4% mana steal	Weapon	4,2
Owl Talon	6% mana steal	Weapon	4,3
Betony Salve	+5% to health regeneration	Melee/Ranged Armor, Shield, Ring, Amulet	1,2
Sandalvine Tincture	+12% to health regeneration	Melee/Ranged Armor, Shield, Ring, Amulet	2,2
Yarrow Balm	+5% to mana regeneration	Mage Armor, Ring, Amulet, Spellbook	2,1
Sage Liniment	+12% to mana regeneration	Mage Armor, Ring, Amulet, Spellbook	2,2
Hide Fragment	+3 to armor	Armor, Shield	1,1
Tanned Skin	+4 to armor	Armor, Shield	2,1
Patterned Shell	+10 to armor	Armor, Shield	3,1
Carved Carapace	+12 to armor	Armor, Shield	2,2
Etched Chrysalis	+18 to armor	Armor, Shield	3,2
Scarab Husk	+24 to armor	Armor, Shield	4,2
Engraved Plating	+32 to armor	Armor, Shield	4,3
Dragon Scale	+40 to armor	Armor, Shield	4,3
Cobalt Bead	+4% ice resistance	Armor, Shield, Ring, Amulet, Spellbook	1,1
Frost Charm	+7% ice resistance	Armor, Shield, Ring, Amulet, Spellbook	2,2
Icicle Talisman	+15% ice resistance	Armor, Shield, Ring, Amulet, Spellbook	3,3
Branded Rune	+4% fire resistance	Armor, Shield, Ring, Amulet, Spellbook	1,1

(continued)

Reagent	Effects	Object Types	Inventory Height, Width
Smoldering Rune	+7% fire resistance	Armor, Shield, Ring, Amulet, Spellbook	2,2
Igneous Rune	+15% fire resistance	Armor, Shield, Ring, Amulet, Spellbook	3,3
Yellow Strand	+4% lightning resistance	Armor, Shield, Ring, Amulet, Spellbook	1,2
Amber Thread	+7% lightning resistance	Armor, Shield, Ring, Amulet, Spellbook	1,4
Gold Ribbon	+15% lightning resistance	Armor, Shield, Ring, Amulet, Spellbook	3,3
Skull Fragment	+4% death resistance	Armor, Shield, Ring, Amulet, Spellbook	1,2
Vai'Kesh Figurine	+7% death resistance	Armor, Shield, Ring, Amulet, Spellbook	4,1
Korven Fetish	+15% death resistance	Armor, Shield, Ring, Amulet, Spellbook	4,3
Aegis Symbol	+3% melee resistance	Armor, Shield	3,3
Azunai Insignia	+4% melee resistance	Armor, Shield	4,4
Half-Giant Pennant	+4% ranged resistance	Armor, Shield	4,2
Agallan Standard	+6% ranged resistance	Armor, Shield	4,3
Stag Crest	+6% chance to block melee attack	Shield	2,2
Lion Crest	+10% chance to block melee attack	Shield	4,3
Griffon Crest	+8% chance to block ranged attack	Shield	2,2
Phoenix Crest	+12% chance to block ranged attack	Shield	4,3
Rainbow Trinket	+5% chance to find magic items	Ring, Amulet, Spellbook	3,3
Prismatic Bauble	+15% chance to find magic items	Ring, Amulet, Spellbook	2,4
Lurnilla's Salve	+5% to health regeneration, +10 to health	Melee/Ranged Armor, Shield, Ring, Amulet	1,2
Viperclaw	+15 to ranged max. damage, +15 to ranged min. damage, +8–12 death damage	Ranged	2,3

Monsters

The following chart presents detailed statistics for each monster in *Dungeon Siege II*'s diverse bestiary. These statistics are for the Mercenary game mode.

* = Boss/Miniboss

Monster	Hit Points	Level	XP	Damage	Defense	Physical Resist	Magic Resist	Fire Resist	Ice Resist	Death Resist	Lightning Resist	Spell
Hak'u Signaler	206	9	156	28–46	36	0%	0%	0%	0%	0%	50%	Resurrect
Hak'u Drummer	112	5	108	17–28	24	0%	0%	0%	0%	0%	25%	Resurrect
*Hak'u Rhythm Signaler	995	11	600	75–125	42	0%	0%	0%	0%	0%	50%	Resurrect
*Hak'u Rhythm Drummer	755	9	520	61–102	36	0%	0%	0%	0%	0%	25%	Resurrect
Hak'u Witch Doctor	124	9	156	27–46	36	0%	0%	0%	0%	0%	50%	Jolt, Summon Raptor
Hak'u Shaman	56	4	96	14–24	22	0%	0%	0%	0%	0%	25%	Jolt, Summon Lesser Raptor
Plagued Hak'u Witch Doctor	184	12	191	37–61	45	0%	0%	0%	0%	0%	50%	Jolt, Summon Raptor
Hrawn the Hak'u	143	10	168	30–51	39	0%	0%	0%	0%	0%	50%	N/A
Hak'u High Priest	760	13	675	90–150	48	0%	0%	0%	0%	0%	50%	Jolt, Summon Raptor
Hak'u Usurper	3396	14	718	146–245	51	0%	0%	0%	0%	0%	50%	Jolt, Earthen Embrace, Blind, Summon Raptor
*Elder Hak'u Witch Doctor	597	11	600	75–125	42	0%	0%	0%	0%	0%	50%	Jolt, Summon Raptor, Blind

(continued)

Monster	Hit Points	Level	XP	Damage	Defense	Physical Resist	Magic Resist	Fire Resist	Ice Resist	Death Resist	Lightning Resist	Spell
*Elder Hak'u Shaman	453	9	520	61–102	36	0%	0%	0%	0%	0%	25%	Jolt, Summon Raptor
*Plagued Elder Hak'u Witch Doctor	849	14	718	98–163	51	0%	0%	0%	0%	0%	50%	Jolt, Summon Raptor, Blind
Hak'u Slayer	51	9	65	13–22	36	0%	0%	0%	0%	0%	0%	N/A
Hak'u Skinner	15	3	35	6–10	19	0%	0%	0%	0%	0%	0%	N/A
Plagued Hak'u Slayer	68	11	75	16–27	42	0%	0%	0%	0%	0%	0%	N/A
*Feral Hak'u Slayer	995	11	600	75–125	41	0%	0%	0%	0%	0%	50%	N/A
*Feral Hak'u Skinner	293	4	320	32–53	22	0%	0%	0%	0%	0%	25%	N/A
*Plagued Feral Hak'u Slayer	1267	13	675	90–150	48	0%	0%	0%	0%	0%	50%	N/A
Hak'u Spearmaster	110	9	117	15–25	36	0%	0%	0%	0%	0%	0%	N/A
Hak'u Hunter	36–43	4	72	8–13	22	0%	0%	0%	0%	0%	0%	N/A
Plagued Hak'u Spearmaster	145	11	135	18–30	42	0%	0%	0%	0%	0%	0%	N/A
*Relentless Hak'u Spearmaster	796	11	600	60–101	42	0%	0%	0%	0%	0%	50%	N/A
*Relentless Hak'u Hunter	604	9	520	49–82	36	0%	0%	0%	0%	0%	25%	N/A
*Plagued Relentless Hak'u Spearmaster	1014	13	675	73–121	48	0%	0%	0%	0%	0%	50%	N/A
Morden-Durvla Purifier	1909	37	1517	228–380	126	0%	0%	50%	0%	0%	0%	Fireball, Plasma Globes, Wrath of Magic
*Morden-Durvla Flawless Purifier	4611	39	4780	386–644	133	0%	0%	50%	0%	0%	0%	Fireball, Plasma Globes, Wrath of Magic
Morden-Durvla Butcher	3182	37	1517	228–380	126	0%	0%	0%	0%	0%	0%	Wrath of the Bear
*Morden-Durvla Cleaving Butcher	7685	39	4780	386	644	133	0%	0%	0%	0%	0%	Wrath of the Bear
Morden-Durvla Enforcer	2546	37	1517	182–303	125	0%	0%	0%	0%	0%	0%	Dehydrate, Fireball
*Morden-Durvla Relentless Enforcer	6148	39	4780	312–520	133	0%	0%	0%	0%	0%	0%	Dehydrate, Fireball
Morden-Gral Igniter	1562	33	1092	192–320	112	0%	0%	75%	0%	0%	0%	Firebolt, Surge of Healing
Morden-Gral Despoiler	1819	36	1396	293–489	122	0%	0%	75%	0%	0%	0%	Firebolt, Surge of Healing
Morden-Gral Mage	307	12	239	53–88	45	0%	0%	0%	-25%	0%	0%	Firebolt, Surge of Healing
Morden-Gral Mage (Finala's Contempt)	729	21	433	103–171	72	0%	0%	75%	0%	0%	0%	Firebolt, Surge of Healing
*Pyrokinetic Morden-Gral Igniter	3810	35	3429	328–547	119	0%	0%	75%	0%	0%	0%	Firebolt, Surge of Healing

(continued)

Monster	Hit Points	Level	XP	Damage	Defense	Physical Resist	Magic Resist	Fire Resist	Ice Resist	Death Resist	Lightning Resist	Spell
*Pyrokinetic Morden-Gral Despoiler	4404	38	4396	346–576	129	0%	0%	75%	0%	0%	0%	Firebolt, Surge of Healing
*Morden-Gral Mage Commander	849	14	718	98–163	51	0%	0%	50%	-25%	0%	0%	Firebolt, Surge of Healing
*Morden-Gral Scout Commander	3810	35	3429	328–547	119	0%	0%	75%	0%	0%	0%	Firebolt, Surge of Healing
Morden-Viir Cavalry	3182	37	1517	227–380	126	0%	0%	0%	0%	0%	0%	N/A
Morden-Urg Prodigy	34	5	81	4–7	24	0%	0%	0%	0%	0%	-50%	Embers, Leech Life
Morden-Urg Savant	786	34	948	67–112	115	0%	0%	0%	0%	0%	0%	Embers, Leech Life, Heal
*Morden-Urg Gifted Prodigy	328	7	440	20–33	30	0%	0%	50%	0%	0%	-50%	Embers, Leech Life
*Morden-Urg Gifted Savant	4003	36	3723	138–230	112	0%	0%	50%	0%	0%	0%	Embers, Leech Life, Heal
Morden-Urg Thug	54	5	81	11–18	24	0%	0%	0%	0%	0%	0%	N/A
Morden-Urg Scrapper	2057	34	948	170–283	115	0%	0%	50%	0%	0%	0%	N/A
*Morden-Urg Strong Thug	546	7	440	49–81	30	50%	0%	0%	0%	0%	-50%	N/A
*Morden-Urg Frenzied Scrapper	6671	36	3723	342–570	122	0%	0%	50%	0%	0%	0%	N/A
Morden-Urg Scavenger	43	5	81	9–15	25	0%	0%	0%	0%	0%	0%	N/A
Morden-Urg Marksman	1060	34	948	94–156	115	0%	0%	50%	0%	0%	0%	N/A
*Morden-Urg Skilled Scavenger	437	7	440	39–65	30	0%	0%	0%	0%	0%	-50%	N/A
*Morden-Urg Uncanny Marksman	5337	36	3723	276–461	122	0%	0%	50%	0%	0%	0%	N/A
Forest Va'arth Avalancher	908	24	540	49–82	82	0%	0%	0%	25%	0%	0%	Iceball, Wrath of Ice, Encase
Forest Va'arth Frostcrusher	729	21	433	41–69	72	0%	0%	0%	15%	0%	0%	Iceball, Wrath of Ice, Encase
Snow Va'arth Avalancher	1402	31	930	70–117	105	0%	0%	-25%	50%	0%	0%	Iceball, Drown, Wrath of Ice, Encase
Snow Va'arth Frostcrusher	1177	28	733	61–101	95	0%	0%	-25%	50%	0%	0%	Iceball, Drown, Wrath of Ice, Encase
*Forest Va'arth Glacial Avalancher	2284	26	1676	86–144	88	0%	0%	0%	50%	0%	0%	Iceball, Wrath of Ice, Encase
*Forest Va'arth Glacial Frostcrusher	1861	23	1337	73–122	79	0%	0%	0%	50%	0%	0%	Iceball, Wrath of Ice, Encase
*Snow Va'arth Glacial Avalancher	3437	33	2912	121–202	112	0%	0%	-25%	50%	0%	0%	Iceball, Drown, Wrath of Ice, Encase
*Snow Va'arth Glacial Frostcrusher	2435	27	1810	91–152	92	0%	0%	-25%	50%	0%	0%	Iceball, Drown, Wrath of Ice, Encase
Forest Va'arth Barbarian	1892	24	540	147–245	82	0%	0%	0%	25%	0%	0%	Wrath of the Bear, Summon Uhn Blaster

(continued)

Monsters

Monster	Hit Points	Level	XP	Damage	Defense	Physical Resist	Magic Resist	Fire Resist	Ice Resist	Death Resist	Lightning Resist	Spell
Forest Va'arth Brute	1518	21	433	123–205	72	0%	0%	0%	15%	0%	0%	Wrath of the Bear, Summon, Uhn Blaster
Snow Va'arth Barbarian	2921	31	930	211–351	105	0%	0%	0%	50%	0%	0%	Wrath of the Bear, Summon Uhn Blaster
Snow Va'arth Brute	2453	28	733	182–303	95	0%	0%	0%	50%	0%	0%	Wrath of the Bear, Summon Uhn Blaster
*Hardened Forest Va'arth Barbarian	3807	26	1676	214–357	88	0%	0%	0%	50%	0%	0%	Wrath of the Bear, Summon Uhn Blaster
*Hardened Forest Va'arth Brute	3102	23	1337	181–302	79	0%	0%	0%	50%	0%	0%	Wrath of the Bear, Summon Uhn Blaster
*Hardened Snow Va'arth Barbarian	5729	33	2912	301–501	112	0%	0%	0%	50%	0%	0%	Wrath of the Bear, Summon Uhn Blaster
*Hardened Snow Va'arth Brute	4858	30	2289	262–437	102	0%	0%	0%	50%	0%	0%	Wrath of the Bear, Summon Uhn Blaster
Forest Va'arth Bombardier	1211	24	540	98–163	82	0%	0%	0%	25%	0%	0%	Summon Rugged Snow Kurgan
Forest Va'arth Cannoneer	972	21	433	82–137	72	0%	0%	0%	15%	0%	0%	Summon Rugged Snow Kurgan
Snow Va'arth Bombardier	1869	31	930	140–234	105	0%	0%	-25%	50%	0%	0%	Summon Rugged Snow Kurgan
Snow Va'arth Cannoneer	1570	28	733	121–202	95	0%	0%	-25%	50%	0%	0%	Summon Rugged Snow Kurgan
*Elite Forest Va'arth Bombardier	3046	26	1676	173–288	88	0%	0%	0%	50%	0%	0%	Summon Rugged Snow Kurgan
*Elite Forest Va'arth Cannoneer	2482	23	1337	146–244	79	0%	0%	0%	50%	0%	0%	Summon Rugged Snow Kurgan
*Elite Snow Va'arth Bombardier	4583	33	2912	243–405	112	0%	0%	-25%	50%	0%	0%	Summon Rugged Snow Kurgan
*Elite Snow Va'arth Cannoneer	3886	30	2289	212–353	102	0%	0%	-25%	50%	0%	0%	Summon Rugged Snow Kurgan
Morden-Viir Cavalry (2)	1732	35	1029	148–247	119	0%	0%	0%	0%	0%	0%	N/A
Morden-Viir Lancer	1185	32	806	110–183	108	0%	0%	0%	0%	0%	0%	N/A
Morden-Viir Impaler	1385	35	1029	125–209	119	0%	0%	0%	0%	0%	0%	N/A
Morden-Viir Spearmen	217	11	180	29–48	42	0%	0%	0%	0%	0%	0%	N/A
Morden-Viir Lancer (Finala's Contempt)	539	20	322	58–96	69	0%	0%	0%	0%	0%	0%	N/A
Morden-Viir City Guard	1385	35	1029	125–209	119	0%	0%	0%	0%	0%	0%	N/A
*Morden-Viir Lancer Captain	6035	34	3159	314–524	115	0%	0%	0%	0%	0%	0%	N/A

(continued)

Monster	Hit Points	Level	XP	Damage	Defense	Physical Resist	Magic Resist	Fire Resist	Ice Resist	Death Resist	Lightning Resist	Spell
*Morden-Viir Impaler Master	7001	37	4045	357–594	125	0%	0%	0%	0%	0%	0%	N/A
*Morden-Viir Spearman Captain	1267	13	675	90–150	48	-25%	0%	0%	0%	0%	0%	N/A
Morden-Viir Soldier	1481	32	806	130–216	108	0%	0%	0%	0%	0%	0%	N/A
Morden-Viir Ripper	1732	35	1029	148–247	119	0%	0%	0%	0%	0%	0%	N/A
Morden-Viir Grunt	70–80	4	96	14–24	22	0%	0%	0%	0%	0%	0%	N/A
Morden-Viir Soldier (Finala's Contempt)	673	20	322	68–113	69	0%	0%	0%	0%	0%	0%	N/A
*Morden-Viir Soldier Captain	6035	34	3159	314–524	115	0%	0%	0%	0%	0%	0%	N/A
*Morden-Viir Ripper Champion	7001	37	4045	357–594	125	0%	0%	0%	0%	0%	0%	N/A
*Morden-Viir Grunt Captain	647	8	480	55–91	33	-25%	0%	0%	0%	0%	0%	N/A
*Morden-Viir City Lieutenant	7001	37	4045	357–594	125	0%	0%	0%	0%	0%	0%	N/A
*Morden-Viir City Lieutenant (Other)	5601	37	4045	288–480	125	0%	0%	0%	0%	0%	0%	N/A
*Morden-Viir Patrol Leader	7001	37	4045	357–594	125	0%	0%	0%	0%	0%	0%	N/A
*Morden-Viir Chief	7001	37	4045	357–594	125	0%	0%	0%	0%	0%	0%	N/A
Morden-Viir Crossbowman	1185	32	806	104–173	108	0%	0%	0%	0%	0%	0%	N/A
Morden-Viir Piercer	1385	35	1029	119–198	119	0%	0%	0%	0%	0%	0%	N/A
Morden-Viir Recruit	72	5	108	13–22	24	0%	0%	0%	0%	0%	0%	N/A
Morden-Viir Recruit Leader	72	5	108	13–22	24	0%	0%	0%	0%	0%	0%	N/A
Morden-Viir Crossbowman (Finala's Contempt)	539	20	322	55–91	69	0%	0%	0%	0%	0%	0%	N/A
*Morden-Viir Crossbowman Captain	4828	34	3159	254–423	115	0%	0%	0%	0%	0%	0%	N/A
*Morden-Viir Heartless Piercer	5601	37	4045	288–480	125	0%	0%	0%	0%	0%	0%	N/A
*Morden-Viir Recruit Captain	604	9	520	49–82	36	-25%	0%	0%	0%	0%	0%	N/A
Qatall Runecaster	2096	39	1793	247–411	133	0%	0%	0%	0%	0%	75%	Lightning Blast, Fork Lightning, Wind Embrace, Wrath of Magic
*Qatall Runeshaper	4823	40	5200	162–270	136	0%	0%	0%	0%	0%	75%	Lightning Blast, Fork Lightning, Wind Embrace, Wrath of Magic

(continued)

Monster	Hit Points	Level	XP	Damage	Defense	Physical Resist	Magic Resist	Fire Resist	Ice Resist	Death Resist	Lightning Resist	Spell
Qatall Minion	3493	39	1793	247–411	133	0%	0%	0%	0%	0%	75%	Wind Embrace, Decay Armor
*Qatall Attendant	8039	40	5200	401–669	136	0%	0%	0%	0%	0%	75%	Wind Embrace, Decay Armor
Skath Disciple	284	16	245	21–34	57	0%	0%	0%	-25%	0%	0%	Firespray, Dehydrate, Summon Ironhorn
Plagued Skath Disciple	341	18	280	24–40	63	0%	0%	0%	-25%	0%	0%	Firespray, Dehydrate, Summon Ironhorn
Plagued Disciple Scout (alerts all friends)	284	16	245	21–34	57	0%	0%	0%	-25%	0%	0%	Firespray, Dehydrate, Summon Ironhorn
*Devoted Skath Disciple	1251	18	935	53–89	63	0%	0%	50%	0%	0%	0%	Firespray, Dehydrate, Summon Ironhorn
*Plagued Devoted Skath Disciple	1481	20	1075	61–101	69	0%	0%	50%	0%	0%	0%	Firespray, Dehydrate, Summon Ironhorn
*Devoted Skath Disciple Stelae Guardian	1251	18	935	53–89	63	0%	0%	50%	0%	0%	0%	Firespray, Dehydrate, Summon Ironhorn
Skath Zealot	473	16	245	52–86	57	0%	0%	0%	-25%	0%	0%	N/A
Plagued Skath Zealot	569	18	280	60–99	63	0%	0%	0%	-25%	0%	0%	N/A
*Devoted Skath Zealot	2086	18	935	132–220	63	0%	0%	50%	0%	0%	0%	N/A
*Plagued Devoted Skath Zealot	2468	20	1075	151–252	69	0%	0%	50%	0%	0%	0%	N/A
*Devoted Skath Zealot Stelae Guardian	2086	18	935	132–220	63	0%	0%	50%	0%	0%	0%	N/A
Skath Avenger	1300	17	328	63–105	60	0%	0%	0%	-25%	0%	0%	N/A
Plagued Skath Avenger	1550	19	376	72–120	66	0%	0%	0%	-25%	0%	0%	N/A
*Devoted Skath Avenger	1819	19	1002	114–190	66	0%	0%	50%	0%	0%	0%	N/A
*Plagued Devoted Skath Avenger	2143	21	1155	130–216	72	0%	0%	50%	0%	0%	0%	N/A
*Devoted Skath Avenger Stelae Guardian	1818	19	1002	114–190	66	0%	0%	50%	0%	0%	0%	N/A
Uhn Scorcher	1146	37	1213	159–266	125	0%	0%	25%	0%	0%	0%	Flamethrower, Punishing Fire
*Blazing Uhn Scorcher	4611	39	4780	386–644	133	0%	0%	25%	0%	0%	0%	Flamethrower, Punishing Fire
Uhn Miner	3336	38	1649	237–395	129	0%	0%	0%	0%	0%	0%	N/A
*Uhn Miner Forebeast	8039	40	5200	401–669	136	0%	0%	0%	0%	0%	0%	Punishing Fire
Uhn Blaster	1528	37	1213	129–215	125	0%	0%	0%	0%	0%	0%	N/A

(continued)

Monster	Hit Points	Level	XP	Damage	Defense	Physical Resist	Magic Resist	Fire Resist	Ice Resist	Death Resist	Lightning Resist	Spell
*Uhn Blaster Demolitionist	6148	39	4780	312–520	133	0%	0%	0%	0%	0%	0%	Punishing Fire
Undead Azunite Mage	706	28	587	106–177	95	0%	0%	0%	0%	50%	50%	Leech Life, Ancestors Revenge, Resurrect, Summon Bone Minion
*Undead Azunite Mage Hero	2915	30	2289	262–437	102	0%	0%	0%	0%	50%	50%	Leech Life, Ancestors Revenge, Resurrect, Summon Bone Minion
Undead Azunite Soldier	1177	28	587	107–179	95	0%	0%	0%	0%	50%	50%	N/A
*Undead Azunite Soldier Hero	4858	30	2289	262–437	102	0%	0%	0%	0%	50%	50%	Ancestors Revenge
Undead Azunite Archer	942	28	587	86–143	95	0%	0%	0%	0%	50%	0%	N/A
*Undead Azunite Archer Hero	3886	30	2289	212–353	102	0%	0%	0%	0%	50%	0%	Ancestors Revenge
Vai'kesh Seer	623	26	503	39–65	88	0%	0%	0%	0%	75%	-50%	Soul Lance, Life Embrace, Heal, Summon Feaster
Vai'kesh Seer Neophyte	583	25	466	37–61	85	0%	0%	0%	0%	75%	-50%	Soul Lance, Life Embrace, Heal, Summon Feaster
Vai'kesh Seer Neophyte Scout	583	25	466	37–61	85	0%	0%	0%	0%	75%	-50%	Soul Lance, Life Embrace, Heal, Summon Feaster
Lesser Vai'kesh Diabolist	583	25	466	37–61	85	0%	0%	0%	0%	75%	-50%	Soul Lance, Vai'kesh Circle Buff
*An'tul Vai'kesh Seer	2590	28	1956	96–160	95	0%	0%	0%	0%	75%	-50%	Soul Lance, Life Embrace, Surge of Healing, Summon Feaster
*An'tul Vai'kesh Seer Neophyte	2435	27	1810	91–152	92	0%	0%	0%	0%	75%	-50%	Soul Lance, Life Embrace, Surge of Healing, Summon Feaster
*Vai'kesh Prophet	2590	28	1956	96–160	95	0%	0%	0%	0%	75%	-50%	Soul Lance, Life Embrace, Surge of Healing, Summon Feaster
Vai'kesh Zealot	1038	26	503	97–161	88	0%	0%	0%	0%	50%	-50%	N/A
Vai'kesh Zealot Neophyte	972	25	466	92–153	85	0%	0%	0%	0%	50%	-50%	N/A

(continued)

Monsters

Monster	Hit Points	Level	XP	Damage	Defense	Physical Resist	Magic Resist	Fire Resist	Ice Resist	Death Resist	Lightning Resist	Spell
*An'tul Vai'kesh Zealot	4316	28	1956	238–396	95	0%	0%	0%	0%	50%	-50%	Life Embrace
*An'tul Vai'kesh Zealot Neophyte	4058	27	1810	226–376	92	0%	0%	0%	0%	50%	-50%	Life Embrace
*Vai'kesh Jailor	4316	28	1956	237–396	95	0%	0%	0%	0%	50%	-50%	Life Embrace
Vai'kesh Fanatic	831	26	503	77–129	88	0%	0%	0%	0%	50%	-50%	N/A
Vai'kesh Fanatic Neophyte	778	25	466	73–122	85	0%	0%	0%	0%	50%	-50%	N/A
*An'tul Vai'kesh Fanatic	3453	28	1956	192–320	95	0%	0%	0%	0%	50%	-50%	Life Embrace
*An'tul Vai'kesh Fanatic Neophyte	3246	27	1810	182–304	92	0%	0%	0%	0%	50%	-50%	Life Embrace
Bracken Defender	8	1	14	4–7	13	0%	0%	-5%	0%	0%	0%	N/A
Plagued Bracken Defender	271	11	180	34–56	42	0%	0%	-5%	0%	0%	0%	N/A
*Plagued Infused Bracken Defender	1267	13	675	90–150	48	0%	0%	-5%	0%	0%	0%	N/A
Forest Golem	23	2	30	5–9	16	0%	0%	-5%	0%	0%	0%	N/A
Plagued Forest Golem	217	11	180	27–45	42	0%	0%	-5%	0%	0%	0%	N/A
*Plagued Infused Forest Golem	1014	13	675	73–121	48	0%	0%	-5%	0%	0%	0%	N/A
Korven Blightwalker	1819	36	1396	87–146	122	0%	0%	0%	0%	50%	0%	Skull Spray, Impale, Summon Thrusk, Resurrect
*Mythic Korven Blightwalker	4404	38	4396	150–250	129	0%	0%	0%	0%	75%	0%	Skull Spray, Impale, Summon Thrusk, Resurrect
Korven Boneslayer	3032	36	1396	219–364	122	0%	0%	0%	0%	50%	0%	Earthen Embrace
*Mythic Korven Boneslayer	7339	38	4396	371–619	129	0%	0%	0%	0%	75%	0%	Earthen Embrace, Cripple, Summon Thrusk
Mystic Protector	24	3	35	8–13	19	0%	0%	-25%	0%	0%	0%	Icebolt
Plagued Mystic Protector	307	12	239	53–88	45	0%	0%	-5%	0%	0%	0%	Icebolt
*Plagued Infused Mystic Protector	849	14	718	98–163	51	0%	0%	-5%	0%	0%	0%	Icebolt
Birath	3493	39	1793	247–411	133	0%	0%	0%	0%	0%	0%	Infect
*Tormented Birath	8039	40	5200	401–669	136	0%	0%	0%	0%	0%	0%	Infect

(continued)

Monster	Hit Points	Level	XP	Damage	Defense	Physical Resist	Magic Resist	Fire Resist	Ice Resist	Death Resist	Lightning Resist	Spell
Black Scorpion	238	10	168	31–51	39	0%	0%	0%	0%	0%	0%	N/A
Young Black Scorpion	48	10	70	12–20	39	0%	0%	0%	0%	0%	0%	Black Scorpion Sting
*King Black Scorpion	1127	12	636	82–137	45	0%	0%	0%	0%	0%	0%	N/A
*Young King Black Scorpion	902	12	636	66–111	45	0%	0%	0%	0%	0%	0%	Black Scorpion Sting
Blastwing	347	17	210	37–61	60	0%	0%	0%	0%	0%	0%	N/A
Blazewing	1385	35	1029	125–209	119	0%	0%	0%	0%	0%	0%	N/A
Fire-Breathing Blastwing	208	17	210	15–24	60	0%	0%	0%	0%	0%	0%	Flamethrower
Fire-Breathing Blazewing	827	35	1029	70–117	119	0%	0%	0%	0%	0%	0%	Flamethrower
*Blastwing Monarch	2273	19	1002	141–236	66	0%	0%	0%	0%	0%	0%	N/A
*Blazewing Monarch	7001	37	4045	357–594	125	0%	0%	0%	0%	0%	0%	N/A
*Fire-Breathing Blastwing Monarch	1364	19	1002	57–95	66	0%	0%	0%	0%	0%	0%	Flamethrower
*Firebreathing Blazewing Monarch	4201	37	4045	144–240	125	0%	0%	0%	0%	0%	0%	Flamethrower
Boarbeast	210	7	165	31–52	30	0%	0%	0%	0%	-25%	0%	N/A
*Greater Boarbeast	647	8	480	55–91	33	0%	0%	0%	0%	-25%	0%	N/A
Plagued Boggrot	246	12	191	31–52	45	0%	0%	0%	0%	0%	0%	N/A
*Plagued Maddened Boggrot	1415	14	718	98–163	51	0%	0%	0%	0%	0%	0%	N/A
*Bone Minion	80	4	96	14–24	22	0%	0%	0%	0%	0%	0%	N/A
Bone Minion Summon	1177	28	0	107–179	95	0%	0%	0%	0%	0%	0%	N/A
Bone Minion (2)	4356	10	560	82–137	39	0%	0%	0%	0%	75%	75%	Grave Beam, Cripple, Embers, Multispark
Borga	370	32	339	62–103	108	0%	0%	0%	0%	0%	0%	N/A
*Shelled Borga	6035	34	3159	314–524	115	0%	0%	0%	0%	0%	0%	N/A
Bortusk	1097	34	758	94–156	115	0%	0%	0%	0%	0%	0%	N/A
*Alpha Bortusk	6671	36	3723	342–570	122	0%	0%	0%	0%	0%	0%	N/A
Bracken	243	25	196	44–72	85	0%	0%	-50%	0%	0%	0%	N/A
Rotten Bracken	227	24	181	41–69	82	0%	0%	-50%	0%	0%	0%	N/A
*Frenzied Bracken	4058	27	1810	226–376	92	0%	0%	-50%	0%	0%	0%	N/A
*Rotten Frenzied Bracken	3807	26	1676	214–357	88	0%	0%	-50%	0%	0%	0%	N/A
Brall	3182	37	1517	220–367	125	0%	0%	0%	0%	0%	0%	N/A
Brall (Snowbrook Haven)	2604	33	1092	186–309	112	0%	0%	0%	0%	0%	0%	N/A
*Brall Demolitionist	6148	39	4780	312–520	133	0%	0%	0%	0%	0%	0%	N/A
Plagued Carver Bat	77	12	80	18–30	45	0%	0%	0%	0%	0%	0%	N/A

(continued)

Monsters

Monster	Hit Points	Level	XP	Damage	Defense	Physical Resist	Magic Resist	Fire Resist	Ice Resist	Death Resist	Lightning Resist	Spell
*Plagued Ravenous Carver Bat	1415	14	718	98–163	51	0%	0%	0%	0%	0%	0%	N/A
Sand Reaper	86	13	85	19–32	48	0%	0%	0%	0%	0%	0%	N/A
Festering Sand Reaper	788	16	306	73–122	57	0%	0%	0%	0%	0%	0%	N/A
*Devouring Sand Reaper	1571	15	766	106–177	54	0%	0%	0%	0%	0%	0%	N/A
*Festering Devouring Sand Reaper	7001	37	4045	357–594	125	0%	0%	0%	0%	0%	0%	N/A
Plagued Crawn	260	35	432	70–117	119	0%	0%	0%	0%	0%	0%	Small Spit
*Plagued Goring Crawn	4201	37	4045	357–594	125	0%	0%	0%	0%	0%	0%	Small Spit
*Demon of the Vai'kesh	6852	26	1676	86–144	88	0%	0%	0%	0%	0%	0%	Multispark, Leech Life, Blind, Infect
Plagued Feaster	1456	36	1117	131–218	122	0%	0%	0%	0%	0%	0%	N/A
*Plagued Maniacal Feaster	7339	38	4396	371–619	129	0%	0%	0%	0%	0%	0%	N/A
Fellspine	413	19	240	42–70	66	0%	0%	0%	0%	0%	50%	N/A
Fellspine Mage	331	19	240	34–57	66	0%	0%	0%	0%	0%	50%	Jolt
*Fellspine Despoiler	2273	19	1002	141–236	66	0%	0%	0%	0%	0%	50%	N/A
*Fellspine Warlock	1818	19	1002	114–190	66	0%	0%	0%	0%	0%	50%	Jolt
Fettershin	778	25	466	174–290	85	0%	0%	0%	0%	0%	0%	N/A
Decrepit Fettershin	726	24	432	73–122	82	0%	0%	0%	0%	0%	0%	N/A
*Chattering Fettershin	4058	27	1810	226–376	92	0%	0%	0%	0%	0%	0%	N/A
*Decrepit Chattering Fettershin	3807	26	1676	214–357	88	0%	0%	0%	0%	0%	0%	N/A
Murky Flaypick	1766	30	858	139–232	102	0%	0%	0%	0%	0%	0%	N/A
Flaypick	1476	27	679	120–200	92	0%	0%	0%	0%	0%	0%	N/A
*Murky Piercing Flaypick	5430	32	2686	288–479	108	0%	0%	0%	0%	0%	0%	N/A
*Piercing Flaypick	4583	29	2115	250–416	98	0%	0%	0%	0%	0%	0%	N/A
*Ganth	12500	34	3159	314–524	115	0%	0%	25%	0%	25%	25%	Ganth Slam Attack
Plagued Gantis Worker	461	13	253	48–80	48	0%	0%	0%	0%	0%	0%	N/A
*Plagued Kithraya Hive Queen	6283	15	765	99–221	54	0%	0%	0%	0%	-25%	0%	Cripple, Impale
*Plagued Gantis Patriarch	1571	15	765	106–177	54	0%	0%	0%	0%	0%	0%	N/A
Slashing Gila	52	5	81	11–18	24	0%	0%	0%	0%	0%	0%	N/A
Spitting Gila	20	5	45	7–11	24	0%	0%	0%	0%	0%	0%	Small Spit
*Alpha Slashing Gila	370	5	360	37–62	24	0%	0%	0%	0%	0%	0%	N/A

(continued)

Monster	Hit Points	Level	XP	Damage	Defense	Physical Resist	Magic Resist	Fire Resist	Ice Resist	Death Resist	Lightning Resist	Spell
*Alpha Spitting Gila	296	5	360	30–50	24	0%	0%	0%	0%	0%	0%	Small Spit
Gorgak	200	8	144	30–49	33	0%	0%	0%	0%	0%	0%	N/A
*Gorgak Firstborn	647	8	480	55–91	33	0%	0%	0%	0%	0%	0%	N/A
Ornate Stabbing Grangefly	312	29	267	53–89	98	0%	0%	0%	0%	0%	0%	N/A
Stabbing Grangefly	260	26	211	46–77	88	0%	0%	0%	0%	0%	0%	N/A
Ornate Spewing Grangefly	187	29	267	53–89	98	0%	0%	0%	0%	0%	0%	Small Spit
Spewing Grangefly	156	26	211	46–77	88	0%	0%	0%	0%	0%	0%	Small Spit
*Ornate Stabbing Slimy Grangefly	5140	31	2479	275–458	105	0%	0%	0%	0%	0%	0%	N/A
*Stabbing Slimy Grangefly	4316	28	1956	237–396	95	0%	0%	0%	0%	0%	0%	N/A
*Ornate Spewing Slimy Grangefly	3084	31	2479	275–458	105	0%	0%	0%	0%	0%	0%	Small Spit
*Spewing Slimy Grangefly	2590	28	1956	238–396	95	0%	0%	0%	0%	0%	0%	Small Spit
Harpy	3336	38	1649	237–395	129	0%	0%	0%	0%	0%	0%	Ancestors Revenge
*Harpy Matriarch	8039	40	5200	401–669	136	0%	0%	0%	0%	0%	0%	Ancestors Revenge
Hulking Shail	3493	39	1793	247–411	133	0%	0%	0%	75%	0%	0%	N/A
Stygian Hulking Shail	2096	39	1793	99–164	133	0%	0%	0%	75%	0%	0%	Iceball, Blind
*Plated Hulking Shail	8039	40	5200	401–669	136	0%	0%	0%	75%	0%	0%	Blind
*Plated Stygian Hulking Shail	4823	40	5200	162–270	136	0%	0%	0%	75%	0%	0%	Iceball, Blind
Hyena	309	14	216	37–62	51	0%	0%	0%	0%	0%	0%	N/A
*Hyena Matron	1734	16	817	114–191	57	0%	0%	0%	0%	0%	0%	N/A
Plagued Impus	3182	37	1517	228–380	125	0%	0%	0%	0%	0%	0%	N/A
*Plagued Spiked Impus	7685	39	4780	386–644	133	0%	0%	0%	0%	0%	0%	N/A
Iraca	758	18	351	70–117	63	0%	0%	50%	-25%	0%	0%	N/A
Iraca (Act III)	2426	36	1396	182–303	122	0%	0%	50%	-25%	0%	0%	N/A
*King Iraca	2468	20	1075	151–252	69	0%	0%	50%	-25%	0%	0%	N/A
*Queen Iraca	7339	38	4396	371–619	129	0%	0%	50%	-25%	0%	0%	N/A
Ironhorn	650	17	262	67–111	60	0%	0%	0%	0%	0%	0%	N/A
*Ironhorn Patron	2273	19	1001	141–236	66	0%	0%	0%	0%	0%	0%	N/A
Ketril	166	2	40	9–14	16	0%	0%	0%	0%	0%	0%	N/A
*Infused Ketril	373	3	152	13–22	19	0%	0%	0%	0%	0%	0%	N/A
Klask	2604	33	1092	192–320	112	0%	0%	0%	0%	0%	0%	N/A
Klask (2)	3182	37	1517	228–380	125	0%	0%	0%	0%	0%	0%	N/A
*Klask Enforcer (Snowbrook Haven)	6349	35	3429	328–547	119	0%	0%	0%	0%	0%	0%	N/A

(continued)

Monsters

Monster	Hit Points	Level	XP	Damage	Defense	Physical Resist	Magic Resist	Fire Resist	Ice Resist	Death Resist	Lightning Resist	Spell
*Klask Enforcer	7685	39	4780	386–644	133	0%	0%	0%	0%	0%	0%	N/A
Kragen	2086	18	935	132–220	63	0%	0%	50%	0%	0%	0%	N/A
*Plagued Kragen	2468	20	1075	151–252	69	0%	0%	50%	0%	0%	0%	N/A
Rugged Kurgan	846	23	401	82–136	79	0%	0%	0%	0%	0%	0%	N/A
Kurgan	673	20	322	68–113	69	0%	0%	0%	0%	0%	0%	N/A
Rugged Snow Kurgan	1060	30	687	100–167	102	0%	0%	0%	0%	0%	0%	N/A
Snow Kurgan	885	27	543	86–144	92	0%	0%	0%	0%	0%	0%	N/A
*Alpha Rugged Kurgan	3564	25	1553	203–338	85	0%	0%	0%	0%	0%	0%	N/A
*Alpha Kurgan	2883	22	1242	171–285	75	0%	0%	0%	0%	0%	0%	N/A
*Alpha Rugged Snow Kurgan	5430	32	2686	288–479	108	0%	0%	0%	0%	0%	0%	N/A
*Alpha Snow Kurgan	4583	29	2115	250–416	98	0%	0%	0%	0%	0%	0%	N/A
Plagued Kurtle	184	12	191	37–61	45	0%	0%	0%	0%	0%	0%	Medium Spit
*Plagued Kurtle Predator	849	14	718	98–163	51	0%	0%	0%	0%	0%	0%	Medium Spit
Plagued Larvax	164	12	153	20–33	45	0%	0%	0%	0%	0%	0%	Larvax Sting
*Plagued Frenzied Larvax	1132	14	718	79–131	51	0%	0%	0%	0%	0%	0%	Larvax Sting
Armored Lertisk	1656	30	687	142–236	102	0%	0%	-25%	50%	0%	0%	N/A
Lertisk	1383	27	543	122–203	92	0%	0%	-25%	50%	0%	0%	N/A
*Dominant Armored Lertisk	5430	32	2686	288–479	108	0%	0%	-25%	50%	0%	0%	N/A
*Dominant Lertisk	4583	29	2115	250–416	98	0%	0%	-25%	50%	0%	0%	N/A
*Letiso the Lich	2915	30	2289	262–437	102	0%	0%	-25%	50%	50%	0%	Leech Life, Ancestors Revenge, Resurrect, Summon Bone Minion
Plagued Lithid	433	35	432	70–117	119	0%	0%	0%	0%	0%	0%	N/A
*Plagued Berzerk Lithid	7001	37	4045	357–594	125	0%	0%	0%	0%	0%	0%	N/A
Maguar	106	8	144	25–41	33	0%	0%	0%	0%	0%	0%	Maguar Spit
*Vile Maguar	388	8	480	55–91	33	0%	0%	0%	0%	0%	0%	Maguar Spit
Plagued Maltratar	346	13	253	58–96	48	0%	0%	0%	0%	0%	0%	Icebolt, Heal
*Plagued Maltratar Overlord	942	15	765	106–177	54	0%	0%	0%	0%	0%	0%	Icebolt, Heal
Mercrus	2604	33	1092	192–320	112	0%	0%	0%	0%	0%	0%	Steal Magic
*Prowling Mercrus	6035	34	3159	314–524	115	0%	0%	0%	0%	0%	0%	Steal Magic
*Mimic (Act I #1)	5071	17	873	99–165	60	0%	0%	0%	0%	0%	0%	Skull Spray, Iceball, Impale
*Mimic (Act I #2)	7145	21	1155	162–270	72	0%	0%	0%	0%	0%	0%	Skull Spray, Iceball, Impale
*Mimic (Act II #1)	10911	27	1810	182–304	92	0%	0%	0%	0%	0%	0%	Skull Spray, Iceball, Impale

(continued)

Monster	Hit Points	Level	XP	Damage	Defense	Physical Resist	Magic Resist	Fire Resist	Ice Resist	Death Resist	Lightning Resist	Spell
*Mimic (Act II #2)	16300	34	3159	317–529	115	0%	0%	0%	0%	0%	0%	Skull Spray, Iceball, Impale
*Mimic (Act III #1)	19861	38	4396	375–624	129	0%	0%	0%	0%	0%	0%	Skull Spray, Iceball, Impale
*Mimic (Act III #2)	21773	40	5200	405–675	136	0%	0%	0%	0%	0%	0%	Skull Spray, Iceball, Impale
Mucrim	370	32	339	62–103	108	0%	0%	0%	0%	0%	0%	N/A
Mucrim Shocker	222	32	339	62–103	108	0%	0%	0%	0%	0%	0%	Multispark
*Mucrim Matriarch	6035	34	3159	314–524	115	0%	0%	0%	0%	0%	0%	N/A
*Mucrim Shocker Matriarch	3621	34	3159	314–524	115	0%	0%	0%	0%	0%	0%	Multispark
Naldrun	389	25	373	60–101	85	0%	0%	0%	0%	0%	50%	Static Bolt
Defiled Naldrun	363	24	346	57–95	82	0%	0%	0%	0%	0%	25%	Static Bolt
*Shadowy Naldrun	2435	27	1810	226–376	92	0%	0%	0%	0%	0%	75%	Static Bolt, Fork Lightning
*Defiled Shadowy Naldrun	2284	26	1676	214–357	88	0%	0%	0%	0%	0%	75%	Static Bolt, Fork Lightning
Nawl Beast	935	31	595	82–136	105	0%	0%	0%	0%	0%	0%	N/A
Nawl Beast (Act I)	65	6	90	13–21	27	0%	0%	0%	0%	0%	0%	N/A
Nawl Beast (Rift)	158	10	126	20–34	39	0%	0%	0%	0%	0%	0%	N/A
*Nawl Beast War Hound	5729	33	2912	301–501	112	0%	0%	0%	0%	0%	0%	N/A
*Nawl Beast Patron	647	8	480	55–91	33	0%	0%	0%	0%	0%	0%	N/A
Orthrac	3429	34	1185	241–401	115	0%	0%	0%	0%	0%	0%	N/A
Dark Orthrac	720	13	253	69–115	48	0%	0%	0%	0%	0%	0%	N/A
*Orthrac Predator	6035	34	3159	314–524	115	0%	0%	0%	0%	0%	0%	N/A
*Dark Orthrac Predator	1571	15	766	106–177	54	0%	0%	0%	0%	0%	0%	N/A
Ralatar	2096	39	1434	174–290	133	0%	0%	0%	0%	0%	0%	N/A
*Voracious Ralatar	8039	40	5200	401–669	136	0%	0%	0%	0%	0%	0%	N/A
Raptor	165	9	156	23–39	36	0%	0%	0%	0%	0%	0%	N/A
Garganturax (Taar's Investigation)	3981	11	600	108–180	42	0%	0%	0%	0%	0%	0%	N/A
*Fierce Raptor	1127	12	636	82–137	45	0%	0%	0%	0%	0%	0%	N/A
Rawk	2002	38	1319	167–279	129	0%	0%	0%	0%	0%	0%	N/A
*Fierce Rawk	8039	40	5200	401–669	136	0%	0%	0%	0%	0%	0%	N/A
Rhinock	495	10	210	52–87	39	0%	0%	0%	0%	-25%	0%	N/A
*Alpha Rhinock	1127	12	636	82–137	45	0%	0%	0%	0%	-25%	0%	N/A
Rustguard	2468	32	1007	184–306	108	0%	0%	0%	0%	0%	0%	N/A
Rustguard (2)	3182	37	1517	228–380	125	0%	0%	0%	0%	0%	0%	N/A
Rustguard (3)	3336	38	1649	237–395	129	0%	0%	0%	0%	0%	0%	N/A
Sangor	1730	26	628	137–228	88	0%	0%	0%	0%	0%	0%	N/A
Diseased Sangor	1620	25	582	130–216	85	0%	0%	0%	0%	0%	0%	N/A
*Colossal Sangor	4316	28	1956	238–396	95	0%	0%	0%	0%	0%	0%	N/A
*Diseased Colossal Sangor	4058	27	1810	226–376	92	0%	0%	0%	0%	0%	0%	N/A

(continued)

Monsters

Monster	Hit Points	Level	XP	Damage	Defense	Physical Resist	Magic Resist	Fire Resist	Ice Resist	Death Resist	Lightning Resist	Spell
Scorpion	986	16	306	88–146	57	0%	0%	50%	-25%	0%	0%	N/A
*King Scorpion	2086	18	935	132–220	63	0%	0%	50%	-25%	0%	0%	N/A
Scrub Boar	315	16	196	34–57	57	0%	0%	0%	0%	0%	0%	N/A
*Scrub Boar Mother	2086	18	935	132–220	63	0%	0%	0%	0%	0%	0%	N/A
Shaggrot	1732	35	1286	210–350	119	0%	0%	0%	0%	0%	0%	Firebolt, Plasma Globes
*Shaggrot Patriarch	3810	35	3429	328–547	119	0%	0%	0%	0%	0%	0%	Firebolt, Plasma Globes
Snow Beast	1570	28	733	121–202	95	0%	0%	0%	50%	0%	0%	N/A
Horned Snow Beast	1869	31	930	235–392	105	0%	0%	0%	50%	0%	0%	N/A
*Horned Digging Snow Beast	4583	33	2912	243–405	112	0%	0%	0%	50%	0%	0%	N/A
*Digging Snow Beast	3886	30	2289	212–353	102	0%	0%	0%	50%	0%	0%	N/A
Shambler Hatchling	50	27	0–1	65	96	0%	0%	0%	0%	0%	0%	N/A
Plagued Snowbrook Haven Soldier	1562	33	874	136–226	112	0%	0%	0%	0%	0%	0%	N/A
Plagued Snowbrook Haven Ranger	1250	33	874	109–181	112	0%	0%	0%	0%	0%	0%	N/A
Plagued Snowbrook Haven Mage	937	33	874	135–224	112	0%	0%	0%	0%	0%	0%	Grave Beam, Summon Twisted Shail, Infect
Plagued Snowbrook Haven Fighter	1562	33	874	136–226	112	0%	0%	0%	0%	0%	0%	N/A
Plagued Snowbrook Haven Archer	1250	33	874	109–181	112	0%	0%	0%	0%	0%	0%	N/a
Plagued Snowbrook Haven Sorceress	937	33	874	135–224	112	0%	0%	0%	0%	0%	0%	Grave Beam, Summon Twisted Shail, Infect
*Plagued Snowbrook Haven Commander	5729	33	2912	301–501	112	0%	0%	0%	0%	0%	0%	N/A
Plagued Windstone Fortress Soldier	496	19	301	54–90	66	0%	0%	0%	0%	0%	0%	N/A
Plagued Windstone Soldier	276	13	203	34–57	48	0%	0%	0%	0%	0%	0%	N/A
Plagued Windstone Fortress Ranger	496	19	301	51–85	66	0%	0%	0%	0%	0%	0%	N/A
Plagued Windstone Fortress Mage	404	20	322	68–113	69	0%	0%	0%	0%	0%	0%	Grave Beam, Summon Twisted Shail, Infect, Shard Soul Embrace
Plagued Windstone Fortress Fighter	496	19	301	54–90	66	0%	0%	0%	0%	0%	0%	N/A

(continued)

Monster	Hit Points	Level	XP	Damage	Defense	Physical Resist	Magic Resist	Fire Resist	Ice Resist	Death Resist	Lightning Resist	Spell
Plagued Windstone Fortress Archer	496	19	301	51–85	66	0%	0%	0%	0%	0%	0%	N/A
Plagued Windstone Fortress Sorceress	404	20	322	68–113	69	0%	0%	0%	0%	0%	0%	Grave Beam, Summon Twisted Shail, Infect, Shard Soul Embrace
*Plagued Windstone Fortress Captain	2672	21	1155	161–268	72	0%	0%	0%	0%	0%	0%	N/A
*Plagued Windstone Fortress Sniper	2137	21	1155	130–216	72	0%	0%	0%	0%	0%	0%	N/A
*Plagued Windstone Fortress Grand Wizard	1730	22	1242	171–285	75	0%	0%	0%	0%	0%	0%	Grave Beam, Summon, Infect, Shard Soul Embrace
Grim Shard Soul	391	33	367	240–401	112	0%	0%	0%	0%	0%	0%	Shard Soul Embrace
Shard Soul	130	17	110	98–164	60	0%	0%	0%	0%	0%	0%	Shard Soul Embrace
Frail Shard Soul	68	10	75	60–100	42	0%	0%	0%	0%	0%	0%	Shard Soul Embrace
*Shard Wraith	2086	18	935	165–275	63	0%	0%	0%	0%	0%	0%	Shard Soul Embrace
*Frail Shard Wraith	1571	15	766	132–221	54	0%	0%	0%	0%	0%	0%	Shard Soul Embrace
Durvla (Khartos' Rift Site)	2604	33	1092	192–320	112	0%	0%	0%	0%	0%	0%	N/A
Durvla (The Siege at Snowbrook Haven)	2886	35	1286	210–350	119	0%	0%	-50%	0%	0%	0%	N/A
*Veteran Durvla	5729	33	2912	301–501	112	0%	0%	0%	0%	0%	0%	Dehydrate
Skath Cat	343	15	230	40–67	54	0%	0%	0%	0%	0%	0%	N/A
*Belligerent Skath Cat	1906	17	873	123–205	60	0%	0%	0%	0%	0%	0%	N/A
Skeen	234	33	367	27–45	112	0%	0%	0%	0%	0%	0%	Firebolt
*Skeen Firespitter	3810	35	3429	132–221	119	0%	0%	0%	0%	0%	0%	Firebolt
Skitter	95	16	103	84–140	57	0%	0%	0%	0%	0%	0%	Small Spit
*Mutant Skitter	1668	18	935	107–178	63	0%	0%	0%	0%	0%	0%	Small Spit
Taclak Basher	524	22	298	51–85	75	0%	0%	0%	0%	0%	0%	N/A
Taclak Tracker	419	22	298	41–69	75	0%	0%	0%	0%	0%	0%	N/A
*Decorated Taclak Basher	3329	24	1440	192–320	82	0%	0%	0%	0%	0%	0%	Blind, Steal Magic
*Decorated Taclak Tracker	2663	24	1440	155–258	82	0%	0%	0%	0%	0%	0%	Blind, Steal Magic
Taugrim	1513	24	540	141–235	82	0%	0%	0%	0%	0%	-50%	N/A
Adolescent Taugrim	1214	21	433	103–171	72	0%	0%	0%	0%	0%	-50%	N/A
*Feral Taugrim	3807	26	1676	214–357	88	0%	0%	0%	0%	0%	-50%	N/A
*Feral Adolescent Taugrim	3102	23	1337	181–302	79	0%	0%	0%	0%	0%	-50%	N/A
Terrak	68	4	96	14–24	22	0%	0%	0%	0%	0%	0%	N/A

(continued)

Monster	Hit Points	Level	XP	Damage	Defense	Physical Resist	Magic Resist	Fire Resist	Ice Resist	Death Resist	Lightning Resist	Spell
*Elder Terrak	370	5	360	37–62	24	0%	0%	0%	0%	0%	0%	N/A
Piercing Tharva	197	22	156	36–61	75	0%	0%	0%	0%	0%	0%	N/A
Jabbing Tharva	155	19	126	30–51	66	0%	0%	0%	0%	0%	0%	N/A
Sniping Tharva	169	23	168	33–55	79	0%	0%	0%	0%	0%	0%	Tharva Sting
Shooting Tharva	124	19	126	26–43	66	0%	0%	0%	0%	0%	0%	Tharva Sting
*Mutant Piercing Tharva	3329	24	1440	192–320	82	0%	0%	0%	0%	0%	0%	N/A
*Mutant Jabbing Tharva	2672	21	1155	161–268	72	0%	0%	0%	0%	0%	0%	N/A
*Mutant Sniping Tharva	2851	25	1553	164–273	85	0%	0%	0%	0%	0%	0%	Tharva Sting
*Mutant Shooting Tharva	2137	21	1155	130–216	72	0%	0%	0%	0%	0%	0%	Tharva Sting
Thrine	518	25	373	49–81	85	0%	0%	0%	0%	0%	0%	Thrine Spike
Diseased Thrine	484	24	346	46–77	81	0%	0%	0%	0%	0%	0%	Thrine Spike
*Devouring Thrine	3246	27	1810	182–304	92	0%	0%	0%	0%	0%	0%	Thrine Spike
*Diseased Devouring Thrine	3046	26	1676	173–288	88	0%	0%	0%	0%	0%	0%	Thrine Spike
Thrusk	257	15	230	47–79	54	0%	0%	0%	0%	0%	0%	Firebolt
Giant Thrusk	2287	17	328	123–205	60	0%	0%	0%	0%	0%	0%	Fireball
*Thrusk Channeler	1144	17	873	123–205	60	0%	0%	0%	0%	0%	0%	Firebolt
*Giant Thrusk Channeler	1715	17	873	117–195	60	0%	0%	50%	-25%	0%	0%	Fireball
Plagued Traglok	1154	35	823	98–163	119	0%	0%	0%	0%	0%	0%	Cripple
*Plagued Berzerk Traglok	7001	37	4045	357–594	125	0%	0%	0%	0%	0%	0%	Cripple
Trasak	147	12	191	46–77	45	0%	0%	0%	0%	0%	0%	Leech Life
*Vampiric Trasak	849	14	718	98–163	51	0%	0%	0%	0%	0%	0%	Leech Life
Twisted Shail	2002	38	1319	167–279	129	0%	0%	0%	0%	75%	0%	N/A
Rotten Twisted Shail	473	16	245	52–86	57	0%	0%	0%	0%	50%	0%	N/A
Stygian Twisted Shail	1201	38	1320	166–277	129	0%	0%	0%	0%	75%	0%	Ice Beam, Ancestors Revenge
*Plated Twisted Shail	8039	40	5200	401–669	136	0%	0%	0%	0%	75%	0%	Ancestors Revenge
*Plated Twisted Shail (Act I)	1734	16	817	114–191	57	0%	0%	0%	0%	50%	0%	Ancestors Revenge
*Plated Stygian Twisted Shail	4823	40	5200	401–669	136	0%	0%	0%	0%	75%	0%	Ice Beam, Ancestors Revenge
Vasp	635	23	401	66–109	79	0%	0%	0%	0%	0%	0%	Multispark
Outcast Vasp	505	20	322	55–91	69	0%	0%	0%	0%	0%	0%	Multispark
*Leeching Vasp	2138	25	1553	203–338	85	0%	0%	0%	0%	0%	0%	Multispark
*Leeching Outcast Vasp	1730	22	1242	171–285	75	0%	0%	0%	0%	0%	0%	Multispark

(continued)

Monster	Hit Points	Level	XP	Damage	Defense	Physical Resist	Magic Resist	Fire Resist	Ice Resist	Death Resist	Lightning Resist	Spell
Plagued Veesh	307	12	191	37–62	45	0%	0%	0%	0%	0%	0%	N/A
*Plagued Veesh Man-Eater	1415	14	718	98–163	51	0%	0%	0%	0%	0%	0%	N/A
Vulk	1127	12	239	75–125	45	0%	0%	0%	0%	-25%	0%	N/A
*Ancient Vulk	2830	14	718	140–234	51	0%	0%	0%	0%	-25%	0%	N/A
Kluun Legionnaire	2002	38	1319	167–279	129	0%	0%	0%	0%	0%	0%	N/A
Conjuring Kluun Legionnaire	1201	38	1319	67–112	129	0%	0%	0%	0%	0%	0%	Fireball, Aquatic Embrace, Drown, Plasma Globes
*Kluun Legionnaire Swordmaster	8039	40	5200	401–669	136	0%	0%	75%	0%	0%	0%	Aquatic Embrace, Drown
Zombie Commander	8039	40	5200	401–669	136	0%	0%	75%	0%	0%	0%	Aquatic Embrace, Drown
*Conjuring Kluun Legionnaire Master	4823	40	5200	162–270	136	0%	0%	75%	0%	0%	0%	Fireball, Aquatic Embrace, Drown, Plasma Globes

Pets

This section reveals the exact formulas applied to the pet-food bonuses and predefined maturity bonuses for each pet at every level of maturity. For more information on the pets, see Part 3, "Combat Strategies and Pets."

Food Bonuses

Feeding your pet increases its growth. After a certain amount of food, the pet increases in maturity. What you feed the pet determines what attribute bonuses the pet receives when it reaches the next level of maturity. For example, feed it exclusively melee weapons to improve its strength, or potions to increase health and mana.

Pet Food	Attribute Bonus	Value
Melee Weapons	Strength	$3 + (6 \times$ character level $\times 0.1)$
Ranged Weapons	Dexterity	$4 + (9.5 \times$ character level $\times 0.1)$
Mage Weapons	Intelligence	$1 + (5.5 \times$ character level $\times 0.1)$
Melee Armor	Armor	+20%
	Strength	$1 + (2.4 \times$ character level $\times 0.1)$
Ranged Armor	Armor	+20%
	Dexterity	$2 + (3.2 \times$ character level $\times 0.1)$
Mage Armor	Armor	+20%
	Intelligence	$1 + (1.8 \times$ character level $\times 0.1)$
Potions	Health	$0.20 \times (50 + 10.6 \times$ character level$)$
	Mana	$0.11 \times (50 + 5.1 \times$ character level$)$
Reagents, Rings, and Amulets	Strength	$1 + (1.1 \times$ character level $\times 0.1)$
	Dexterity	$1 + (1.7 \times$ character level $\times 0.1)$
	Intelligence	$1 + (0.9 \times$ character level $\times 0.1)$
	Armor	+5%
	Health	$0.05 \times (50 + 10.6 \times$ character level$)$
	Mana	$0.055 \times (50 + 5.1 \times$ character level$)$

Predefined Maturity Bonuses

When your pet reaches the next level of maturity, it receives a predefined bonus to a particular attribute or resistance. The pet may also learn a stronger attack, spell, power, or Emanation. These tables reveal the exact formulas for each pet's predefined bonus at each maturity level.

Pack Mule

Maturity Level	Predefined Bonus	New Ability
Baby	N/A	Attack: Kick
Fledgling	+Health by 0.10 × (50 + 10.6 × character level)	N/A
Juvenile	+Armor by 10%	Attack: Strong Kick; Power: Staggering Kick
Adolescent	+Strength by 1+ (2.4 × character level × 0.1)	N/A
Young Adult	+Health by 0.10 × (50 + 10.6 × character level)	Attack: Mighty Kick
Mature	+Strength by 1+ (2.4 × character level × 0.1)	Emanation: Reveal Treasure

Pack Mule Power

Power	% Normal damage to enemies	Stun Duration	Stun Radius
Staggering Kick	30 × melee level + 250	8 s	3.5 m (4 enemies)

Ice Elemental

Maturity Level	Predefined Bonus	New Ability
Baby	N/A	Attack: Lesser Icestrike
Fledgling	+Mana by 0.11 × (50 + 13.7 × character level), +5% ice resistance	N/A
Juvenile	+Intelligence by 1 + (1.8 × character level × 0.1)	Attack: Icestrike; Power: Frost Aura
Adolescent	+Armor by 10%, +5% ice resistance	N/A
Young Adult	+Health by 0.10 × (50 + 8.0 × character level)	Attack: Greater Icestrike
Mature	+Intelligence by 1 + (1.8 × character level × 0.1), +5% ice resistance	Emanation: Ice Resistance

Ice Elemental Power

Power	Aura Duration	Ice Damage per Wave	Radius
Frost Aura	20 s	2 + 0.5 × nature magic level × ((0.06 × nature magic level) + 0.5)	2 m

Scorpion Queen

Maturity Level	Predefined Bonus	New Ability
Baby	N/A	Attack: Lesser Scorpion Sting
Fledgling	+Dexterity by 2 + (3.2 × character level × 0.1)	N/A
Juvenile	+Armor by 10%	Attack: Scorpion Sting
Power: Explosive Sting		
Adolescent	+Dexterity by 2 + (3.2 × character level × 0.1)	N/A
Young Adult	+Health by 0.10 × (50 + 8.0 × character level)	Attack: Greater Scorpion Sting
Mature	+Dexterity by 2 + (3.2 × character level × 0.1)	Emanation: Evasion Aura

Scorpion Queen Power

Power	% Normal damage to enemies	Radius
Explosive Sting	(60 + 15 × ranged level) × (0.06 × ranged level + 0.5)	3.5 m

Dire Wolf

Maturity Level	Predefined Bonus	New Ability
Baby	N/A	Attack: Bite
Fledgling	+Strength by 1+ (2.4 × character level × 0.1)	N/A
Juvenile	+Health by 0.10 × (50 + 10.6 × character level)	Attack: Rending Bite; Power: Furious Howl
Adolescent	+Strength by 1+ (2.4 × character level × 0.1)	N/A
Young Adult	+Armor by 10%	Attack: Devastating Bite
Mature	+Strength by 1+ (2.4 × character level × 0.1)	Emanation: Vicious Counter

Dire Wolf Power

Power	Damage	Radius
Furious Howl	(60 + 16 × melee level) × ((0.06 × melee level) + 0.5)	5 m

Fire Elemental

Maturity Level	Predefined Bonus	New Ability
Baby	N/A	Attack: Lesser Firestrike
Fledgling	+Intelligence by 1 + (1.8 × character level × 0.1), +5% fire resistance	N/A
Juvenile	+Mana by 0.11 × (50 + 13.7 × character level)	Attack: Firestrike; Power: Inferno
Adolescent	+Intelligence by 1 + (1.8 × character level × 0.1), +5% fire resistance	N/A
Young Adult	+Health by 0.10 × (50 + 8.0 × character level), +5% fire resistance	Attack: Greater Firestrike
Mature	+Mana by 0.11 × (50 + 13.7 × character level), +5% fire resistance	Emanation: Fire Resistance

Fire Elemental Power

Power	Fire damage per second	Duration	Range
Inferno	(22 + 5.5 × combat magic level) × ((0.06 × combat magic level) + 0.5)	5 s	6

Dark Naiad

Maturity Level	Predefined Bonus	New Ability
Baby	N/A	Attack: Duskbeam; Spell: Lesser Fade Wounds
Fledgling	+Intelligence by 1 + (1.8 × character level × 0.1)	N/A
Juvenile	+Armor by 10%	Spell: Fade Wounds; Power: Arboreal Rejuvenation
Adolescent	+Mana by 0.11 × (50 + 13.7 × character level)	N/A
Young Adult	+Health by 0.10 × (50 + 8.0 × character level)	Spell: Greater Fade Wounds
Mature	+Armor by 10%	Emanation: Regeneration

Dark Naiad Power

Power	Amount Healed	Radius
Arboreal Rejuvenation	30 + 6 × nature magic level	10 m

Light Naiad

Maturity Level	Predefined Bonus	New Ability
Baby	N/A	Attack: Duskbeam; Spell: Lesser Abolish Wounds
Fledgling	+Intelligence by 1 + (1.8 × character level × 0.1), +5% magic damage resistance	N/A
Juvenile	+Armor by 10%	Spell: Abolish Wounds; Power: Arboreal Rejuvenation
Adolescent	+Mana by 0.11 × (50 + 13.7 × character level), +5% magic damage resistance	N/A
Young Adult	+Health by 0.10 × (50 + 8.0 × character level)	Spell: Greater Abolish Wounds
Mature	+Armor by 10%, +5% magic damage resistance	Emanation: Regeneration

Light Naiad Power

Power	Amount Healed	Radius
Arboreal Rejuvenation	30 + 6 × nature magic level	10 m

Mythrilhorn

Maturity Level	Predefined Bonus	New Ability
Baby	N/A	Attack: Lesser Claw Strike
Fledgling	+Armor by 10%	N/A
Juvenile	+Health by 0.10 × (50 + 10.6 × character level)	Attack: Claw Strike; Power: Enrage
Adolescent	+Armor by 10%	N/A
Young Adult	+Health by 0.10 × (50 + 10.6 × character level)	Attack: Grievous Claw Strike
Mature	+Strength by 1+ (2.4 × character level × 0.1)	Emanation: Defense Aura

Mythrilhorn Power

Power	Radius	
Enrage	10 m	

Lap Dragon

Maturity Level	Predefined Bonus	New Ability
Baby	N/A	Attack: Dragon Breath; Spell: Baby Dragon Scales
Fledgling	+Armor by 10%	N/A
Juvenile	+Intelligence by 1 + (1.8 × character level × 0.1)	Spell: Dragon Scales; Power: Draconic Inspiration
Adolescent	+Mana by 0.11 × (50 + 13.7 × character level)	Attack: Dragon Fire
Young Adult	+Health by 0.10 × (50 + 10.6 × character level)	Spell: Infused Dragon Scales
Mature	+Armor by 10%	Emanation: Dragon Vitality

Lap Dragon Power

Power	Power Damage Bonus %	Duration	Radius
Draconic Inspiration	35%	20 s	5 m

Necrolithid

Maturity Level	Predefined Bonus	New Ability
Baby	N/A	Attack: Deathstrike; Spell: Wasting
Fledgling	+Intelligence by 1 + (1.8 × character level × 0.1), +5% death resistance	N/A
Juvenile	+Mana by 0.11 × (50 + 13.7 × character level)	Spell: Necrosis; Power: Decompose
Adolescent	+Health by 0.10 × (50 + 8.0 × character level), +5% death resistance	N/A
Young Adult	+Armor by 10%, +5% death resistance	Spell: Dissolution
Mature	+Health by 0.10 × (50 + 8.0 × character level), +5% death resistance	Emanation: Mana Steal

Necrolithid Power

Power	Health Restored % of Maximum Enemy Health	Duration	Radius
Decompose	2.5%	20 s	3 m

Potions

The following chart reveals potions, their effects, and their cost in town. In *Dungeon Siege II*, a character can benefit from the potions held by another character. Using a potion makes it disappear from the entire party's inventory, not just one character's. Also, a character drinks only the amount of potion necessary to replenish his or her health or mana reserve.

Potion	Effect(s)	Cost
Small Health Potion	+125 to health	15
Normal Health Potion	+250 to health	75
Large Health Potion	+450 to health	225
Super Health Potion	+700 to health	375
Colossal Health Potion	+1100 to health	750
Small Mana Potion	+150 to mana	15
Normal Mana Potion	+300 to mana	75
Large Mana Potion	+500 to mana	225
Super Mana Potion	+900 to mana	375
Colossal Mana Potion	+1400 to mana	750
Small Rejuvenation Potion	+125 to health, +150 to mana	30
Normal Rejuvenation Potion	+250 to health, +250 to mana	150
Large Rejuvenation Potion	+450 to health, +450 to mana	450
Super Rejuvenation Potion	+700 to health, +700 to mana	750
Colossal Rejuvenation Potion	+1100 to health, +1100 to mana	1500

Incantations

Locate Chant Lecterns throughout the game; select a lectern to pick up its chant. Find an Incantation Shrine and invoke the chant to receive its benefits. This table reveals all incantations, their effects, and locations.

Incantation	Chant	Duration	Value	Description	Lectern Location
Lesser Chant of Fighter Power	Vigorus Adeptus Es	40	N/A	Instantly recharges powers for all fighters in the party for a short duration.	An Elven Shrine (Secrets of the Elven Shrine)

(continued)

Incantation	Chant	Duration	Value	Description	Lectern Location
Lesser Chant of Ranger Power	Agilus Adeptus Es	40	N/A	Instantly recharges powers for all rangers in the party for a short duration.	An Elven Shrine (Secrets of the Elven Shrine)
Lesser Chant of Mage Power	Ingenus Adeptus Es	40	N/A	Instantly recharges powers for all mages in the party for a short duration.	An Elven Shrine (Secrets of the Elven Shrine)
Chant of Fighter Power	Vigorus Adeptus	60	N/A	Instantly recharges powers for all fighters in the party for a moderate duration.	The Vai'kesh Sanctuary
Chant of Ranger Power	Agilus Adeptus	60	N/A	Instantly recharges powers for all rangers in the party for a moderate duration.	The Vai'kesh Sanctuary (behind a ranged Sanctuary Door)
Chant of Mage Power	Ingenus Adeptus	60	N/A	Instantly recharges powers for all mages in the party for a moderate duration.	The Vai'kesh Sanctuary
Chant of Power	Multus Adeptus	60	N/A	Instantly recharges powers for any party members nearby. Powers continue to recharge instantly until the chant wears off.	Zaramoth's Horns
Greater Chant of Fighter Power	Vigorus Adeptus Ix	75	N/A	Instantly recharges powers for all fighters in the party for a long duration.	Some Ancient Ruins
Greater Chant of Ranger Power	Agilus Adeptus Ix	75	N/A	Instantly recharges powers for all rangers in the party for a large duration.	A Large Abandoned Shelter
Greater Chant of Mage Power	Ingenus Adeptus Ix	75	N/A	Instantly recharges powers for all mages in the party for a long duration.	A Large Abandoned Shelter
Lesser Chant of Fighter Health	Vigorus Vitalis Es	180	+100% to health regeneration rate	Gives a small boost to the health regeneration rate of all fighters in the party.	Western Greilyn Jungle
Lesser Chant of Ranger Health	Agilus Vitalis Es	180	+100% to health regeneration rate	Gives a small boost to the health regeneration rate of all rangers in the party.	Western Greilyn Jungle
Lesser Chant of Mage Health	Ingenus Vitalis Es	180	+100% to health regeneration rate	Gives a small boost to the health regeneration rate of all mages in the party.	Western Greilyn Jungle
Chant of Fighter Health	Vigorus Vitalis	240	+150% to health regeneration rate	Gives a moderate boost to the health regeneration rate of all fighters in the party.	The Levreth Estate (A Servant's Haunt)
Chant of Ranger Health	Agilus Vitalis	240	+150% to health regeneration rate	Gives a moderate boost to the health regeneration rate of all rangers in the party.	The Levreth Estate (A Servant's Haunt)
Chant of Mage Health	Ingenus Vitalis	240	+150% to health regeneration rate	Gives a moderate boost to the health regeneration rate of all mages in the party.	The Levreth Estate (A Servant's Haunt)
Greater Chant of Fighter Health	Vigorus Vitalis Ix	300	+200% to health regeneration rate	Gives a large boost to the health regeneration rate of all fighters in the party.	The Ruins of Okaym
Greater Chant of Ranger Health	Agilus Vitalis Ix	300	+200% to health regeneration rate	Gives a large boost to the health regeneration rate of all rangers in the party.	The Eastern Plain of Tears
Greater Chant of Mage Health	Ingenus Vitalis Ix	300	+200% to health regeneration rate	Gives a large boost to the health regeneration rate of all mages in the party.	The Eastern Plain of Tears
Chant of Health	Multus Vitalis	240	+150% to health regeneration rate	Temporarily boosts the health regeneration rate of any party members nearby.	A Magical Oasis (Deru's Treasure Hunt)
Lesser Chant of Strength	Elevato Vigorum Es	180	3.0+(6 × character level × 0.1)	Gives a small boost to the Strength of all party members.	Northern Greilyn Jungle
Chant of Strength	Elevato Vigorum	240	4.5+(9 × character level × 0.1)	Gives a moderate boost to the Strength of all party members.	Northern Vai'lutra Forest
Greater Chant of Strength	Elevato Vigorum Ix	300	6.0+(12 × character level × 0.1)	Gives a large boost to the Strength of all party members.	The Snowbrook Haven Reliquary
Lesser Chant of Dexterity	Elevato Agilum Es	180	4.0+(9.5 × character level × 0.1)	Gives a small boost to the Dexterity of all party members.	Tower dungeon in Northern Greilyn Jungle

(continued)

Incantations

Incantation	Chant	Duration	Value	Description	Lectern Location
Chant of Dexterity	Elevato Agilum	240	5.5+(12.6 × character level × 0.1)	Gives a moderate boost to the Dexterity of all party members.	Northern Vai'lutra Forest
Greater Chant of Dexterity	Elevato Agilum Ix	300	7.0 +(16 × character level × 0.1)	Gives a large boost to the Dexterity of all party members.	The Snowbrook Haven Reliquary
Lesser Chant of Intelligence	Elevato Ingenum Es	180	2+(5.4 × character level × 0.1)	Gives a small boost to the Intelligence of all party members.	Northern Greilyn Jungle
Chant of Intelligence	Elevato Ingenum	240	2.6+(7.1 × character level × 0.1)	Gives a moderate boost to the Intelligence of all party members.	Northern Vai'lutra Forest
Greater Chant of Intelligence	Elevato Ingenum Ix	300	4.0+(9 × character level × 0.1)	Gives a large boost to the Intelligence of all party members.	The Snowbrook Haven Reliquary
Chaotic Chant of Might	Elevato Rando Ixo	240	Strength: 7+(14 × character level × 0.1); Dexterity: 8+(18 × character level × 0.1); Intelligence: 6+(10 × character level × 0.1)	Gives all party members a huge boost to a random primary stat.	The Azunite Burial Grounds
Lesser Chant of Fortification	Dono Armorum Es	180	+25% to armor	Gives a small boost to the Armor rating of all party members.	Northern Greilyn Jungle (at first Incantation Shrine)
Chant of Fortification	Dono Armorum	240	+40% to armor	Gives a moderate boost to the Armor rating of all party members.	A Small Vai'kesh Cave (A Dark Ohm secondary quest)
Greater Chant of Fortification	Dono Armorum Ix	300	+50% to armor	Gives a large boost to the Armor rating of all party members.	In a treasure room accessible upon completing The Morden Riders
Chant of Scholars	Dono Experium	300	Experience Boost: 50%; Decrease to Health: -0.20 × (50+10.6 × character level)	Gives a boost to the amount of experience earned and a decrease to the maximum health of all party members.	Temple of Xeria
Lesser Chant of Prosperity	Dono Fortunam Es	180	Chance to find magic items: 50%; Increase to gold dropped: 100%	Gives a small boost to the party's chance to find magic items and to the amount of gold dropped.	An Elven Shrine
Chant of Prosperity	Dono Fortunam	240	Chance to find magic items: 75%; Increase to gold dropped: 150%	Gives a moderate boost to the party's chance to find magic items and to the amount of gold dropped.	Reward from the Dwarven Song of Ore secondary quest
Greater Chant of Prosperity	Dono Fortunam Ix	300	Chance to find magic items: 100%; Increase to gold dropped: 200%	Gives a large boost to the party's chance to find magic items and to the amount of gold dropped.	Reward from the Dwarven Song of Ore secondary quest (for retrieving fourth stanza)
Lesser Chant of Magic Awareness	Incantum Percepto Es	180	+40% to magic resistance	Gives a small boost to magic resistance for all party members.	Eastern Greilyn Jungle
Chant of Magic Awareness	Incantum Percepto	240	+60% to magic resistance	Gives a moderate boost to magic resistance for all party members.	Snowbrook Valley

(continued)

Incantation	Chant	Duration	Value	Description	Lectern Location
Greater Chant of Magic Awareness	Incantum Percepto Ix	300	+80% to magic resistance	Gives a large boost to magic resistance for all party members.	The Upper Mines of Kaderak, Part 2
Lesser Chant of Ranged Awareness	Propelum Percepto Es	180	+40% to ranged resistance	Gives a small boost to ranged resistance for all party members.	Eastern Greilyn Jungle
Chant of Ranged Awareness	Propelum Percepto	240	+60% to ranged resistance	Gives a moderate boost to ranged resistance for all party members.	The Garden of the Ancients (secret southern area)
Greater Chant of Ranged Awareness	Propelum Percepto Ix	300	+80% to ranged resistance	Gives a large boost to ranged resistance for all party members.	The Desert of Kaderak
Lesser Chant of Melee Awareness	Physium Percepto Es	180	+20% to melee resistance	Gives a small boost to melee resistance for all party members.	An Ancient Azunite Shrine
Chant of Melee Awareness	Physium Percepto	240	+30% to melee resistance	Gives a moderate boost to melee resistance for all party members.	The Garden of the Ancients (secret southern area)
Greater Chant of Melee Awareness	Physium Percepto Ix	300	+40% to melee resistance	Gives a large boost to melee resistance for all party members.	The Desert of Kaderak
Chant of Master Self Awareness	Ipsum Percepto Ixo	300	+95% to melee, ranged, or magic resistance	Gives each party member complete resistance to their primary damage type (whichever type matches the highest class)	A Frozen Crypt (without Champion's Mask)
Lesser Chant of Casting	Incanta Rapida Es	180	Reduces spell mana cost to 0	Party members will instantly recover all mana for a short duration.	Western Greilyn Jungle
Chant of Casting	Incanta Rapida	240	Reduces spell mana cost to 0	Party members will instantly recover all mana for a moderate duration.	The Vai'kesh Sanctuary
Greater Chant of Casting	Incanta Rapida Ix	300	Reduces spell mana cost to 0	Party members will instantly recover all mana for a long duration.	Some Ancient Ruins
Lesser Chant of Purity	Vexori Impedio Es	360	100% resistance to freeze, stun, ignite, immobilize, knockback, silence, slow, and curses	Gives all party members resistance to status altering affects for a short duration.	An Ancient Azunite Shrine
Chant of Purity	Vexori Impedio	420	100% resistance to freeze, stun, ignite, immobilize, knockback, silence, slow, and curses	Gives all party members resistance to status altering affects for a moderate duration.	The Azunite Catacombs in Letiso the Lich's chamber (Rahvan's Curse)
Greater Chant of Purity	Vexori Impedio Ix	600	100% resistance to freeze, stun, ignite, immobilize, knockback, silence, slow, and curses	Gives all party members resistance to status altering affects for a long duration.	Some Crumbling Ruins
Lesser Chant of Melee Skill	Vigorus Artifex Es	180	+1 to melee skills	Gives a small boost to melee skills for all party members.	Eastern Windstone Fortress Gatehouse
Chant of Melee Skill	Vigorus Artifex	240	+2 to melee skills	Gives a moderate boost to melee skills for all party members.	The Snowbrook Grotto
Greater Chant of Melee Skill	Vigorus Artifex Ix	300	+3 to melee skills	Gives a large boost to melee skills for all party members.	Zaramoth's Horns
Lesser Chant of Ranged Skill	Agilus Artifex Es	180	+1 to ranged skills	Gives a small boost to ranged skills for all party members.	Windstone Fortress Barracks
Chant of Ranged Skill	Agilus Artifex	240	+2 to ranged skills	Gives a moderate boost to ranged skills for all party members.	The Snowbrook Foothills

(continued)

Incantations

Incantation	Chant	Duration	Value	Description	Lectern Location
Greater Chant of Ranged Skill	Agilus Artifex Ix	300	+3 to ranged skills	Gives a large boost to ranged skills for all party members.	Zaramoth's Horns
Lesser Chant of Magic Skill	Ingenus Artifex Es	180	+1 to combat magic and nature magic skills	Gives a small boost to magic skills for all party members.	Western Windstone Fortress Gatehouse
Chant of Magic Skill	Ingenus Artifex	240	+2 to combat magic and nature magic skills	Gives a moderate boost to magic skills for all party members.	The Snowbrook Grotto
Greater Chant of Magic Skill	Ingenus Artifex Ix	300	+3 to combat magic and nature magic skills	Gives a large boost to magic skills for all party members.	Zaramoth's Horns
Chaotic Chant of Skill	Rando Artifex Ixo	300	+4 to all skills	Gives all party members a huge boost to a random class's skills.	Zaramoth's Horns
Lesser Chant of Random Item	Rando Conjurum Es	N/A	N/A	Provides a lesser random item.	A Tranquil Cave
Chant of Random Item	Rando Conjurum	N/A	N/A	Provides a random item.	A Flooded Chamber
Greater Chant of Random Item	Rando Conjurum Ix	N/A	N/A	Provides a greater random item.	A Mysterious Vault, in southern treasure room (The Lost Jewels of Soranith)
Lesser Chant of Summon Enemies	Requo Malum Es	N/A	N/A	Summons lesser enemies.	An Ancient Azunite Shrine
Chant of Summon Enemies	Requo Malum	N/A	N/A	Summons enemies.	The Snowbrook Haven Living Quarters
Greater Chant of Summon Enemies	Requo Malum Ix	N/A	N/A	Summons greater enemies.	The Agallan Chambers Beneath Kalrathia
Lesser Chant of Summon Friends	Requo Amicum Es	N/A	N/A	Summons lesser friends.	Provided by Master Thestrin in The Family Heirloom, Part 1 if you return the Heirloom Sword
Chant of Summon Friends	Requo Amicum	N/A	N/A	Summons friends.	The Snowbrook Haven Servants' Quarters (near ghostly spirit)
Greater Chant of Summon Friends	Requo Amicum Ix	N/A	N/A	Summons greater friends.	The Agallan Chambers Beneath Kalrathia
Chant of the Dead	Vox Mortem	300	Speak with the ghostly spirits.	Received from Mage Lyssanore upon completion of the A Dark Ohm secondary quest.	Mage Lyssanore in Aman'lu
Explosion	Magrum Erupto	N/A	N/A	A "curse" chant received from Master Thestrin upon completing the A Family Heirloom secondary quest.	Master Thestrin in Azunite Desert

Lore Books

The following chart reveals *Dungeon Siege II*'s Lore Books and their locations in the game.

Name	Location
The Mothers of Eirulan	Great Hall in Eirulan
Tome of Smithing	Great Hall in Eirulan
The Hak'u	Merchant Shop in Eirulan
Tattered Diary	Hak'u Caves
The Path of Life	A mysterious shrine in Eastern Greilyn jungle (part of the Amren's Vision quest)
The Skath	Near Vix in Eastern Greilyn Jungle.
Living and Working with Half-Giants	Windstone Fortress Western Gatehouse
The Deeds of Xeria	Windstone Fortress Gatehouse
The Death of Xeria	Temple of Xeria
The War of Legions	Temple of Xeria

(continued)

Name	Location
Letter from Drevin	From Drevin's sister in Aman'lu
The Legend of Arinth the Mad	From Eolanda in Aman'lu
Guard's Report	From Eldoriath Wilwarin in south Aman'lu
A Burned Letter	The Levreth Estate
Turmanar and its Aftermath	Alt'ron Hall in the Town of Aman'lu
The Dryads and Their Customs	Near Eolanda in Aman'lu
Zaramoth's Ascendance and Downfall	Aman'lu Magic Shop
Elandir's Life and Teachings	Aman'lu Tavern and Inn
Valdis and His Armies	Tywlis the Mage's home in Aman'lu
Fables of Ancient Artifacts	Near Eolanda in Aman'lu
Symbology of the Azunites	Aman'lu Magic Shop
Downfall of the Manu Ostar	Alar'ithil in south Aman'lu
Taclak Perversity	Aman'lu Armory
The Dark Wizards	Vai'kesh Sanctuary
Kings and Queens of the Northern Reaches	Snowbrook Haven Living Quarters
Elves and Elvish Culture	Kalrathia Tavern and Inn
The Legacy of Azunai	Kalrathia, in a room on the northeastern side
The Morden: Allies or Enemies?	A cellar beneath Kalrathia
Journal of the Mage Apprentice	From Darek the Mage Apprentice
The Mercenary and the Scholar	From Telgrey the Scholar for completing the secondary quest The Lore of Aranna
The Path of the Sighted Eye	A mysterious shrine in the Southern Vai'lutra Forest (part of the Amren's Vision quest)
The Path of Death	A mysterious shrine in The Garden of the Ancients (part of the Amren's Vision quest)
The Path of Blindness	A mysterious shrine in The Ruins of Okaym (part of the Amren's Vision quest)

Experience Progression

This table reveals the number of experience points required to reach each level from 0 to 100. The experience required applies to all classes.

Level	XP Required
0	0
1	300
2	900
3	2000
4	4000
5	7600
6	12,800
7	19,600
8	26,600
9	34,200
10	43,000
11	53,200
12	65,000
13	78,428
14	93,334
15	109,879
16	128,243
17	148,628
18	171,256
19	196,372
20	224,251
21	255,197
22	289,547
23	327,676
24	369,998
25	416,976

Level	XP Required
26	469,122
27	527,004
28	591,252
29	662,568
30	741,729
31	829,597
32	927,131
33	1,035,394
34	1,115,565
35	1,288,956
36	1,437,019
37	1,601,370
38	1,783,799
39	1,986,295
40	2,211,065
41	2,460,561
42	2,737,501
43	3,044,904
44	3,386,122
45	3,764,873
46	4,185,288
47	4,651,948
48	5,169,940
49	5,744,912
50	6,383,130
51	7,091,553
52	7,877,902
53	8,750,749
54	9,719,610
55	10,795,045
56	11,988,778

(continued)

(continued)

Level	XP Required
57	13,313,822
58	14,784,621
59	16,417,207
60	18,229,378
61	20,240,888
62	22,473,664
63	24,952,046
64	27,703,049
65	30,756,663
66	34,146,174
67	37,908,531
68	42,084,748
69	46,720,348
70	51,865,865
71	57,577,388
72	63,917,179
73	70,954,347
74	78,765,603
75	87,436,098
76	97,060,347
77	107,743,263
78	119,601,300
79	132,763,722
80	147,374,009
81	164,591,429
82	181,592,764
83	201,574,246
84	223,753,692
85	248,372,876
86	275,700,171
87	306,033,468
88	339,703,427
89	377,077,083
90	418,561,840
91	464,609,920
92	515,723,290
93	572,459,130
94	635,435,913
95	705,340,141
96	782,933,835
97	869,062,835
98	964,666,025
99	1,070,785,566
100	1,188,578,257

Combat-Magic Spells

This section reveals stats for every combat-magic damage, curse, summon, and utility spell. Range is the spell's range in meters; radius is area-of-effect radius for applicable spells; and cast time is the spell's rate of fire. The higher the cast time, the slower the spell's firing rate.

Damage and summon spell statistics are governed by a character's Intelligence, not combat-magic level. A curse spell's mana cost and damage per second are governed by Intelligence. Our tables are level-specific, so actual curse spell mana cost and damage values may vary.

In this section, we've presented a sampling of stats at a large number of Intelligence levels to provide relative mana cost and spell effectiveness at a variety of levels. These spells increase in effectiveness until reaching a maximum Intelligence level, at which point a stronger spell must be acquired.

Firebolt

Firebolt throws a bolt of searing flame at target enemy. Increase the power of this spell with the Searing Flames, Ignite, and Devastation skills.

♦ **Range: 10** ♦ **Cast Time: 1.39** ♦ **Lesser: Maximum Intelligence 59** ♦ **Normal: Requires combat-magic level 13; Maximum Intelligence 136** ♦ **Greater: Requires cobat-magic level 30; Maximum Intelligence 256** ♦ **Master: Requires combat-magic level 56; Maximum Intelligence 424**

LESSER

INT	Mana Cost	Damage
10	3	12–14
16	5	17–21
22	8	23–28
28	10	29–35
34	12	34–42
40	15	40–49
46	17	45–55
54	21	53–65
59	23	58–70

NORMAL

INT	Mana Cost	Damage
64	25	62–76
70	27	68–83
76	30	74–90
82	32	79–97
88	35	85–103
94	37	90–110
100	40	96–117
106	42	102–124
112	44	107–131
124	49	118–145
136	54	130–158

GREATER

INT	Mana Cost	Damage
148	59	141–172
160	64	152–186
172	69	163–200
184	74	175–213
196	79	186–227
208	84	197–241
220	89	208–254
232	94	220–268
248	100	235–287
256	103	242–296

MASTER

INT	Mana Cost	Damage
268	108	253–309
280	113	264–323
292	118	276–337
304	123	287–351
316	128	298–364

(continued)

INT	Mana Cost	Damage
328	133	309–378
340	138	321–392
352	143	332–405
364	148	343–419
376	153	354–433
388	158	366–447
400	163	377–460
412	167	388–474
424	172	399–488

Firespray

The Firespray spell shoots five embers in an arc in front of the caster. Damage is per ember. Increase the power of this spell with the Searing Flames, Ignite, and Devastation skills.

◆ Range: 10 ◆ Cast Time: 1.04 ◆ Enemies Hit per Cast: 3 ◆ Lesser: Requires combat-magic level 4; Maximum Intelligence 78 ◆ Normal: Requires combat-magic level 17; Maximum Intelligence 198 ◆ Greater: Requires combat-magic level 43; Maximum Intelligence 300 ◆ Master: Requires combat-magic level 65; Maximum Intelligence 467

LESSER

INT	Mana Cost	Damage
22	6	5–6
30	8	7–8
38	11	8–10
46	13	10–12
54	16	12–14
62	18	13–16
70	21	15–18
78	23	16–20

NORMAL

INT	Mana Cost	Damage
90	27	19–23
102	31	21–26
114	34	23–29
126	38	26–31
138	42	28–34
150	46	31–37
162	49	33–40
174	53	35–43
186	57	38–46
198	60	40–49

GREATER

INT	Mana Cost	Damage
204	62	41–50
216	66	44–53
228	70	46–56
240	73	48–59
252	77	51–62
264	81	53–65
276	85	56–68
288	88	58–71
300	92	60–74

MASTER

INT	Mana Cost	Damage
312	96	63–76
324	99	65–79
336	103	67–82

INT	Mana Cost	Damage
348	107	70–85
360	111	72–88
372	114	75–91
384	118	77–94
396	122	79–97
408	125	82–100
420	129	84–103
432	133	86–106
444	137	89–108
456	140	91–111
467	144	93–114

Embers

The Embers spell shoots multiple projectiles in rapid succession at the target enemy. Damage is per projectile. Increase the power of this spell with the Searing Flames, Ignite, and Devastation skills.

◆ Range: 10 ◆ Cast Time: 1.04 ◆ Lesser: Requires combat-magic level 8; Maximum Intelligence 117 ◆ Normal: Requires combat-magic level 25; Maximum Intelligence 218 ◆ Greater: Requires combat-magic level 47; Maximum Intelligence 347 ◆ Master: Requires combat-magic level 75; Maximum Intelligence 500

LESSER

INT	Mana Cost	Damage
34	17	11–14
42	21	14–16
50	25	16–19
58	29	18–22
64	32	20–24
72	36	22–27
80	40	25–30
88	44	27–33
98	49	30–37
107	54	33–40
117	59	36–44

NORMAL

INT	Mana Cost	Damage
134	68	41–50
146	74	44–54
158	80	48–59
170	86	52–63
182	92	55–67
194	98	59–72
206	105	62–76
218	111	66–80

GREATER

INT	Mana Cost	Damage
239	121	72–88
251	128	76–92
263	134	79–97
275	140	83–101
287	146	86–105
299	152	90–110
311	158	93–114
323	164	97–118
335	170	101–123
347	176	104–127

(continued)

(continued)

Combat-Magic Spells

INT	Mana Cost	Damage
356	181	107–130
368	187	110–135
380	193	114–139
392	199	118–144
404	206	121–148
416	212	125–152
428	218	128–157
440	224	132–161
452	230	135–165
464	236	139–170
476	242	142–174
488	248	146–178
500	255	150–183

Plasma Globes

Plasma Globes throws several balls of plasma that bounce along the ground and detonate on contact. Damage is per plasma ball. Increase the power of this spell with the Searing Flames, Ignite, and Devastation skills.

♦ **Range: 8** ♦ **Cast Time: 1.66** ♦ **Lesser: Requires combat-magic level 21; Maximum Intelligence 184** ♦ **Normal: Requires combat-magic level 39; Maximum Intelligence 285** ♦ **Greater: Requires combat-magic level 61; Maximum Intelligence 371** ♦ **Master: Requires combat-magic level 80; Maximum Intelligence 500**

LESSER

INT	Mana Cost	Damage
73	40	53–65
86	48	62–76
98	54	71–86
110	61	79–97
123	69	88–108
135	75	97–118
147	82	105–128
160	90	114–139
172	97	123–150
184	103	131–160

NORMAL

INT	Mana Cost	Damage
201	113	143–175
213	120	151–185
225	127	160–195
237	134	168–206
249	140	177–216
261	147	185–226
273	154	194–236
285	161	202–247

GREATER

INT	Mana Cost	Damage
299	169	212–259
311	176	220–269
323	183	229–279
335	189	237–290
347	196	245–300
359	203	254–310
371	210	262–321

INT	Mana Cost	Damage
392	222	277–339
404	229	286–349
416	236	294–359
428	242	302–369
440	249	311–380
452	256	319–390
464	263	328–400
476	270	336–411
480	277	344–421
500	284	353–431

Fireball

The Fireball spell throws a ball of fire, which explodes on contact with an enemy or the ground, dealing fire damage to nearby enemies. Increase the power of this spell with the Searing Flames, Ignite, and Devastation skills.

♦ **Range: 10** ♦ **Radius: 2.5** ♦ **Cast Time: 1.66** ♦ **Lesser: Requires combat-magic level 34; Maximum Intelligence 246** ♦ **Normal: Requires combat-magic level 52; Maximum Intelligence 328** ♦ **Greater: Requires combat-magic level 70; Maximum Intelligence 400** ♦ **Master: Requires combat-magic level 85; Maximum Intelligence 500**

LESSER

INT	Mana Cost	Damage
112	91	54–66
124	101	59–73
136	111	65–79
148	121	71–86
160	131	76–93
172	141	82–100
184	150	88–107
196	160	93–114
208	170	99–121
220	180	104–127
234	191	111–135
246	201	117–142

NORMAL

INT	Mana Cost	Damage
256	209	121–148
268	219	127–155
280	229	132–162
292	239	138–169
304	249	144–176
316	259	149–182
328	268	155–189

GREATER

INT	Mana Cost	Damage
340	278	161–196
352	288	166–203
364	298	172–210
376	308	177–217
388	318	183–224
400	328	189–230

MASTER

INT	Mana Cost	Damage
416	341	196–240

(continued)

(continued)

INT	Mana Cost	Damage
428	350	202–246
440	360	207–253
452	370	213–260
464	380	219–267
476	390	224–274
488	400	230–281
500	410	235–288

Grave Beam

Grave Beam damages the target enemy with a beam of concentrated death energy. Increase the power of this spell with the Grim Necromancy, Vampirism, and Devastation skills.

◆ **Range: 10** ◆ **Cast Time: 1.04** ◆ Lesser Grave Beam is slightly more powerful in relation to its upper levels because Grim Necromancy isn't available until level 12. ◆ **Lesser: Requires combat-magic level 3; Maximum Intelligence 83** ◆ **Normal: Requires combat-magic level 18; Maximum Intelligence 165** ◆ **Greater: Requires combat-magic level 36; Maximum Intelligence 285** ◆ **Master: Requires combat-magic level 62; Maximum Intelligence 434**

LESSER

INT	Mana Cost	Damage
19	4	9–25
27	5	12–34
35	7	15–43
43	9	18–52
51	11	21–62
59	13	24–71
67	15	27–80
75	17	30–89
83	19	33–99

NORMAL

INT	Mana Cost	Damage
93	21	34–100
101	23	37–109
109	25	39–117
117	27	42–125
125	29	45–134
133	31	48–142
141	33	51–151
149	35	53–159
157	37	56–167
165	39	59–176

GREATER

INT	Mana Cost	Damage
177	41	63–188
189	44	67–201
201	47	72–214
213	50	76–226
225	53	80–239
237	56	84–251
249	59	88–264
261	62	93–277
273	65	97–289
285	67	101–302

MASTER

INT	Mana Cost	Damage
302	71	107–320

INT	Mana Cost	Damage
314	74	111–332
326	77	115–345
338	80	120–358
350	83	124–370
362	86	128–383
374	89	132–395
386	92	136–408
398	95	141–421
410	97	145–433
422	100	149–446
434	103	153–458

Leech Life

Leech Life draws the life out of the target enemy, replenishing the caster's health. Increase the power of this spell with the Grim Necromancy, Vampirism, and Devastation skills.

◆ **Range: 10** ◆ **Cast Time: 1.25** ◆ **Lesser: Requires combat-magic level 10; Maximum Intelligence 102; 4% health steal** ◆ **Normal: Requires combat-magic level 22; Maximum Intelligence 227; 7% health steal** ◆ **Greater: Requires combat-magic level 49; Maximum Intelligence 333; 10% health steal** ◆ **Master: Requires combat-magic level 72; Maximum Intelligence 458; 12% health steal**

LESSER

INT	Mana Cost	Damage
40	19	18–53
47	22	21–62
54	25	24–71
61	29	27–80
68	32	30–89
74	35	32–96
81	39	35–105
88	42	38–114
95	46	41–123
102	49	44–132

NORMAL

INT	Mana Cost	Damage
107	51	46–138
119	57	51–153
131	63	56–168
143	69	61–183
155	75	66–198
167	81	71–213
179	87	77–229
191	93	82–244
203	98	87–259
215	104	92–274
227	110	97–289

GREATER

INT	Mana Cost	Damage
237	115	101–302
249	121	106–317
261	127	111–332
273	133	116–347
285	139	121–362
297	145	126–377
309	150	131–392
321	156	136–407
333	162	141–423

(continued)

(continued)

Combat-Magic Spells

MASTER

INT	Mana Cost	Damage
350	171	148–444
362	176	153–459
374	182	158–474
386	188	163–489
398	194	169–505
410	200	174–520
422	206	179–535
434	212	184–550
446	218	189–565
458	223	194–580

Soul Lance

Soul Lance fires a long bolt of soul-crushing energy that penetrates all enemies it hits. Increase the power of this spell with the Grim Necromancy, Vampirism, and Devastation skills.

◆ **Range: 10** ◆ **Cast Time: 1.66** ◆ **Lesser: Requires combat-magic level 14; Maximum Intelligence 146** ◆ **Normal: Requires combat-magic level 31; Maximum Intelligence 246** ◆ **Greater: Requires combat-magic level 53; Maximum Intelligence 366** ◆ **Master: Requires combat-magic level 79; Maximum Intelligence 500**

LESSER

INT	Mana Cost	Damage
52	24	23–68
60	28	26–78
68	32	30–88
76	36	33–98
84	40	36–108
92	44	40–118
100	48	43–127
108	51	46–137
116	55	49–147
124	59	53–157
132	63	56–167
139	67	59–176
146	70	62–185

NORMAL

INT	Mana Cost	Damage
150	72	64–190
162	78	69–205
174	84	74–220
186	79	79–235
198	96	84–250
210	101	88–264
222	107	93–279
234	113	98–294
246	119	103–309

GREATER

INT	Mana Cost	Damage
258	125	108–324
270	131	113–339
282	137	118–354
294	143	123–369
306	148	128–384
318	154	133–399
330	160	138–414
342	166	143–429

INT	Mana Cost	Damage
354	172	148–444
366	178	153–459

MASTER

INT	Mana Cost	Damage
380	185	159–476
392	191	164–491
404	196	169–506
416	202	174–521
428	208	179–536
440	214	184–551
452	220	189–566
464	226	194–581
476	232	199–596
488	238	204–611
500	244	209–625

Skull Spray

The Skull Spray spell throws three energy skulls at nearby enemies. Damage is per energy skull. Increase the power of this spell with the Grim Necromancy, Vampirism, and Devastation skills.

◆ **Range: 8** ◆ **Cast Time: 2.08** ◆ **Lesser: Requires combat-magic level 27; Maximum Intelligence 213** ◆ **Normal: Requires combat-magic level 45; Maximum Intelligence 314** ◆ **Greater: Requires combat-magic level 67; Maximum Intelligence 390** ◆ **Master: Requires combat-magic level 84; Maximum Intelligence 500**

LESSER

INT	Mana Cost	Damage
91	50	37–109
103	57	41–123
115	64	46–137
127	71	51–151
140	78	56–167
152	85	61–181
164	92	65–195
176	99	70–209
188	106	75–223
200	113	79–237
213	120	84–252

NORMAL

INT	Mana Cost	Damage
230	130	91–272
242	136	96–286
254	143	100–300
266	150	105–314
278	157	110–328
290	164	114–342
302	171	119–356
314	177	124–370

GREATER

INT	Mana Cost	Damage
318	180	125–375
330	187	130–389
342	193	135–403
354	200	139–417
366	207	144–431
378	214	149–445

(continued)

(continued)

INT	Mana Cost	Damage
390	221	153–459

MASTER

INT	Mana Cost	Damage
404	229	159–476
416	236	164–490
428	242	168–504
440	249	173–518
452	256	178–532
464	263	182–546
476	270	187–560
488	277	192–574
500	284	196–588

Impale

Impale causes spikes to erupt from the ground within a cloud of death corruption, damaging enemies. Increase the power of this spell with the Grim Necromancy, Vampirism, and Devastation skills.

♦ **Range: 8** ♦ **Radius: 2** ♦ **Cast Time: 2.5** ♦ **Lesser: Requires combat-magic level 41; Maximum Intelligence 270** ♦ **Normal: Requires combat-magic level 57; Maximum Intelligence 352** ♦ **Greater: Requires combat-magic level 75; Maximum Intelligence 424** ♦ **Master: Requires combat-magic level 90; Maximum Intelligence 500**

LESSER

INT	Mana Cost	Damage
133	162	53–158
145	176	58–172
157	191	63–187
169	206	67–201
181	221	72–215
193	235	77–229
205	250	81–243
218	266	86–258
230	281	91–272
242	296	96–286
256	313	101–302
270	330	107–319

NORMAL

INT	Mana Cost	Damage
280	342	110–330
292	357	115–344
304	372	120–359
316	387	125–373
328	401	129–387
340	416	134–401
352	431	139–415

GREATER

INT	Mana Cost	Damage
364	446	143–429
376	460	148–443
388	475	153–457
400	490	157–471
412	505	162–485
424	520	167–499

MASTER

INT	Mana Cost	Damage
440	539	173–518
452	554	178–532

INT	Mana Cost	Damage
464	569	182–546
476	583	187–560
488	598	192–574
500	613	196–588

Jolt

Jolt strikes the target enemy with a blast of electricity. Increase the power of this spell with the Amplified Lightning, Arcing, and Devastation skills.

♦ **Range: 10** ♦ **Cast Time: 1.04** ♦ **Lesser: Requires combat-magic level 1; Maximum Intelligence 69** ♦ **Normal: Requires combat-magic level 15; Maximum Intelligence 150** ♦ **Greater: Requires combat-magic level 33; Maximum Intelligence 275** ♦ **Master: Requires combat-magic level 60; Maximum Intelligence 429**

LESSER

INT	Mana Cost	Damage
13	2	8–14
20	4	12–20
27	5	16–26
34	7	19–32
41	9	23–38
48	11	27–44
55	12	30–50
62	14	34–57
69	16	38–63

NORMAL

INT	Mana Cost	Damage
78	18	43–71
86	20	47–78
94	22	51–85
102	23	55–92
110	25	59–99
118	27	64–106
126	29	68–113
134	31	72–120
142	33	76–127
150	35	80–134

GREATER

INT	Mana Cost	Damage
167	39	89–148
179	42	96–159
191	45	102–169
203	48	108–180
215	51	114–190
227	53	121–201
239	56	127–211
251	59	133–222
263	62	140–232
275	65	146–243

MASTER

INT	Mana Cost	Damage
285	67	151–252
297	70	157–262
309	73	164–273
321	76	170–283
333	79	176–294
345	82	183–304
357	85	189–315

(continued)

(continued)

INT	Mana Cost	Damage
369	88	195–325
381	90	202–336
393	93	208–346
405	96	214–357
417	99	220–367
429	102	227–378

Multispark

Multispark releases three sparks toward nearby enemies. Damage is per spark. Increase the power of this spell with the Amplified Lightning, Arcing, and Devastation skills.

♦ **Range: 8** ♦ **Cast Time: 1.39** ♦ **Lesser: Requires combat-magic level 6; Maximum Intelligence 88** ♦ **Normal: Requires combat-magic level 19; Maximum Intelligence 213** ♦ **Greater: Requires combat-magic level 46; Maximum Intelligence 314** ♦ **Master: Requires combat-magic level 68; Maximum Intelligence 462**

LESSER

INT	Mana Cost	Damage
28	10	8–14
34	12	10–16
40	15	12–19
46	17	13–22
52	20	15–24
58	22	16–27
64	25	18–29
70	27	19–32
76	30	21–35
82	32	23–37
88	35	24–40

NORMAL

INT	Mana Cost	Damage
93	37	25–42
105	42	29–47
117	46	32–53
129	51	35–58
141	56	38–63
153	61	41–68
165	66	44–74
177	71	47–79
189	76	51–84
201	81	54–89
213	86	57–96

GREATER

INT	Mana Cost	Damage
230	93	61–102
242	98	65–107
254	103	68–113
266	108	71–118
278	112	74–123
290	117	77–128
302	122	80–134
314	127	83–139

MASTER

INT	Mana Cost	Damage
330	134	88–146
342	139	91–151
354	144	94–156

INT	Mana Cost	Damage
366	149	97–162
378	153	100–167
390	158	103–172
402	163	107–177
414	168	110–183
426	173	113–188
438	178	116–193
450	183	119–198
462	188	122–204

Static Bolt

Static Bolt blasts the target enemy with a bolt of static, damaging it and briefly slowing its attacks. Increase the power of this spell with the Amplified Lightning, Arcing, and Devastation skills.

♦ **Range: 9** ♦ **Cast Time: 1.04** ♦ **Struck monster attacks slowed 50% for 2 seconds.** ♦ **Lesser: Requires combat-magic level 11; Maximum Intelligence 131** ♦ **Normal: Requires combat-magic level 28; Maximum Intelligence 232** ♦ **Greater: Requires combat-magic level 50; Maximum Intelligence 352** ♦ **Master: Requires combat-magic level 76; Maximum Intelligence 500**

LESSER

INT	Mana Cost	Damage
43	12	24–40
51	15	28–47
59	17	33–54
67	20	37–61
75	22	41–68
83	25	45–75
91	27	49–82
99	30	54–89
107	32	58–96
115	35	62–103
123	37	66–110
131	40	70–117

NORMAL

INT	Mana Cost	Damage
136	41	73–121
148	45	79–132
160	49	86–142
172	52	92–153
184	56	98–163
196	60	104–174
208	63	111–184
220	67	117–195
232	71	123–205

GREATER

INT	Mana Cost	Damage
244	75	130–216
256	78	136–226
268	82	142–237
280	86	149–247
292	90	155–258
304	93	161–268
316	97	167–279
328	101	174–289
340	104	180–300
352	108	186–310

(continued)

(continued)

MASTER

INT	Mana Cost	Damage
368	113	195–324
380	117	201–335
392	121	207–345
404	124	214–356
416	128	220–366
428	132	226–377
440	135	233–387
452	139	239–398
464	143	245–408
476	147	251–419
488	150	258–429
500	154	264–440

Lightning Blast

The Lightning Blast spell shoots a long, straight bolt of lightning that penetrates all enemies it hits. Increase the power of this spell with the Amplified Lightning, Arcing, and Devastation skills.

◆ **Range: 10** ◆ **Radius: 1** ◆ **Cast Time: 1.66** ◆ **Lesser:** Requires combat-magic level 23; Maximum Intelligence 198 ◆ **Normal:** Requires combat-magic level 42; Maximum Intelligence 300 ◆ **Greater:** Requires combat-magic level 64; Maximum Intelligence 380 ◆ **Master:** Requires combat-magic level 82; Maximum Intelligence 500

LESSER

INT	Mana Cost	Damage
79	64	64–106
91	74	73–121
102	83	82–136
114	93	91–151
126	103	100–167
138	113	110–183
150	123	119–198
162	132	128–214
174	142	138–229
186	152	147–245
198	162	157–261

NORMAL

INT	Mana Cost	Damage
204	167	161–268
216	177	171–284
228	186	180–300
240	196	189–315
252	206	199–331
264	216	208–346
276	226	217–362
288	236	227–378
300	246	236–393

GREATER

INT	Mana Cost	Damage
308	252	242–404
320	262	252–419
332	272	261–435
344	282	270–450
356	291	280–466
368	301	289–482
380	311	298–497

MASTER

INT	Mana Cost	Damage
392	321	308–513
404	331	317–528
416	341	327–544
428	350	336–560
440	360	345–575
452	370	355–591
464	380	364–606
476	390	373–622
488	400	383–638
500	410	392–653

Call Lightning

Lightning strikes from the sky at up to two enemies. Damage is per lightning strike. Increase the power of this spell with the Amplified Lightning, Arcing, and Devastation skills.

◆ **Range: 8** ◆ **Radius: 2** ◆ **Cast Time: 1.39** ◆ **Lesser:** Requires combat-magic level 37; Maximum Intelligence 261 ◆ **Normal:** Requires combat-magic level 55; Maximum Intelligence 333 ◆ **Greater:** Requires combat-magic level 71; Maximum Intelligence 410 ◆ **Master:** Requires combat-magic level 87; Maximum Intelligence 500

LESSER

INT	Mana Cost	Damage
121	77	60–100
135	86	67–112
149	95	74–123
163	104	81–135
177	113	88–146
191	122	95–157
205	131	101–169
219	140	108–180
233	149	115–191
247	158	122–203
261	167	129–214

NORMAL

INT	Mana Cost	Damage
273	174	135–224
285	182	140–234
297	190	146–243
309	197	152–253
321	205	158–263
333	213	164–273

GREATER

INT	Mana Cost	Damage
338	216	166–277
350	224	172–287
362	231	178–296
374	239	184–306
386	247	190–316
398	254	196–326
410	262	201–335

MASTER

INT	Mana Cost	Damage
416	266	204–340
428	273	210–350
440	281	216–360
452	289	222–369
464	296	228–379
476	304	234–389

(continued)

(continued)

Combat-Magic Spells

INT	Mana Cost	Damage
488	312	239–399
500	320	245–408

Dehydrate

Dehydrate withers and weakens enemies, reducing damage dealt by their melee attacks and increasing their vulnerability to fire. Increase the power of this spell with the Debilitation skill.

♦ **Range: 10** ♦ **Radius: 3** ♦ **Cast Time: 1.5** ♦ **Requires combat-magic level 3; Mana cost depends on Intelligence; other stats depend on combat-magic level.**

Combat Magic Level	Mana Cost	-% Melee Attack Damage	+% Fire Vulnerability	Duration
3	6	-5%	+15%	10
4	8	-5%	+15%	10
5	9	-5%	+16%	10
6	10	-5%	+16%	10
7	12	-6%	+17%	11
8	13	-6%	+17%	11
9	14	-6%	+18%	11
10	15	-6%	+18%	12
11	17	-6%	+19%	12
12	18	-6%	+19%	12
13	19	-7%	+20%	13
14	20	-7%	+20%	13
15	22	-7%	+21%	13
16	23	-7%	+21%	14
17	24	-7%	+22%	14
18	25	-7%	+22%	14
19	27	-8%	+23%	15
20	28	-8%	+23%	15
21	29	-8%	+24%	15
22	30	-8%	+24%	16
23	32	-8%	+25%	16
24	33	-8%	+25%	16
25	34	-9%	+26%	16
26	35	-9%	+26%	17
27	37	-9%	+27%	17
28	38	-9%	+27%	18
29	39	-9%	+28%	18
30	41	-9%	+28%	18
31	42	-9%	+29%	19
32	43	-10%	+29%	19
33	44	-10%	+30%	19

Decay Armor

This curse causes armor and natural defenses of enemies to rot and weaken, increasing their vulnerability to nonmagical attacks. Increase the power of this spell with the Debilitation skill.

♦ **Range: 10** ♦ **Radius: 3** ♦ **Cast Time: 1.5** ♦ **Requires combat-magic level 8; Mana cost depends on Intelligence; other stats are affected by combat-magic level.**

Combat Magic Level	Mana Cost	Armor Reduced by %	Duration
8	13	8%	10
9	14	8%	10
10	15	8%	10
11	17	8%	10
12	18	8%	11
13	19	9%	11
14	20	9%	11
15	22	9%	12
16	23	9%	12
17	24	10%	12
18	25	10%	13
19	27	10%	13
20	28	10%	13
21	29	11%	14
22	30	11%	14
23	32	11%	14
24	33	11%	15
25	34	12%	15
26	35	12%	15
27	37	12%	16
28	38	12%	16
29	39	13%	16
30	41	13%	17
31	42	13%	17
32	43	13%	17
33	44	14%	18
34	46	14%	18
35	47	14%	18
36	48	14%	19
37	49	15%	19
38	51	15%	19

Steal Magic

Steal Magic rips magic power from enemies, temporarily reducing damage dealt by their spells. Increase the power of this spell with the Debilitation skill.

♦ **Range: 8** ♦ **Radius: 3** ♦ **Cast Time: 1.5** ♦ **Requires combat-magic level 13; Mana cost depends on Intelligence; other stats are affected by combat-magic level.**

Combat Magic Level	Mana Cost	% to Magic Attack Damage	Duration
13	9	-18%	20
14	9	-18%	20
15	10	-19%	21
16	11	-19%	21
17	11	-20%	22
18	12	-20%	23
19	13	-21%	23
20	13	-22%	24
21	14	-22%	25
22	14	-23%	25
23	15	-23%	26
24	16	-24%	27
25	16	-24%	27
26	17	-25%	28
27	18	-26%	29
28	18	-26%	29
29	19	-27%	30
30	20	-27%	31
31	20	-28%	31
32	21	-28%	32
33	21	-29%	33
34	22	-30%	33
35	23	-30%	34

(continued)

(continued)

Combat Magic Level	Mana Cost	% to Magic Attack Damage	Duration
36	23	-31%	35
37	24	-31%	35
38	25	-32%	36
39	25	-33%	37
40	26	-33%	37
41	26	-34%	38
42	27	-34%	39
43	28	-35%	39

Drown

This curse floods enemies' lungs with magical poison, causing drowning damage and increasing their vulnerability to ice and lightning. Increase the power of this spell with the Debilitation skill.

◆ **Range: 10** ◆ **Radius: 3** ◆ **Cast Time: 1.5** ◆ **Requires combat-magic level 18; Mana cost and damage per second are dependent on Intelligence; other stats depend on combat-magic level.**

Combat Magic Level	Mana Cost	+ Damage Per Second	+% Ice and Lightning Vulnerability	Duration
18	25	8	+11%	10
19	27	8	+11%	10
20	28	9	+12%	10
21	29	9	+12%	10
22	30	10	+12%	11
23	32	10	+13%	11
24	33	10	+13%	11
25	34	11	+14%	12
26	35	11	+14%	12
27	37	11	+14%	12
28	38	12	+15%	13
29	39	12	+15%	13
30	41	13	+15%	13
31	42	13	+16%	14
32	43	13	+16%	14
33	44	14	+16%	14
34	46	14	+17%	15
35	47	14	+17%	15
36	48	15	+18%	15
37	49	15	+18%	16
38	51	16	+18%	16
39	52	16	+19%	16
40	53	16	+19%	17
41	54	17	+19%	17
42	56	17	+20%	17
43	57	17	+20%	18
44	58	18	+20%	18
45	59	18	+21%	18
46	61	19	+21%	19
47	62	19	+22%	19
48	63	19	+22%	20

Blind

This curse blinds enemies, causing some of their melee attacks to miss and making their ranged attacks fly wide. Increase the power of this spell with the Debilitation skill.

◆ **Range: 10** ◆ **Radius: 3** ◆ **Cast Time: 1.5** ◆ **Increases aiming error of ranged attacks.** ◆ **Requires combat-magic level 23; Mana cost depends on Intelligence; other stats depend on combat-magic level.**

Combat Magic Level	Mana Cost	+% Chance for Melee Attacks to Miss	Duration
23	32	6%	10
24	33	6%	10
25	34	6%	10
26	35	7%	10
27	37	7%	11
28	38	7%	11
29	39	7%	11
30	41	7%	12
31	42	8%	12
32	43	8%	12
33	44	8%	13
34	46	8%	13
35	47	8%	13
36	48	9%	14
37	49	9%	14
38	51	9%	14
39	52	9%	15
40	53	9%	15
41	54	10%	15
42	56	10%	16
43	57	10%	16
44	58	10%	16
45	59	10%	17
46	61	11%	17
47	62	11%	17
48	63	11%	18
49	64	11%	18
50	66	11%	18
51	67	12%	19
52	68	12%	19
53	69	12%	19

Punishing Fire

Punishing Fire burns enemies from within, increasing the damage they deal with weapons, but punishing them when they harm others. Increase the power of this spell with the Debilitation skill.

◆ **Range: 8** ◆ **Radius: 3** ◆ **Cast Time: 1.5** ◆ **+10% to enemy melee and ranged damage** ◆ **Requires combat-magic level 28; Mana cost is dependent on Intelligence; other stats are dependent on combat-magic level.**

Combat Magic Level	Mana Cost	Returns % of Melee and Ranged Damage Dealt	Duration
28	38	30%	10
29	39	31%	10
30	41	32%	10
31	42	33%	10
32	43	34%	11
33	44	35%	11
34	46	36%	11
35	47	37%	12
36	48	38%	12
37	49	39%	12
38	51	40%	13
39	52	41%	13
40	53	42%	13
41	54	43%	14

(continued)

Combat Magic Level	Mana Cost	Returns % of Melee and Ranged Damage Dealt	Duration
42	56	44%	14
43	57	45%	14
44	58	46%	15
45	59	47%	15
46	61	48%	15
47	62	49%	16
48	63	50%	16
49	64	51%	16
50	66	52%	17
51	67	53%	17
52	68	54%	17
53	69	55%	18
54	71	56%	18
55	72	57%	18
56	73	58%	19
57	75	59%	19
58	76	60%	19

Infect

Infect inflicts enemies with plague, slowing the cast rate of their spells, increasing their vulnerability to death magic, and hurting them slowly over time. Increase the power of this spell with the Debilitation skill.

◆ **Range: 10** ◆ **Radius: 3** ◆ **Cast Time: 1.5** ◆ **Requires combat-magic level 33; Mana cost and damage per second are dependent on Intelligence; other stats depend on combat-magic level.**

Combat Magic Level	Mana Cost	Cast Rate Reduced by %	+% Death Vulnerability	+ Damage per Second	Duration
33	44	15%	+15%	10	10
34	46	15%	+15%	11	10
35	47	16%	+16%	11	10
36	48	16%	+16%	11	10
37	49	17%	+17%	11	11
38	51	17%	+17%	12	11
39	52	18%	+18%	12	11
40	53	18%	+18%	12	12
41	54	19%	+19%	13	12
42	56	19%	+19%	13	12
43	57	20%	+20%	13	13
44	58	20%	+20%	13	13
45	59	21%	+21%	14	13
46	61	21%	+21%	14	14
47	62	22%	+22%	14	14
48	63	22%	+22%	15	14
49	64	23%	+23%	15	15
50	66	23%	+23%	15	15
51	67	24%	+24%	15	15
52	68	24%	+24%	16	16
53	69	25%	+25%	16	16
54	71	25%	+25%	16	16
55	72	26%	+26%	16	17
56	73	26%	+26%	17	17
57	75	27%	+27%	17	17
58	76	27%	+27%	17	18
59	77	28%	+28%	18	18
60	78	28%	+28%	18	18
61	80	29%	+29%	18	19
62	81	29%	+29%	18	19
63	82	30%	+30%	19	19

Cripple

Cripple wracks enemies with crippling pain, reducing their maximum health and slowing their attack rate with melee and ranged weapons. Increase the power of this spell with the Debilitation skill.

◆ **Range: 10** ◆ **Radius: 3** ◆ **Cast Time: 1.5** ◆ **Requires combat-magic level 38; Mana cost is dependent on Intelligence; other stats depend on combat-magic level.**

Combat Magic Level	Mana Cost	Melee and Ranged Attack Speed Reduced by %	Health Reduced by %	Duration
38	51	8%	4%	10
39	52	8%	4%	10
40	53	8%	4%	10
41	54	8%	4%	10
42	56	8%	5%	11
43	57	9%	5%	11
44	58	9%	5%	11
45	59	9%	5%	12
46	61	9%	5%	12
47	62	10%	5%	12
48	63	10%	5%	13
49	64	10%	5%	13
50	66	10%	6%	13
51	67	11%	6%	14
52	68	11%	6%	14
53	69	11%	6%	14
54	71	11%	6%	15
55	72	12%	6%	15
56	73	12%	6%	15
57	75	12%	7%	16
58	76	12%	7%	16
59	77	13%	7%	16
60	78	13%	7%	17
61	80	13%	7%	17
62	81	13%	7%	17
63	82	14%	7%	18
64	83	14%	7%	18
65	85	14%	8%	18
66	86	14%	8%	19
67	87	15%	8%	19
68	88	15%	8%	19

Summon Trasak

Summons a deadly Trasak to fight for the caster. The Trasak uses Leech Life to inflict death damage. Increase the power of this spell with the Summon Alacrity skill as well as the nature-magic skills Summon Fortitude and Summon Might.

◆ **Duration: 600** ◆ **Attack Duration: 2 seconds** ◆ **Lesser: Requires combat-magic level 9; Maximum Intelligence 112; 4% health steal** ◆ **Normal: Requires combat-magic level 24; Maximum Intelligence 208; 7% health steal** ◆ **Greater: Requires combat-magic level 45; Maximum Intelligence 294; 10% health steal** ◆ **Paragon: Requires combat-magic level 64; Maximum Intelligence 410; 12% health steal.**

(continued)

LESSER

INT	Mana Cost	Average Damage Per Second	Life	Armor
37	151	7	128	39
53	209	9	166	52
65	258	11	199	64
77	307	13	231	75
89	356	15	263	86
101	406	17	296	98
112	451	19	325	108

NORMAL

INT	Mana Cost	Average Damage Per Second	Life	Armor
124	500	21	358	120
136	549	23	390	131
148	598	25	423	142
160	648	28	455	154
172	697	30	487	165
184	746	32	520	177
196	795	34	552	188
208	844	36	585	199

GREATER

INT	Mana Cost	Average Damage Per Second	Life	Armor
222	902	38	622	213
234	951	40	655	224
246	1000	42	687	236
258	1049	44	720	247
270	1099	46	752	258
282	1148	48	784	270
294	1197	50	817	281

PARAGON

INT	Mana Cost	Average Damage Per Second	Life	Armor
314	1279	54	871	300
326	1328	56	903	312
338	1377	58	936	323
350	1427	60	968	334
362	1476	62	1000	346
374	1525	64	1033	357
386	1574	66	1065	369
398	1623	68	1098	380
410	1673	70	1130	391

Summon Thrusk

Summons a Thrusk to fight for the caster. The incendiary beast blasts enemies with fire. Increase the power of this spell with the Summon Alacrity skill as well as the nature-magic skills Summon Fortitude and Summon Might.

◆ **Duration: 600** ◆ **Attack Duration: 2 seconds** ◆ **Lesser: Requires combat-magic level 14; Maximum Intelligence 136; +20% Fire resistance** ◆ **Normal: Requires combat-magic level 29; Maximum Intelligence 227; +40% Fire resistance** ◆ **Greater: Requires combat-magic level 49; Maximum Intelligence 318; +70% Fire resistance** ◆ **Paragon: Requires combat-magic level 69; Maximum Intelligence 424; Immune to fire**

LESSER

INT	Mana Cost	Average Damage Per Second	Life	Armor
52	205	9	163	51

(continued)

INT	Mana Cost	Average Damage Per Second	Life	Armor
64	254	11	196	63
76	303	13	228	74
88	352	15	261	85
100	402	17	293	97
112	451	19	325	108
124	500	21	358	120
136	549	23	390	131

NORMAL

INT	Mana Cost	Average Damage Per Second	Life	Armor
143	578	25	409	138
155	627	27	442	149
167	676	29	474	161
179	725	31	506	172
191	775	33	539	183
203	824	35	571	195
215	873	37	604	206
227	922	39	636	218

GREATER

INT	Mana Cost	Average Damage Per Second	Life	Armor
234	951	40	655	224
246	1000	42	687	236
258	1049	44	720	247
270	1099	46	752	258
282	1148	48	784	270
294	1197	50	817	281
306	1246	52	849	293
318	1295	54	882	304

PARAGON

INT	Mana Cost	Average Damage Per Second	Life	Armor
328	1336	56	909	313
340	1386	58	941	325
352	1435	60	973	336
364	1484	62	1006	348
376	1533	64	1038	359
388	1582	66	1071	370
400	1632	68	1103	382
412	1681	70	1135	393
424	1730	72	1168	405

Summon Stygian Twisted Shail

Summons a Stygian Twisted Shail to fight for the caster. The macabre construct blasts enemies with ice. Increase the power of this spell with the Summon Alacrity skill as well as the nature-magic skills Summon Fortitude and Summon Might.

◆ **Duration: 600** ◆ **Attack Duration: 2 seconds** ◆ **Lesser: Requires combat-magic level 19; Maximum Intelligence 189; +20% death resistance** ◆ **Normal: Requires combat-magic level 40; Maximum Intelligence 275; +40% death resistance** ◆ **Greater: Requires combat-magic level 59; Maximum Intelligence 371; +70% death resistance** ◆ **Paragon: Requires combat-magic level 80; Maximum Intelligence 486; Immune to death magic**

LESSER

INT	Mana Cost	Average Damage Per Second	Life	Armor
67	266	12	204	66

(continued)

Combat-Magic Spells

INT	Mana Cost	Average Damage Per Second	Life	Armor
79	315	14	236	77
90	361	16	266	87
102	410	18	298	99
114	450	20	331	110
126	508	22	363	122
138	557	24	396	133
150	607	26	428	144
164	664	28	466	158
176	713	30	498	169
189	766	32	533	181

NORMAL

INT	Mana Cost	Average Damage Per Second	Life	Armor
191	775	33	539	183
203	824	35	571	195
215	873	37	604	206
227	922	39	636	218
239	971	41	668	229
251	1021	43	701	240
263	1070	45	733	252
275	1119	47	766	263

GREATER

INT	Mana Cost	Average Damage Per Second	Life	Armor
287	1168	49	798	275
299	1217	51	830	286
311	1267	53	863	297
323	1316	55	895	309
335	1365	57	928	320
347	1414	59	960	332
359	1463	61	992	343
371	1513	63	1025	354

PARAGON

INT	Mana Cost	Average Damage Per Second	Life	Armor
388	1582	66	1071	370
400	1632	68	1103	382
412	1681	70	1135	393
424	1730	72	1168	405
436	1779	74	1200	416
448	1828	76	1233	427
460	1878	79	1265	439
472	1972	81	1297	450
484	1976	83	1330	462

LESSER

INT	Mana Cost	Average Damage Per Second	Life	Armor
112	451	19	325	108
124	500	21	358	120
136	549	23	390	131
148	598	25	423	142
160	648	28	455	154
172	697	30	487	165
184	746	32	520	177
196	795	34	552	188
208	844	36	585	199
220	894	38	617	211
232	943	40	649	222
244	992	42	682	234
256	1041	44	714	245

NORMAL

INT	Mana Cost	Average Damage Per Second	Life	Armor
275	1119	47	766	263
287	1168	49	798	275
299	1217	51	830	286
311	1267	53	863	297
323	1316	55	895	309
335	1365	57	928	320
347	1414	59	960	332

GREATER

INT	Mana Cost	Average Damage Per Second	Life	Armor
359	1463	61	992	343
371	1513	63	1025	354
383	1562	65	1057	366
390	1591	67	1076	372
400	1632	68	1103	382
410	1673	70	1130	391

PARAGON

INT	Mana Cost	Average Damage Per Second	Life	Armor
424	1730	72	1168	405
436	1779	74	1200	416
448	1828	76	1233	427
460	1878	79	1265	439
472	1927	81	1297	450
486	1984	83	1335	464

Summon Mucrim Shocker

Summons a Mucrim Shocker to fight for the caster. The flying creature shocks enemies with lightning. Increase the power of this spell with the Summon Alacrity skill as well as the nature-magic skills Summon Fortitude and Summon Might.

◆ **Duration: 600 ◆ Attack Duration: 2 seconds ◆ Lesser: Requires combat-magic level 34; Maximum Intelligence 256; +20% lightning resistance ◆ Normal: Requires combat-magic level 54; Maximum Intelligence 347; +40% lightning resistance ◆ Greater: Requires combat-magic level 74; Maximum Intelligence 410; +70% lightning resistance ◆ Paragon: Requires combat-magic level 86; Maximum Intelligence 486; immune to lightning**

Corpse Transmutation

Corpse Transmutation absorbs a target corpse and uses its essence to create a temporary magical shield around the caster.

◆ **Range: 10 ◆ Duration: 20 ◆ Requires combat-magic level 35; Mana cost is dependent on the maximum health of the target.**

Combat Magic Level	+ Armor
35	+36
36	+37
37	+39
38	+41
39	+43
40	+44
41	+46
42	+48

(continued)

Combat Magic Level	+ Armor
43	+50
44	+52
45	+54
46	+56
47	+58
48	+60
49	+63
50	+65
51	+67
52	+69
53	+72
54	+74
55	+76
56	+79
57	+81
58	+84
59	+86
60	+89
61	+92
62	+94
63	+97
64	+100
65	+103
66	+106
67	+108
68	+111
69	+114
70	+117
71	+120
72	+123
73	+126
74	+130
75	+133
76	+136
77	+139
78	+142
79	+146
80	+149
81	+153
82	+156
83	+160
84	+163
85	+167
86	+170
87	+174
88	+178
89	+181
90	+185
91	+189
92	+193
93	+196
94	+200
95	+204
96	+208
97	+212
98	+216
99	+221
100	+225

Nature-Magic Spells

This section reveals stats for every nature-magic spell at every available level. Range is the spell's range in meters; radius is area-of-effect radius for applicable spells; and cast time is the spell's rate of fire. The higher the cast time, the slower the spell's rate of fire.

Damage, heal, and summon spells are governed by a character's Intelligence. Embrace and Wrath spell mana cost are governed by Intelligence. In these tables, we assume base Intelligence at the corresponding nature-magic level.

In this section, we've presented a sampling of stats at a large number of Intelligence levels to provide relative mana cost and spell effectiveness at a variety of levels. These spells increase in effectiveness until reaching a maximum Intelligence level, at which point a stronger spell must be acquired.

Icebolt

Icebolt throws a bolt of chilling cold at target enemy. Increase the power of this spell with Aquatic Affinity, Arctic Mastery, and Freezing skills.

♦ **Range: 10** ♦ **Cast Time: 1.39** ♦ **Lesser: Maximum Intelligence 64** ♦ **Normal: Requires nature-magic level 14, Maximum Intelligence 140** ♦ **Greater: Requires nature-magic level 31, Maximum Intelligence 270** ♦ **Master: Requires nature-magic level 59, Maximum Intelligence 414**

LESSER

INT	Mana Cost	Damage
10	3	8–12
16	5	11–18
22	6	15–24
28	10	18–30
34	12	22–36
40	14	25–42
48	17	30–50
52	19	32–54
58	21	36–60
64	23	40–66

NORMAL

INT	Mana Cost	Damage
70	26	43–72
77	28	47–49
84	31	51–85
91	34	56–92
98	36	60–99
105	39	64–106
112	42	68–113
119	44	72–120
126	47	76–127
133	50	80–134
140	52	85–141

GREATER

INT	Mana Cost	Damage
150	56	91–151
162	61	98–162
174	65	105–174
186	70	112–186
198	74	119–198

(continued)

INT	Mana Cost	Damage
210	79	126–210
222	83	133–222
234	88	140–234
246	92	147–245
258	97	155–257
270	102	162–269

MASTER

INT	Mana Cost	Damage
294	111	176–293
306	115	183–305
318	120	190–316
330	124	197–328
342	129	204–340
354	134	211–352
366	138	219–364
378	143	226–376
390	147	233–388
402	152	240–399
414	156	247–411

Encase

The Encase spell blasts target enemies with spikes of cold, chilling them to the bone and briefly slowing their attacks. Increase the power of this spell with Aquatic Affinity, Arctic Mastery, and Freezing skills.

◆ **Range: 8** ◆ **Radius: 3** ◆ **Cast Time: 2.5** ◆ **Slows monster attack speed by 50% for 4 seconds while encased** ◆ **Lesser: Requires nature-magic level 3, Maximum Intelligence 112** ◆ **Normal: Requires nature-magic level 24, Maximum Intelligence 212** ◆ **Greater: Requires nature-magic level 46, Maximum Intelligence 290** ◆ **Master: Requires nature-magic level 62, Maximum Intelligence 440**

LESSER

INT	Mana Cost	Damage
19	13	21–34
27	20	28–47
35	26	36–60
43	32	44–72
51	39	51–85
59	45	59–98
68	52	68–112
76	59	75–125
84	65	83–138
92	72	91–151
102	80	100–167
112	88	110–183

NORMAL

INT	Mana Cost	Damage
116	91	114–189
128	100	125–208
140	110	137–228
152	120	148–247
164	129	160–266
176	139	171–285
188	148	183–304
200	158	194–324
212	168	206–343

GREATER

INT	Mana Cost	Damage
234	185	227–378
242	192	235–391
250	198	242–404
258	204	250–416
266	211	258–429
274	217	265–442
282	224	273–455
290	230	281–468

MASTER

INT	Mana Cost	Damage
306	243	296–493
318	252	308–512
330	262	319–532
342	272	331–551
354	281	342–570
366	291	354–589
378	300	365–608
390	310	377–628
402	320	388–647
414	329	400–666
426	339	411–685
440	350	425–708

Cold Snap

The Cold Snap spell launches a sharp blast of cold that damages all enemies caught inside it. Increase the power of this spell with Aquatic Affinity, Arctic Mastery, and Freezing skills.

◆ **Range: 8** ◆ **Radius: 2** ◆ **Cast Time: 1.25** ◆ **Lesser: Requires nature-magic level 10, Maximum Intelligence 131** ◆ **Normal: Requires nature-magic level 28, Maximum Intelligence 227** ◆ **Greater: Requires nature-magic level 49, Maximum Intelligence 342** ◆ **Master: Requires nature-magic level 74, Maximum Intelligence 500**

LESSER

INT	Mana Cost	Damage
40	13	8–13
49	16	10–16
58	19	11–18
67	22	13–21
76	25	15–24
85	28	16–27
94	31	18–29
103	34	19–32
112	37	21–35
122	40	23–38
131	44	24–40

NORMAL

INT	Mana Cost	Damage
137	46	26–42
146	49	27–45
155	52	29–48
164	55	30–50
173	58	32–53
182	61	34–56
191	64	35–58
200	67	37–61
209	70	38–64

(continued)

(continued)

INT	Mana Cost	Damage
218	73	40–66
227	76	42–69

GREATER

INT	Mana Cost	Damage
246	83	45–75
258	87	47–78
270	91	49–82
282	95	52–86
294	99	54–89
306	103	56–93
318	107	58–96
330	111	60–100
342	115	62–104

MASTER

INT	Mana Cost	Damage
356	120	65–108
368	124	67–111
380	128	69–115
392	132	71–119
404	136	74–122
416	140	76–126
428	145	78–129
440	149	80–133
452	153	82–137
464	157	84–140
476	161	87–144
488	165	89–147
500	169	91–151

INT	Mana Cost	Damage
234	111	131–219
246	117	138–230
258	123	145–241
270	129	151–252
282	134	158–263
294	140	165–274
306	146	171–285
318	152	178–296

GREATER

INT	Mana Cost	Damage
330	157	185–308
342	163	191–319
354	169	198–330
366	175	205–341
378	180	211–352
385	184	215–358

MASTER

INT	Mana Cost	Damage
397	190	222–370
409	195	229–381
421	201	235–392
433	207	242–403
445	213	249–414
457	218	255–425
469	224	262–436
481	230	269–447
490	234	274–456
500	239	279–465

Frost Beam

Frost Beam shoots a beam of frost at the target enemy. Increase the power of this spell with Aquatic Affinity, Arctic Mastery, and Freezing skills.

◆ **Range: 10** ◆ **Cast Time: 1.04** ◆ **Lesser: Requires nature-magic level 21, Maximum Intelligence 203** ◆ **Normal: Requires nature-magic level 43, Maximum Intelligence 318** ◆ **Greater: Requires nature-magic level 68, Maximum Intelligence 385** ◆ **Master: Requires nature-magic level 81, Maximum Intelligence 500**

LESSER

INT	Mana Cost	Damage
73	34	42–70
82	38	47–78
91	43	52–87
100	47	57–95
109	51	62–103
118	56	67–111
127	60	72–120
136	64	77–128
145	69	82–136
155	73	88–146
164	78	93–154
174	83	98–163
183	87	103–172
193	92	109–181
203	96	114–190

NORMAL

INT	Mana Cost	Damage
222	106	125–208

Iceball

Iceball throws a ball of ice at the target enemy. The ball explodes on contact, dealing ice damage to nearby enemies. Increase the power of this spell with Aquatic Affinity, Arctic Mastery, and Freezing skills.

◆ **Range: 10** ◆ **Radius: 2** ◆ **Cast Time: 1.66** ◆ **Lesser: Requires nature-magic level 34, Maximum Intelligence 266** ◆ **Normal: Requires nature-magic level 50, Maximum Intelligence 362** ◆ **Greater: Requires nature-magic level 67, Maximum Intelligence 420** ◆ **Master: Requires nature-magic level 85, Maximum Intelligence 500**

LESSER

INT	Mana Cost	Damage
112	85	34–56
124	94	37–62
136	103	41–68
148	112	44–74
160	121	48–79
172	130	51–85
184	139	55–91
196	148	58–97
208	158	62–103
220	167	65–109
232	176	69–115
244	185	72–120
256	194	76–126
266	202	79–131

NORMAL

INT	Mana Cost	Damage
278	211	82–137

(continued)

(continued)

INT	Mana Cost	Damage
290	220	86–143
302	229	89–149
314	238	93–155
326	247	96–160
338	256	100–166
350	266	103–172
362	275	107–178

GREATER

INT	Mana Cost	Damage
366	278	108–180
372	282	110–183
378	287	112–186
384	291	113–189
390	296	115–192
396	300	117–195
402	305	119–197
408	310	120–200
414	314	122–203
420	319	124–206

GREATER

INT	Mana Cost	Damage
432	328	127–212
444	337	131–218
456	346	134–224
468	355	138–230
480	364	141–235
490	372	144–240
500	380	147–245

Ripple

The earth ripples at the feet of the target enemy, damaging all nearby enemies.

♦ **Range: 8** ♦ **Radius: 2** ♦ **Cast Time: 1.66** ♦ **Lesser: Requires nature-magic level 7, Maximum Intelligence 83** ♦ **Normal: Requires nature-magic level 18, Maximum Intelligence 184** ♦ **Greater: Requires nature-magic level 40, Maximum Intelligence 300** ♦ **Master: Requires nature-magic level 65, Maximum Intelligence 458**

LESSER

INT	Mana Cost	Damage
31	13	11–13
37	16	13–16
43	18	15–18
49	21	17–21
56	24	20–24
62	27	22–27
68	30	25–30
75	33	28–24
83	37	31–38

NORMAL

INT	Mana Cost	Damage
88	39	33–41
100	45	39–47
112	50	44–54
124	56	50–61
136	61	56–69
148	67	63–77
160	72	70–85
172	78	76–93

INT	Mana Cost	Damage
184	83	84–102

GREATER

INT	Mana Cost	Damage
204	92	96–117
216	98	104–127
228	103	112–137
240	109	120–147
252	114	129–157
264	120	138–168
276	125	147–179
288	131	156–191
300	137	166–202

MASTER

INT	Mana Cost	Damage
326	148	187–229
338	154	198–242
350	160	208–254
362	165	219–268
374	171	230–281
386	176	242–295
398	182	253–309
410	187	265–324
422	193	277–339
434	198	290–354
446	204	302–369
458	209	315–385

Grasping Vine

A constricting vine wraps around the target enemy, immobilizing him for the spell's duration.

♦ **Range: 10** ♦ **Radius: 3** ♦ **Cast Time: 2.5** ♦ **Lesser: Requires nature-magic level 34, Maximum Intelligence 251** ♦ **Normal: Requires nature-magic level 53, Maximum Intelligence 332** ♦ **Greater: Requires nature-magic level 71, Maximum Intelligence 405** ♦ **Master: Requires nature-magic level 85, Maximum Intelligence 500**

LESSER

INT	Mana Cost	Damage
112	113	234–287
124	125	267–326
136	138	299–366
148	150	334–408
160	162	369–451
172	175	406–497
184	187	445–543
198	201	491–600
210	214	532–650
222	226	575–702
230	234	604–738
242	247	649–793
251	256	683–835

NORMAL

INT	Mana Cost	Damage
260	265	718–878
272	278	766–936
284	290	816–997
296	302	866–1059
308	315	918–1122
320	327	972–1188

(continued)

(continued)

INT	Mana Cost	Damage
332	339	1026–1254

GREATER

INT	Mana Cost	Damage
345	353	1087–1329
351	359	1116–1364
357	365	1145–1399
363	371	1174–1435
369	378	1203–1471
375	384	1233–1507
381	390	1264–1544
387	396	1294–1582
393	402	1325–1619
399	408	1356–1658
405	415	1388–1696

MASTER

INT	Mana Cost	Damage
416	426	1447–1768
428	438	1512–1848
440	451	1579–1929
452	463	1647–2012
464	475	1716–2097
476	488	1787–2183
488	500	1859–2271
500	513	1932–2361

Heal

This powerful heal envelops the target character with replenishing water, instantly restoring a large amount of health. Increase the effectiveness of this spell with the Aquatic Affinity and Nurturing Gift skills.

◆ Range: 10 ◆ Cast Time: 1.66 ◆ Lesser: Requires nature-magic level 1; Maximum Intelligence 70 ◆ Normal: Requires nature-magic level 24; Maximum Intelligence 208 ◆ Greater: Requires nature-magic level 45; Maximum Intelligence 314 ◆ Master: Requires nature-magic level 67; Maximum Intelligence 500

LESSER

INT	Mana Cost	Life Restored to Target Instantly
13	13	15
17	18	19
21	22	22
25	27	26
29	31	29
33	35	33
37	40	36
41	44	40
44	47	42
48	52	46
52	56	50
56	61	53
60	65	57
65	71	61
70	76	65

NORMAL

INT	Mana Cost	Life Restored to Target Instantly
78	85	73
91	99	84

INT	Mana Cost	Life Restored to Target Instantly
104	113	95
117	128	107
130	142	118
143	156	130
156	171	141
169	185	153
182	199	164
195	214	176
208	228	187

GREATER

INT	Mana Cost	Life Restored to Target Instantly
218	239	196
226	248	203
234	256	210
242	265	217
250	274	224
258	283	231
266	292	238
274	300	245
282	309	253
290	318	260
298	327	267
306	336	274
314	344	281

MASTER

INT	Mana Cost	Life Restored to Target Instantly
320	351	286
344	377	307
368	404	328
389	427	347
413	453	368
443	486	395
461	506	410
485	533	432
500	549	445

Healing Rain

Curative rain heals nearby allies a small amount over a long duration. Increase the effectiveness of this spell with the Aquatic Affinity and Nurturing Gift skills.

◆ Range: 10 ◆ Radius: 10 ◆ Cast Time: 3 ◆ Lesser: Requires nature-magic level 12; Maximum Intelligence 136 ◆ Normal: Requires nature-magic level 29; Maximum Intelligence 232 ◆ Greater: Requires nature-magic level 50; Maximum Intelligence 342 ◆ Master: Requires nature-magic level 73; Maximum Intelligence 500

LESSER

INT	Mana Cost	Life Restored to Party Over 8 Seconds
36	64	35
45	80	43
54	96	51
63	112	59
72	129	67
81	145	75
90	161	83
99	177	91
108	193	99

(continued)

(continued)

INT	Mana Cost	Life Restored to Party Over 8 Seconds
117	210	107
125	224	114
136	244	124

NORMAL

INT	Mana Cost	Life Restored to Party Over 8 Seconds
144	258	131
152	273	138
160	287	145
168	301	152
176	316	159
184	330	166
192	345	173
200	359	180
208	373	187
216	388	194
224	402	201
232	417	208

GREATER

INT	Mana Cost	Life Restored to Party Over 8 Seconds
246	442	221
254	456	228
262	471	235
270	485	242
278	499	249
286	514	256
294	528	263
302	543	270
310	557	277
318	571	284
326	586	291
334	600	298
342	615	305

MASTER

INT	Mana Cost	Life Restored to Party Over 8 Seconds
356	640	318
368	661	328
380	683	339
392	705	350
404	726	360
416	748	371
428	769	381
440	791	392
452	813	403
464	834	413
476	856	424
488	877	434
500	899	445

LESSER

INT	Mana Cost	Life Restored to Target Instantly	Life Restored to Target over 6 Seconds
31	15	5	20
45	22	7	28
59	29	9	36
74	36	11	44
88	43	13	52
102	50	15	60
116	57	17	68
130	64	19	76
144	71	21	84
160	79	23	93

NORMAL

INT	Mana Cost	Life Restored to Target Instantly	Life Restored to Target over 6 Seconds
170	84	25	98
182	90	26	105
194	96	28	112
206	102	30	119
218	108	31	125
230	114	33	132
242	120	35	139
254	126	36	146
266	132	38	153

GREATER

INT	Mana Cost	Life Restored to Target Instantly	Life Restored to Target over 6 Seconds
275	137	39	158
287	143	41	164
299	149	43	171
311	155	44	178
323	161	46	185
335	167	48	192
347	173	50	198
359	179	51	205
371	185	53	212

MASTER

INT	Mana Cost	Life Restored to Target Instantly	Life Restored to Target over 6 Seconds
383	191	55	219
395	197	56	225
407	203	58	232
419	209	60	239
431	215	61	246
443	221	63	253
455	227	65	259
467	233	67	266
479	239	68	272
491	245	70	280
500	249	71	285

Nourish

This inexpensive heal imbues the target character with curative water, restoring a moderate amount of health over a moderate duration. Increase the effectiveness of this spell with the Aquatic Affinity and Nurturing Gift skills.

◆ Range: 10 ◆ Cast Time: 1.39 ◆ Lesser: Requires nature-magic level 7; Maximum Intelligence 160 ◆ Normal: Requires nature-magic level 34; Maximum Intelligence 266 ◆ Greater: Requires nature-magic level 56; Maximum Intelligence 371 ◆ Master: Requires nature-magic level 79; Maximum Intelligence 500

Healing Cascade

This powerful heal creates a ball of healing water that bounces to all nearby allies, restoring health instantly. Increase the effectiveness of this spell with the Aquatic Affinity and Nurturing Gift skills.

◆ Range: 10 ◆ Radius: 10 ◆ Duration: 3 ◆ Lesser: Requires nature-magic level 19; Maximum Intelligence 184 ◆ Normal: Requires nature-magic level 39; Maximum Intelligence 285 ◆ Greater: Requires nature-magic level 61; Maximum Intelligence 400 ◆ Master: Requires nature-magic level 85; Maximum Intelligence 500

LESSER

INT	Mana Cost	Life Restored to Party Instantly
67	89	38
79	105	44
90	120	50
102	136	56
114	152	63
126	169	69
138	185	75
150	201	82
162	217	88
174	233	94
184	247	100

NORMAL

INT	Mana Cost	Life Restored to Party Instantly
189	254	102
201	270	109
213	286	115
225	302	121
237	318	128
249	335	134
261	351	140
273	367	147
285	383	153

GREATER

INT	Mana Cost	Life Restored to Party Instantly
304	409	163
316	425	170
328	441	176
340	458	182
352	474	189
364	490	195
376	506	201
388	522	208
400	539	214

MASTER

INT	Mana Cost	Life Restored to Party Instantly
416	560	222
428	576	229
440	593	235
452	609	242
464	625	248
476	641	254
488	657	261
500	674	267

Earthen Embrace

This enchantment imbues nearby allies with the strength of Earth, increasing maximum health. Increase the effectiveness of this spell with Enveloping Embrace.

◆ Range: 8 ◆ Cast Time: 3 ◆ Mana is affected by Intelligence; other stats are affected by nature-magic level.

Nature Magic Level	Mana Cost	+% Maximum Health	Duration
2	15	5%	600
3	19	5%	619
4	22	5%	639
5	26	5%	659

Nature Magic Level	Mana Cost	+% Maximum Health	Duration
6	29	6%	679
7	32	6%	699
8	36	6%	718
9	39	6%	738
10	42	6%	758
11	46	6%	778
12	49	7%	798
13	52	7%	817
14	56	7%	837
15	59	7%	857
16	62	7%	877
17	66	7%	897
18	69	8%	916
19	73	8%	936
20	76	8%	956
21	79	8%	976
22	83	8%	996
23	86	8%	1015
24	89	9%	1035
25	93	9%	1055
26	96	9%	1075
27	99	9%	1095
28	103	9%	1114
29	106	9%	1135
30	110	10%	1154
31	113	10%	1174
32	116	10%	1194

Wind Embrace

Wind Embrace imbues nearby allies with the swiftness of wind, granting a chance to dodge melee and ranged attacks. Increase the effectiveness of this spell with Enveloping Embrace.

◆ Range: 8 ◆ Cast Time: 3 ◆ Mana is affected by Intelligence; other stats are affected by nature-magic level.

Nature Magic Level	Mana Cost	+% Chance to Dodge Melee and Ranged Attacks	Duration
10	42	+4%	600
11	46	+4%	619
12	49	+4%	639
13	52	+4%	659
14	56	+5%	679
15	59	+5%	699
16	62	+5%	718
17	66	+5%	738
18	69	+5%	758
19	73	+5%	778
20	76	+5%	798
21	79	+5%	817
22	83	+6%	837
23	86	+6%	857
24	89	+6%	877
25	93	+6%	897
26	96	+6%	916
27	99	+6%	936
28	103	+6%	956
29	106	+7%	976

(continued)

(continued)

Nature-Magic Spells

Nature Magic Level	Mana Cost	+% Chance to Dodge Melee and Ranged Attacks	Duration
30	110	+7%	996
31	113	+7%	1015
32	116	+7%	1035
33	120	+7%	1055
34	123	+7%	1075
35	126	+7%	1095
36	130	+7%	1114
37	133	+8%	1134
38	136	+8%	1154
39	140	+8%	1174
40	143	+8%	1194

Spirit Embrace

Spirit Embrace imbues nearby allies with nature's spirits, granting resistance to ice, lightning, and fire damage, and protecting them from curses. Increase the effectiveness of this spell with Enveloping Embrace.

◆ **Range: 8** ◆ **Cast Time: 3** ◆ **Mana is affected by Intelligence; other stats are affected by nature-magic level.** ◆ **Immunity to curses**

Nature Magic Level	Mana Cost	+% to Ice, Fire, and Lightning resistances	Duration
18	69	+8%	600
19	73	+8%	619
20	76	+9%	639
21	79	+9%	659
22	83	+9%	679
23	86	+9%	699
24	89	+10%	718
25	93	+10%	738
26	96	+10%	758
27	99	+10%	778
28	103	+11%	798
29	106	+11%	817
30	110	+11%	837
31	113	+11%	857
32	116	+12%	877
33	120	+12%	897
34	123	+12%	916
35	126	+12%	936
36	130	+13%	956
37	133	+13%	976
38	136	+13%	996
39	140	+14%	1015
40	143	+14%	1035
41	146	+14%	1055
42	150	+14%	1075
43	153	+15%	1095
44	157	+15%	1114
45	160	+15%	1134
46	163	+15%	1154
47	167	+15%	1174
48	170	+16%	1194

Aquatic Embrace

This enchantment imbues nearby allies with the vitality of water, vastly hastening mana regeneration. Increase the effectiveness of this spell with Enveloping Embrace.

◆ **Range: 8** ◆ **Cast Time: 3** ◆ **Mana is affected by Intelligence; other stats depend on nature-magic level.**

Nature Magic Level	Mana Cost	+% to Mana Regeneration	Duration
26	96	+10%	600
27	99	+10%	619
28	103	+11%	639
29	106	+11%	659
30	110	+11%	679
31	113	+12%	699
32	116	+12%	718
33	120	+12%	738
34	123	+13%	758
35	126	+13%	778
36	130	+13%	798
37	133	+14%	817
38	136	+14%	837
39	140	+14%	857
40	143	+15%	877
41	146	+15%	897
42	150	+15%	916
43	153	+16%	936
44	157	+16%	956
45	160	+16%	976
46	163	+17%	996
47	167	+17%	1015
48	170	+17%	1035
49	173	+18%	1055
50	177	+18%	1075
51	180	+18%	1095
52	183	+19%	1114
53	187	+19%	1134
54	190	+19%	1154
55	194	+20%	1174
56	197	+20%	1194

Life Embrace

Life Embrace imbues nearby allies with the spirit of life, allowing them to absorb health from enemies they damage. Increase the effectiveness of this spell with Enveloping Embrace.

◆ **Range: 8** ◆ **Cast Time: 3** ◆ **Mana is affected by Intelligence; other stats depend on nature-magic level.**

Nature Magic Level	Mana Cost	% Health Steal	Duration
34	123	3%	600
35	126	3%	619
36	130	3%	639
37	133	3%	659
38	136	3%	679
39	140	3%	699
40	143	4%	718
41	146	4%	738
42	150	4%	758
43	153	4%	778
44	157	4%	798
45	160	4%	817
46	163	4%	837
47	167	4%	857

(continued)

Nature Magic Level	Mana Cost	% Health Steal	Duration
48	170	4%	877
49	173	4%	897
50	177	5%	916
51	180	5%	936
52	183	5%	956
53	187	5%	976
54	190	5%	996
55	194	5%	1015
56	197	5%	1035
57	200	5%	1055
58	204	5%	1075
59	207	5%	1095
60	210	6%	1114
61	214	6%	1134
62	217	6%	1154
63	220	6%	1174
64	224	6%	1194

Wrath of the Bear

This enchantment energizes nearby allies with the strength of bears, amplifying the potency of their critical hits. Increase the effectiveness of this spell with Feral Wrath.

◆ **Range: 8** ◆ **Cast Time: 3** ◆ **Mana is affected by Intelligence; other stats are affected by nature-magic level.**

Nature Magic Level	Mana Cost	+% to Extra Damage from Critical Hits	Duration
6	29	+38%	600
7	32	+39%	619
8	36	+40%	639
9	39	+41%	659
10	42	+42%	679
11	46	+44%	699
12	49	+45%	718
13	52	+46%	738
14	56	+47%	758
15	59	+49%	778
16	62	+50%	798
17	66	+51%	817
18	69	+52%	837
19	73	+54%	857
20	76	+55%	877
21	79	+56%	897
22	83	+57%	916
23	86	+59%	936
24	89	+60%	956
25	93	+61%	976
26	96	+62%	996
27	99	+63%	1015
28	103	+65%	1035
29	106	+66%	1055
30	110	+67%	1075
31	113	+68%	1095
32	116	+70%	1114
33	120	+71%	1134
34	123	+72%	1154
35	126	+73%	1174
36	130	+75%	1194

Wrath of Magic

This enchantment energizes nearby allies with the force of magic, increasing the damage of their spells. Increase the effectiveness of this spell with Feral Wrath.

◆ **Range: 8** ◆ **Cast Time: 3** ◆ **Mana is affected by Intelligence; other stats depend on nature-magic level.**

Nature Magic Level	Mana Cost	+% Magic Damage	Duration
14	56	+6%	600
15	59	+6%	619
16	62	+6%	639
17	66	+7%	659
18	69	+7%	679
19	73	+7%	699
20	76	+7%	718
21	79	+7%	738
22	83	+8%	758
23	86	+8%	778
24	89	+8%	798
25	93	+8%	817
26	96	+8%	837
27	99	+9%	857
28	103	+9%	877
29	106	+9%	897
30	110	+9%	916
31	113	+9%	936
32	116	+10%	956
33	120	+10%	976
34	123	+10%	996
35	126	+10%	1015
36	130	+10%	1035
37	133	+11%	1055
38	136	+11%	1075
39	140	+11%	1095
40	143	+11%	1114
41	146	+11%	1134
42	150	+12%	1154
43	153	+12%	1174
44	157	+12%	1194

Wrath of Ice

Wrath of Ice energizes nearby allies with the power of ice, adding ice damage to their melee and ranged attacks and giving their attacks a chance to freeze enemies. Increase the effectiveness of this spell with Feral Wrath.

◆ **Range: 8** ◆ **Cast Time: 3** ◆ **5% Chance to Freeze Enemies for 1 second** ◆ **Mana is affected by Intelligence; other stats are affected by nature-magic level.**

Nature Magic Level	Mana Cost	+ Ice Damage per Attack	Duration
22	83	+3	600
23	86	+3	619
24	89	+3	639
25	93	+3	659
26	96	+4	679
27	99	+4	699
28	103	+4	718
29	106	+4	738

(continued)

Nature-Magic Spells

Nature Magic Level	Mana Cost	+ Ice Damage per Attack	Duration
30	110	+4	758
31	113	+5	778
32	116	+5	798
33	120	+5	817
34	123	+5	837
35	126	+6	857
36	130	+6	877
37	133	+6	897
38	136	+7	916
39	140	+7	936
40	143	+7	956
41	146	+7	976
42	150	+8	996
43	153	+8	1015
44	157	+8	1035
45	160	+9	1055
46	163	+9	1075
47	167	+9	1095
48	170	+10	1114
49	173	+10	1134
50	177	+11	1154
51	180	+11	1174
52	183	+11	1194

Wrath of the Fallen

Wrath of the Fallen energizes nearby allies with the anger of fallen warriors, automatically inflicting on their attackers a percentage of melee and ranged damage received, but it also reduces their armor. Increase the effectiveness of this spell with Feral Wrath.

◆ **Range: 8** ◆ **Cast Time: 3** ◆ **-5% to Armor** ◆ Mana is affected by Intelligence; other stats depend on nature-magic level.

Nature Magic Level	Mana Cost	+% to Physical Damage Reflected to Enemy	Duration
30	110	21%	600
31	113	22%	619
32	116	22%	639
33	120	23%	659
34	123	24%	679
35	126	24%	699
36	130	25%	718
37	133	26%	738
38	136	27%	758
39	140	27%	778
40	143	28%	798
41	146	29%	817
42	150	29%	837
43	153	30%	857
44	157	31%	877
45	160	31%	897
46	163	32%	916
47	167	33%	936
48	170	33%	956
49	173	34%	976
50	177	35%	996
51	180	36%	1015
52	183	36%	1035

Nature Magic Level	Mana Cost	+% to Physical Damage Reflected to Enemy	Duration
53	187	37%	1055
54	190	38%	1075
55	194	38%	1095
56	197	39%	1114
57	200	40%	1134
58	204	40%	1154
59	207	41%	1174
60	210	42%	1194

Wrath of Ancestors

This enchantment energizes nearby allies with the rage of ancestral spirits, increasing the rate at which they recover from using their powers. Increase the effectiveness of this spell with Feral Wrath.

◆ **Range: 8** ◆ **Cast Time: 3** ◆ Mana is affected by Intelligence; other stats are affected by nature-magic level.

Nature Magic Level	Mana Cost	+% Power Recharge Rate	Duration
38	136	+4%	600
39	140	+4%	619
40	143	+4%	639
41	146	+4%	659
42	150	+5%	679
43	153	+5%	699
44	157	+5%	718
45	160	+5%	738
46	163	+5%	758
47	167	+5%	778
48	170	+5%	798
49	173	+5%	817
50	177	+6%	837
51	180	+6%	857
52	183	+6%	877
53	187	+6%	897
54	190	+6%	916
55	194	+6%	936
56	197	+6%	956
57	200	+7%	976
58	204	+7%	996
59	207	+7%	1015
60	210	+7%	1035
61	214	+7%	1055
62	217	+7%	1075
63	220	+7%	1095
64	224	+7%	1114
65	227	+8%	1134
66	230	+8%	1154
67	234	+8%	1174
68	237	+8%	1194

Summon Bracken Defender

Summons a Bracken Defender to fight for the caster. The stalwart, wooden construct will defend the caster with its life. Increase the power of this spell with Summon Fortitude and Summon Might skills, as well as the combat-magic skill Summon Alacrity.

◆ **Duration: 600** ◆ **Attack Duration: 2 seconds** ◆ **Lesser: Requires nature-magic level 4, Maximum Intelligence 64** ◆ **Normal: Requires nature-magic level 14, Maximum**

(continued)

Intelligence 126; +5% health regeneration, 10% of physical damage reflected to enemy ◆ Greater: Requires nature-magic level 28, Maximum Intelligence 280; +10% health regeneration, 20% of physical damage reflected to enemy ◆ Paragon: Requires nature-magic level 61, Maximum Intelligence 419; +20% health regeneration, 40% of physical damage reflected to enemy

LESSER

INT	Mana Cost	Average Damage Per Second	Life	Armor
22	82	6	111	32
29	110	8	140	41
36	139	10	170	51
43	168	12	200	60
50	197	14	229	69
57	225	16	259	78
64	254	18	289	88

NORMAL

INT	Mana Cost	Average Damage Per Second	Life	Armor
68	306	19	306	93
76	340	21	340	104
84	336	23	373	114
92	469	25	407	125
100	402	28	441	136
108	434	30	475	146
117	471	32	513	158
126	508	35	551	170

GREATER

INT	Mana Cost	Average Damage Per Second	Life	Armor
142	574	39	619	192
158	639	43	687	213
174	705	47	755	234
206	836	56	890	277
222	902	60	958	298
238	967	65	1026	319
268	1090	73	1153	359
280	1140	76	1204	375

PARAGON

INT	Mana Cost	Average Damage Per Second	Life	Armor
297	1209	81	1276	398
309	1258	84	1327	414
321	1304	87	1373	428
333	1357	90	1428	446
345	1406	94	1479	462
357	1455	97	1530	477
369	1504	100	1581	493
381	1554	103	1632	509
393	1603	107	1682	525
405	1652	110	1733	541
419	1709	114	1792	560

Summon Raptor

Summons a Raptor to fight for the caster. The vicious, wily reptile rends the caster's foes with its claws. Increase the power of this spell with Summon Fortitude and Summon Might skills, as well as the combat-magic skill Summon Alacrity.

◆ **Duration: 600** ◆ **Attack Duration: 1.333 seconds** ◆ **Lesser: Requires nature-magic level 7; Maximum Intelligence 83** ◆ **Normal: Requires nature-magic level 18;**

Maximum Intelligence 189 ◆ Greater: Requires nature-magic level 41; Maximum Intelligence 309 ◆ Paragon: Requires nature-magic level 67; Maximum Intelligence 434

LESSER

INT	Mana Cost	Average Damage per Second	Life	Armor
31	119	11	149	35
38	147	13	179	43
45	176	16	208	50
52	205	18	238	57
61	242	21	276	67
69	274	24	310	76
76	303	26	340	83
83	332	29	369	90

NORMAL

INT	Mana Cost	Average Damage per Second	Life	Armor
90	361	31	399	98
102	410	35	450	111
114	459	39	501	123
128	516	44	560	138
140	566	48	611	151
152	615	52	661	164
164	664	56	712	177
172	697	59	746	185
189	766	64	818	203

GREATER

INT	Mana Cost	Average Damage per Second	Life	Armor
201	816	68	869	216
213	865	73	920	229
225	914	77	971	242
237	963	81	1022	254
249	1012	85	1072	267
261	1062	89	1123	280
273	1111	93	1174	293
285	1160	97	1225	305
297	1209	101	1276	318
309	1258	105	1327	331

PARAGON

INT	Mana Cost	Average Damage per Second	Life	Armor
315	1283	107	1352	337
321	1304	109	1373	343
332	1353	113	1424	355
344	1402	117	1475	368
356	1451	121	1526	381
368	1500	125	1576	394
383	1562	130	1640	410
395	1611	134	1691	422
409	1668	139	1750	437
434	1771	147	1856	464

Summon Rhinock

Summons a Rhinock to fight for the caster. The stalwart beast will stand between the caster and his foes. Increase the power of this spell with Summon Fortitude and Summon Might skills, as well as the combat-magic skill Summon Alacrity.

◆ **Duration: 600** ◆ **Attack Duration: 3 seconds** ◆ **Lesser: Requires nature-magic level 11, Maximum Intelligence**

Nature-Magic Spells

112 ◆ Normal: Requires nature-magic level 24, Maximum Intelligence 218 ◆ Greater: Requires nature-magic level 47, Maximum Intelligence 347 ◆ Paragon: Requires nature-magic level 75, Maximum Intelligence 453

LESSER

INT	Mana Cost	Average Damage Per Second	Life	Armor
43	168	10	200	75
54	213	12	246	93
64	254	14	289	110
76	303	17	340	130
88	352	19	390	150
98	393	22	433	166
107	430	24	471	181
112	451	25	492	190

NORMAL

INT	Mana Cost	Average Damage Per Second	Life	Armor
120	484	26	526	203
131	529	29	573	221
142	574	31	619	239
153	619	33	666	258
164	664	36	712	276
175	709	38	759	294
186	754	41	805	313
197	799	43	852	331
208	844	45	899	349
218	885	47	941	366

GREATER

INT	Mana Cost	Average Damage Per Second	Life	Armor
230	935	50	992	386
243	998	53	1047	407
256	1041	56	1102	429
269	1094	59	1157	451
282	1148	61	1212	472
295	1201	64	1267	494
308	1254	67	1322	515
321	1308	70	1377	537
335	1365	73	1437	560
347	1414	75	1487	580

PARAGON

INT	Mana Cost	Average Damage Per Second	Life	Armor
359	1463	78	1538	600
371	1513	81	1589	620
383	1562	83	1640	640
397	1619	86	1699	663
410	1673	89	1754	685
422	1722	92	1722	705
434	1771	94	1856	725
453	1849	98	1937	756

Summon Scorpion

Summons a Scorpion to fight for the caster. Its protective carapace belies its offensive strength. Increase the power of this spell with Summon Fortitude and Summon Might skills, as well as the combat-magic skill Summon Alacrity.

◆ Duration: 600 ◆ Attack Duration: 3 seconds ◆ Fast Movement Speed ◆ Lesser: Requires nature-magic level 21, Maximum Intelligence 160; +10% magic-dam-

age resistance ◆ Normal: Requires nature-magic level 34, Maximum Intelligence 266; +18% magic-damage resistance ◆ Greater: Requires nature-magic level 57, Maximum Intelligence 381; +30% magic-damage resistance ◆ Paragon: Requires nature-magic level 82, Maximum Intelligence 500; +45% magic-damage resistance

LESSER

INT	Mana Cost	Average Damage Per Second	Life	Armor
73	291	20	327	100
81	324	22	361	110
89	356	25	395	121
97	389	27	428	132
105	422	29	462	142
112	451	31	492	152
120	484	33	526	162
128	516	35	560	173
136	549	37	594	184
144	582	39	628	194
152	615	42	661	205
160	648	44	695	215

NORMAL

INT	Mana Cost	Average Damage Per Second	Life	Armor
170	689	46	738	229
182	738	50	789	245
194	787	53	839	261
206	836	56	890	277
218	885	59	941	293
230	935	63	992	309
242	984	66	1043	325
254	1033	69	1094	340
266	1082	72	1144	356

GREATER

INT	Mana Cost	Average Damage Per Second	Life	Armor
285	1160	77	1225	382
297	1209	81	1276	398
309	1258	84	1327	414
321	1308	87	1377	430
333	1357	90	1428	446
345	1406	94	1479	462
357	1455	97	1530	477
369	1504	100	1581	493
381	1554	103	1632	509

PARAGON

INT	Mana Cost	Average Damage Per Second	Life	Armor
416	1697	113	1780	556
428	1746	116	1831	572
440	1796	119	1881	588
452	1845	123	1932	604
464	1894	126	1983	620
476	1943	129	2034	636
488	1992	132	2085	652
500	2042	136	2136	668

Summon Lertisk

Summons a Lertisk to fight for the caster. The aggressive predator is a formidable companion. Increase the power of this spell with Summon

Fortitude and Summon Might skills, as well as the combat-magic skill Summon Alacrity.

♦ Duration: 600 ♦ Attack Duration: 1.333 seconds ♦ Lesser: Requires nature-magic level 31, Maximum Intelligence 208 ♦ Normal: Requires nature-magic level 44, Maximum Intelligence 300 ♦ Greater: Requires nature-magic level 64, Maximum Intelligence 420 ♦ Paragon: Requires nature-magic level 75, Maximum Intelligence 500

LESSER

INT	Mana Cost	Average Damage Per Second	Life	Armor
93	373	36	412	95
105	422	40	462	107
118	475	45	517	120
130	525	50	568	132
142	574	54	619	144
154	623	59	670	156
166	672	63	721	168
178	721	68	772	180
192	779	73	831	194
208	844	79	899	209

NORMAL

INT	Mana Cost	Average Damage Per Second	Life	Armor
216	877	82	933	217
228	926	87	983	229
240	976	91	1034	241
252	1025	96	1085	253
264	1074	100	1136	265
276	1123	105	1187	277
288	1172	110	1238	289
300	1222	114	1288	301

GREATER

INT	Mana Cost	Average Damage Per Second	Life	Armor
324	1320	123	1390	325
336	1369	128	1441	337
348	1418	132	1492	349
360	1468	137	1543	361
372	1517	141	1593	373
384	1566	146	1644	385
396	1615	150	1695	397
408	1664	155	1746	409
420	1714	159	1797	421

PARAGON

INT	Mana Cost	Average Damage Per Second	Life	Armor
432	1763	164	1848	433
444	1812	169	1898	445
456	1861	173	1949	457
468	1910	178	2000	469
470	1960	182	2051	481
484	2009	187	2102	493
500	2042	190	2136	501

Summon Ketril

Summons a Ketril to fight for the caster. The giant lizard combines durability with potent swiping attacks. Increase the power of this spell with Summon Fortitude and Summon Might skills, as well as the combat-magic skill Summon Alacrity.

♦ Duration: 600 ♦ Attack Duration: 3 seconds ♦ Lesser: Requires nature-magic level 37, Maximum Intelligence 256 ♦ Normal: Requires nature-magic level 54, Maximum Intelligence 366 ♦ Greater: Requires nature-magic level 78, Maximum Intelligence 438 ♦ Paragon: Requires nature-magic level 94, Maximum Intelligence 500

LESSER

INT	Mana Cost	Average Damage Per Second	Life	Armor
121	488	23	530	229
135	545	26	589	255
149	602	29	649	281
163	660	31	708	307
180	730	34	780	339
194	787	37	839	365
208	844	40	899	391
224	910	43	966	421
238	967	45	1026	447
256	1041	49	1102	480

NORMAL

INT	Mana Cost	Average Damage Per Second	Life	Armor
270	1099	51	1161	506
282	1148	54	1212	529
294	1197	56	1263	551
306	1246	58	1314	574
318	1295	60	1365	596
330	1345	63	1415	618
342	1394	65	1466	641
354	1443	67	1517	663
366	1492	70	1568	685

GREATER

INT	Mana Cost	Average Damage Per Second	Life	Armor
378	1541	72	1619	708
390	1591	74	1670	730
402	1640	76	1720	752
414	1689	79	1771	775
426	1738	81	1822	797
438	1787	83	1873	819

PARAGON

INT	Mana Cost	Average Damage Per Second	Life	Armor
450	1837	85	1924	842
462	1886	88	1975	864
474	1935	90	2025	886
488	1992	93	2085	912
500	2042	95	2136	935

Summon Forest Golem

Summons a massive Forest Golem to fight for the caster. The animated tree is a potent manifestation of nature's vengeance. Increase the power of this spell with Summon Fortitude and Summon Might skills, as well as the combat-magic skill Summon Alacrity.

♦ Duration: 600 ♦ Attack Duration: 2 seconds ♦ Lesser: Requires nature-magic level 51, Maximum Intelligence 338; +100% of physical damage reflected to enemy ♦ Normal: Requires nature-magic level 71, Maximum Intelligence 405; +160% of physical damage reflected to enemy ♦ Greater: Requires nature-magic level 86, Maximum Intelligence 467; +225% of physical damage reflected to enemy ♦ Paragon: Requires nature-magic level 97, Maximum Intelligence 500; +300% of physical damage reflected to enemy

LESSER

INT	Mana Cost	Average Damage Per Second	Life	Armor
163	660	45	708	219
180	730	49	780	242
195	791	53	844	262
210	853	57	907	282
225	914	61	971	302
240	976	65	1034	322
255	1037	69	1098	342
270	1099	73	1161	362
290	1181	79	1246	388
310	1263	84	1331	415
325	1324	88	1394	435
338	1377	92	1449	452

NORMAL

INT	Mana Cost	Average Damage Per Second	Life	Armor
345	1406	94	1479	462
357	1455	97	1530	477
369	1504	100	1581	493
381	1554	103	1632	509
393	1603	107	1682	525
405	1652	110	1733	541

GREATER

INT	Mana Cost	Average Damage Per Second	Life	Armor
417	1701	113	1784	557
429	1750	116	1835	573
441	1800	120	1886	589
453	1849	123	1937	605
467	1906	127	1996	624

PARAGON

INT	Mana Cost	Average Damage Per Second	Life	Armor
473	1931	128	2021	632
479	1955	130	2047	640
485	1980	131	2072	648
491	2005	133	2097	656
500	2042	136	2136	668

Transmute

Transforms objects on the ground into gold; amount of gold is based on the item's power and the caster's nature-magic level.

◆ Range: 5 ◆ Cast Time: 1.25 ◆ Transmutes all items in a 3-meter radius ◆ Mana cost equals nature-magic level plus 3 ◆ Caster is most efficient (more gold) transmuting items that are less powerful than his character. If caster's nature-magic skill is less than an item's level, efficiency falls off sharply (approximately 50% if item and character power differ by 7).

Resurrect

The Resurrect spell draws upon the water of life to raise the dead. ◆ Range: 5 ◆ Cast Time: 7 ◆ Mana Cost: Dependent on the maximum health of the target. The higher the corpse's health, the higher the mana cost. ◆ Lesser: Requires nature-magic level 4; restores 15% of target's health ◆ Normal: Requires nature-magic level 25; restores 30% of target's health ◆ Greater: Requires nature-magic level 45; restores 50% of target's health ◆

Master: Requires nature-magic level 72; restores 75% of target's health

Summon Town Portal

Summons a teleporter that can return the party to the nearest town and then bring them back.